SPICE&WOLF

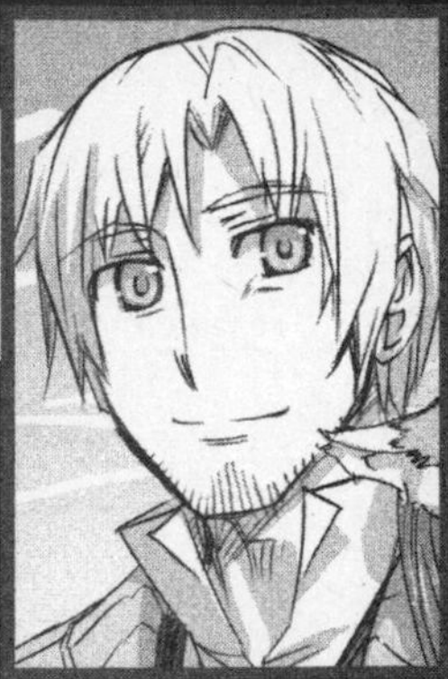

Lawrence
A merchant traveling with Holo. Collecting information about Holo's homeland.

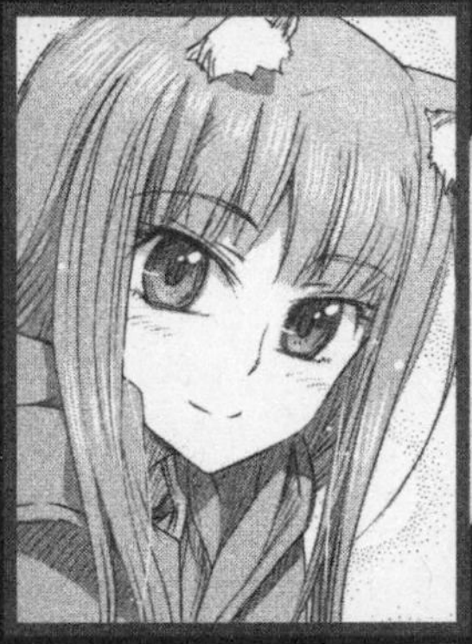

Holo
Lawrence's traveling companion, a beautiful girl. Her true form is that of the wolf-god of the harvest.

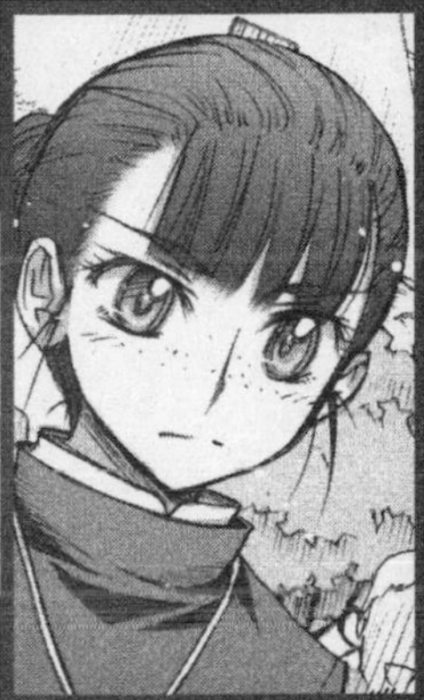

Elsa
The church deaconess of the village of Tereo, successor to the late Father Franz.

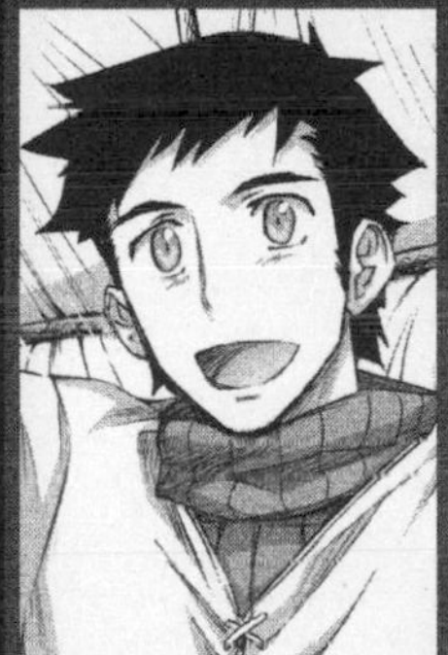

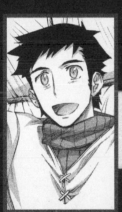

Evan
A young miller. Romantically involved with Elsa.

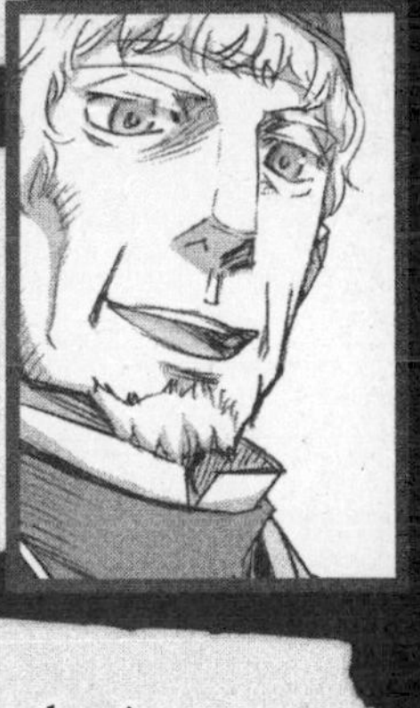

Bishop Van
The bishop of St. Rio's Church in the town of Enberch. Conspiring with the town to control Tereo.

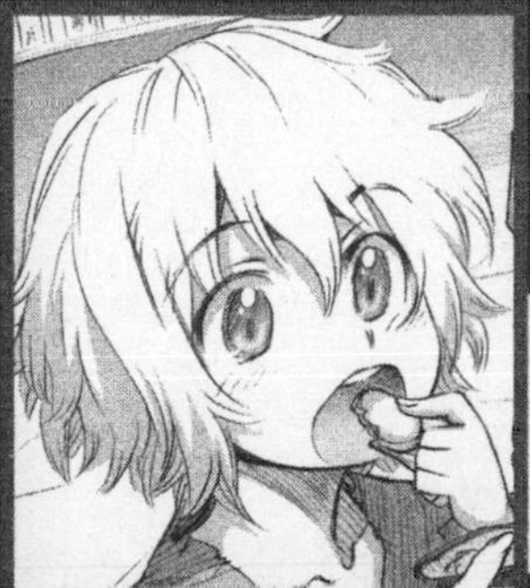

Col
A boy saved by Lawrence at the river checkpoint. A naive but clever lad.

Introduction

Caught in the schemes of Bishop Van, the town of Tereo finds both its faith and its autonomy threatened. Made a scapegoat via the plotting, Lawrence proposes escape to Elsa and Evan. Elsa first chooses to flee but soon returns to fight for her place in her hometown. Will Lawrence be able to rescue the town from the forces that threaten it…!?

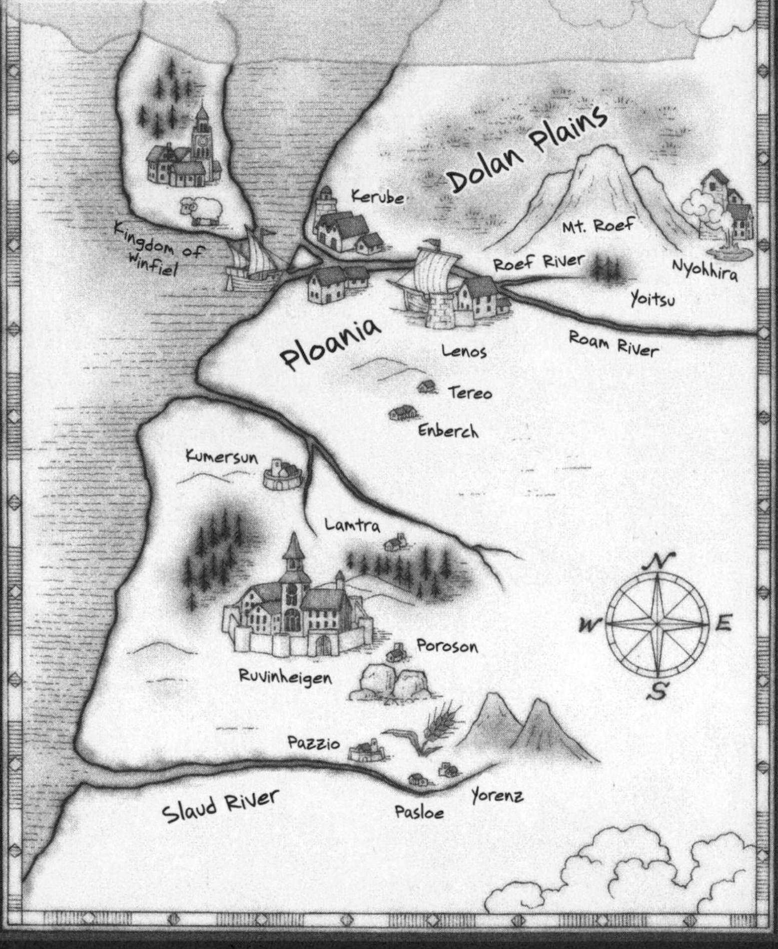

Dolan Plains
Kerube
Mt. Roef
Kingdom of Winfiel
Roef River
Nyohhira
Yoitsu
Ploania
Lenos
Roam River
Tereo
Enberch
Kumersun
Lamtra
N
W
E
S
Poroson
Ruvinheigen
Pazzio
Slaud River
Yorenz
Pasloe

Map Illustration: Hidetada Idemitsu

SPICE & WOLF

CONTENTS

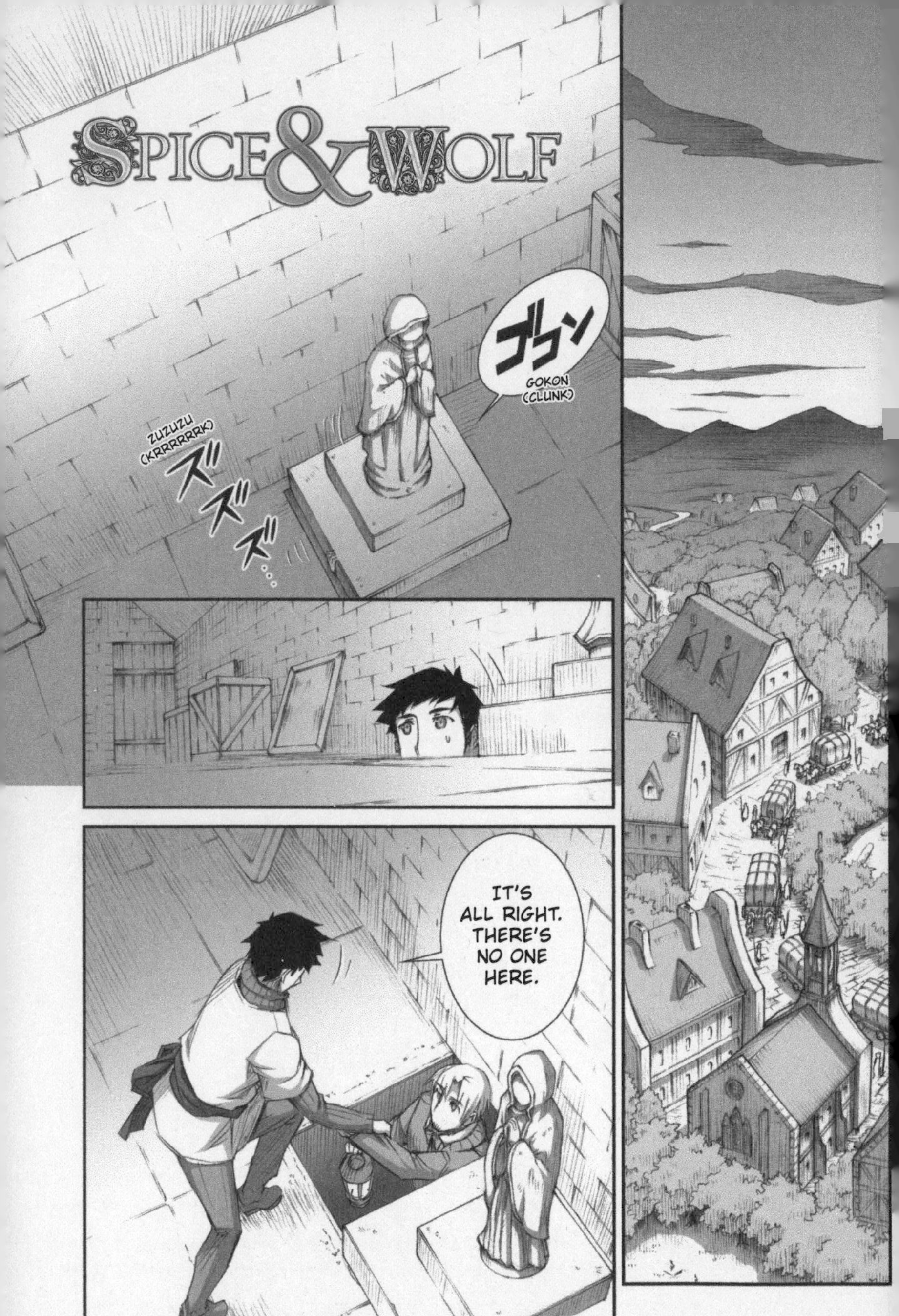
SPICE & WOLF
ゴコン
GOKON (CLUNK)
ズズズ…
ZUZUZU (KRRRRRRK)
IT'S ALL RIGHT. THERE'S NO ONE HERE.

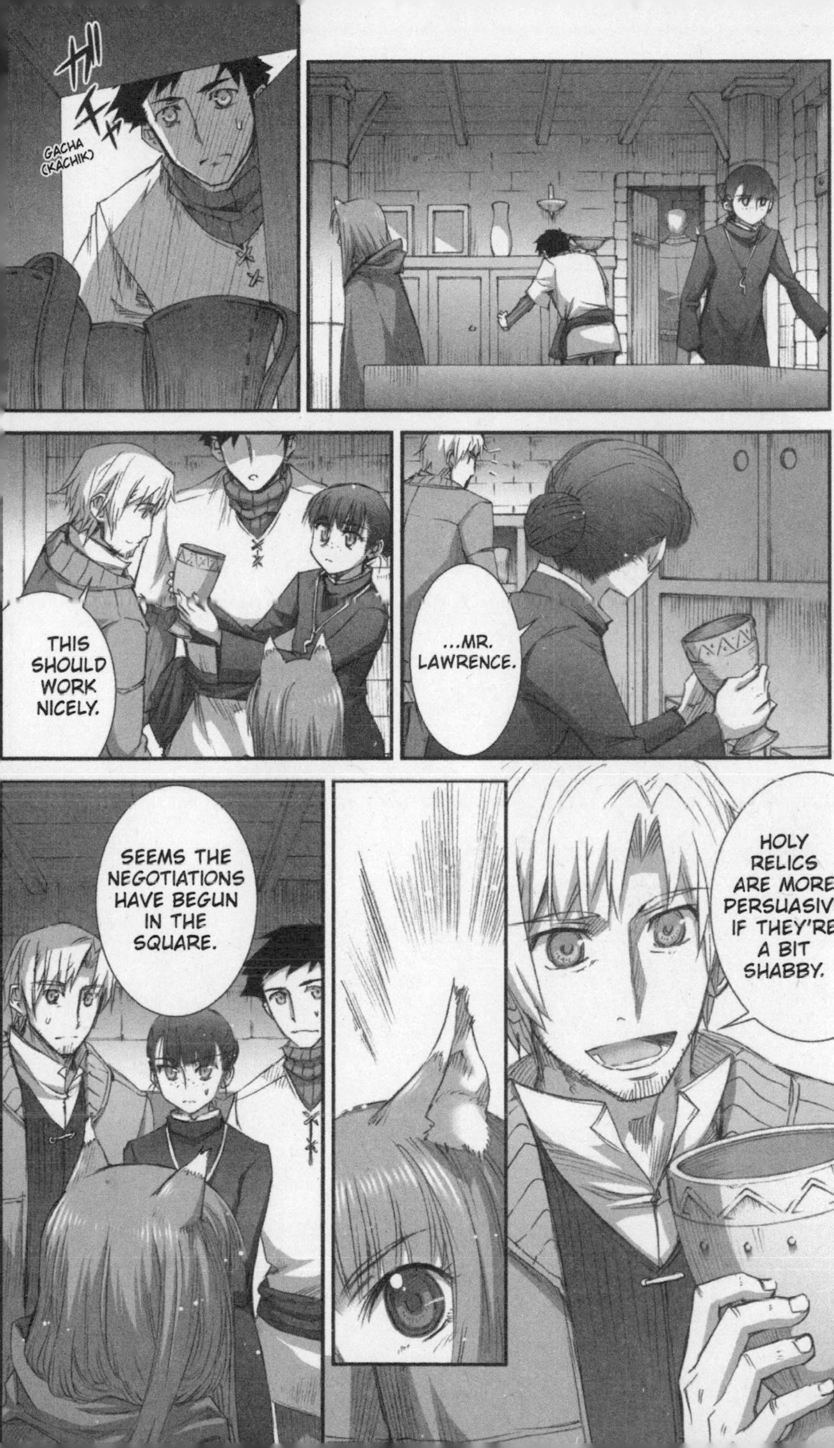
GACHA (KACHIK)
...MR. LAWRENCE.
THIS SHOULD WORK NICELY.
HOLY RELICS ARE MORE PERSUASIVE IF THEY'RE A BIT SHABBY.
SEEMS THE NEGOTIATIONS HAVE BEGUN IN THE SQUARE.

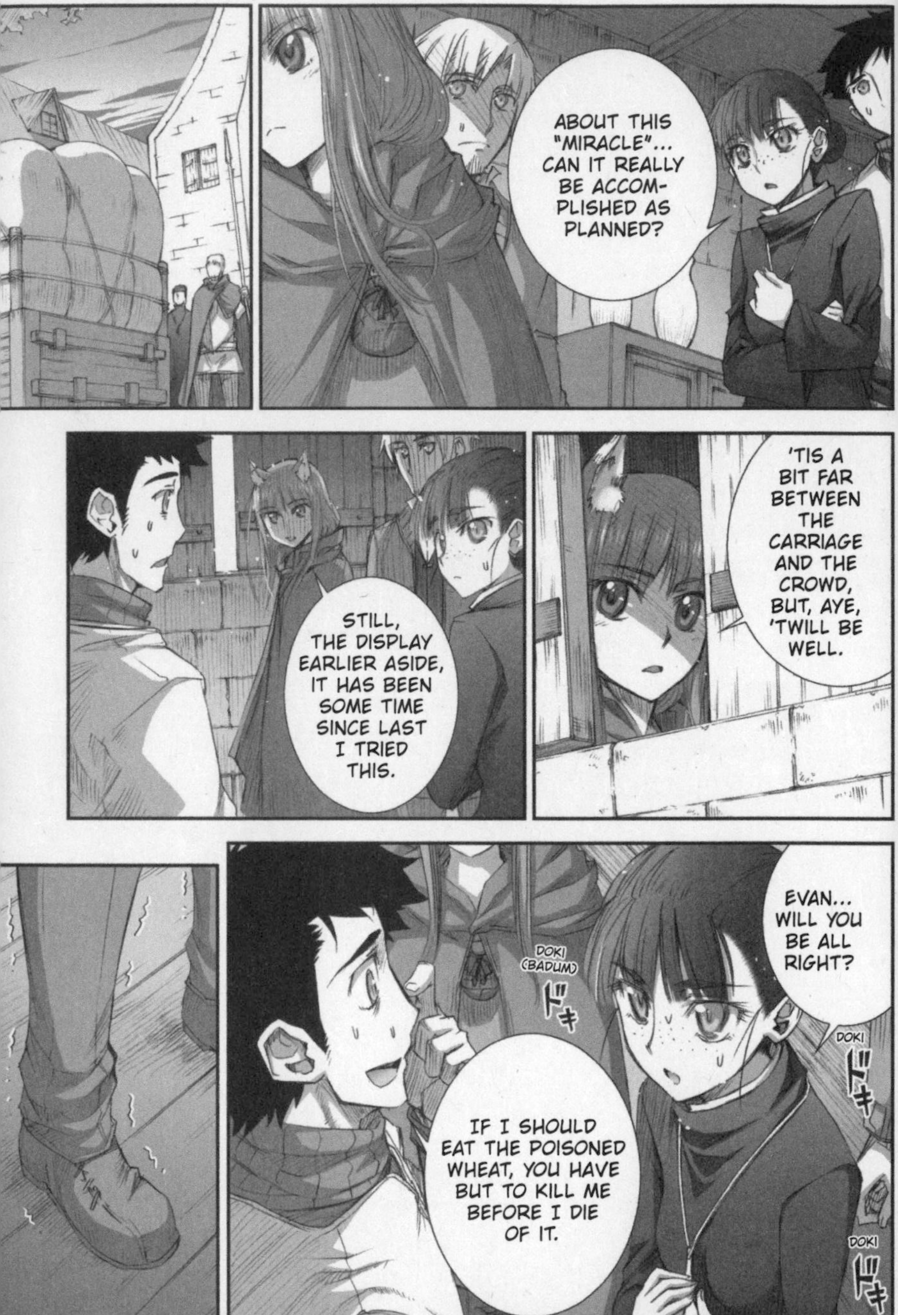
ABOUT THIS "MIRACLE"... CAN IT REALLY BE ACCOMPLISHED AS PLANNED?
'TIS A BIT FAR BETWEEN THE CARRIAGE AND THE CROWD, BUT, AYE, 'TWILL BE WELL.
STILL, THE DISPLAY EARLIER ASIDE, IT HAS BEEN SOME TIME SINCE LAST I TRIED THIS.
EVAN... WILL YOU BE ALL RIGHT?
DOKI
ドキ
DOKI (BADUM)
ドキ
IF I SHOULD EAT THE POISONED WHEAT, YOU HAVE BUT TO KILL ME BEFORE I DIE OF IT.
DOKI
ドキ

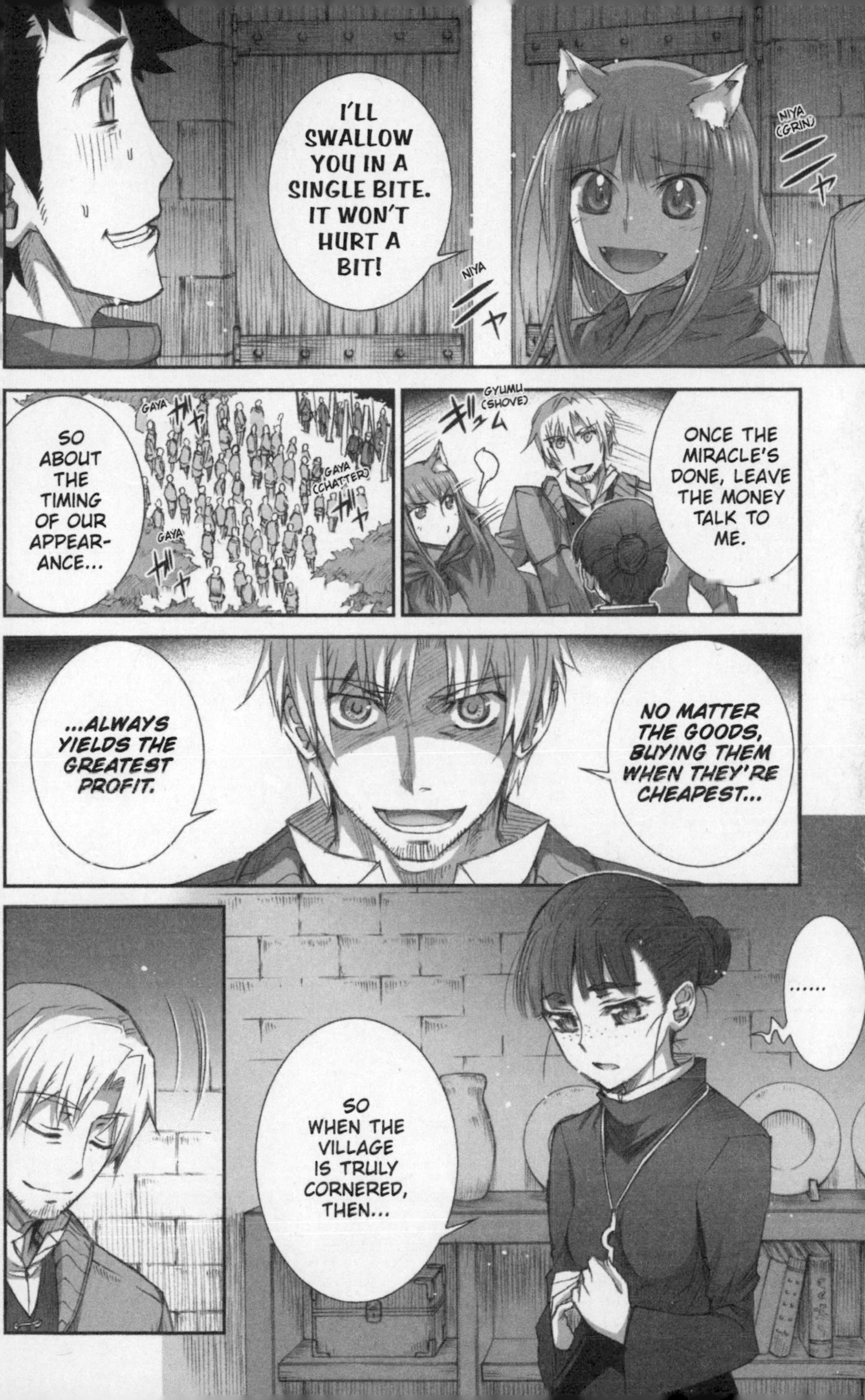
NIYA (GRIN)
I'LL SWALLOW YOU IN A SINGLE BITE. IT WON'T HURT A BIT!
NIYA
GYUMU (SHOVE)
ONCE THE MIRACLE'S DONE, LEAVE THE MONEY TALK TO ME.
SO ABOUT THE TIMING OF OUR APPEARANCE...
GAYA
GAYA (CHATTER)
GAYA
NO MATTER THE GOODS, BUYING THEM WHEN THEY'RE CHEAPEST...
...ALWAYS YIELDS THE GREATEST PROFIT.
......
SO WHEN THE VILLAGE IS TRULY CORNERED, THEN...

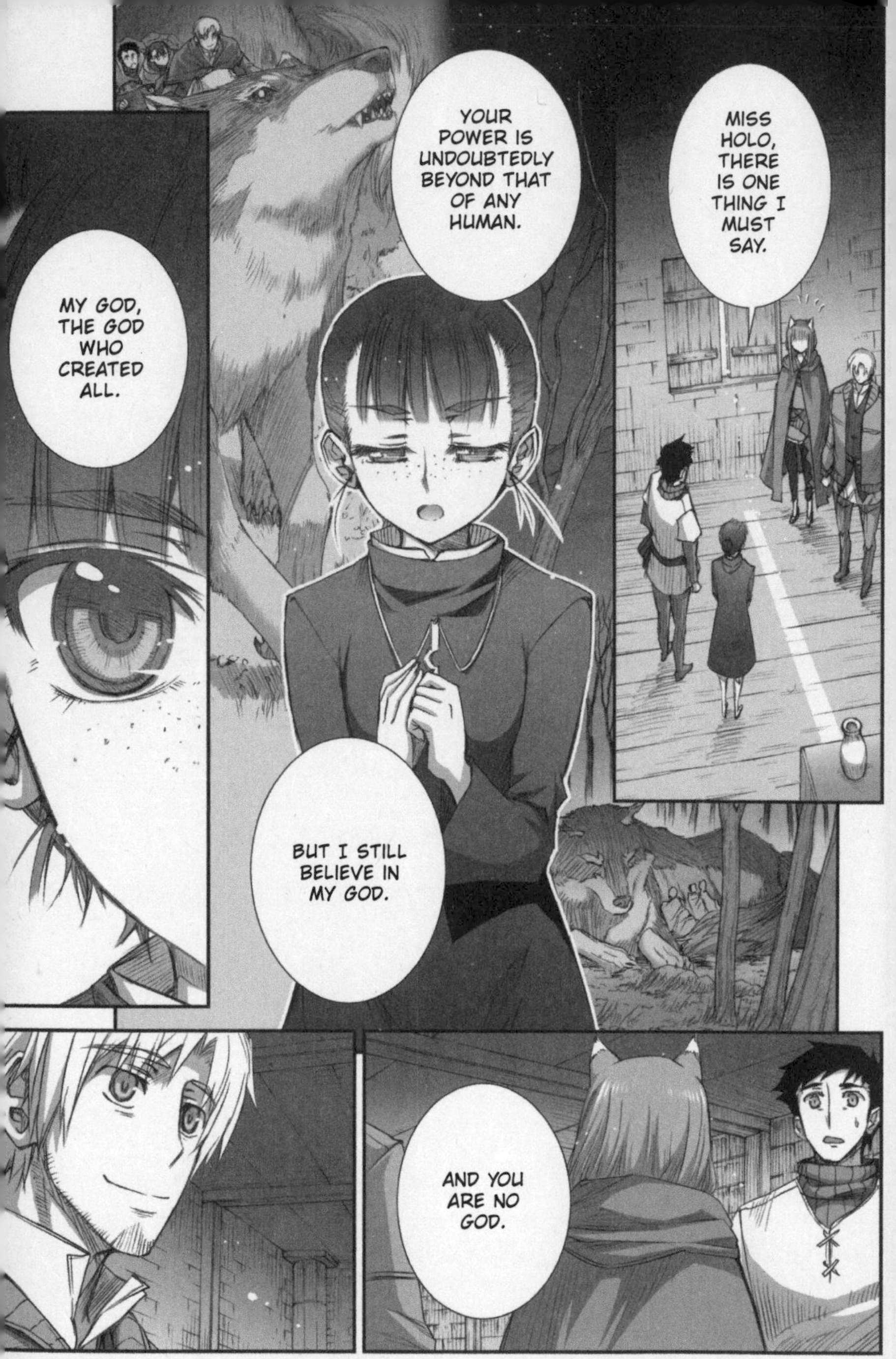
MISS HOLO, THERE IS ONE THING I MUST SAY.
YOUR POWER IS UNDOUBTEDLY BEYOND THAT OF ANY HUMAN.
BUT I STILL BELIEVE IN MY GOD.
MY GOD, THE GOD WHO CREATED ALL.
AND YOU ARE NO GOD.

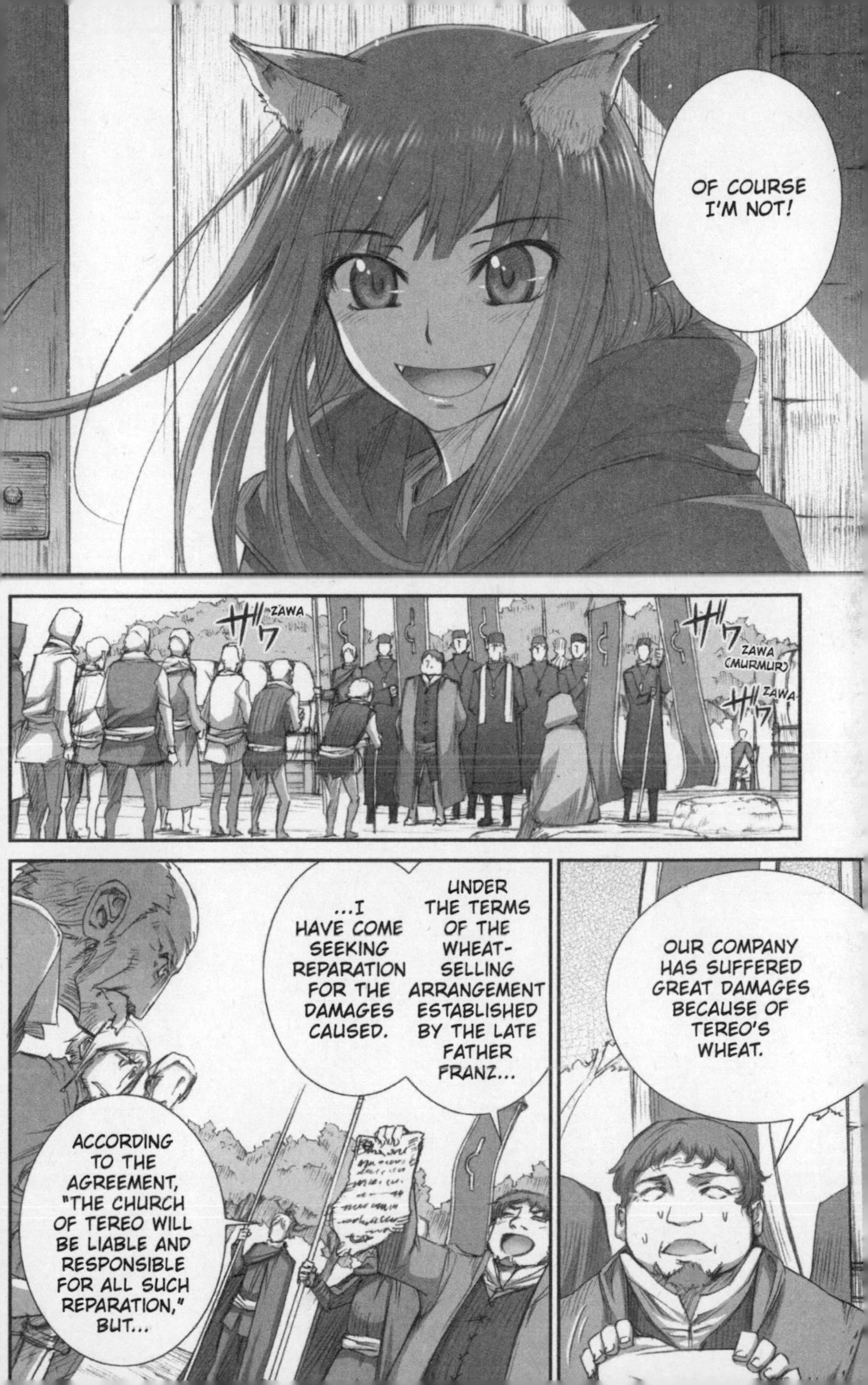
OF COURSE I'M NOT!
ザワ ZAWA (MURMUR)
ザワ ZAWA
ザワ ZAWA
OUR COMPANY HAS SUFFERED GREAT DAMAGES BECAUSE OF TEREO'S WHEAT.
UNDER THE TERMS OF THE WHEAT-SELLING ARRANGEMENT ESTABLISHED BY THE LATE FATHER FRANZ...
...I HAVE COME SEEKING REPARATION FOR THE DAMAGES CAUSED.
ACCORDING TO THE AGREEMENT, "THE CHURCH OF TEREO WILL BE LIABLE AND RESPONSIBLE FOR ALL SUCH REPARATION," BUT...

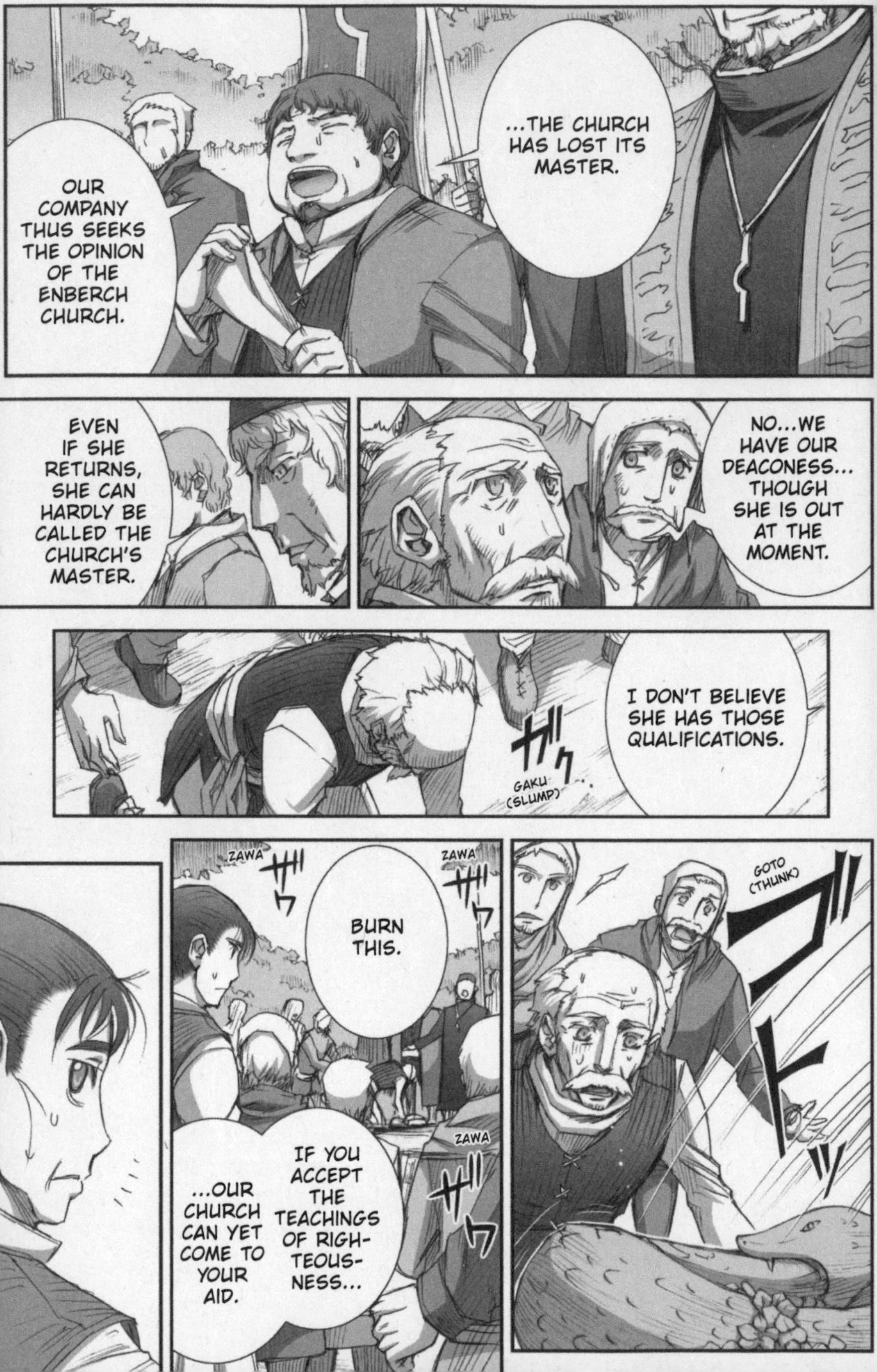
...THE CHURCH HAS LOST ITS MASTER.
OUR COMPANY THUS SEEKS THE OPINION OF THE ENBERCH CHURCH.
NO...WE HAVE OUR DEACONESS... THOUGH SHE IS OUT AT THE MOMENT.
EVEN IF SHE RETURNS, SHE CAN HARDLY BE CALLED THE CHURCH'S MASTER.
I DON'T BELIEVE SHE HAS THOSE QUALIFICATIONS.
GAKU (SLUMP)
GOTO (THUNK)
ZAWA
ZAWA
BURN THIS.
ZAWA
IF YOU ACCEPT THE TEACHINGS OF RIGHTEOUSNESS...
...OUR CHURCH CAN YET COME TO YOUR AID.

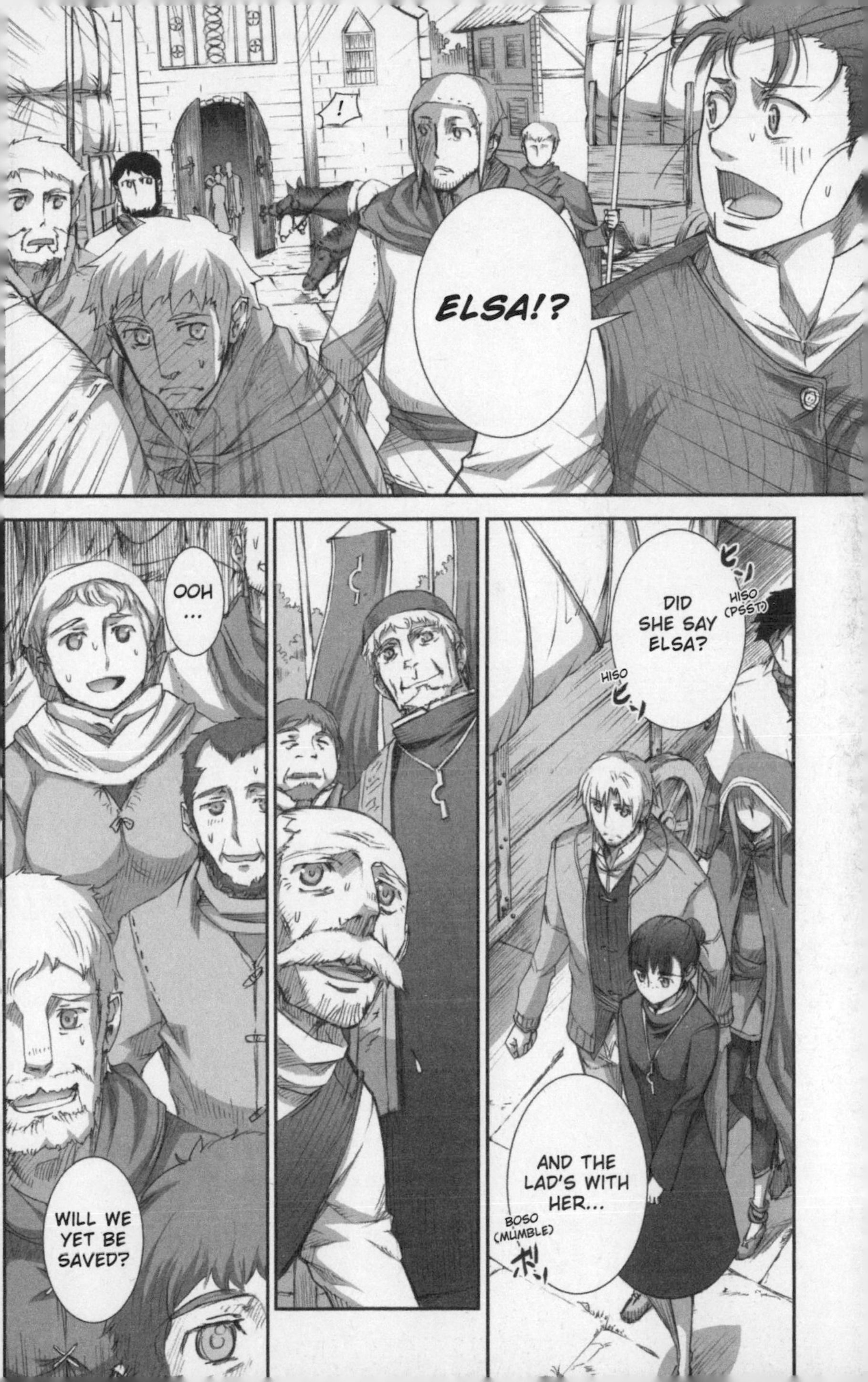
!
ELSA!?
HISO (PSST)
DID SHE SAY ELSA?
HISO
AND THE LAD'S WITH HER...
BOSO (MUMBLE)
OOH ...
WILL WE YET BE SAVED?

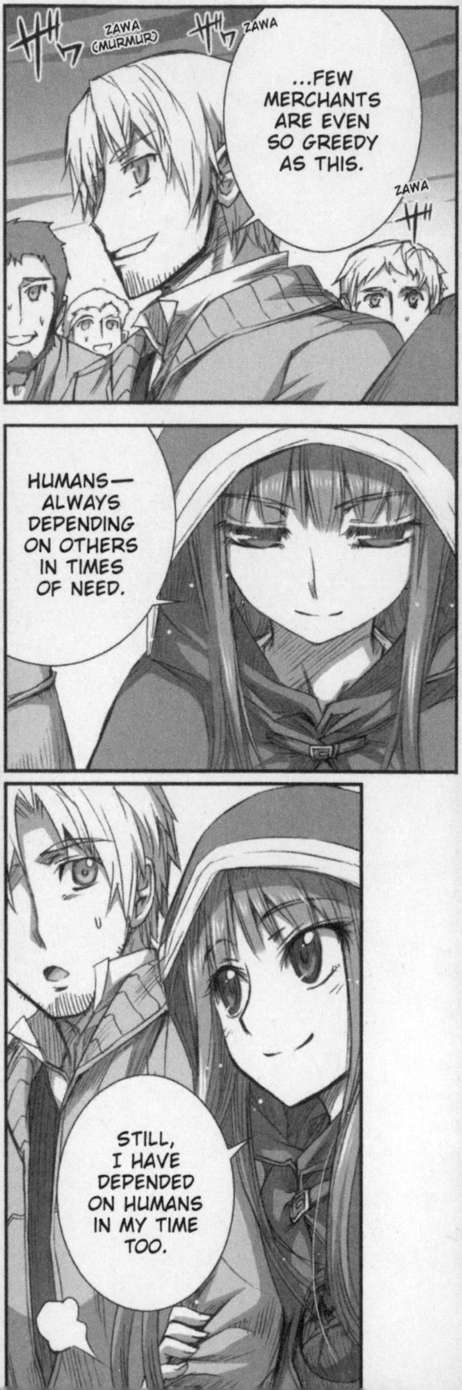
ZAWA (MURMUR)
ZAWA
...FEW MERCHANTS ARE EVEN SO GREEDY AS THIS.
ZAWA
HUMANS—ALWAYS DEPENDING ON OTHERS IN TIMES OF NEED.
STILL, I HAVE DEPENDED ON HUMANS IN MY TIME TOO.
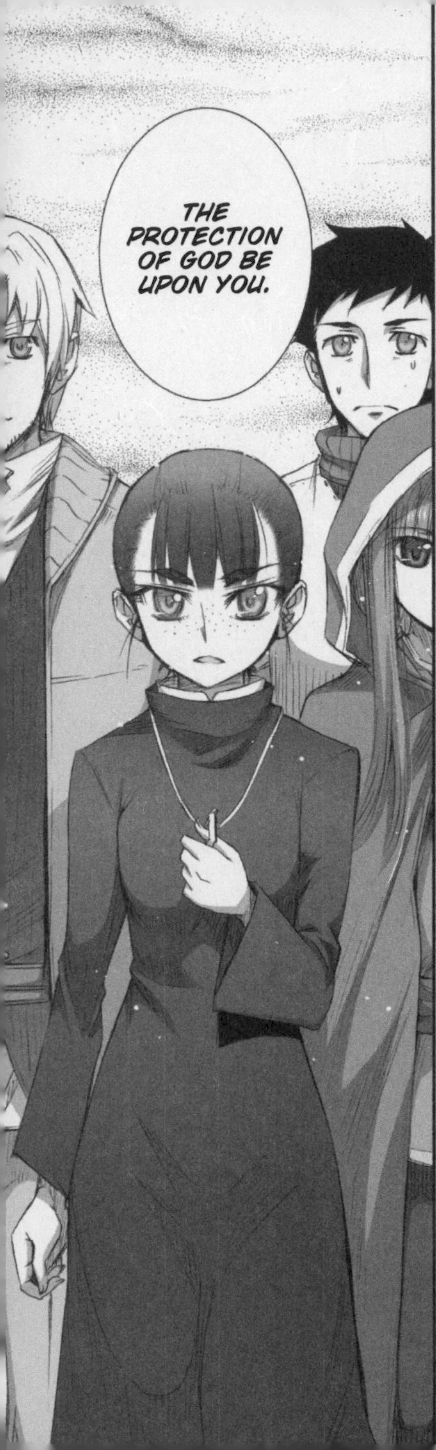
THE PROTECTION OF GOD BE UPON YOU.

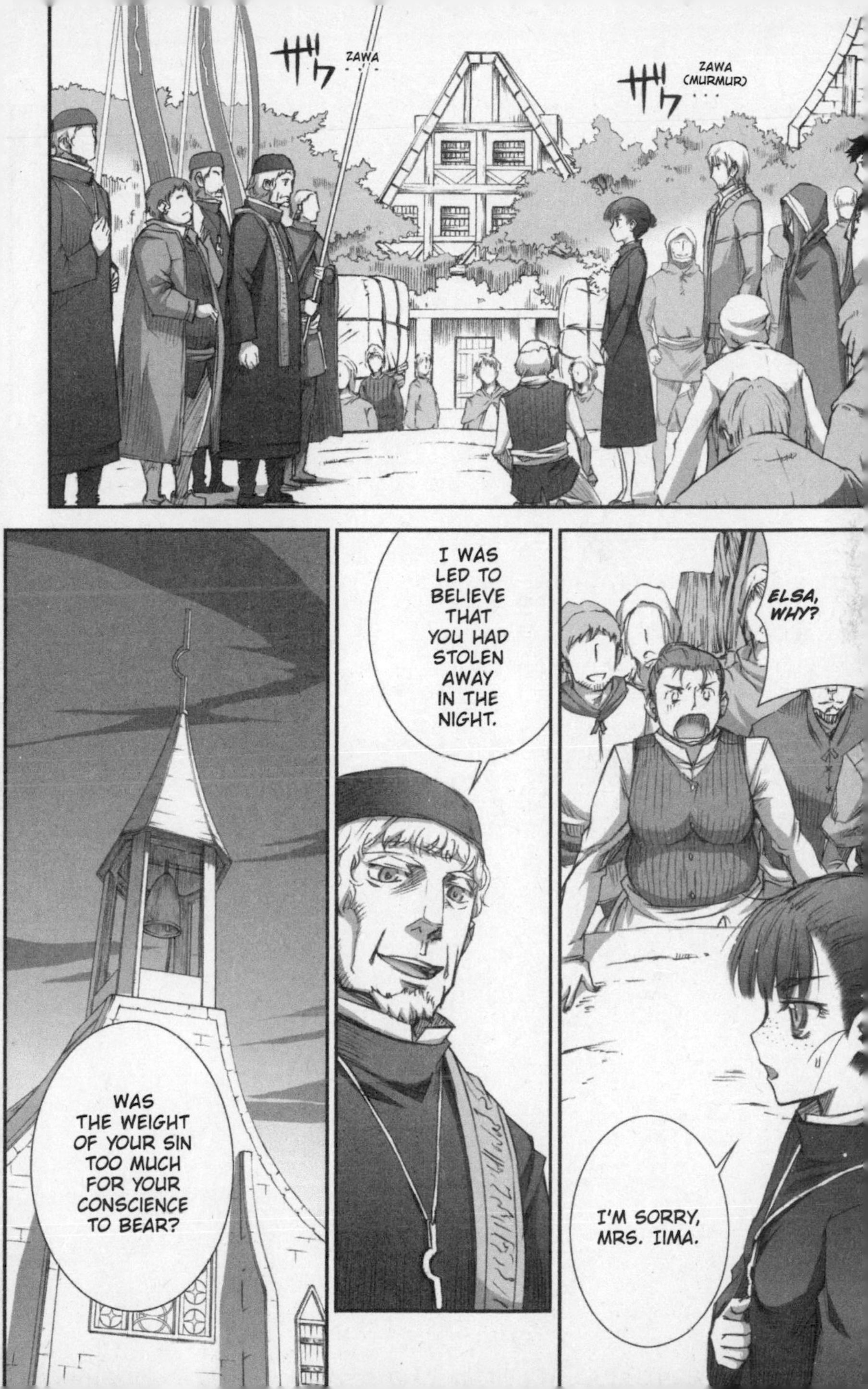
ザワ
ZAWA (MURMUR)
ザワ
ZAWA
ELSA, WHY?
I'M SORRY, MRS. IIMA.
I WAS LED TO BELIEVE THAT YOU HAD STOLEN AWAY IN THE NIGHT.
WAS THE WEIGHT OF YOUR SIN TOO MUCH FOR YOUR CONSCIENCE TO BEAR?

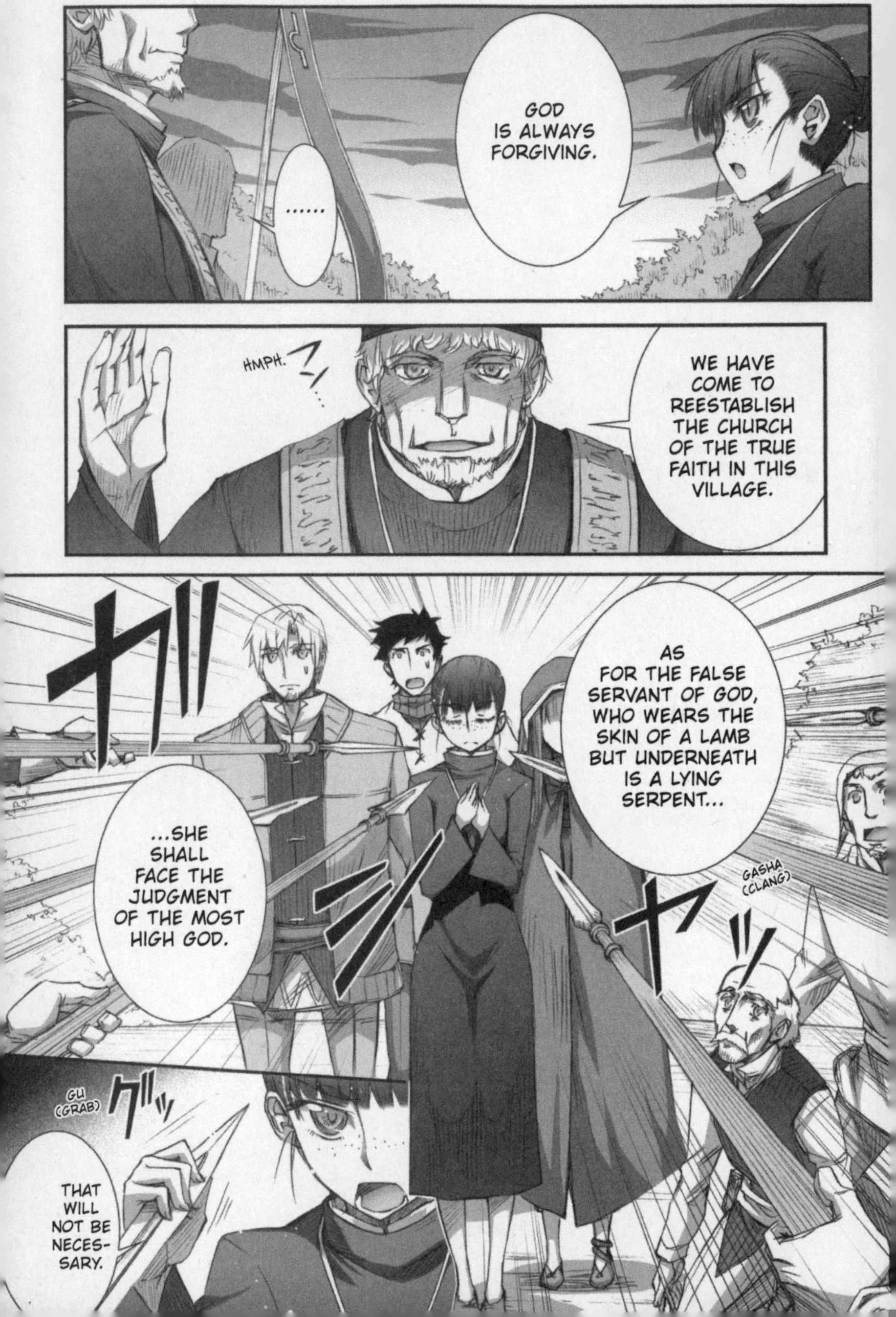
GOD IS ALWAYS FORGIVING.
......
WE HAVE COME TO REESTABLISH THE CHURCH OF THE TRUE FAITH IN THIS VILLAGE.
HMPH.
AS FOR THE FALSE SERVANT OF GOD, WHO WEARS THE SKIN OF A LAMB BUT UNDERNEATH IS A LYING SERPENT...
...SHE SHALL FACE THE JUDGMENT OF THE MOST HIGH GOD.
GASHA (CLANG)
GU (GRAB)
THAT WILL NOT BE NECES-SARY.

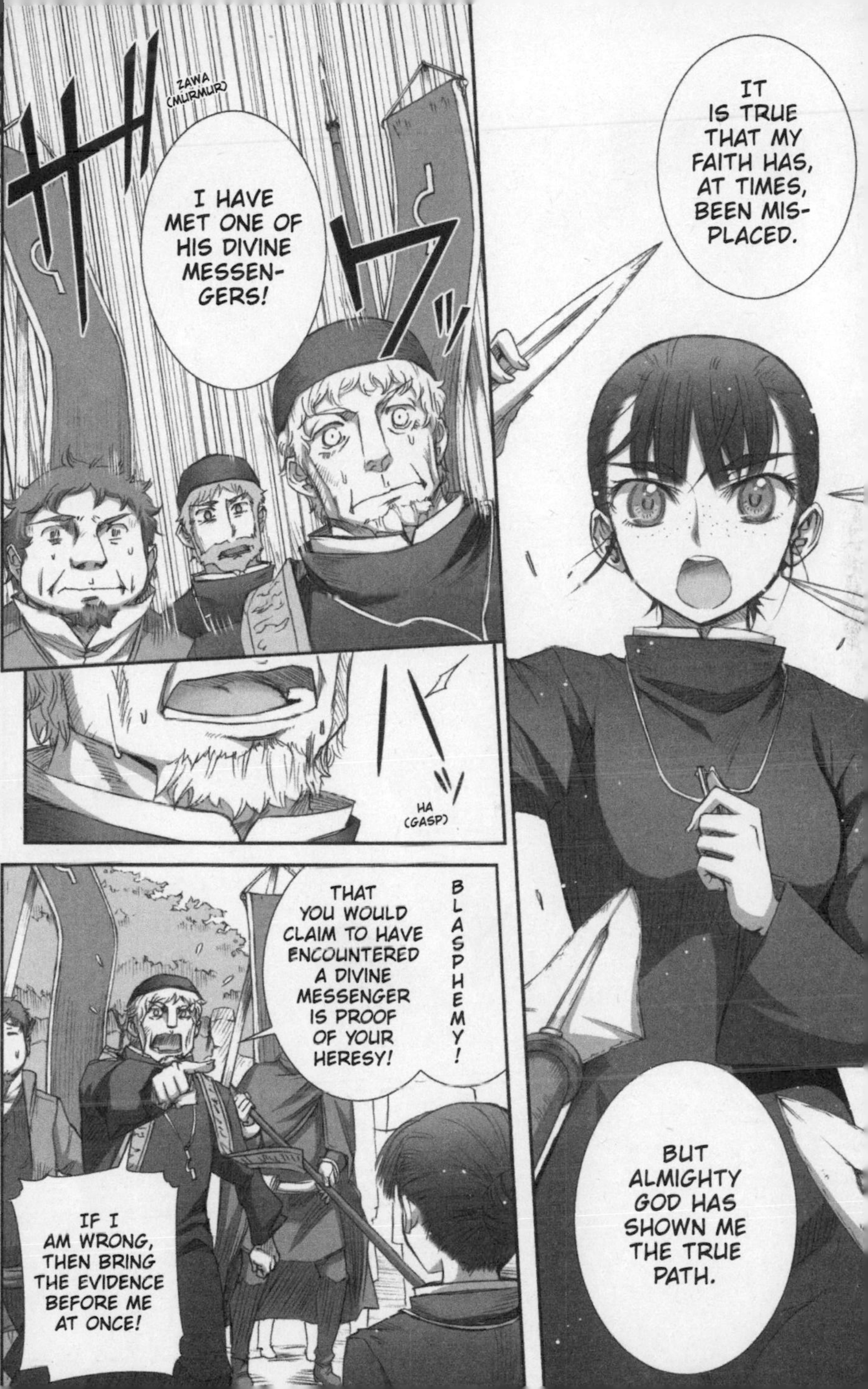
IT IS TRUE THAT MY FAITH HAS, AT TIMES, BEEN MIS-PLACED.
BUT ALMIGHTY GOD HAS SHOWN ME THE TRUE PATH.
ZAWA (MURMUR)
I HAVE MET ONE OF HIS DIVINE MESSEN-GERS!
HA (GASP)
BLASPHEMY!
THAT YOU WOULD CLAIM TO HAVE ENCOUNTERED A DIVINE MESSENGER IS PROOF OF YOUR HERESY!
IF I AM WRONG, THEN BRING THE EVIDENCE BEFORE ME AT ONCE!

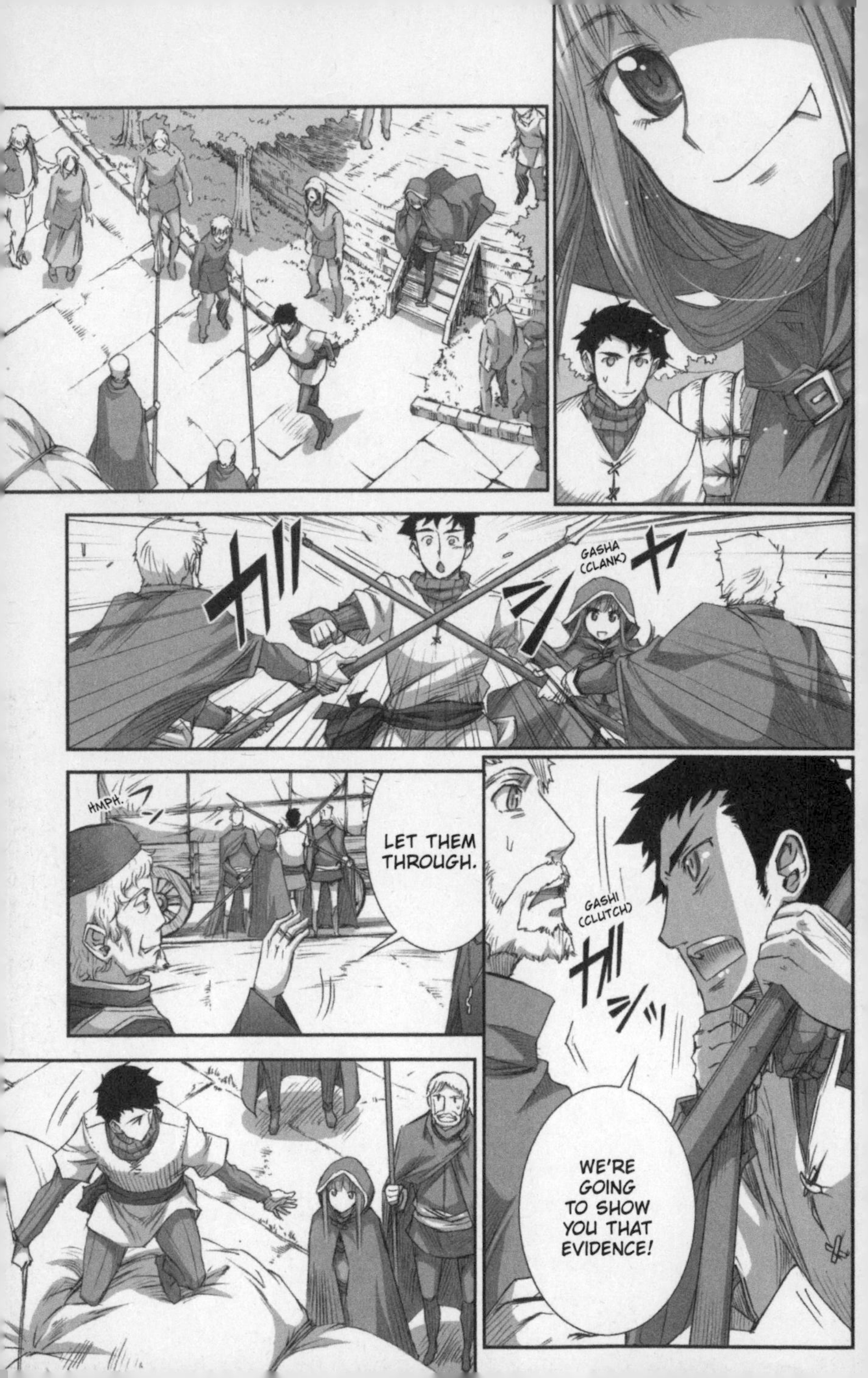
GASHA (CLANK)
GASHI (CLUTCH)
WE'RE GOING TO SHOW YOU THAT EVIDENCE!
HMPH.
LET THEM THROUGH.

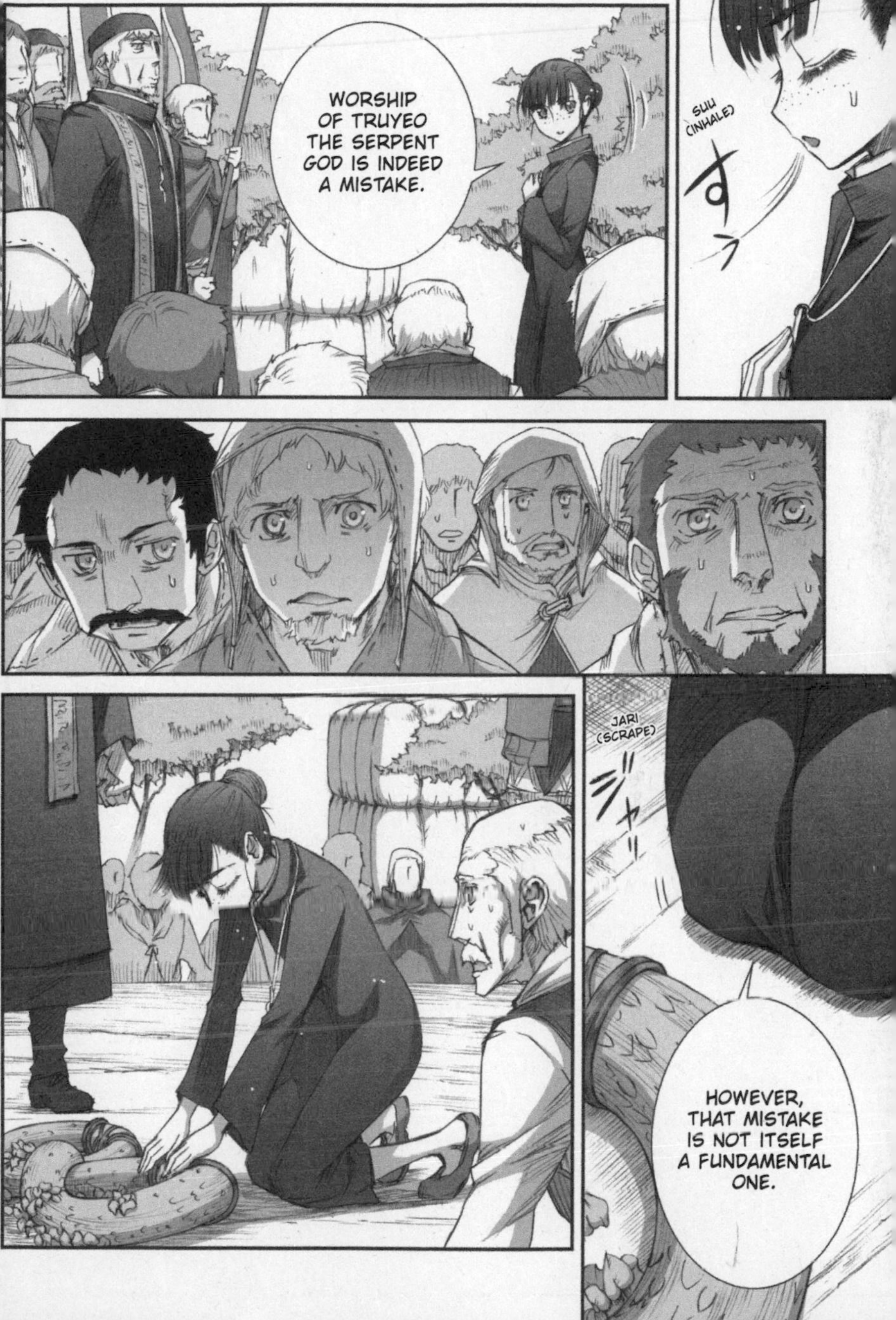
SUU (INHALE)
す
WORSHIP OF TRUYEO THE SERPENT GOD IS INDEED A MISTAKE.
JARI (SCRAPE)
ジャリ!!
HOWEVER, THAT MISTAKE IS NOT ITSELF A FUNDAMENTAL ONE.

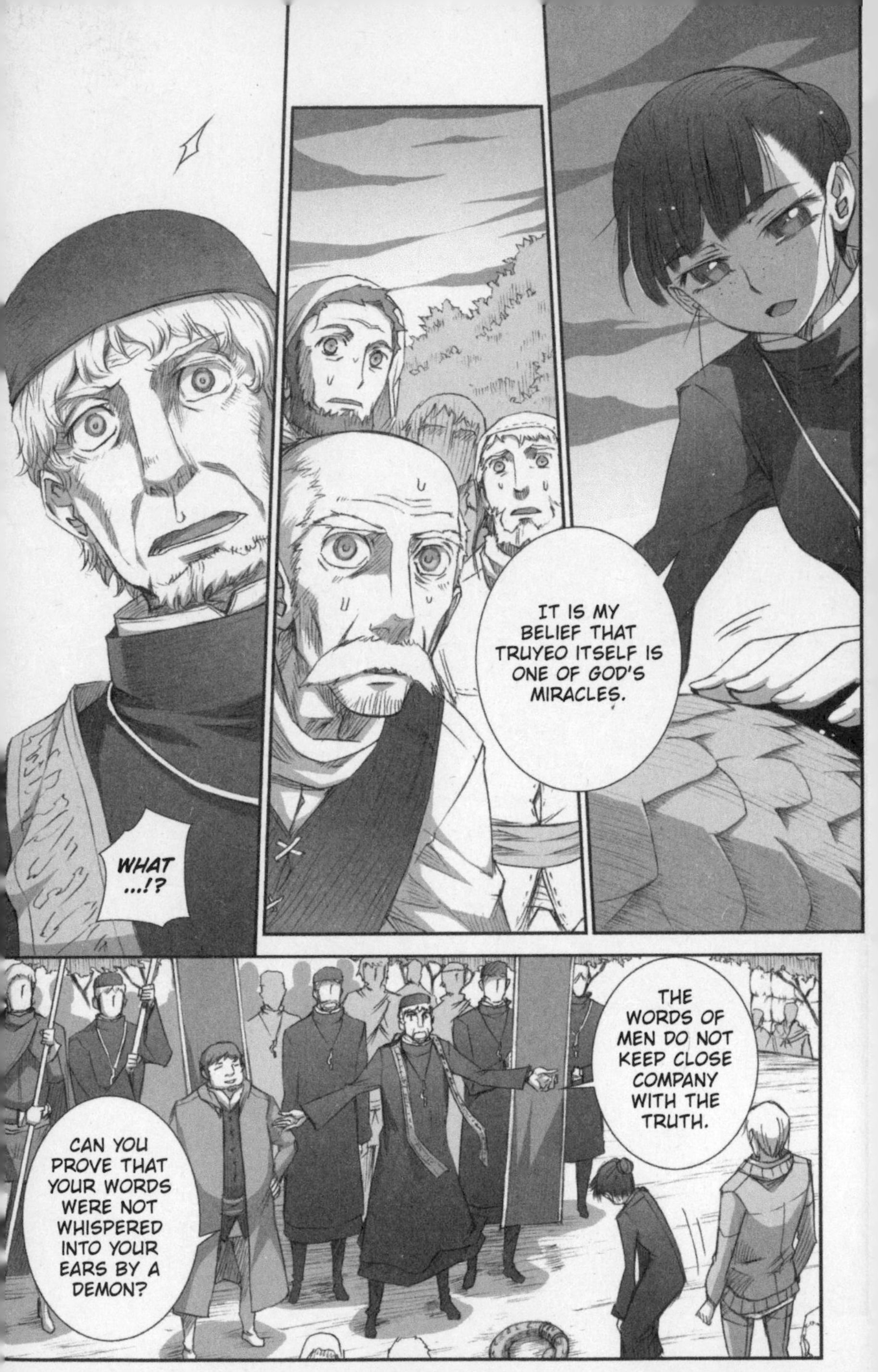
IT IS MY BELIEF THAT TRUYEO ITSELF IS ONE OF GOD'S MIRACLES.
WHAT ...!?
THE WORDS OF MEN DO NOT KEEP CLOSE COMPANY WITH THE TRUTH.
CAN YOU PROVE THAT YOUR WORDS WERE NOT WHISPERED INTO YOUR EARS BY A DEMON?

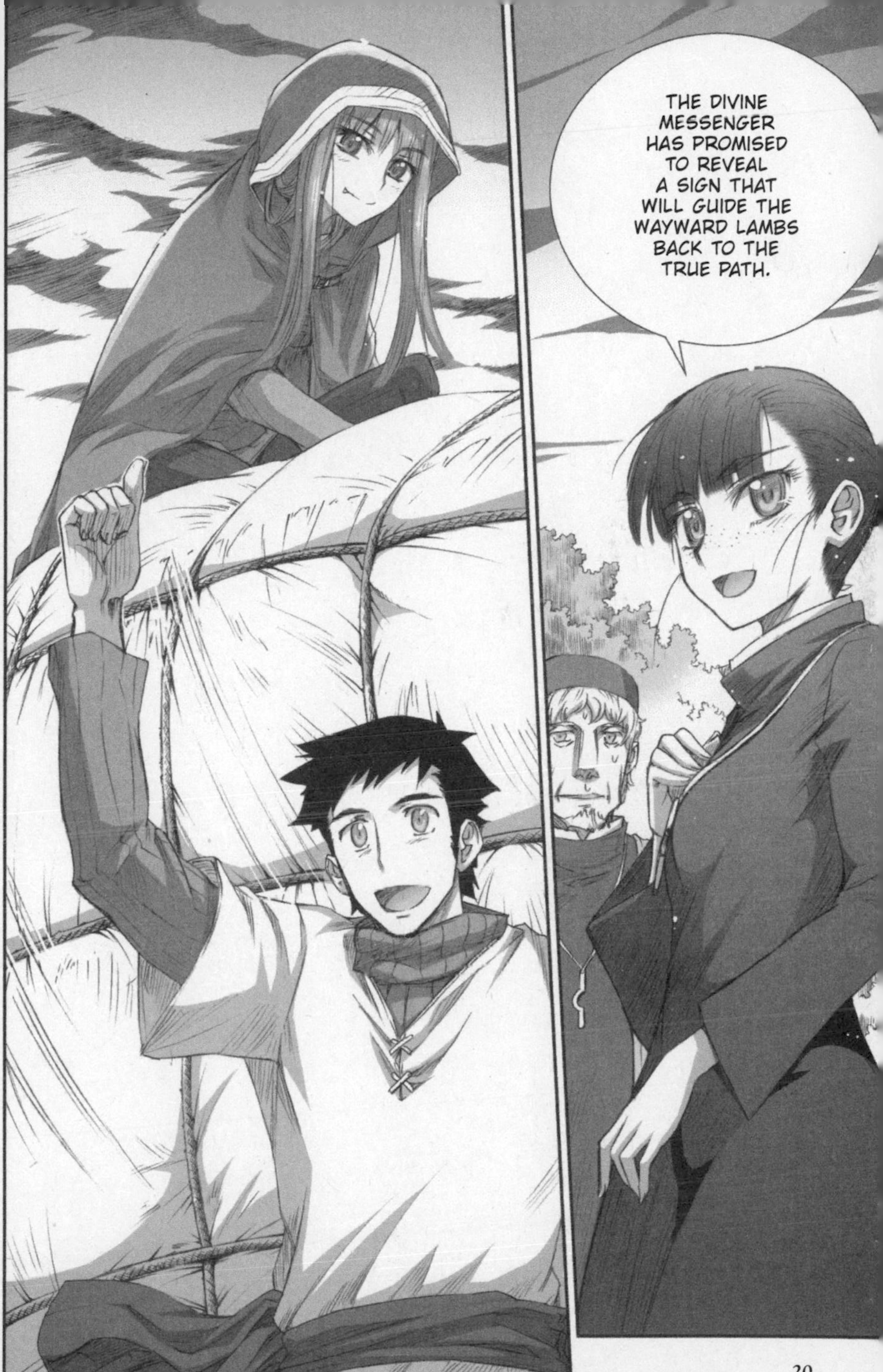
THE DIVINE MESSENGER HAS PROMISED TO REVEAL A SIGN THAT WILL GUIDE THE WAYWARD LAMBS BACK TO THE TRUE PATH.

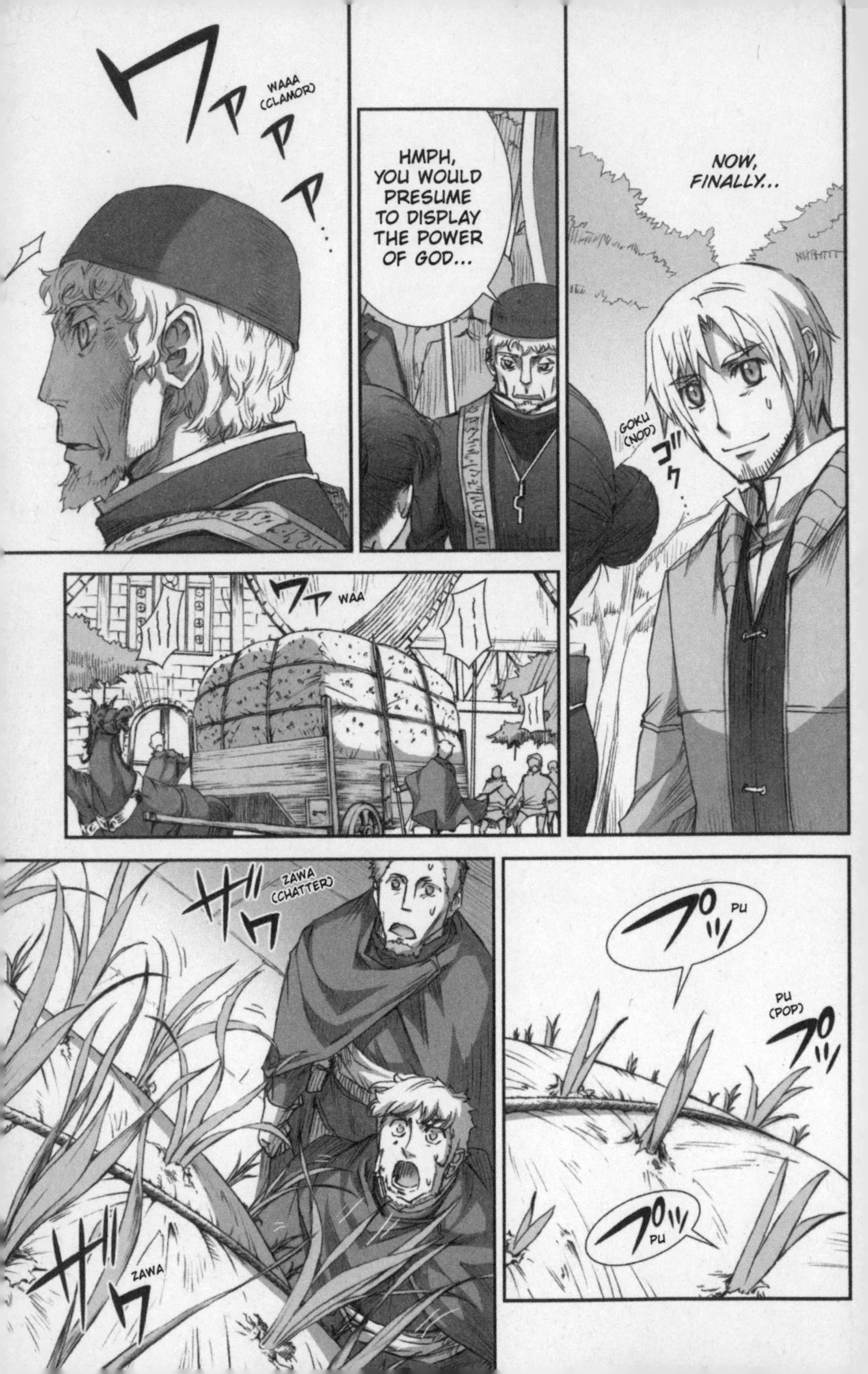

NOW, FINALLY...
GOKU (NOD)
HMPH, YOU WOULD PRESUME TO DISPLAY THE POWER OF GOD...
WAAA (CLAMOR)
WAA
PU
PU (POP)
PU
ZAWA (CHATTER)
ZAWA

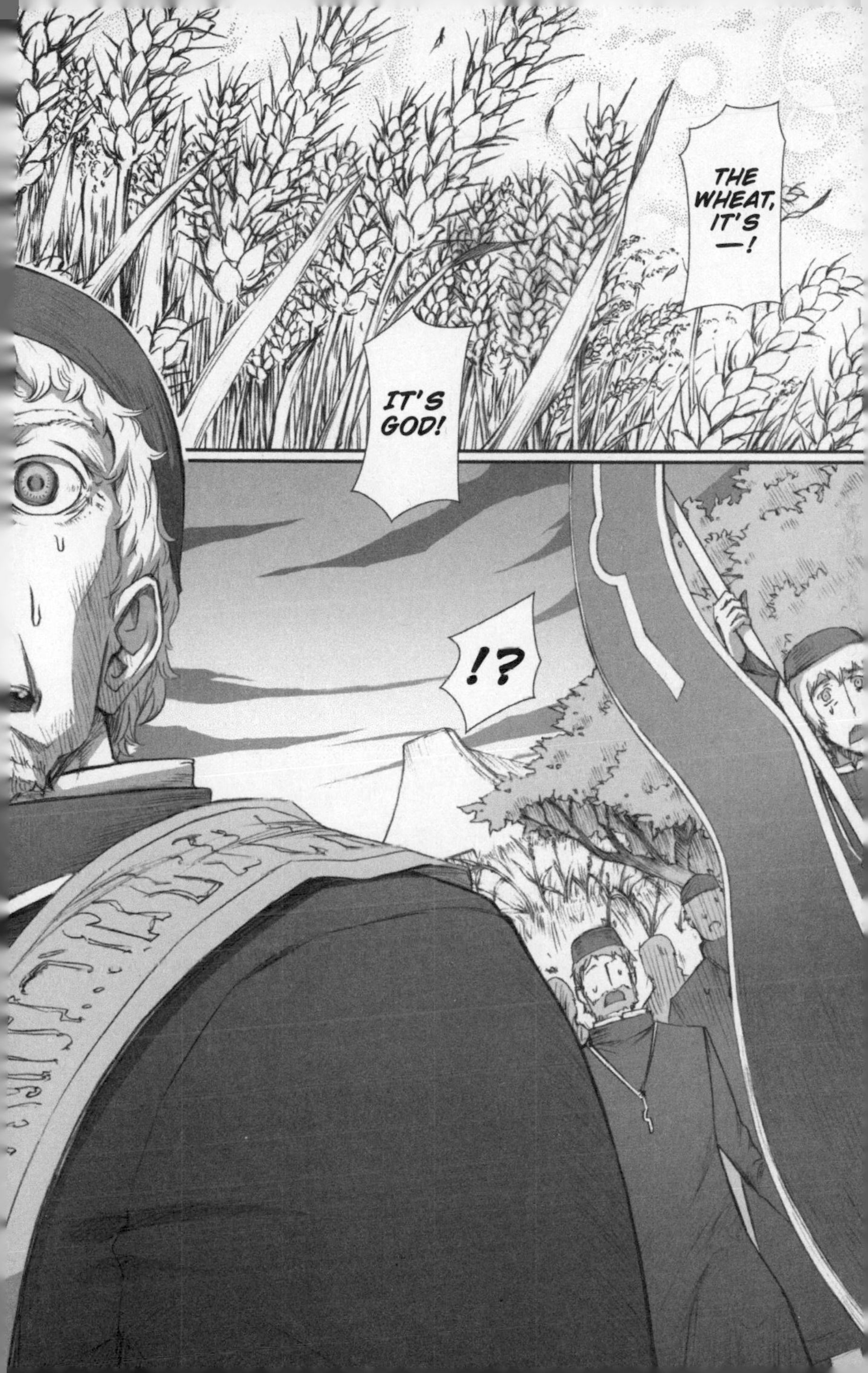
THE WHEAT, IT'S —!
IT'S GOD!
!?

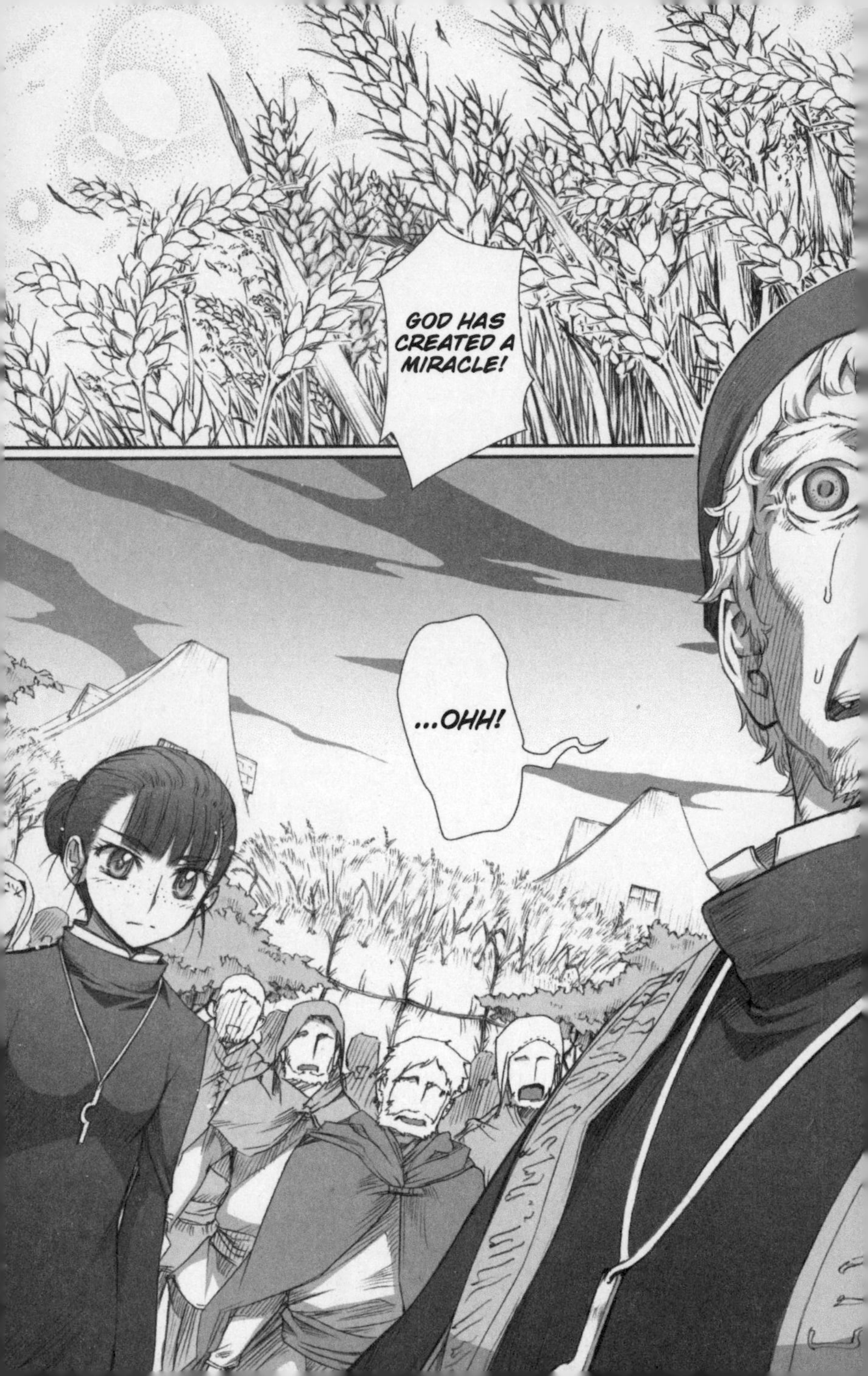
GOD HAS CREATED A MIRACLE!
...OHH!

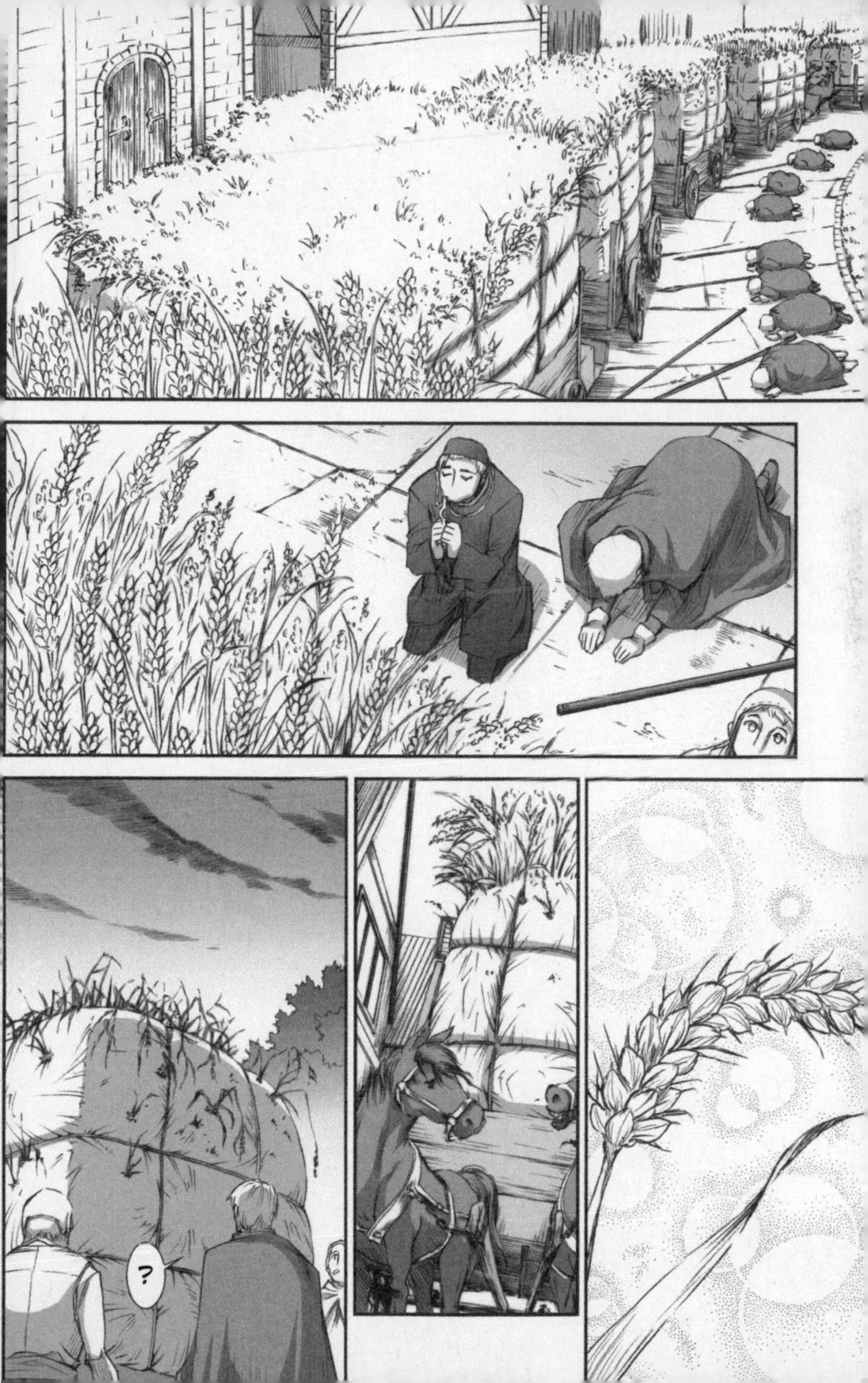
?

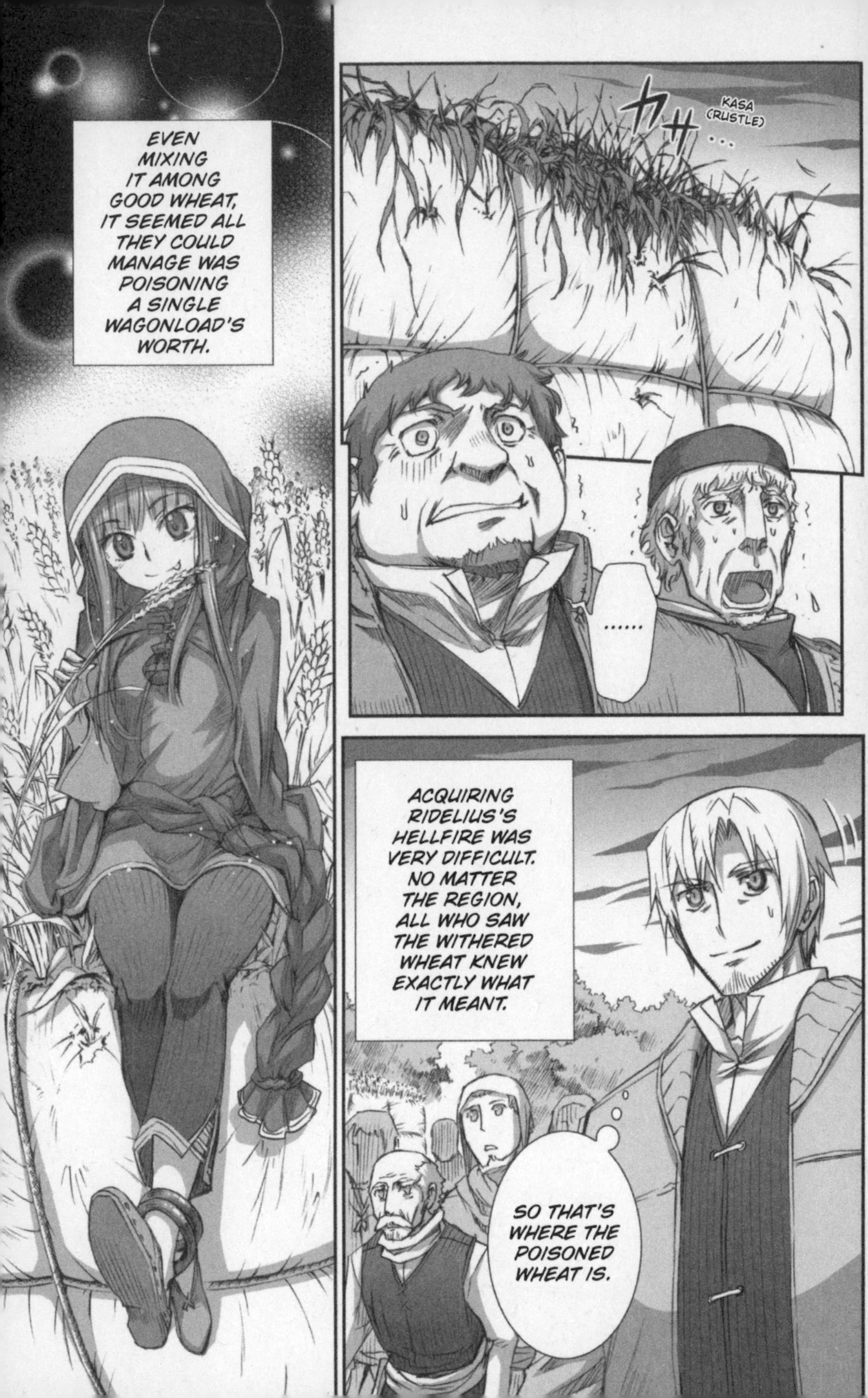
KASA (RUSTLE)
......
ACQUIRING RIDELIUS'S HELLFIRE WAS VERY DIFFICULT. NO MATTER THE REGION, ALL WHO SAW THE WITHERED WHEAT KNEW EXACTLY WHAT IT MEANT.
SO THAT'S WHERE THE POISONED WHEAT IS.
EVEN MIXING IT AMONG GOOD WHEAT, IT SEEMED ALL THEY COULD MANAGE WAS POISONING A SINGLE WAGONLOAD'S WORTH.

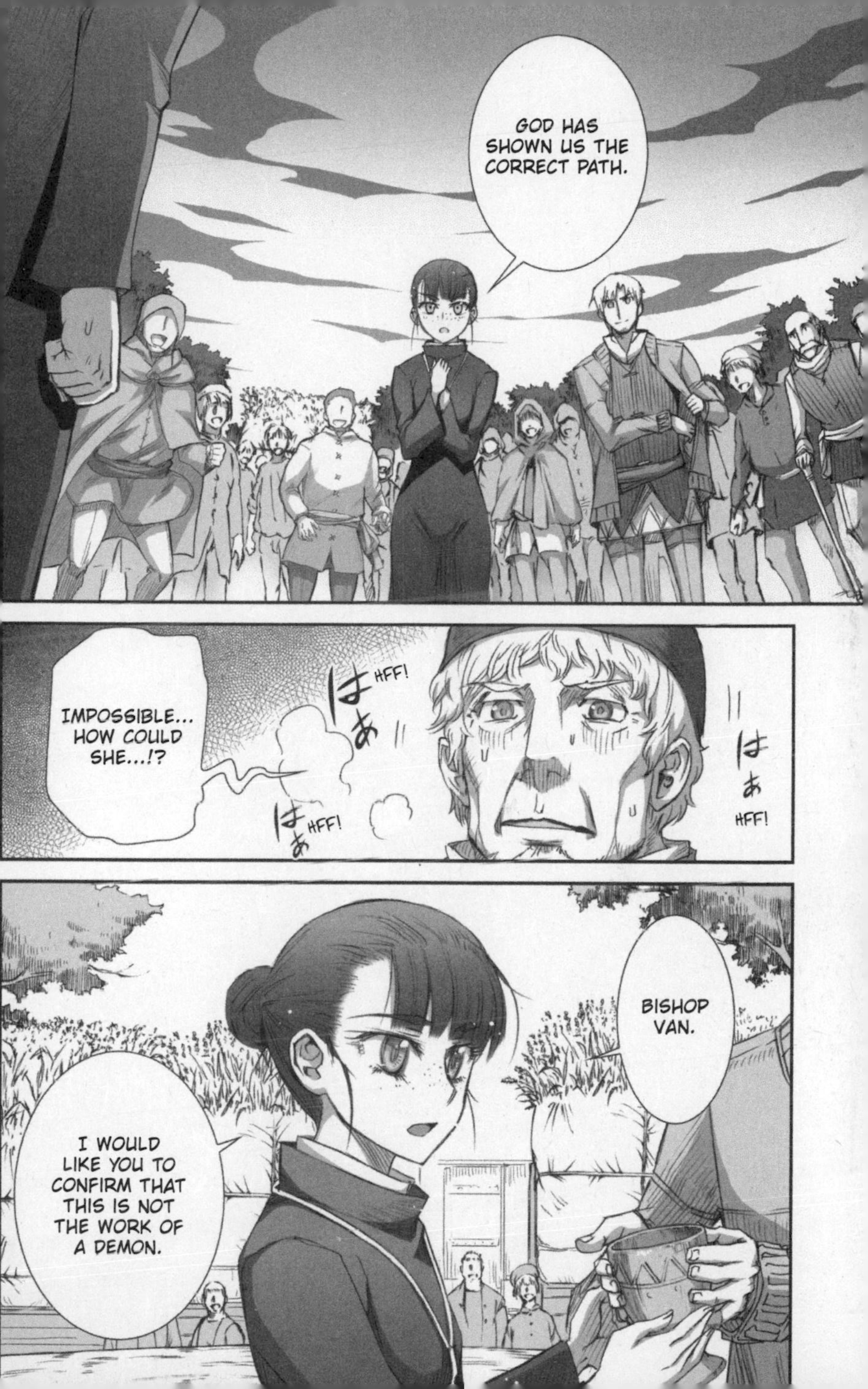
GOD HAS SHOWN US THE CORRECT PATH.
はぁ HFF!
はぁ HFF!
IMPOSSIBLE... HOW COULD SHE...!?
はぁ HFF!
BISHOP VAN.
I WOULD LIKE YOU TO CONFIRM THAT THIS IS NOT THE WORK OF A DEMON.

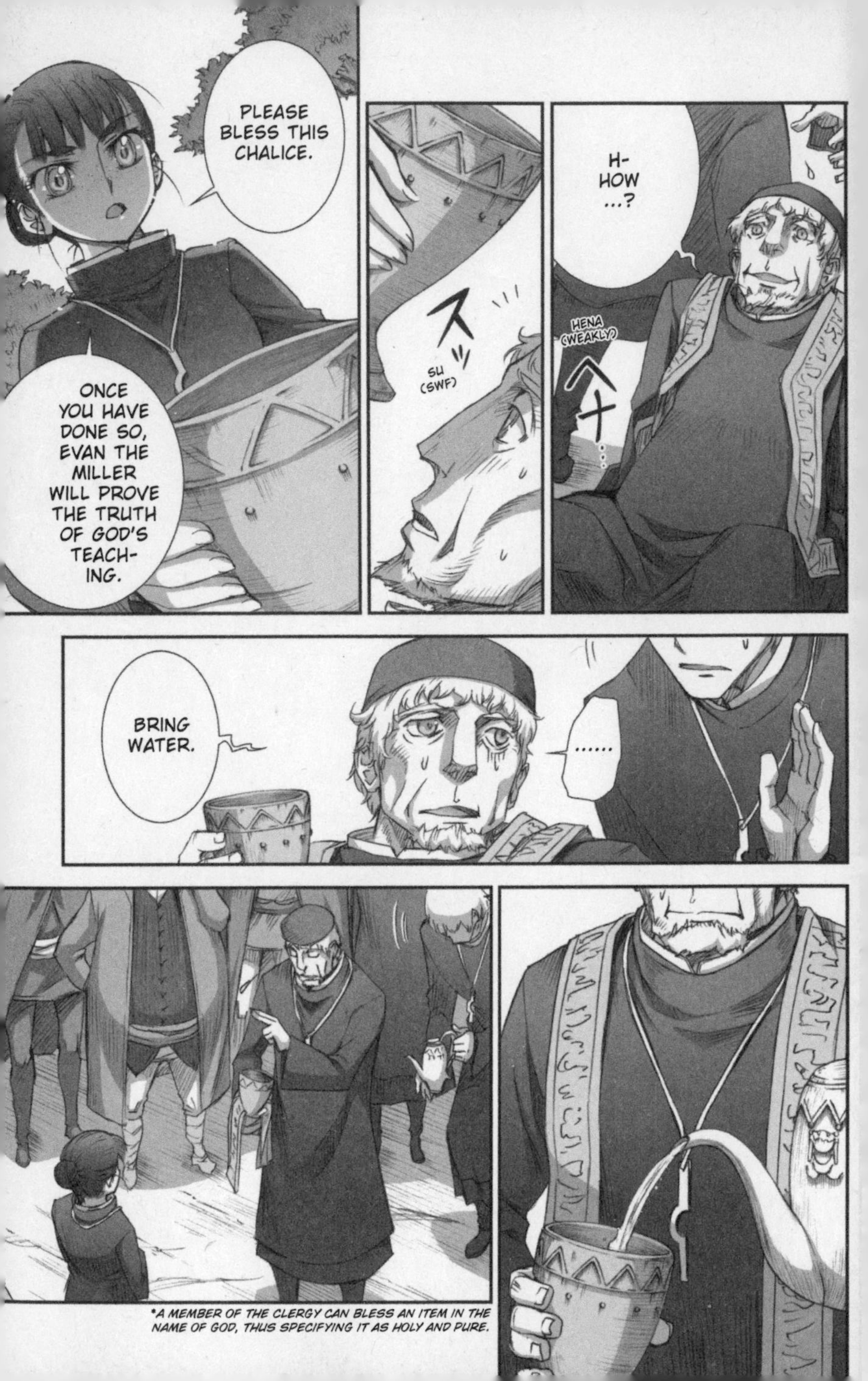
H-HOW ...?
HENA (WEAKLY)
ヘナ…
スッ
SU (SWF)
PLEASE BLESS THIS CHALICE.
ONCE YOU HAVE DONE SO, EVAN THE MILLER WILL PROVE THE TRUTH OF GOD'S TEACHING.
....
BRING WATER.

*A MEMBER OF THE CLERGY CAN BLESS AN ITEM IN THE NAME OF GOD, THUS SPECIFYING IT AS HOLY AND PURE.

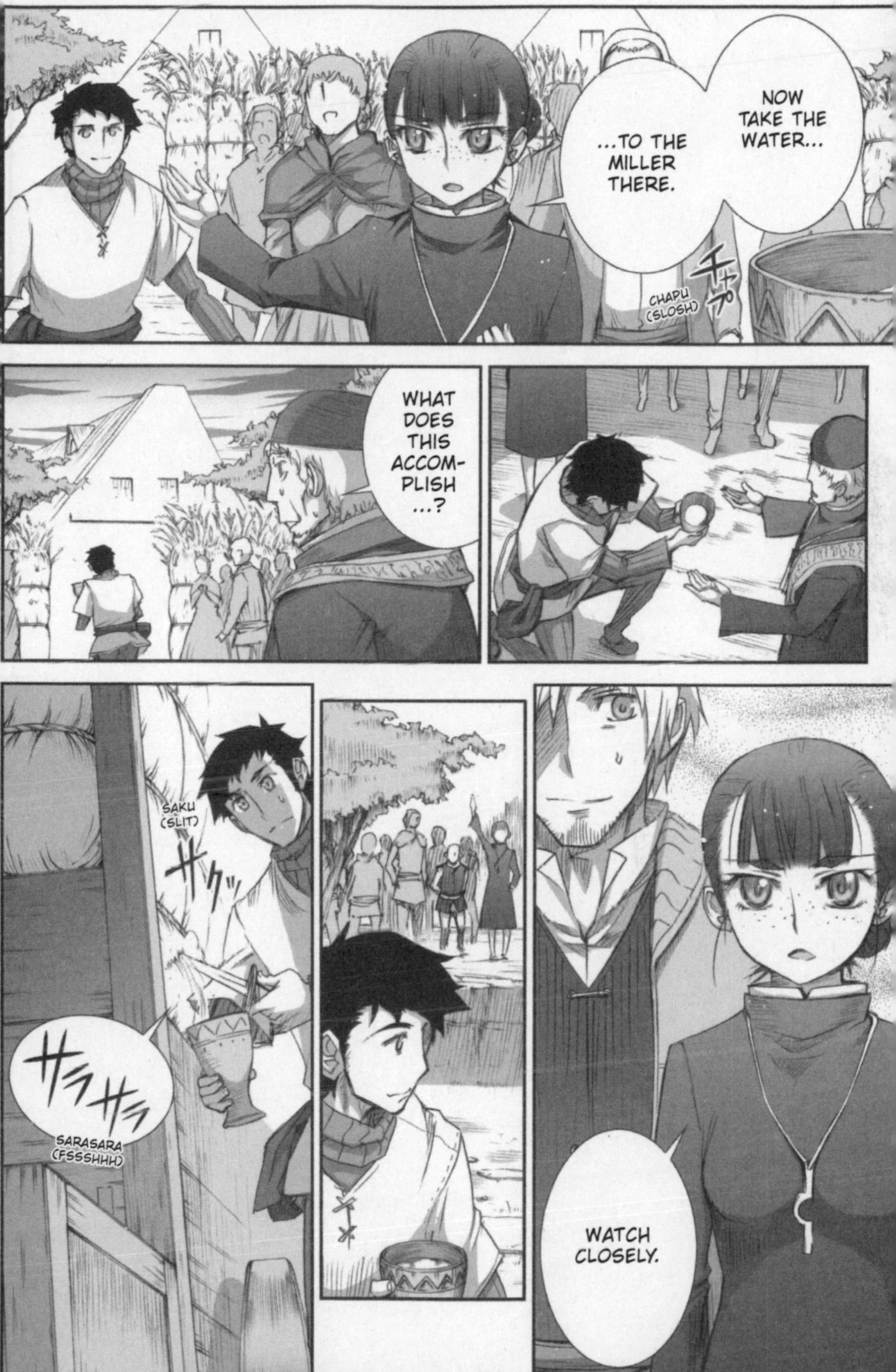
NOW TAKE THE WATER...
...TO THE MILLER THERE.
チャプ
CHAPU (SLOSH)
WHAT DOES THIS ACCOMPLISH...?
WATCH CLOSELY.
ザクッ
SAKU (SLIT)
サラサラ
SARASARA (FSSSHHH)

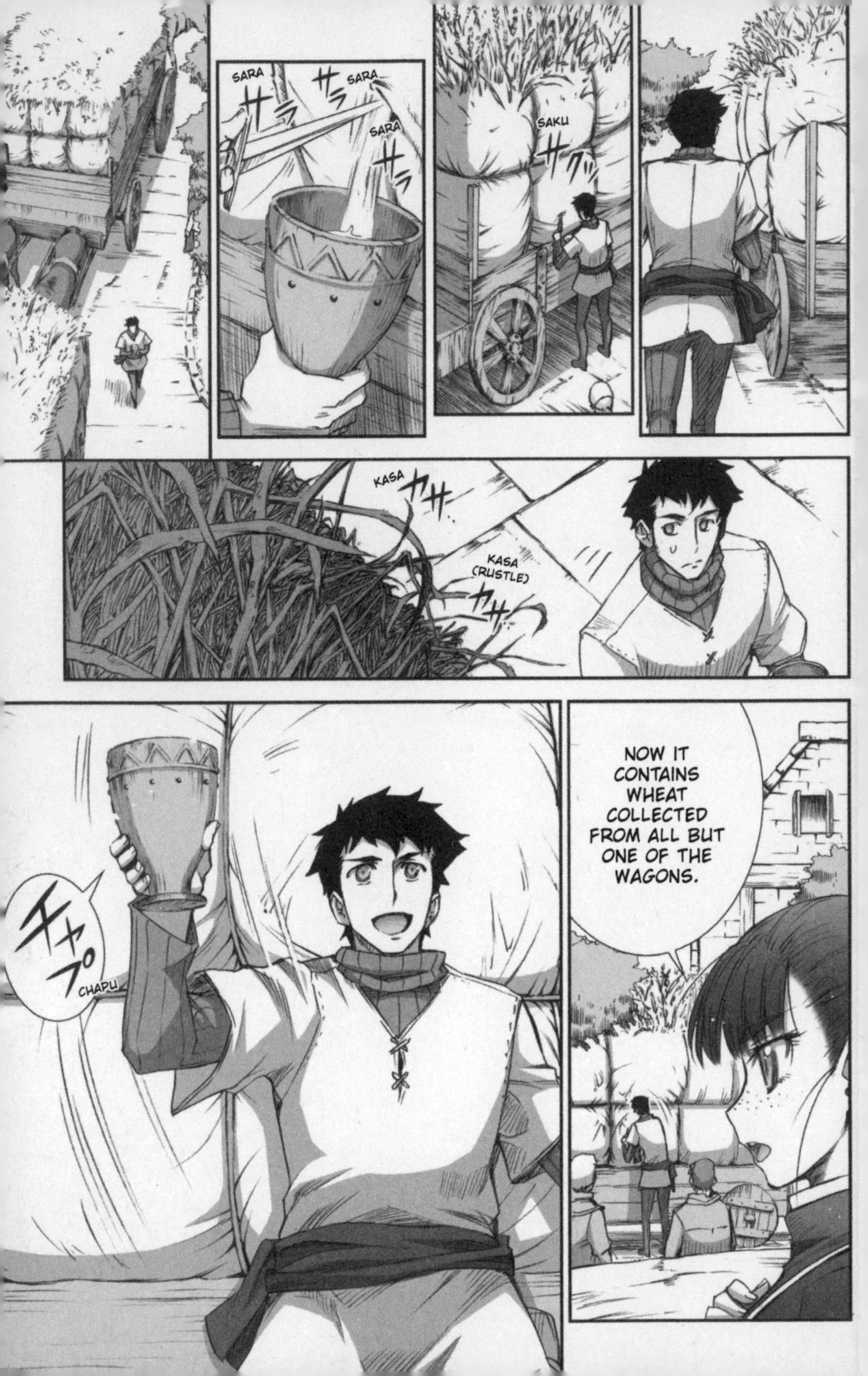
SAKU
SARA
SARA
SARA
KASA
KASA (RUSTLE)
NOW IT CONTAINS WHEAT COLLECTED FROM ALL BUT ONE OF THE WAGONS.
CHAPU

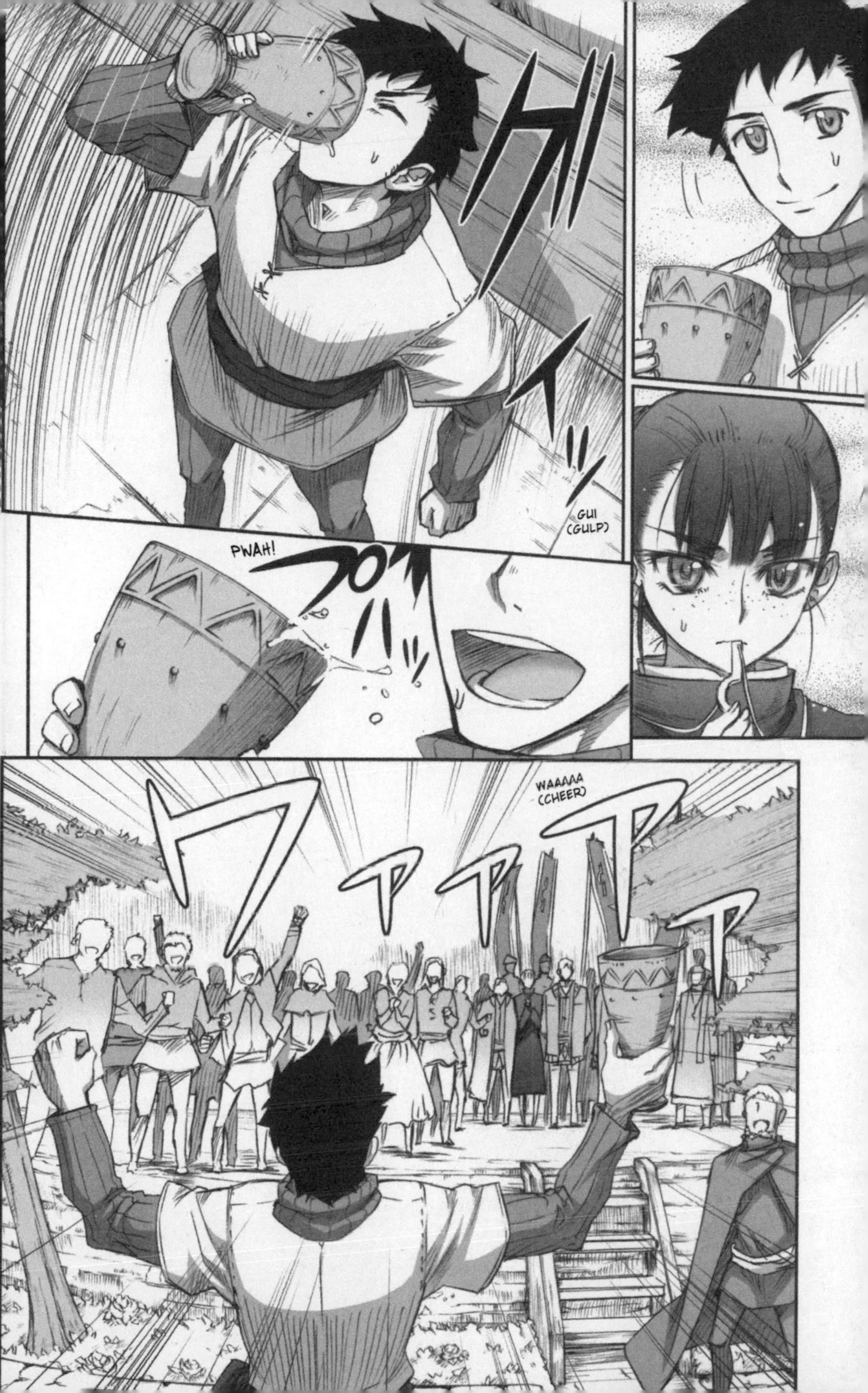
GUI (GULP)
PWAH!
WAAAAA (CHEER)

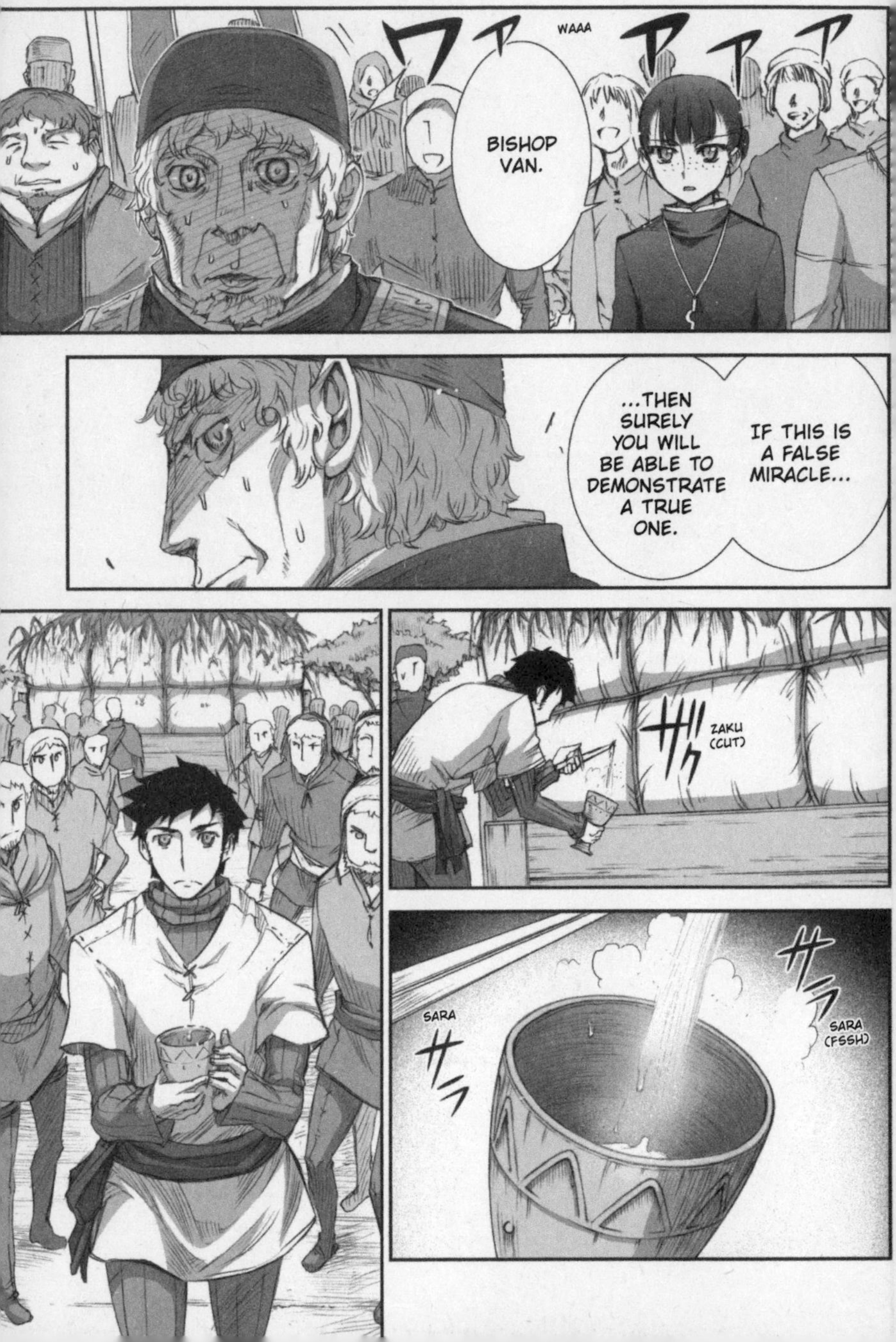
WAAA
BISHOP VAN.
IF THIS IS A FALSE MIRACLE...
...THEN SURELY YOU WILL BE ABLE TO DEMONSTRATE A TRUE ONE.
ZAKU (CUT)
SARA (FSSH)
SARA

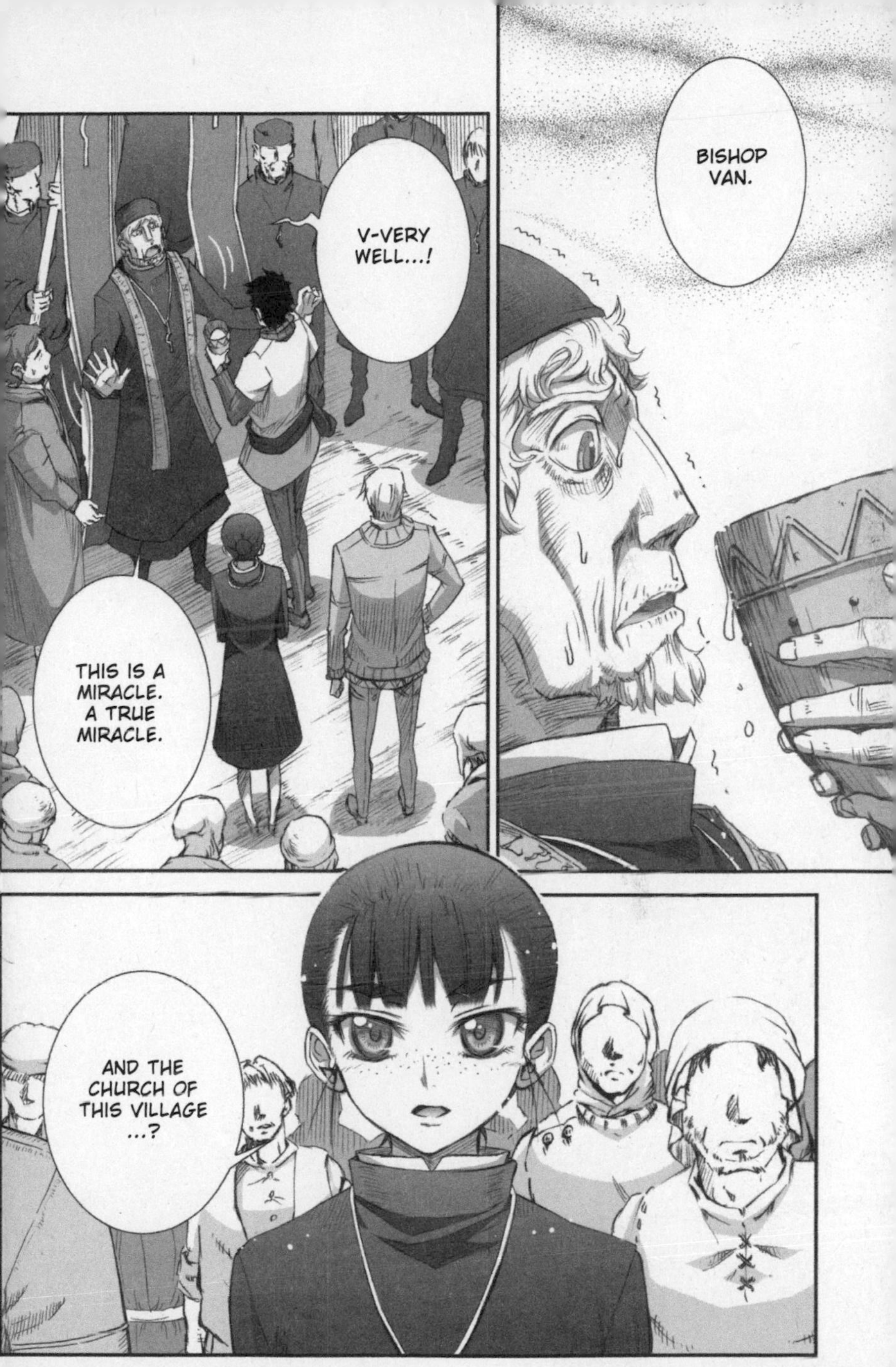
BISHOP VAN.
V-VERY WELL...!
THIS IS A MIRACLE. A TRUE MIRACLE.
AND THE CHURCH OF THIS VILLAGE ...?

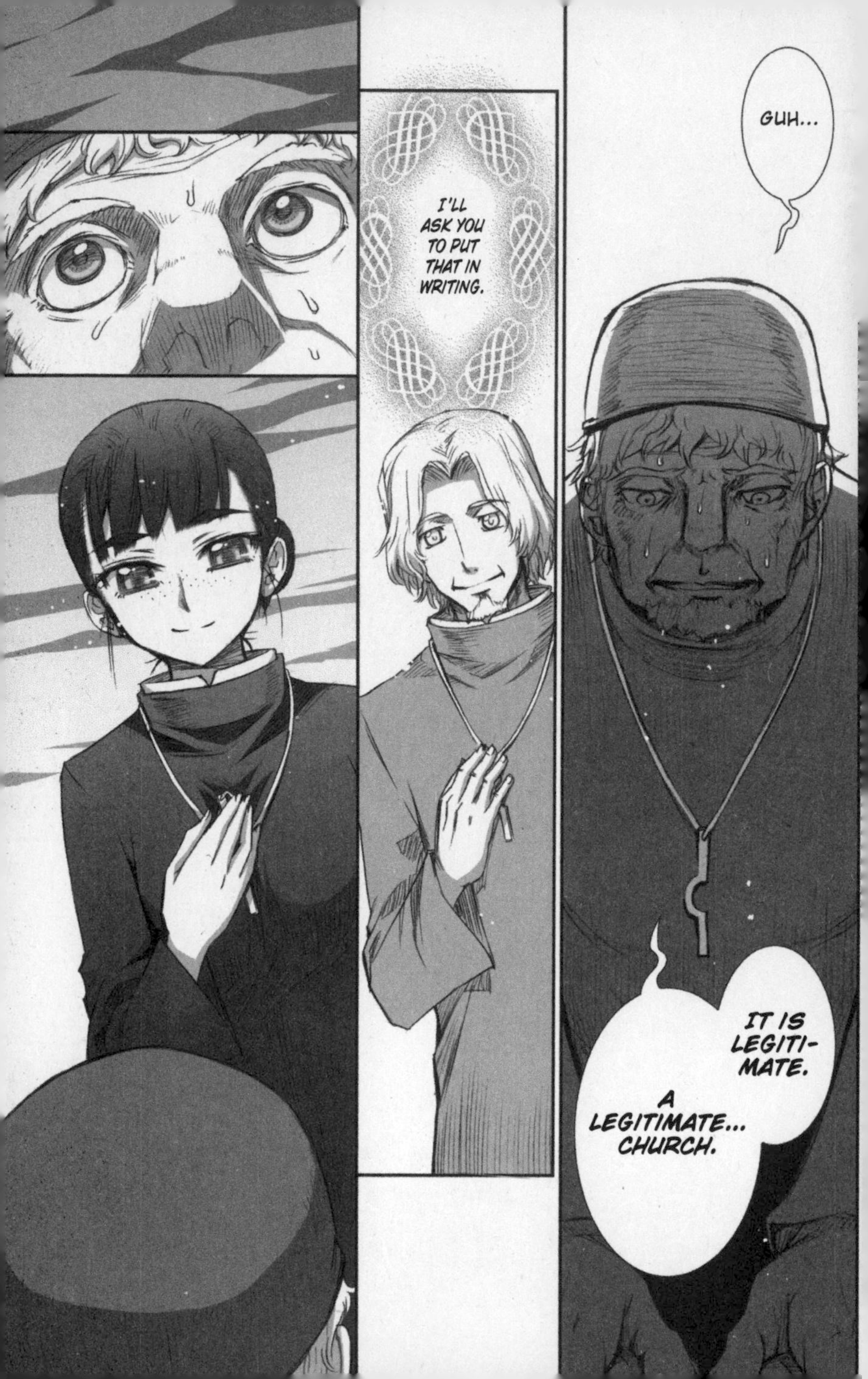
GUH...
IT IS LEGITIMATE.
A LEGITIMATE... CHURCH.
I'LL ASK YOU TO PUT THAT IN WRITING.

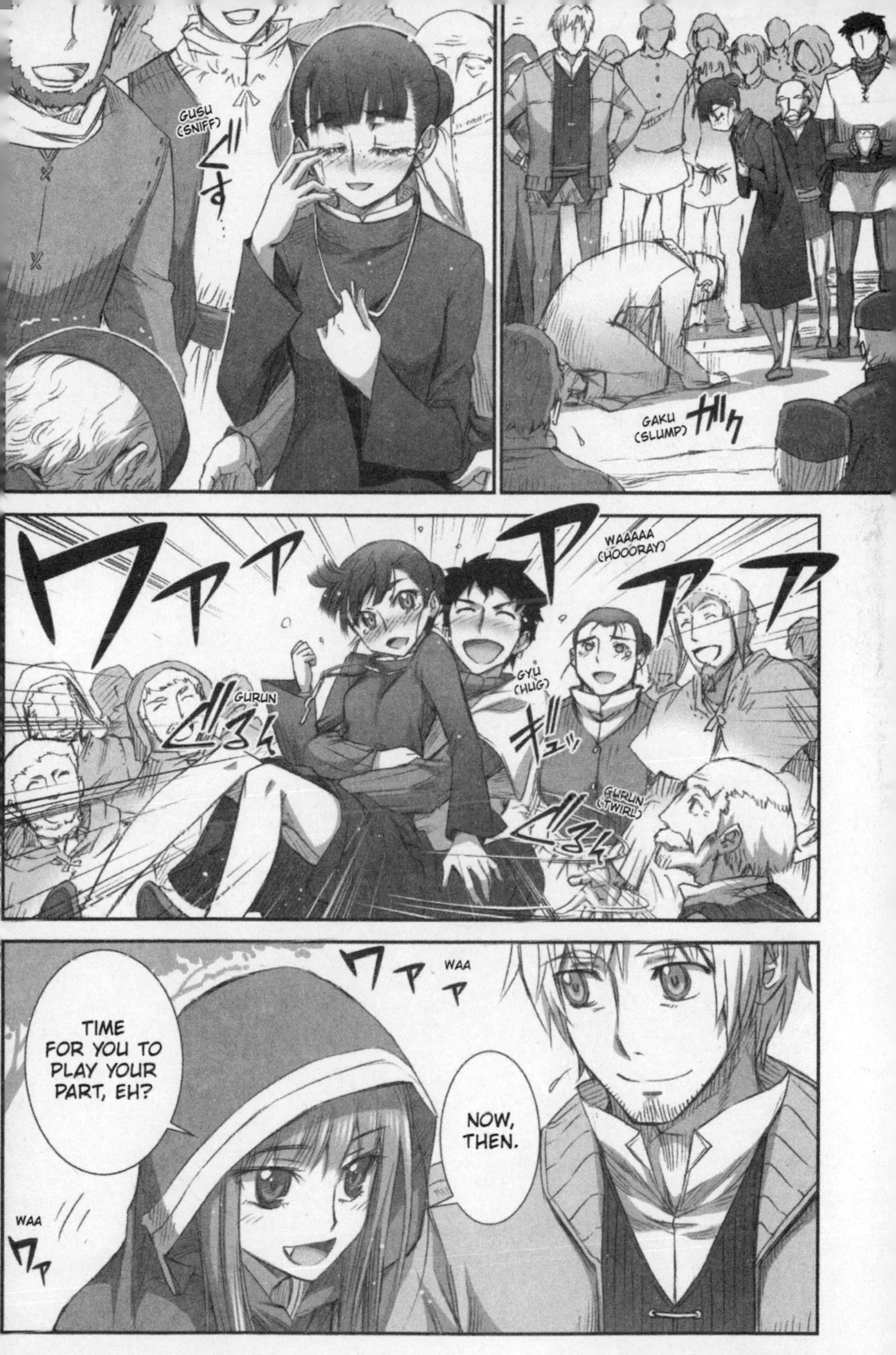
GAKU (SLUMP)
ガク
GUSU (SNIFF)
ぐす
WAAAAA (HOOORAY)
ワァァァァァ
GYU (HUG)
ぎゅっ
GURUN (TWIRL)
ぐるん
GURUN
ぐるん
ワァ
WAA
NOW, THEN.
TIME FOR YOU TO PLAY YOUR PART, EH?
WAA
ワァ

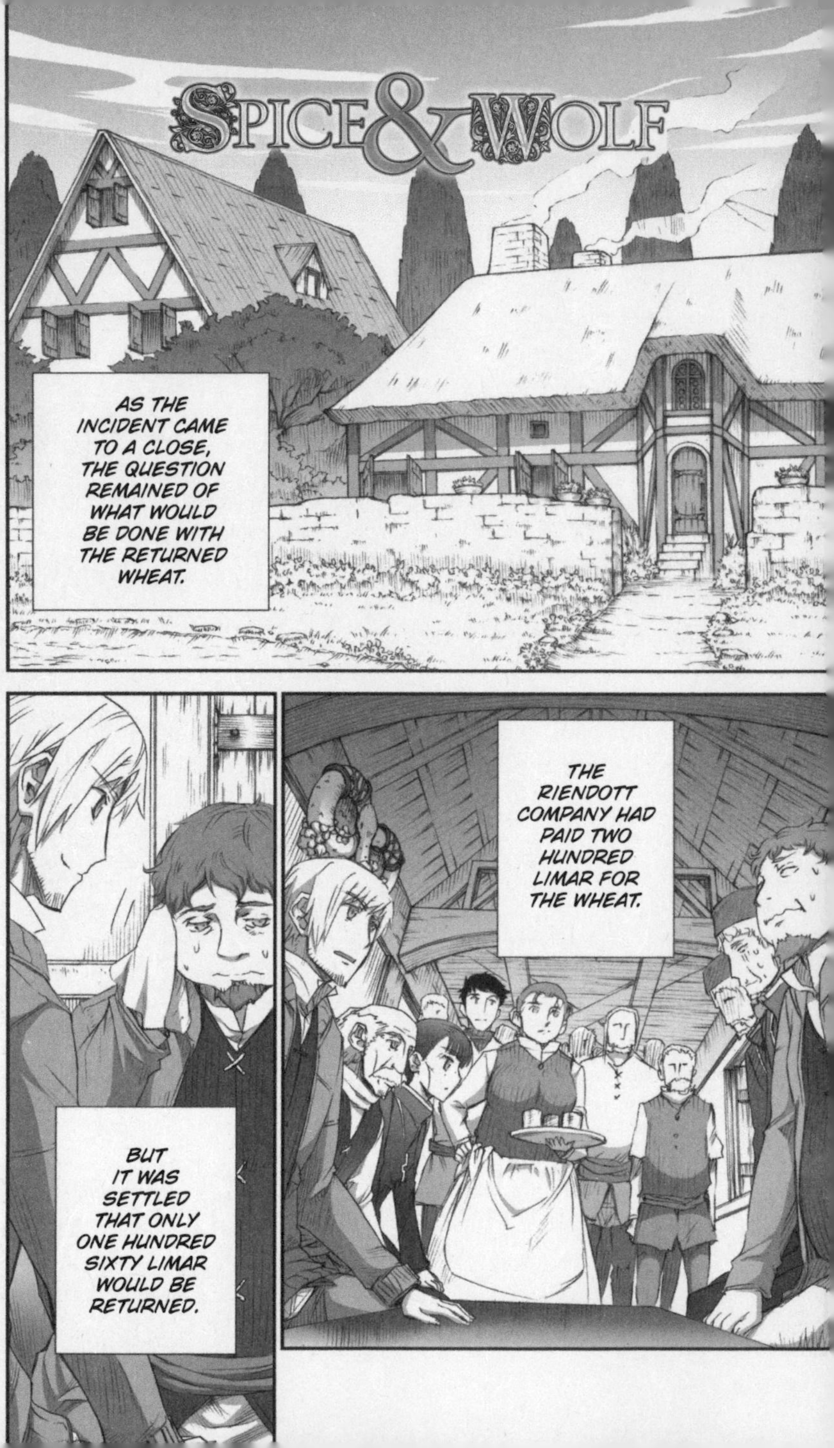
SPICE & WOLF
AS THE INCIDENT CAME TO A CLOSE, THE QUESTION REMAINED OF WHAT WOULD BE DONE WITH THE RETURNED WHEAT.
THE RIENDOTT COMPANY HAD PAID TWO HUNDRED LIMAR FOR THE WHEAT.
BUT IT WAS SETTLED THAT ONLY ONE HUNDRED SIXTY LIMAR WOULD BE RETURNED.

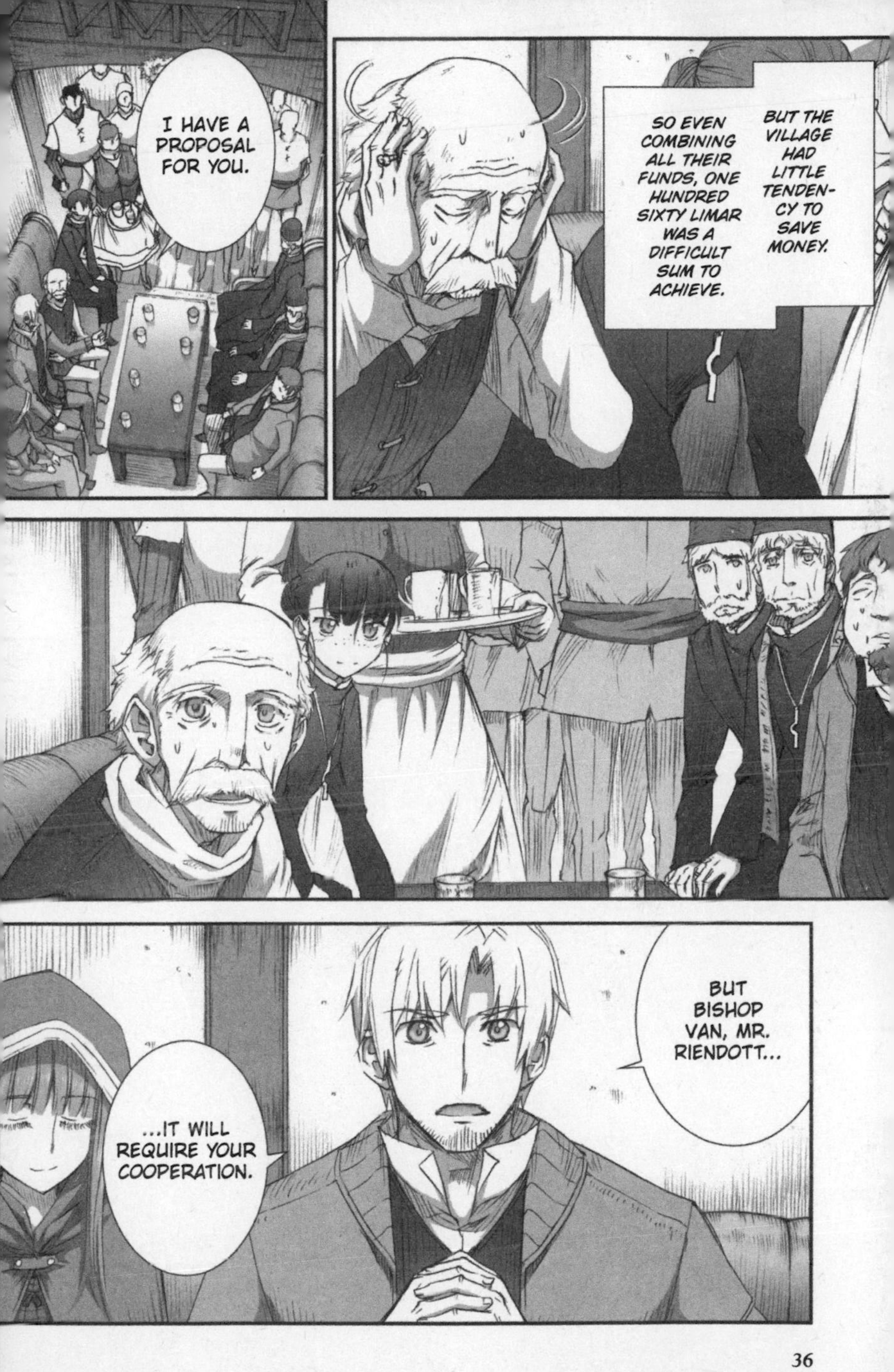
BUT THE VILLAGE HAD LITTLE TENDENCY TO SAVE MONEY.
SO EVEN COMBINING ALL THEIR FUNDS, ONE HUNDRED SIXTY LIMAR WAS A DIFFICULT SUM TO ACHIEVE.
I HAVE A PROPOSAL FOR YOU.
BUT BISHOP VAN, MR. RIENDOTT...
...IT WILL REQUIRE YOUR COOPERATION.

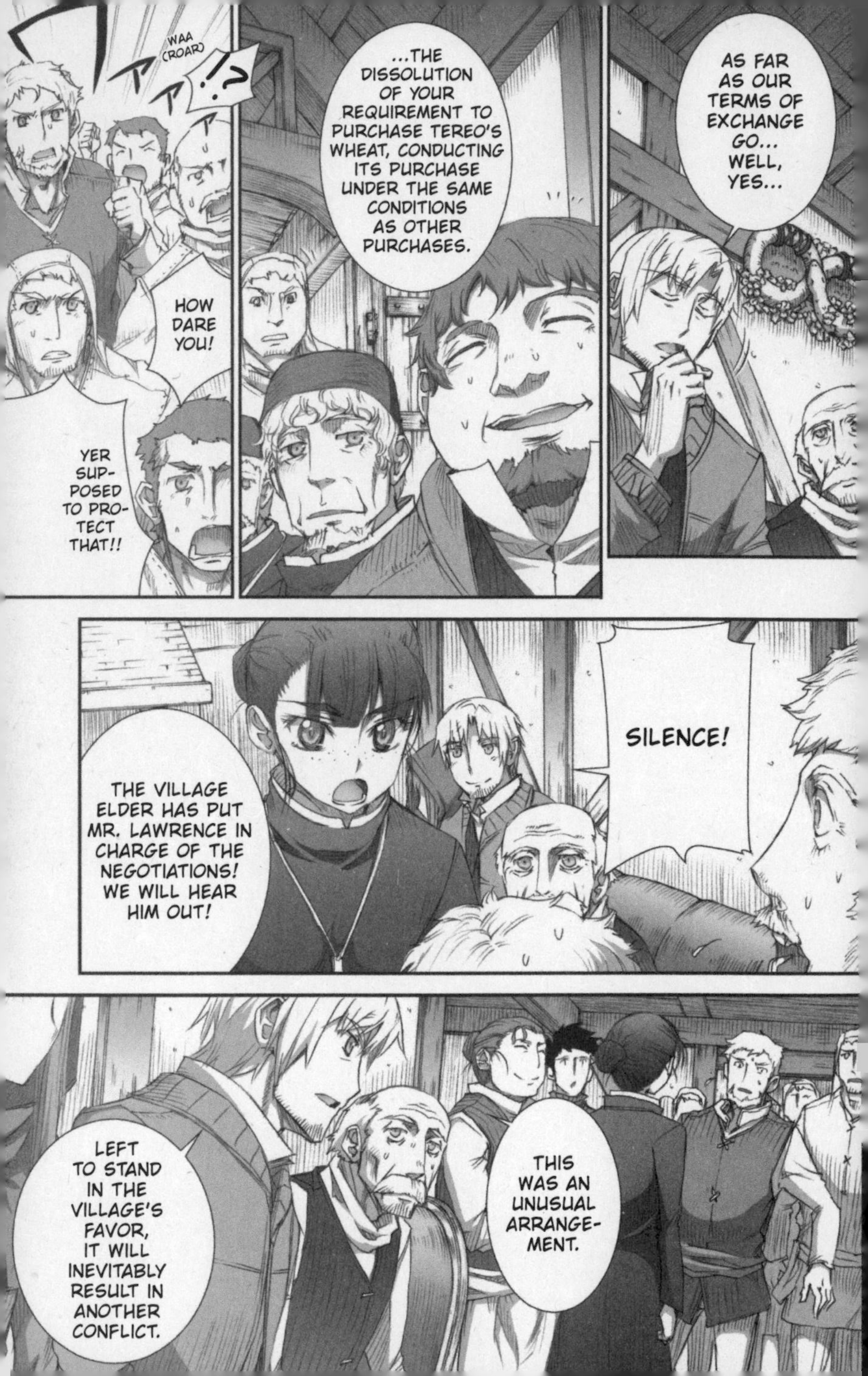
AS FAR AS OUR TERMS OF EXCHANGE GO... WELL, YES...
...THE DISSOLUTION OF YOUR REQUIREMENT TO PURCHASE TEREO'S WHEAT, CONDUCTING ITS PURCHASE UNDER THE SAME CONDITIONS AS OTHER PURCHASES.
WAA (ROAR)
!?
HOW DARE YOU!
YER SUP-POSED TO PRO-TECT THAT!!
SILENCE!
THE VILLAGE ELDER HAS PUT MR. LAWRENCE IN CHARGE OF THE NEGOTIATIONS! WE WILL HEAR HIM OUT!
THIS WAS AN UNUSUAL ARRANGE-MENT.
LEFT TO STAND IN THE VILLAGE'S FAVOR, IT WILL INEVITABLY RESULT IN ANOTHER CONFLICT.

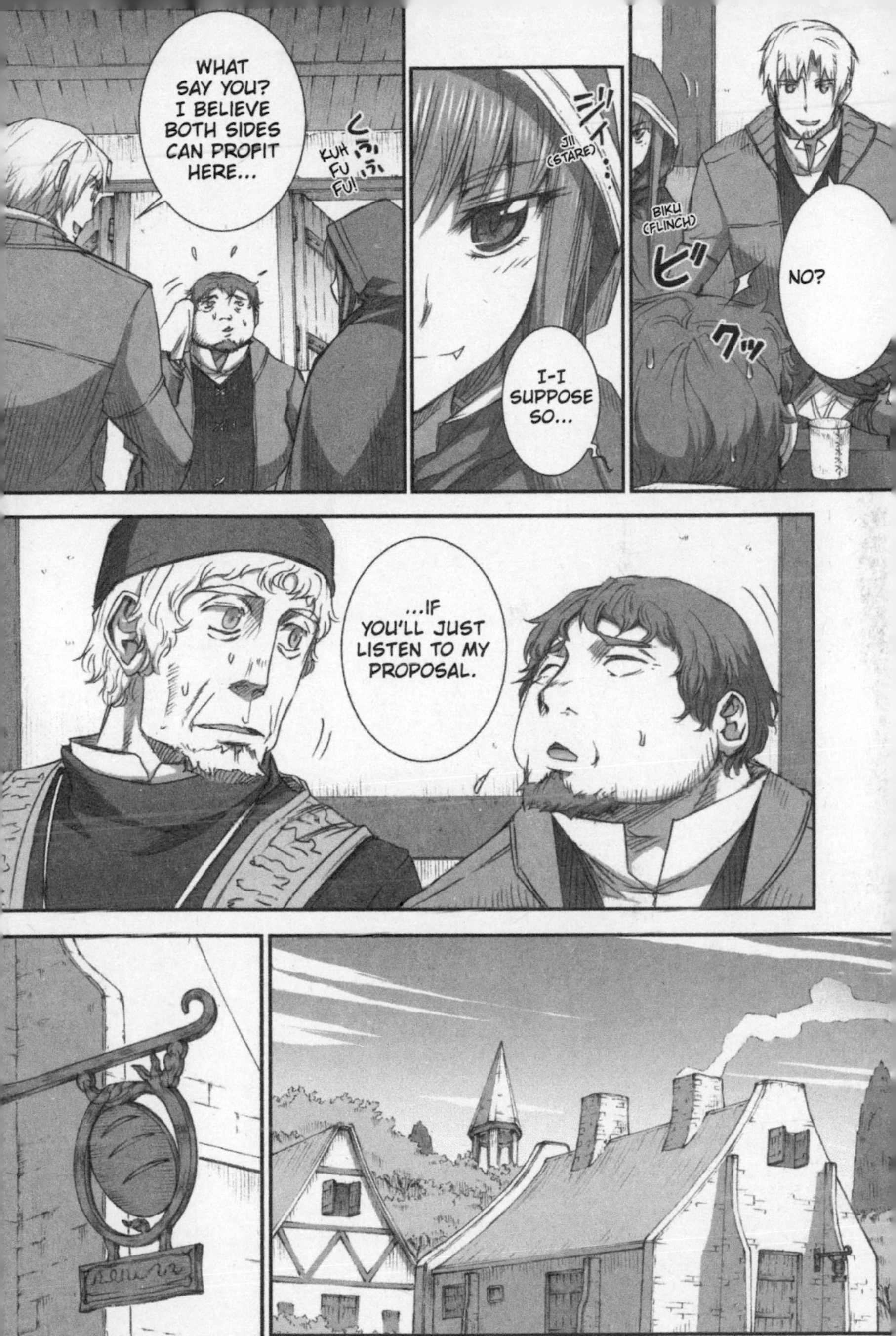
NO?
BIKU (FLINCH)
ビ
クッ
ジィ…
JII (STARE)
I-I SUPPOSE SO...
WHAT SAY YOU? I BELIEVE BOTH SIDES CAN PROFIT HERE...
くふふ
KUH FU FU!
...IF YOU'LL JUST LISTEN TO MY PROPOSAL.

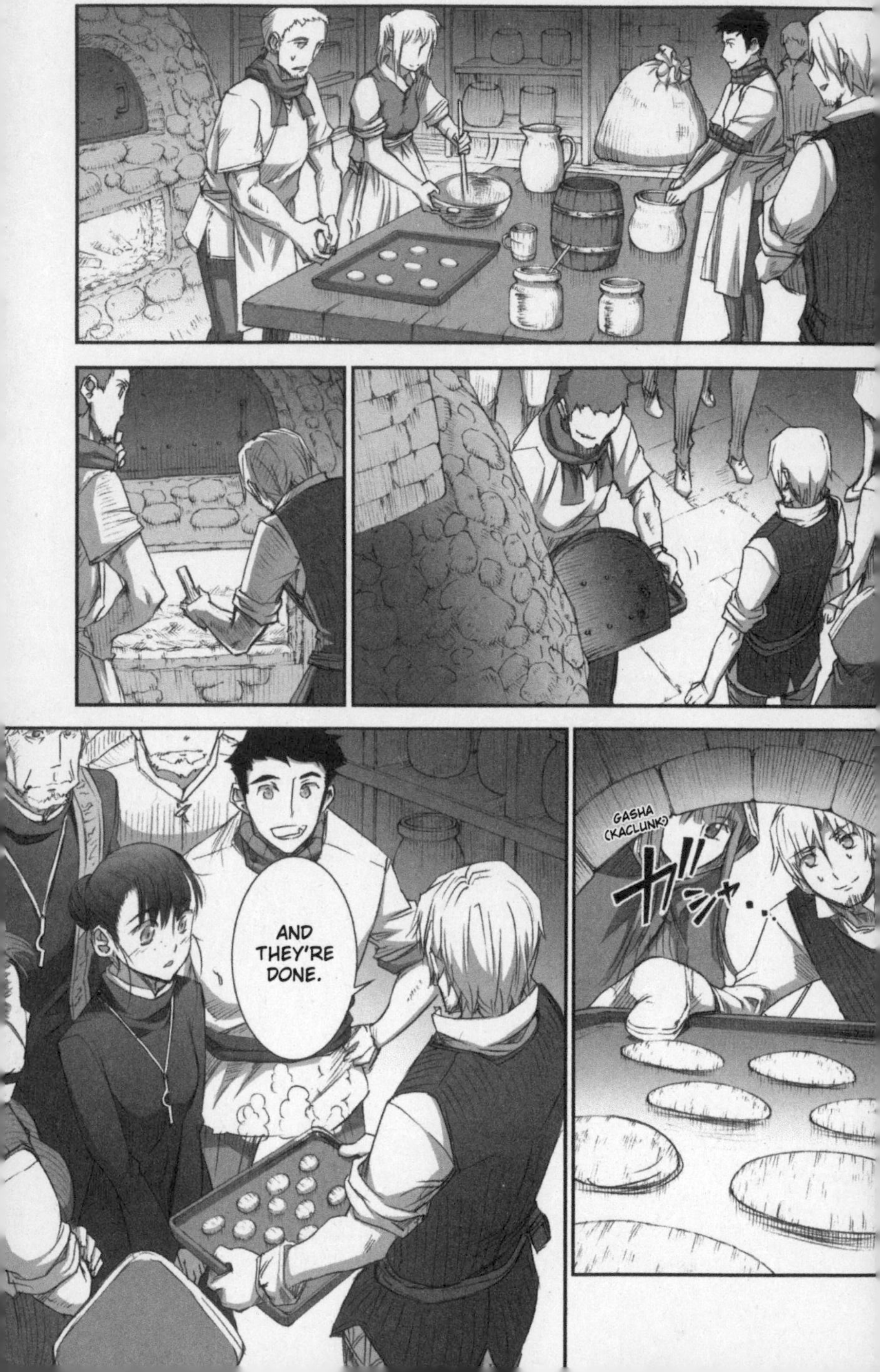
GASHA (KACLUNK)
AND THEY'RE DONE.

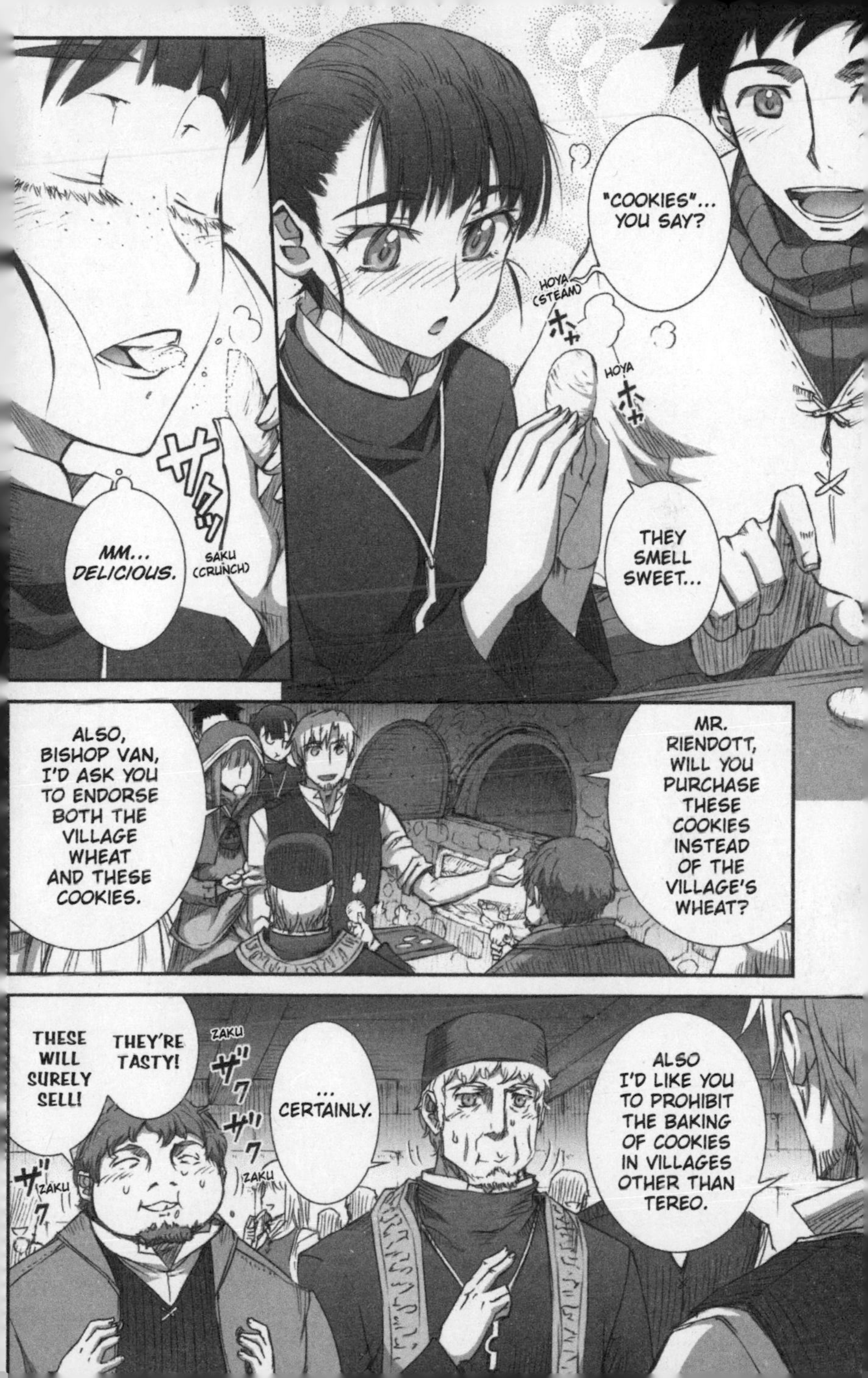
"COOKIES"... YOU SAY?
HOYA (STEAM)
HOYA
THEY SMELL SWEET...
SAKU (CRUNCH)
MM... DELICIOUS.
MR. RIENDOTT, WILL YOU PURCHASE THESE COOKIES INSTEAD OF THE VILLAGE'S WHEAT?
ALSO, BISHOP VAN, I'D ASK YOU TO ENDORSE BOTH THE VILLAGE WHEAT AND THESE COOKIES.
ALSO I'D LIKE YOU TO PROHIBIT THE BAKING OF COOKIES IN VILLAGES OTHER THAN TEREO.
... CERTAINLY.
ZAKU
ZAKU
THEY'RE TASTY!
THESE WILL SURELY SELL!
ZAKU

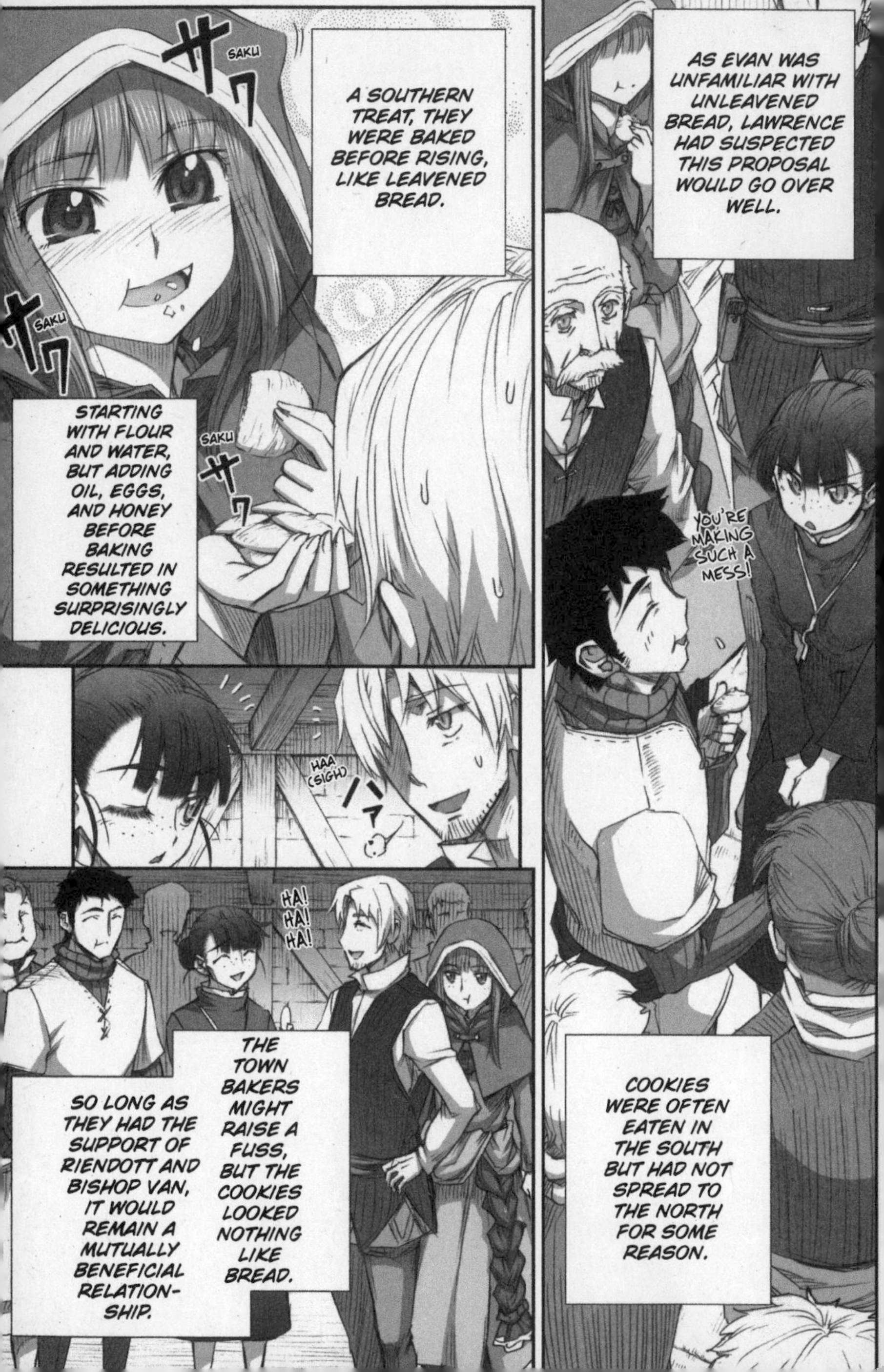
AS EVAN WAS UNFAMILIAR WITH UNLEAVENED BREAD, LAWRENCE HAD SUSPECTED THIS PROPOSAL WOULD GO OVER WELL.
YOU'RE MAKING SUCH A MESS!
COOKIES WERE OFTEN EATEN IN THE SOUTH BUT HAD NOT SPREAD TO THE NORTH FOR SOME REASON.
A SOUTHERN TREAT, THEY WERE BAKED BEFORE RISING, LIKE LEAVENED BREAD.
SAKU
SAKU
SAKU
STARTING WITH FLOUR AND WATER, BUT ADDING OIL, EGGS, AND HONEY BEFORE BAKING RESULTED IN SOMETHING SURPRISINGLY DELICIOUS.
HAA (SIGH)
HA! HA! HA!
THE TOWN BAKERS MIGHT RAISE A FUSS, BUT THE COOKIES LOOKED NOTHING LIKE BREAD.
SO LONG AS THEY HAD THE SUPPORT OF RIENDOTT AND BISHOP VAN, IT WOULD REMAIN A MUTUALLY BENEFICIAL RELATION-SHIP.

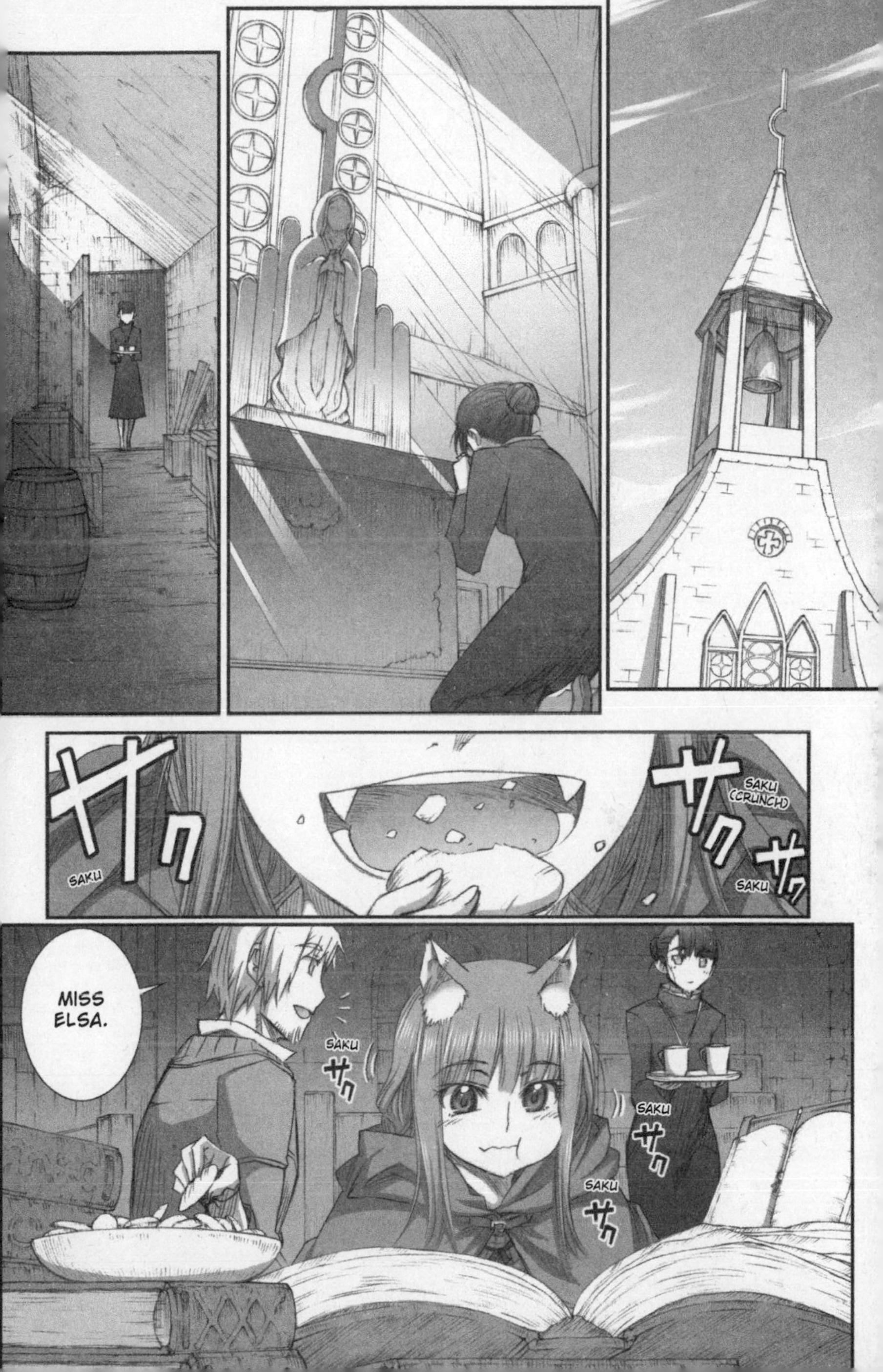

SAKU (CRUNCH)
SAKU
SAKU
SAKU
MISS ELSA.
SAKU
SAKU

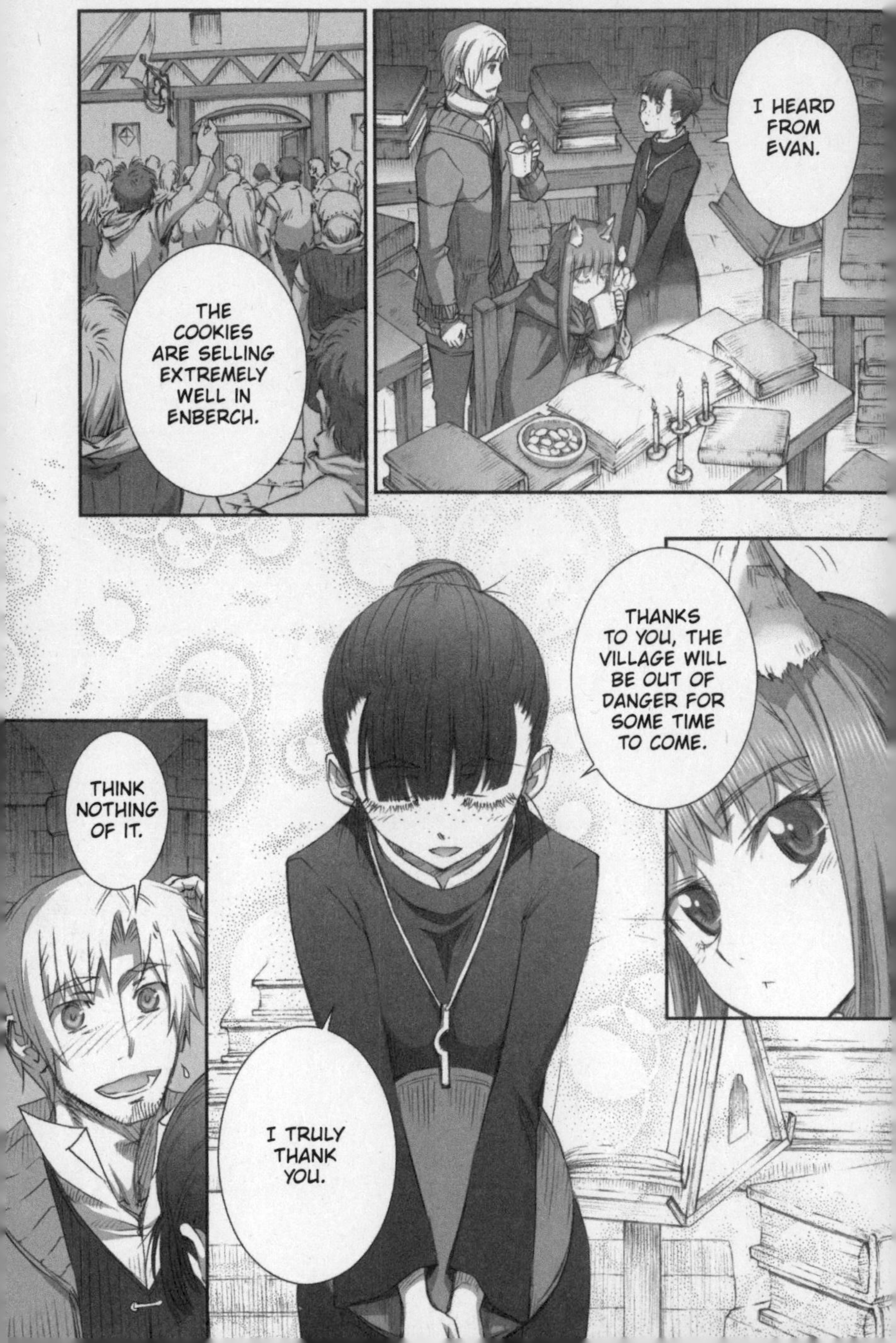
I HEARD FROM EVAN.
THE COOKIES ARE SELLING EXTREMELY WELL IN ENBERCH.
THANKS TO YOU, THE VILLAGE WILL BE OUT OF DANGER FOR SOME TIME TO COME.
I TRULY THANK YOU.
THINK NOTHING OF IT.

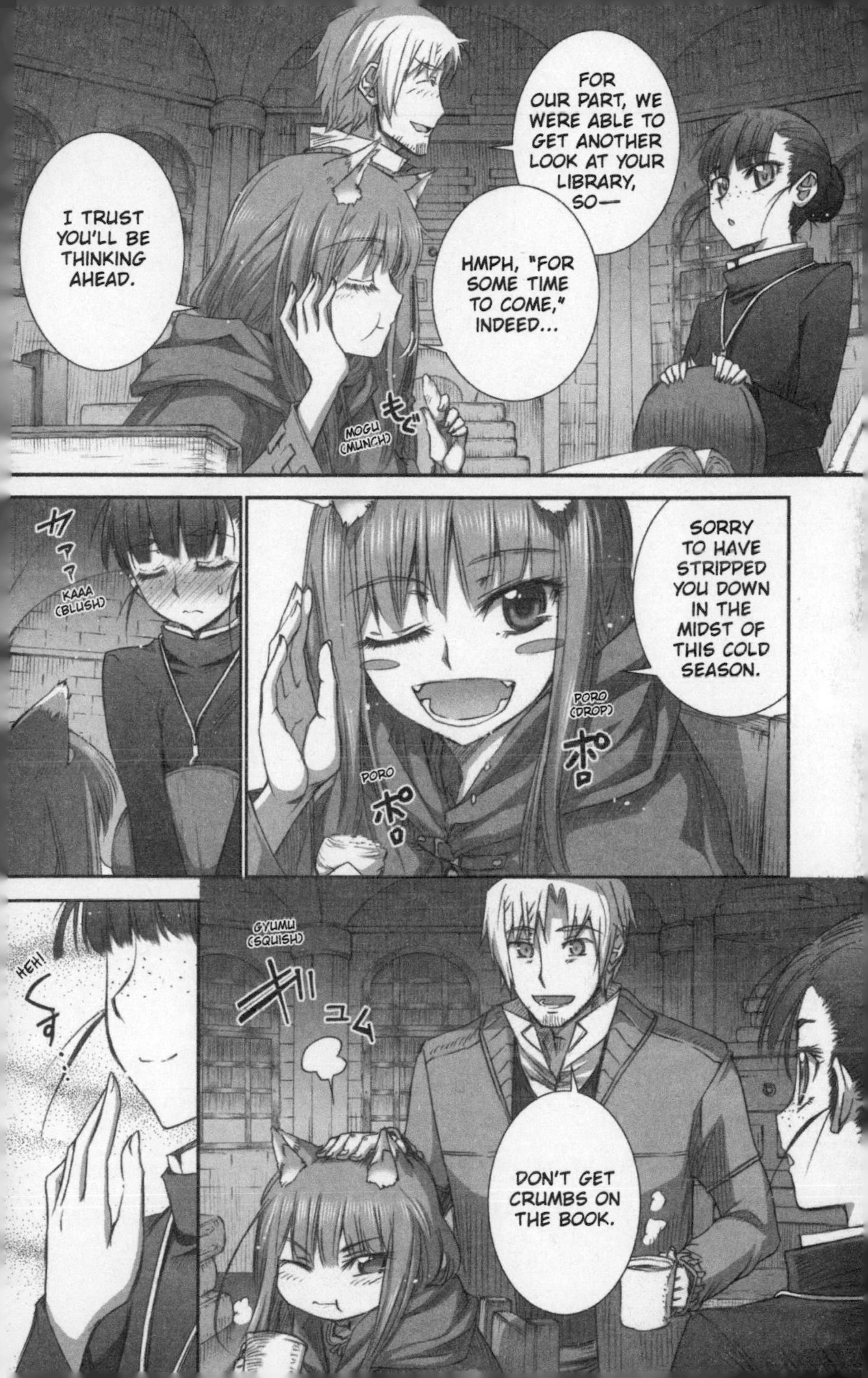

FOR OUR PART, WE WERE ABLE TO GET ANOTHER LOOK AT YOUR LIBRARY, SO—
HMPH, "FOR SOME TIME TO COME," INDEED...
I TRUST YOU'LL BE THINKING AHEAD.
MOGU (MUNCH)
SORRY TO HAVE STRIPPED YOU DOWN IN THE MIDST OF THIS COLD SEASON.
PORO (DROP)
PORO
KAAA (BLUSH)
GYUMU (SQUISH)
DON'T GET CRUMBS ON THE BOOK.
HEH!

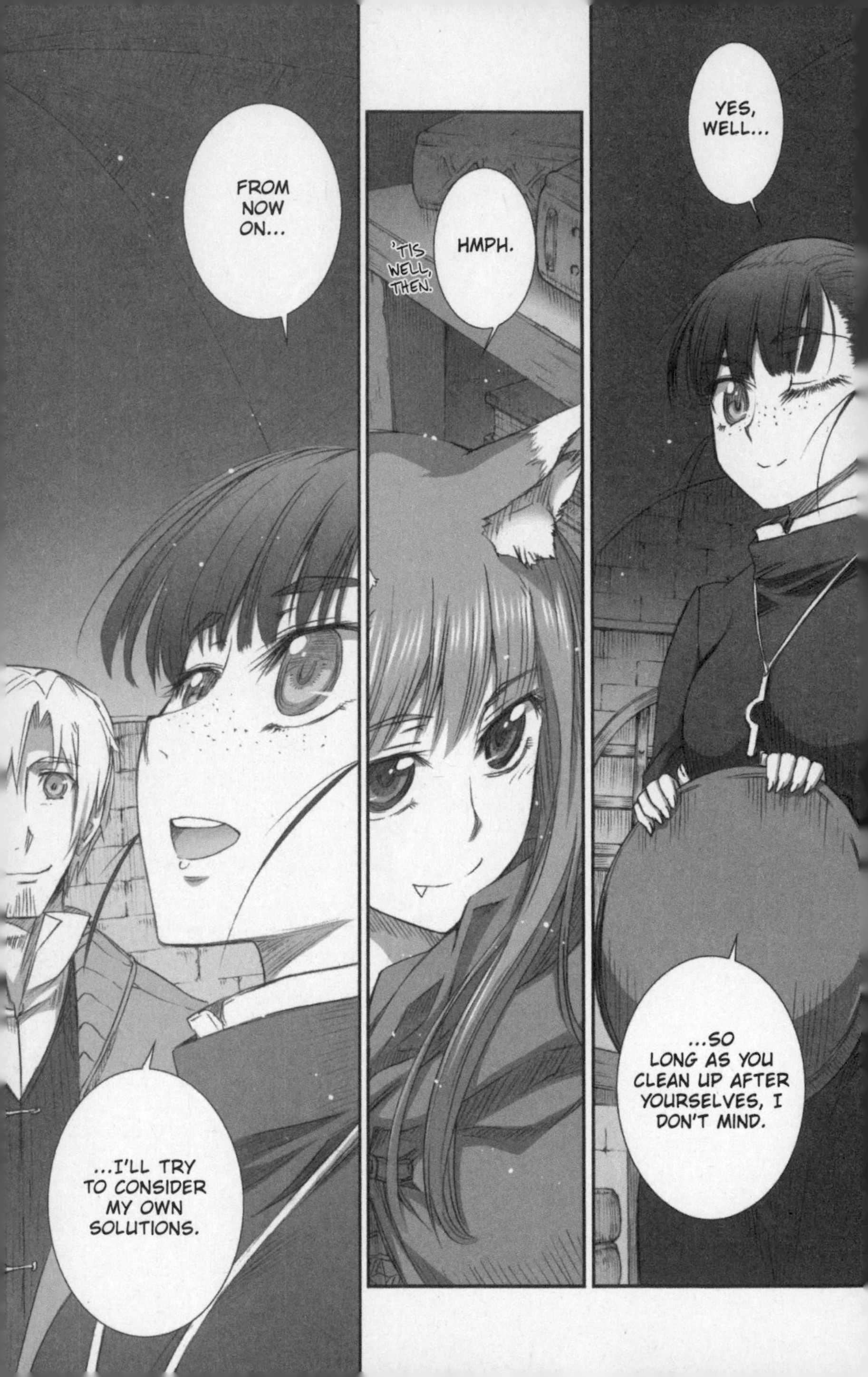
YES, WELL...
...SO LONG AS YOU CLEAN UP AFTER YOURSELVES, I DON'T MIND.
HMPH.
'TIS WELL, THEN.
FROM NOW ON...
...I'LL TRY TO CONSIDER MY OWN SOLUTIONS.

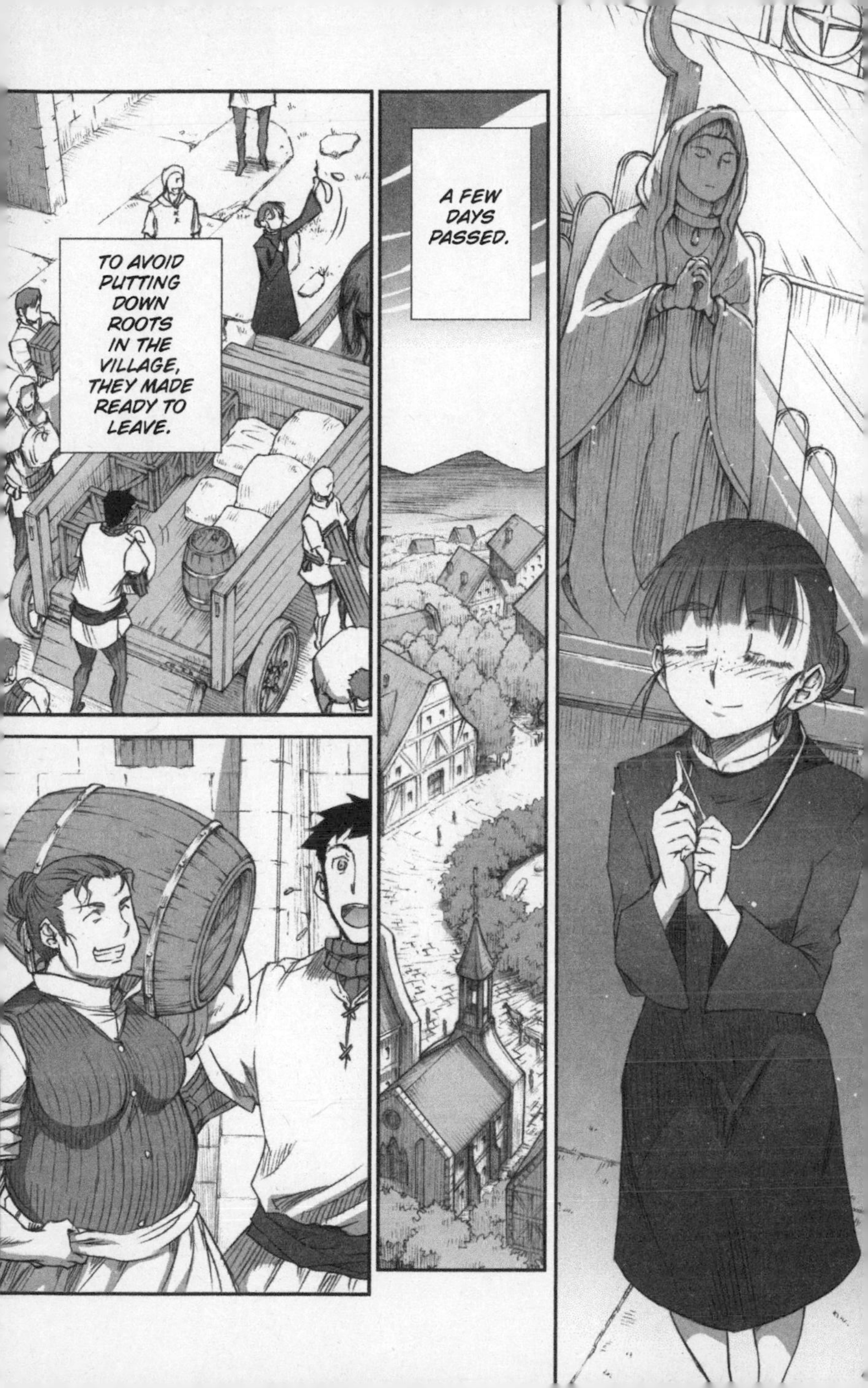
A FEW DAYS PASSED.
TO AVOID PUTTING DOWN ROOTS IN THE VILLAGE, THEY MADE READY TO LEAVE.

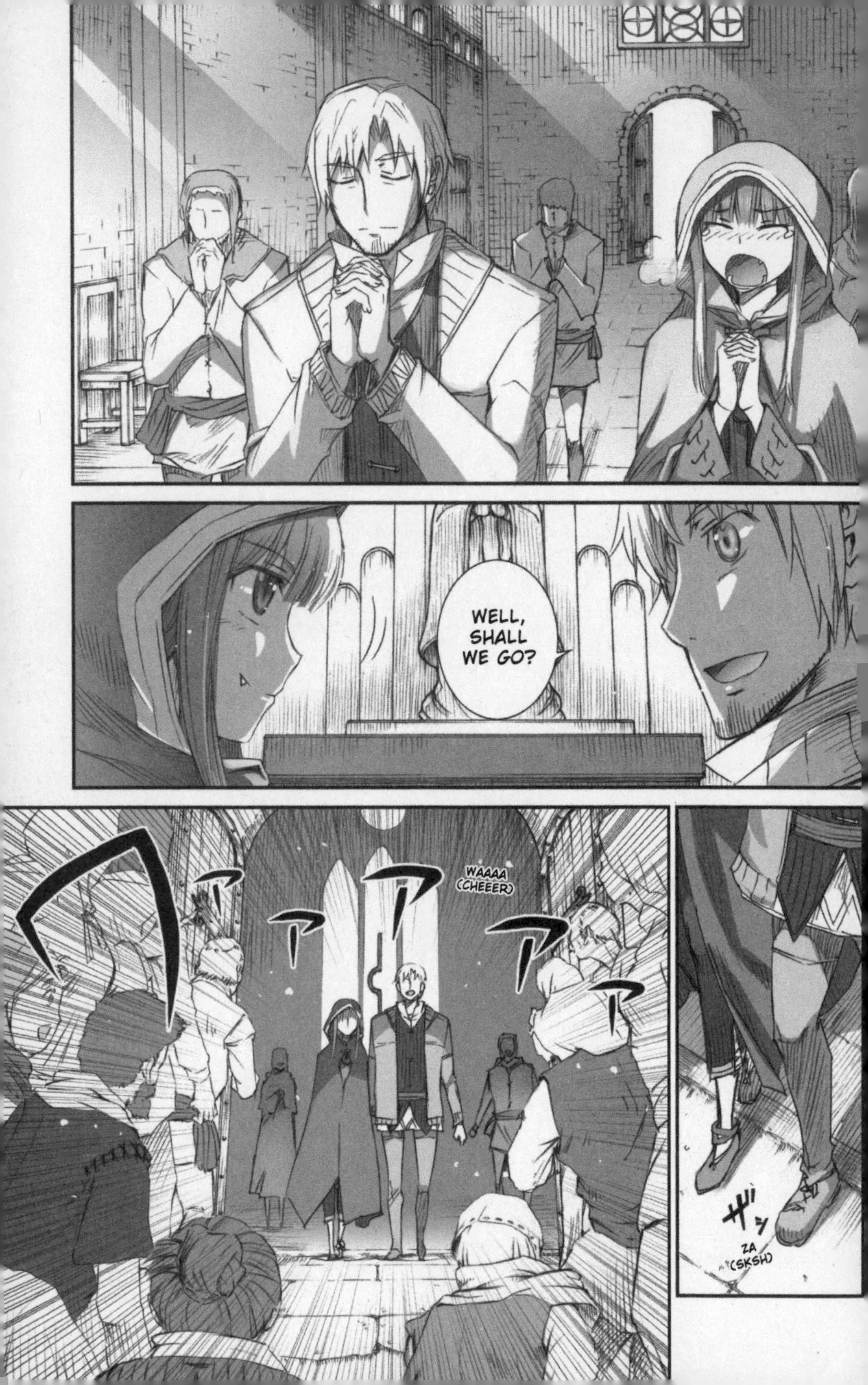
WELL, SHALL WE GO?
ZA (SKSH)
WAAAA (CHEEER)

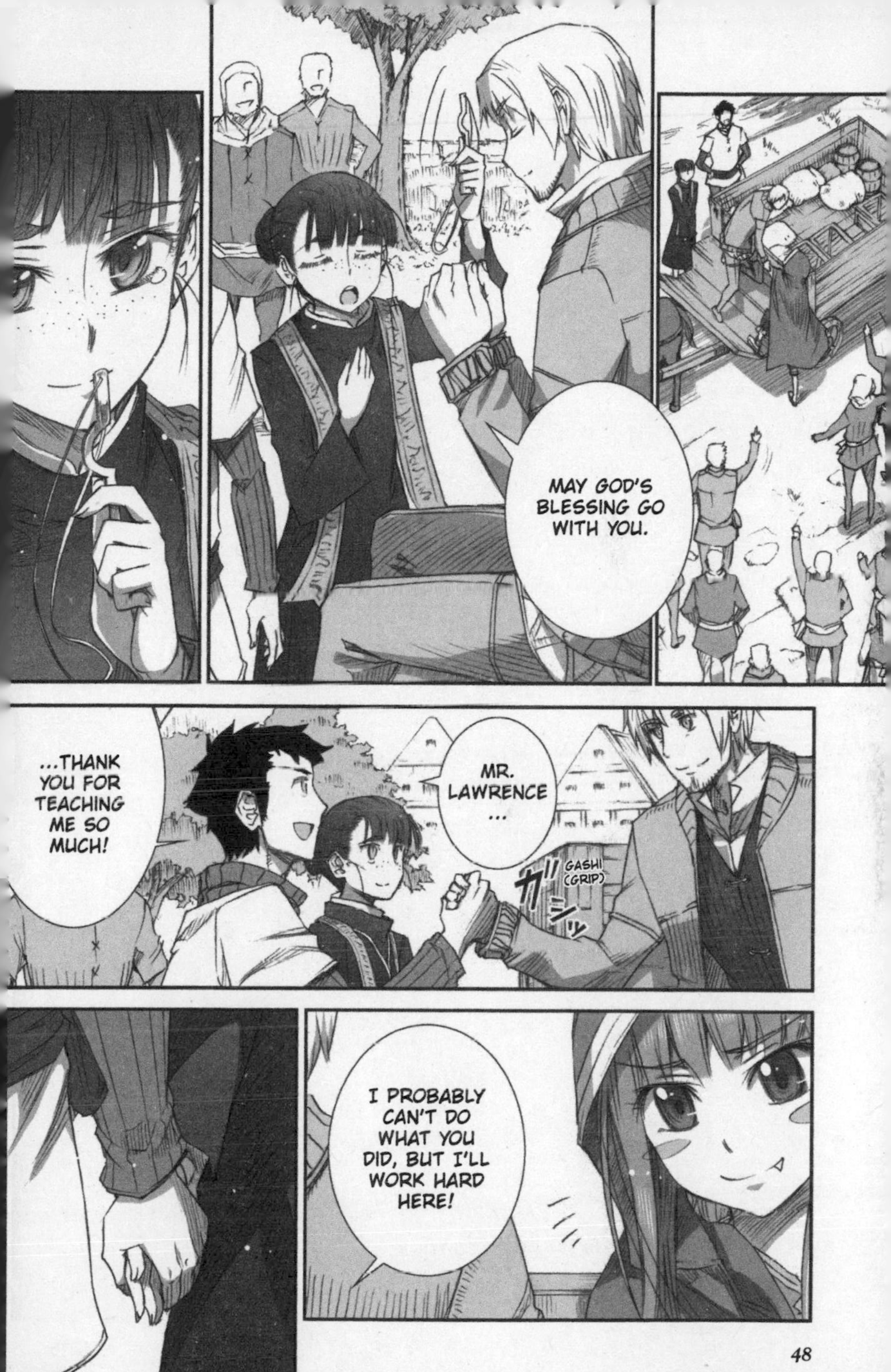
MAY GOD'S BLESSING GO WITH YOU.
MR. LAWRENCE ...
GASHI (GRIP)
...THANK YOU FOR TEACHING ME SO MUCH!
I PROBABLY CAN'T DO WHAT YOU DID, BUT I'LL WORK HARD HERE!

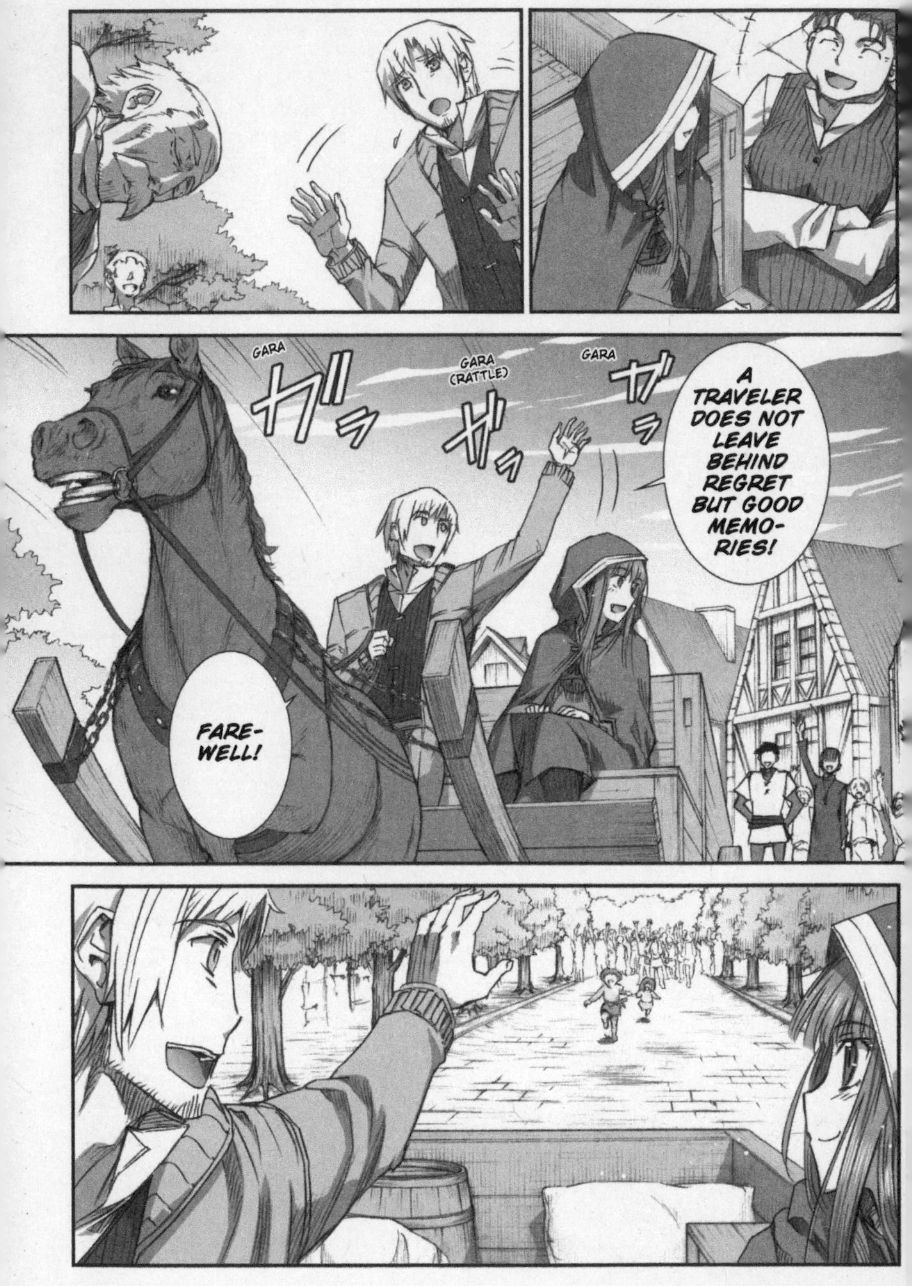
A TRAVELER DOES NOT LEAVE BEHIND REGRET BUT GOOD MEMO-RIES!
GARA
GARA (RATTLE)
GARA
FARE-WELL!

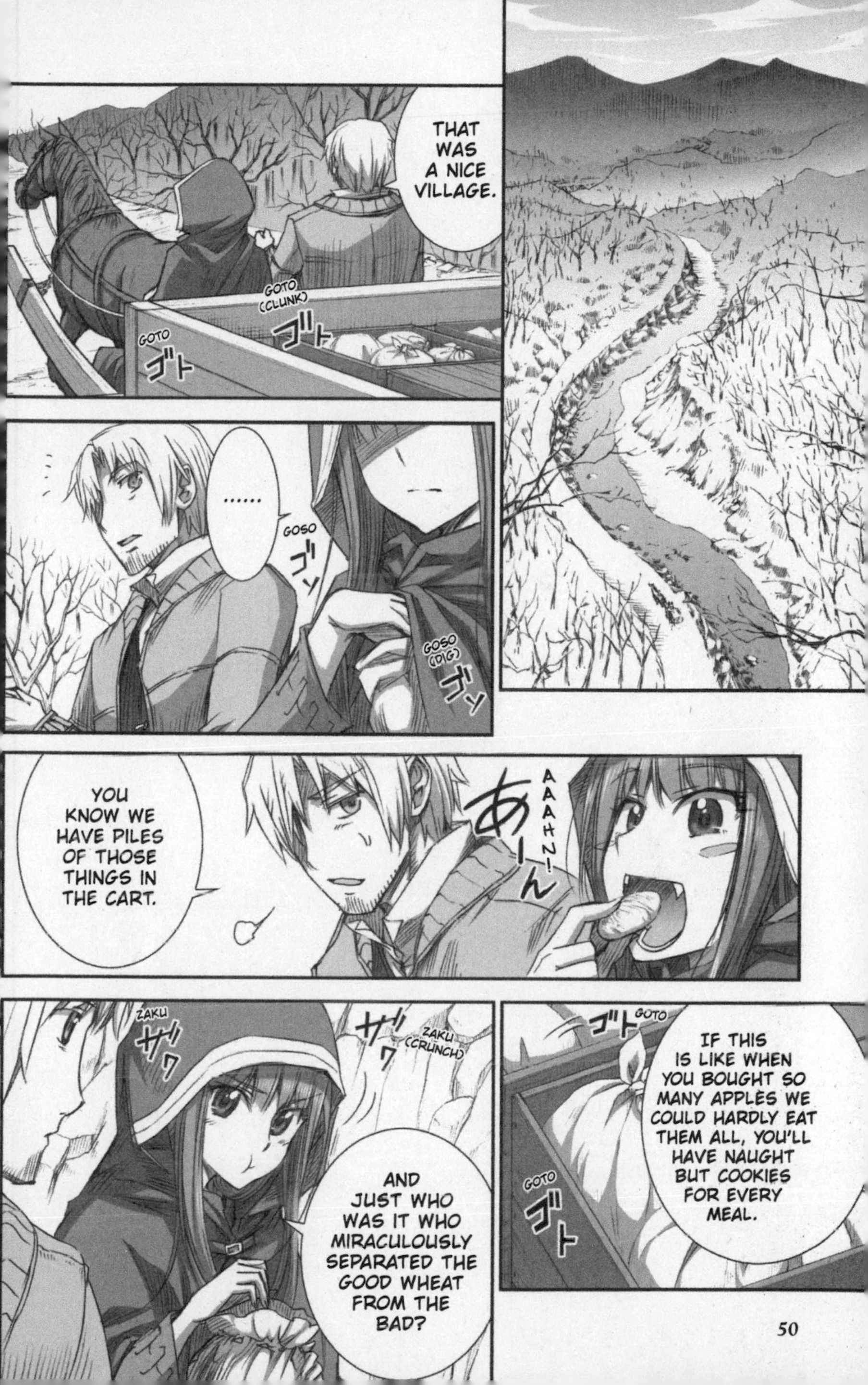
THAT WAS A NICE VILLAGE.
GOTO (CLUNK)
GOTO
......
GOSO
GOSO (DIG)
AAAHN!
YOU KNOW WE HAVE PILES OF THOSE THINGS IN THE CART.
GOTO
IF THIS IS LIKE WHEN YOU BOUGHT SO MANY APPLES WE COULD HARDLY EAT THEM ALL, YOU'LL HAVE NAUGHT BUT COOKIES FOR EVERY MEAL.
GOTO
ZAKU (CRUNCH)
ZAKU
AND JUST WHO WAS IT WHO MIRACULOUSLY SEPARATED THE GOOD WHEAT FROM THE BAD?

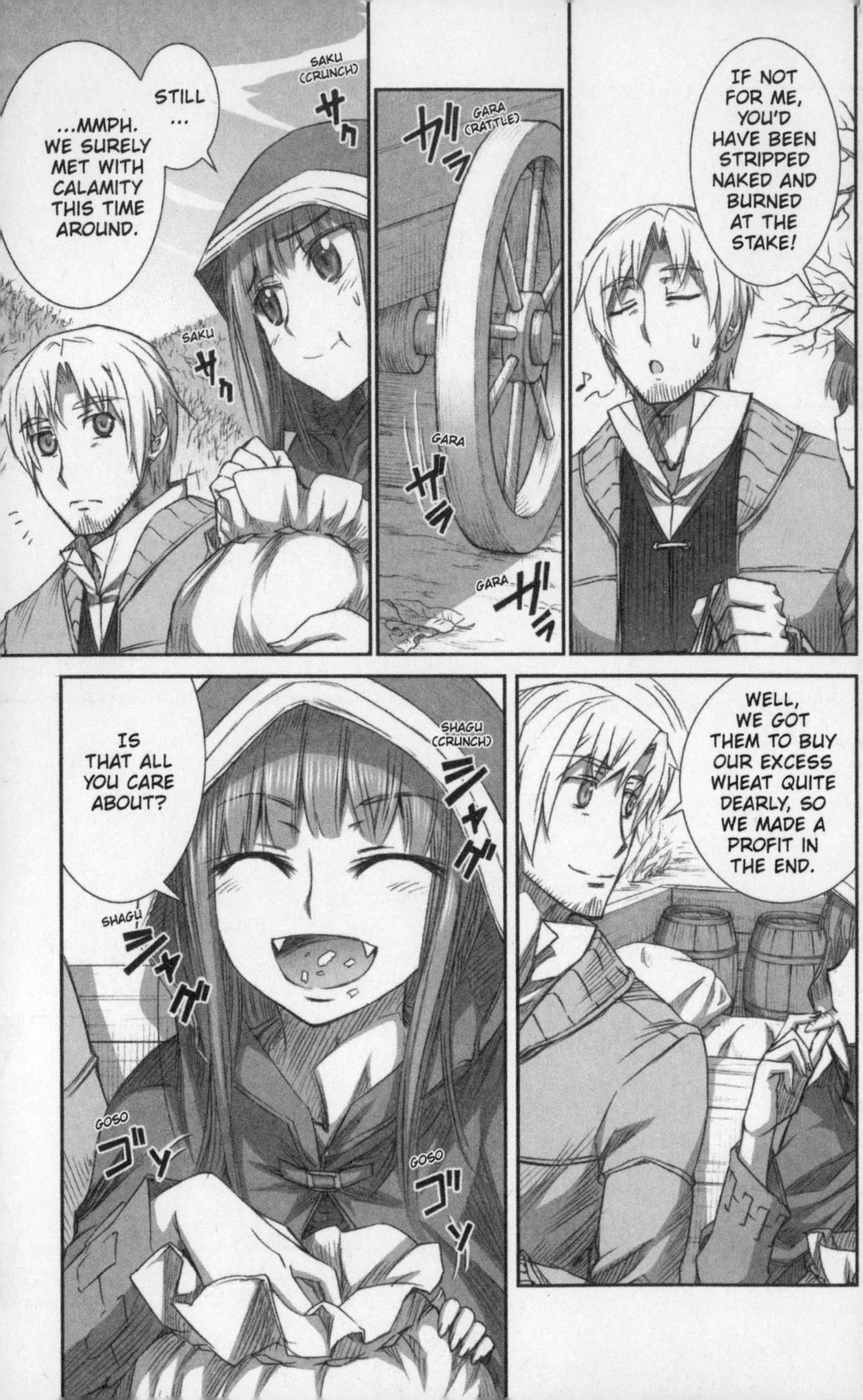
IF NOT FOR ME, YOU'D HAVE BEEN STRIPPED NAKED AND BURNED AT THE STAKE!
GARA (RATTLE)
GARA
GARA
SAKU (CRUNCH)
STILL ...
...MMPH. WE SURELY MET WITH CALAMITY THIS TIME AROUND.
SAKU
WELL, WE GOT THEM TO BUY OUR EXCESS WHEAT QUITE DEARLY, SO WE MADE A PROFIT IN THE END.
SHAGU (CRUNCH)
IS THAT ALL YOU CARE ABOUT?
SHAGU
GOSO
GOSO

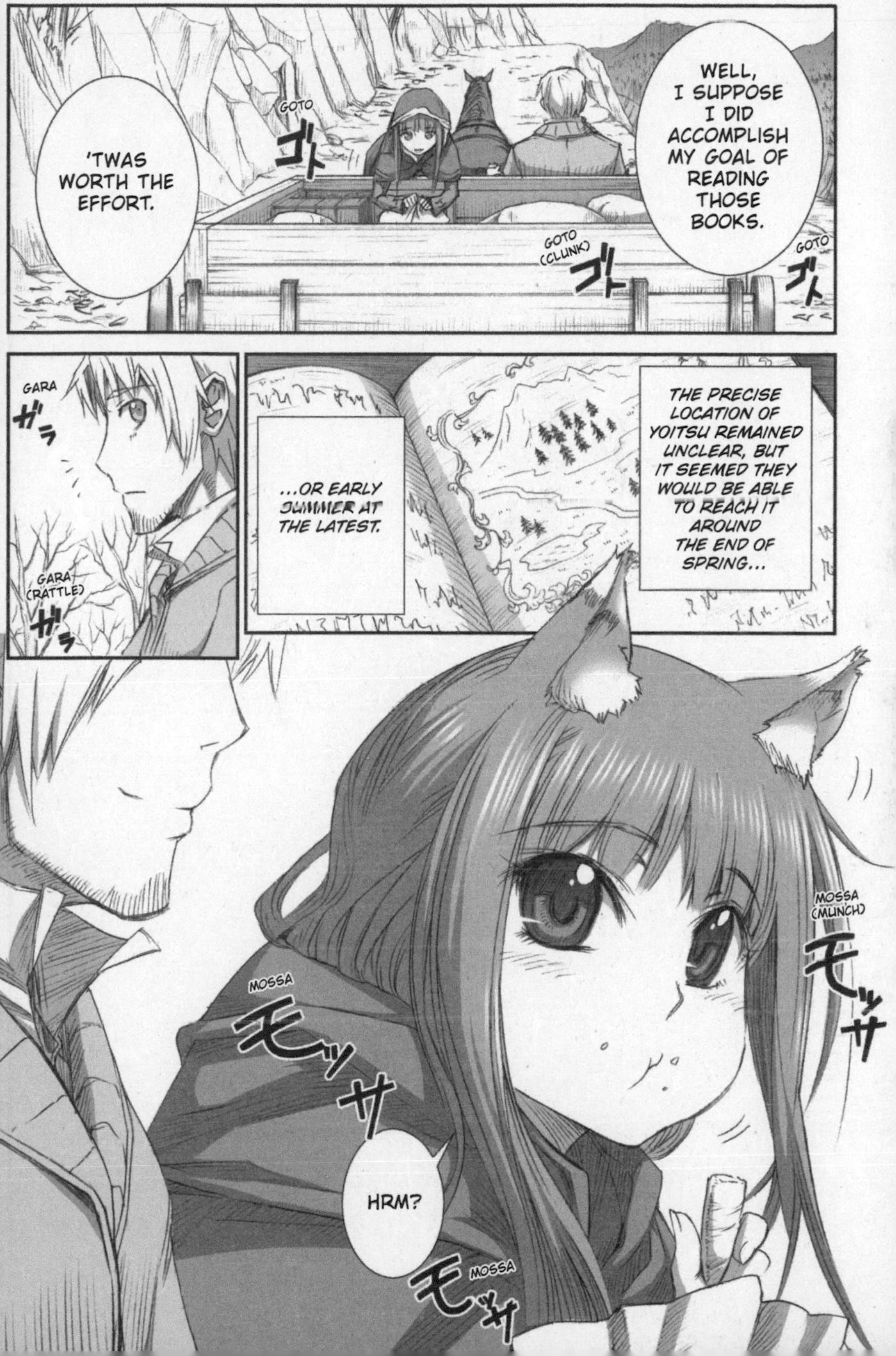
WELL, I SUPPOSE I DID ACCOMPLISH MY GOAL OF READING THOSE BOOKS.
GOTO
GOTO (CLUNK)
'TWAS WORTH THE EFFORT.
GOTO
THE PRECISE LOCATION OF YOITSU REMAINED UNCLEAR, BUT IT SEEMED THEY WOULD BE ABLE TO REACH IT AROUND THE END OF SPRING...
...OR EARLY SUMMER AT THE LATEST.
GARA
GARA (RATTLE)
MOSSA (MUNCH)
MOSSA
HRM?
MOSSA

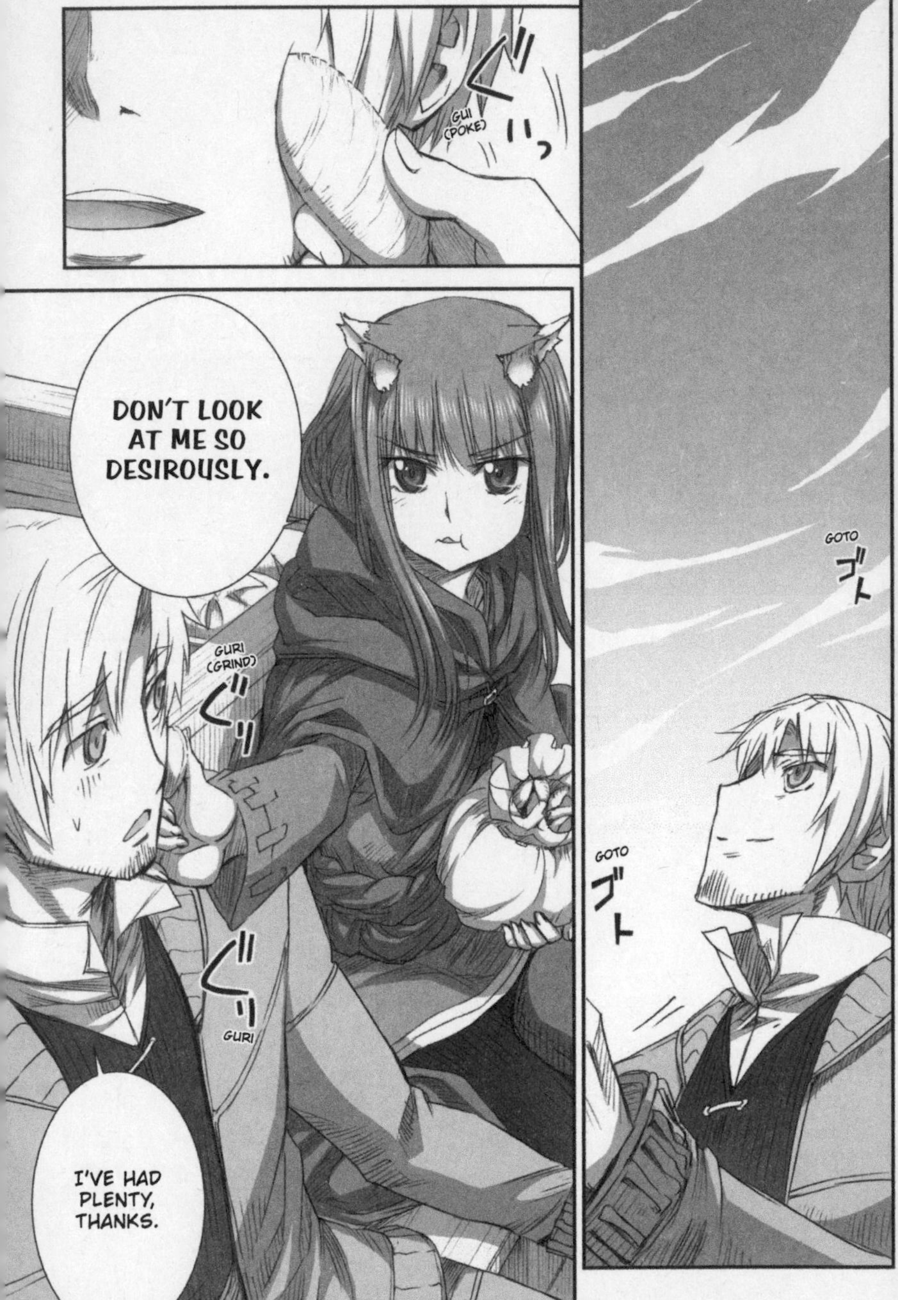
GOTO
ゴト
GOTO
ゴト
GUI (POKE)
ぐいっ
DON'T LOOK AT ME SO DESIROUSLY.
GURI (GRIND)
ぐり
ぐり
GURI
I'VE HAD PLENTY, THANKS.

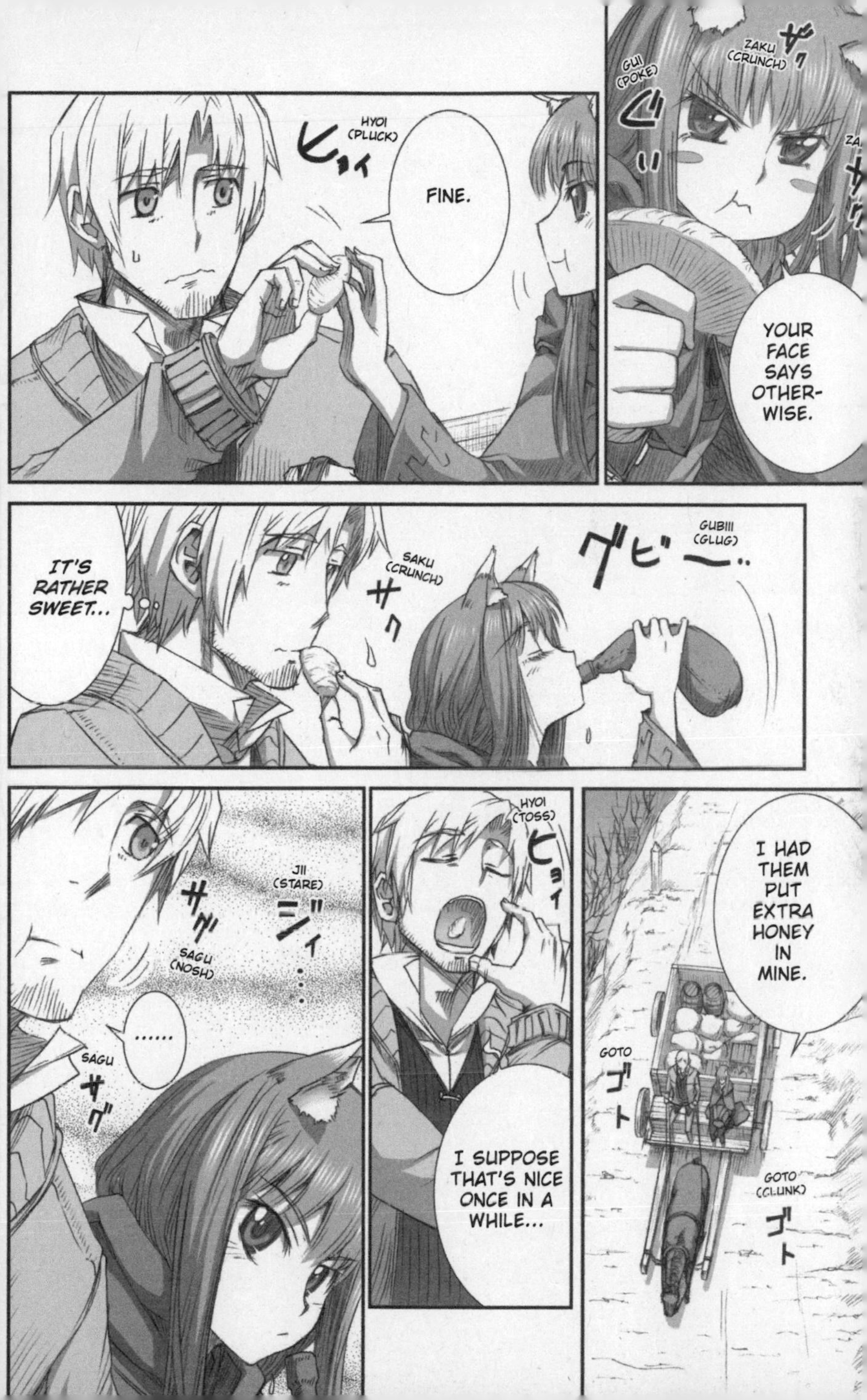
ZAKU (CRUNCH)
ザク
GUI (POKE)
ぐい
YOUR FACE SAYS OTHER-WISE.
HYOI (PLUCK)
ヒョイ
FINE.
GUBIII (GLUG)
グビー..
SAKU (CRUNCH)
サク
IT'S RATHER SWEET...
I HAD THEM PUT EXTRA HONEY IN MINE.
GOTO
ゴト
GOTO (CLUNK)
ゴト
HYOI (TOSS)
ヒョイ
I SUPPOSE THAT'S NICE ONCE IN A WHILE...
JII (STARE)
ジィ...
SAGU (NOSH)
サグ
......
SAGU
サグ

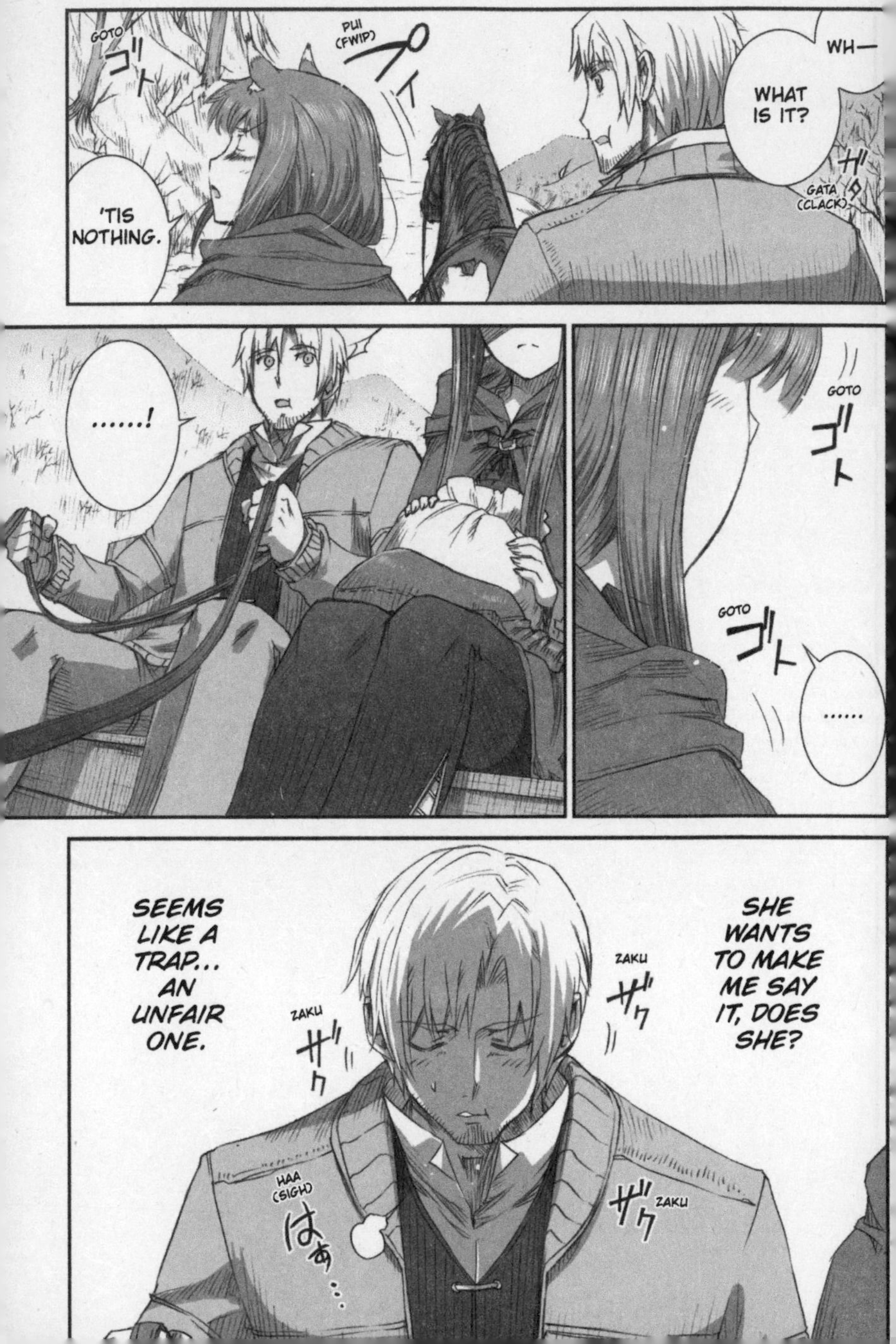
WH— WHAT IS IT?
GATA (CLACK)
PUI (FWIP)
GOTO
'TIS NOTHING.
GOTO
GOTO
......
......!
SHE WANTS TO MAKE ME SAY IT, DOES SHE?
ZAKU
ZAKU
SEEMS LIKE A TRAP... AN UNFAIR ONE.
HAA (SIGH)
ZAKU

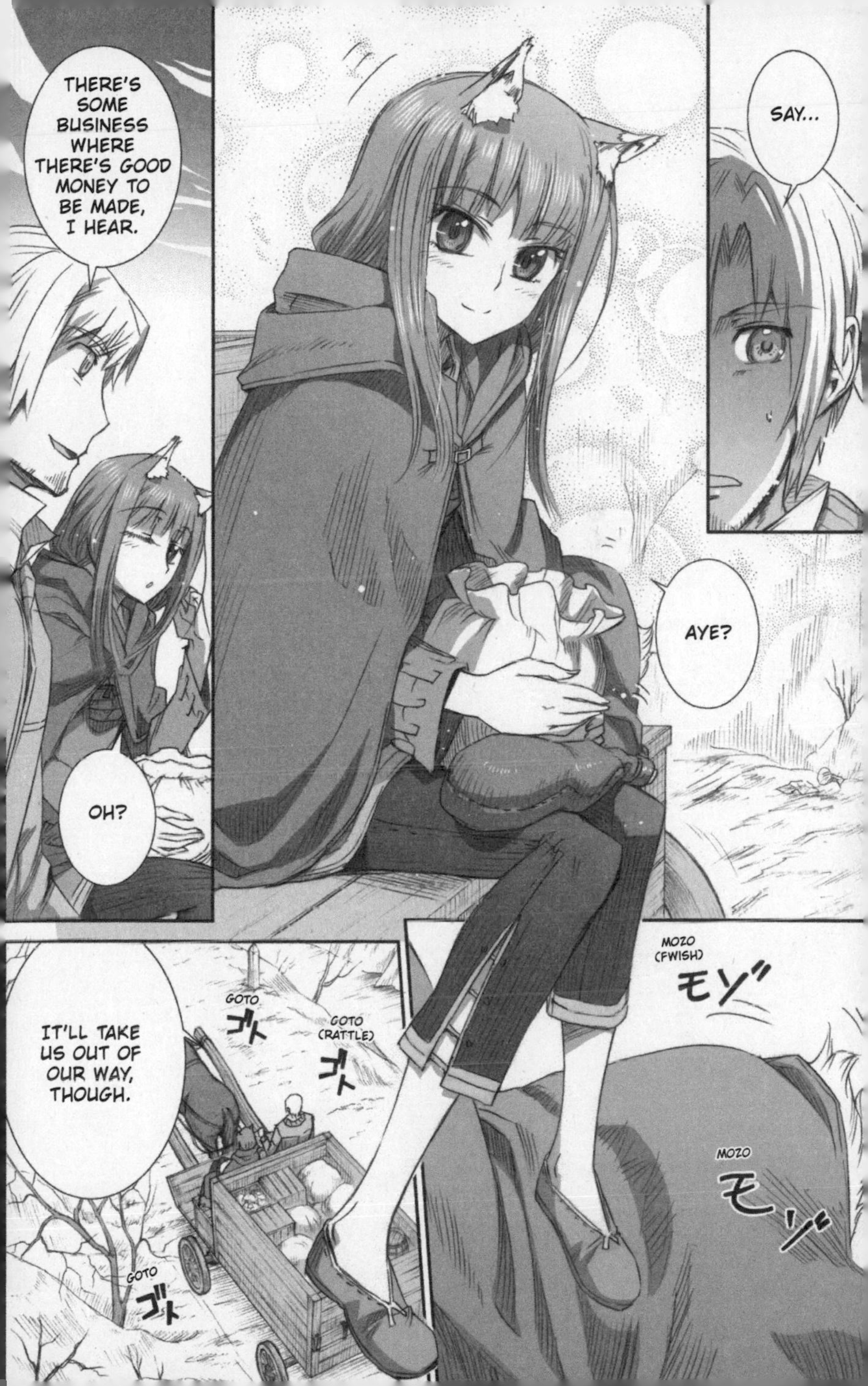
SAY...
AYE?
THERE'S SOME BUSINESS WHERE THERE'S GOOD MONEY TO BE MADE, I HEAR.
OH?
MOZO (FWISH)
モゾ
MOZO
モゾ
IT'LL TAKE US OUT OF OUR WAY, THOUGH.
GOTO
ゴト
GOTO (RATTLE)
ゴト
GOTO
ゴト

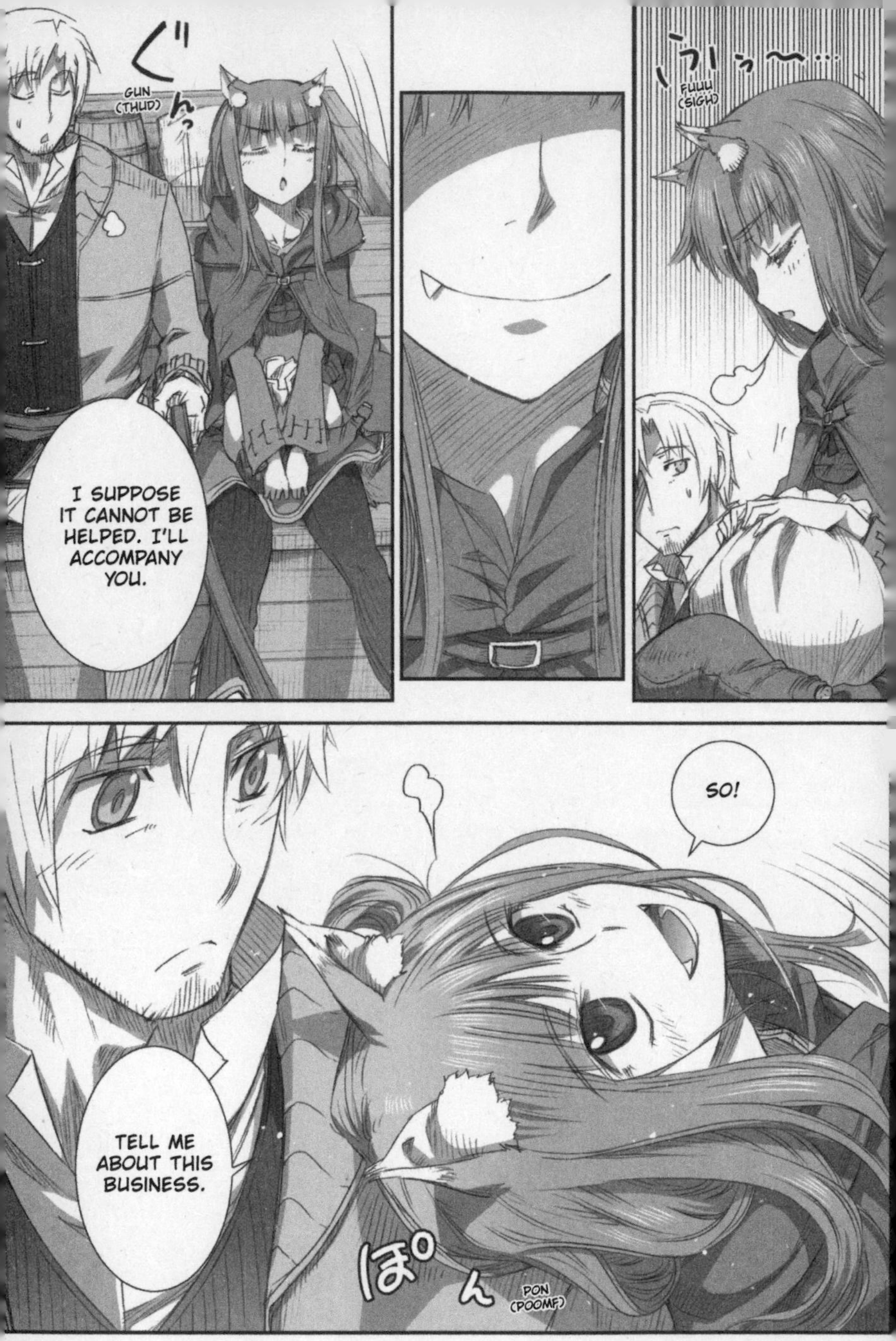
ふぅっ～…
FUUU (SIGH)
ぐんっ
GUN (THUD)
I SUPPOSE IT CANNOT BE HELPED. I'LL ACCOMPANY YOU.
SO!
TELL ME ABOUT THIS BUSINESS.
ぽん
PON (POOMF)

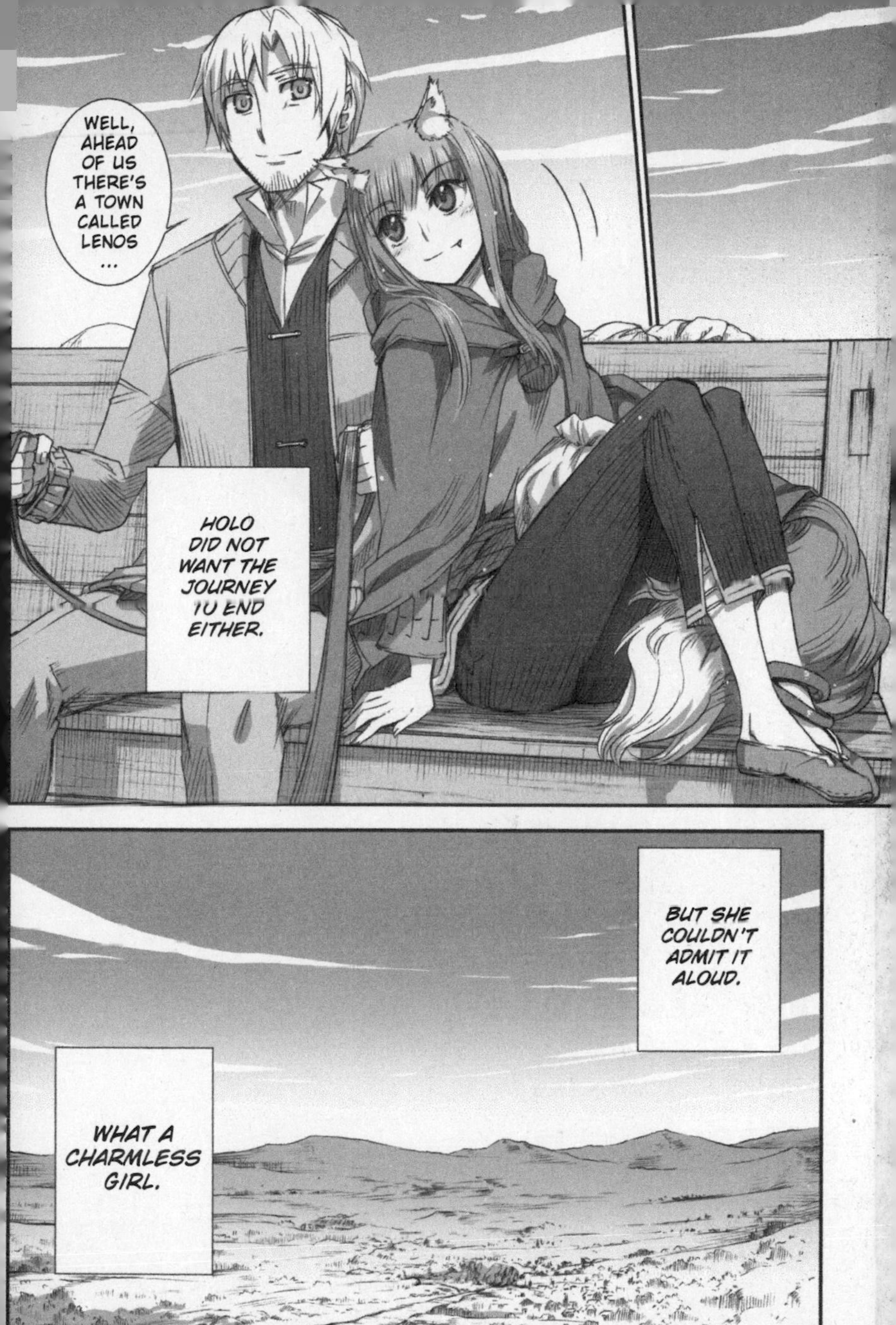
WELL, AHEAD OF US THERE'S A TOWN CALLED LENOS ...
HOLO DID NOT WANT THE JOURNEY TO END EITHER.
BUT SHE COULDN'T ADMIT IT ALOUD.
WHAT A CHARMLESS GIRL.

SPICE & WOLF

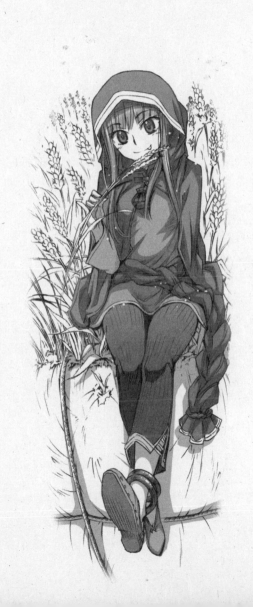

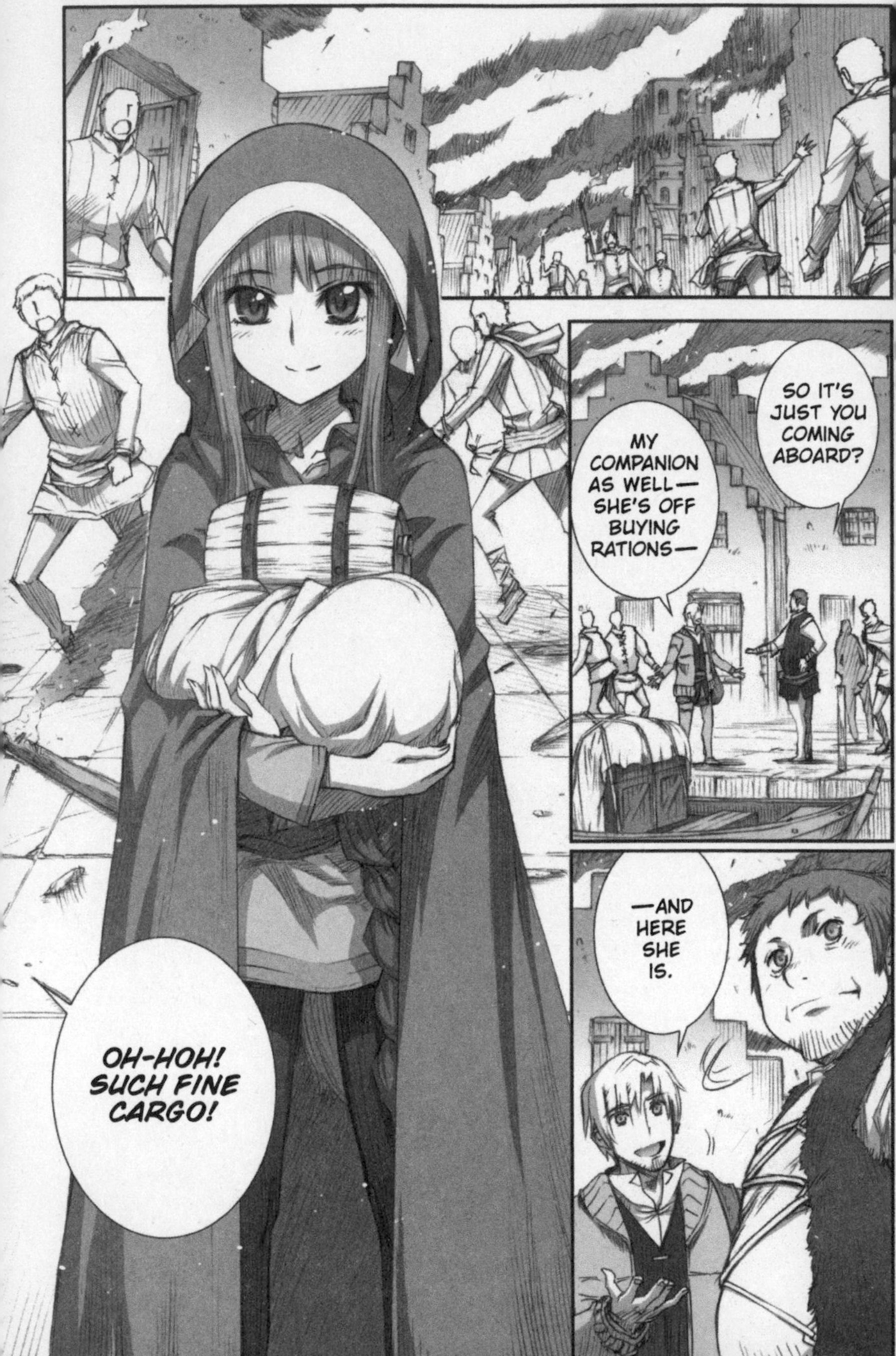
SO IT'S JUST YOU COMING ABOARD?
MY COMPANION AS WELL—SHE'S OFF BUYING RATIONS—
—AND HERE SHE IS.
OH-HOH! SUCH FINE CARGO!

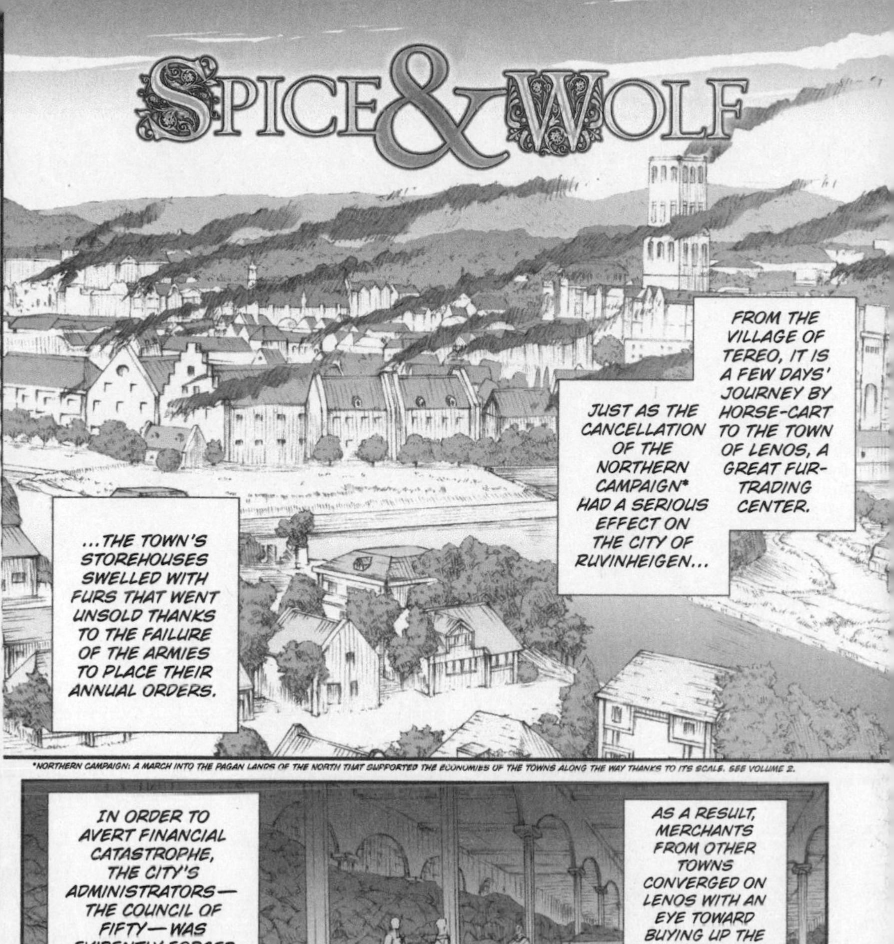
SPICE & WOLF
FROM THE VILLAGE OF TEREO, IT IS A FEW DAYS' JOURNEY BY HORSE-CART TO THE TOWN OF LENOS, A GREAT FUR-TRADING CENTER.
JUST AS THE CANCELLATION OF THE NORTHERN CAMPAIGN* HAD A SERIOUS EFFECT ON THE CITY OF RUVINHEIGEN...
...THE TOWN'S STOREHOUSES SWELLED WITH FURS THAT WENT UNSOLD THANKS TO THE FAILURE OF THE ARMIES TO PLACE THEIR ANNUAL ORDERS.

*NORTHERN CAMPAIGN: A MARCH INTO THE PAGAN LANDS OF THE NORTH THAT SUPPORTED THE ECONOMIES OF THE TOWNS ALONG THE WAY THANKS TO ITS SCALE. SEE VOLUME 2.

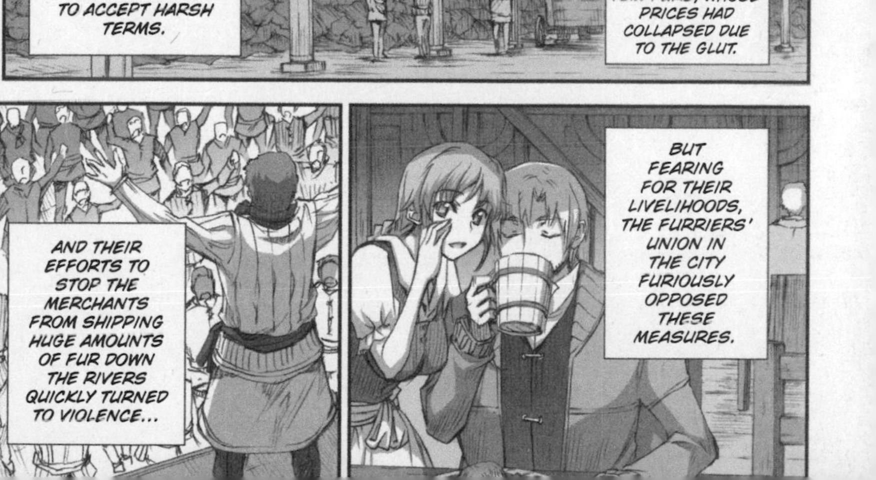
AS A RESULT, MERCHANTS FROM OTHER TOWNS CONVERGED ON LENOS WITH AN EYE TOWARD BUYING UP THE RAW FURS, WHOSE PRICES HAD COLLAPSED DUE TO THE GLUT.
IN ORDER TO AVERT FINANCIAL CATASTROPHE, THE CITY'S ADMINISTRATORS—THE COUNCIL OF FIFTY—WAS EVIDENTLY FORCED TO ACCEPT HARSH TERMS.
BUT FEARING FOR THEIR LIVELIHOODS, THE FURRIERS' UNION IN THE CITY FURIOUSLY OPPOSED THESE MEASURES.
AND THEIR EFFORTS TO STOP THE MERCHANTS FROM SHIPPING HUGE AMOUNTS OF FUR DOWN THE RIVERS QUICKLY TURNED TO VIOLENCE...

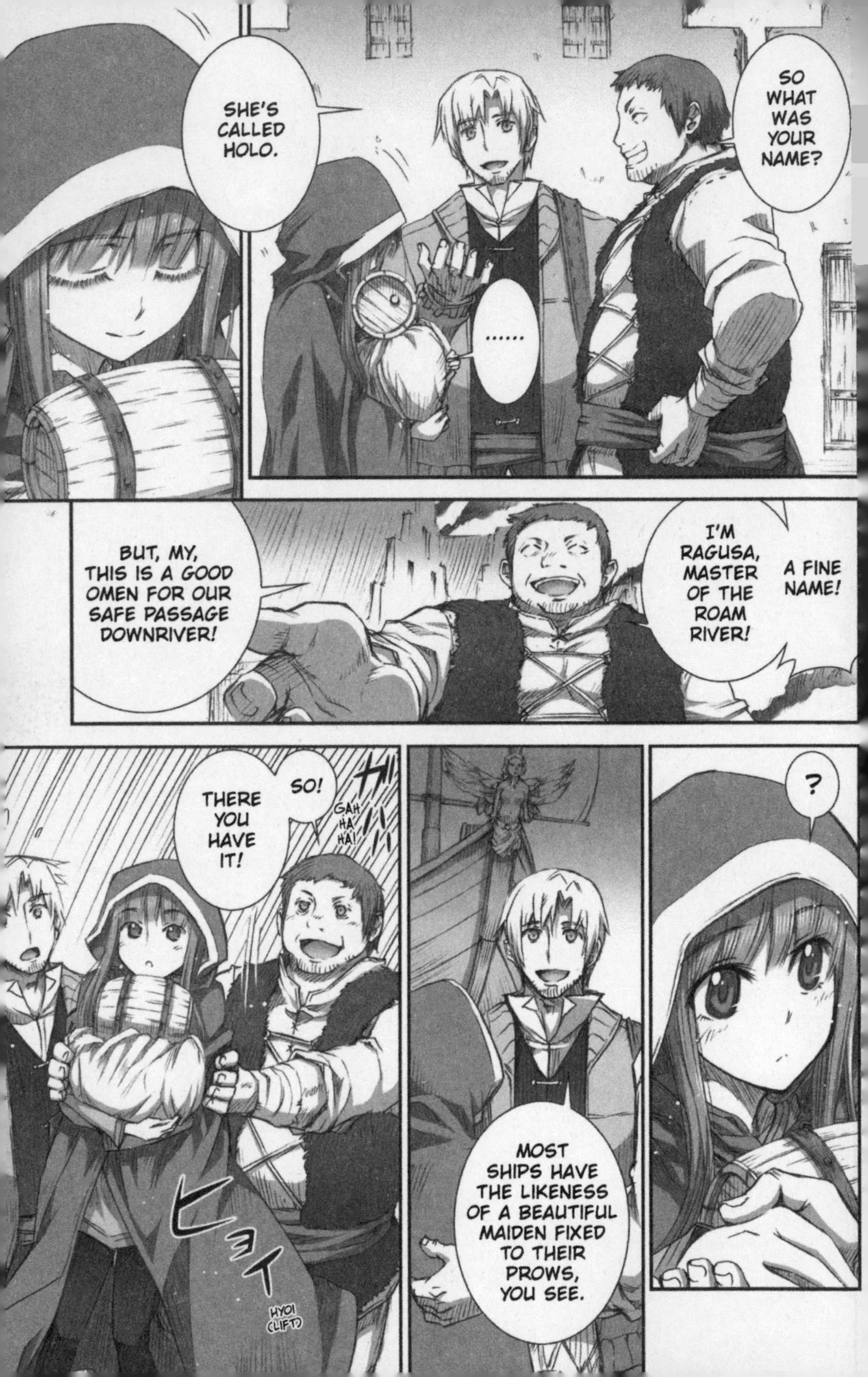
SO WHAT WAS YOUR NAME?
......
SHE'S CALLED HOLO.
A FINE NAME!
I'M RAGUSA, MASTER OF THE ROAM RIVER!
BUT, MY, THIS IS A GOOD OMEN FOR OUR SAFE PASSAGE DOWNRIVER!
?
MOST SHIPS HAVE THE LIKENESS OF A BEAUTIFUL MAIDEN FIXED TO THEIR PROWS, YOU SEE.
SO!
GAH HA HA!
THERE YOU HAVE IT!
HYOI (LIFT)

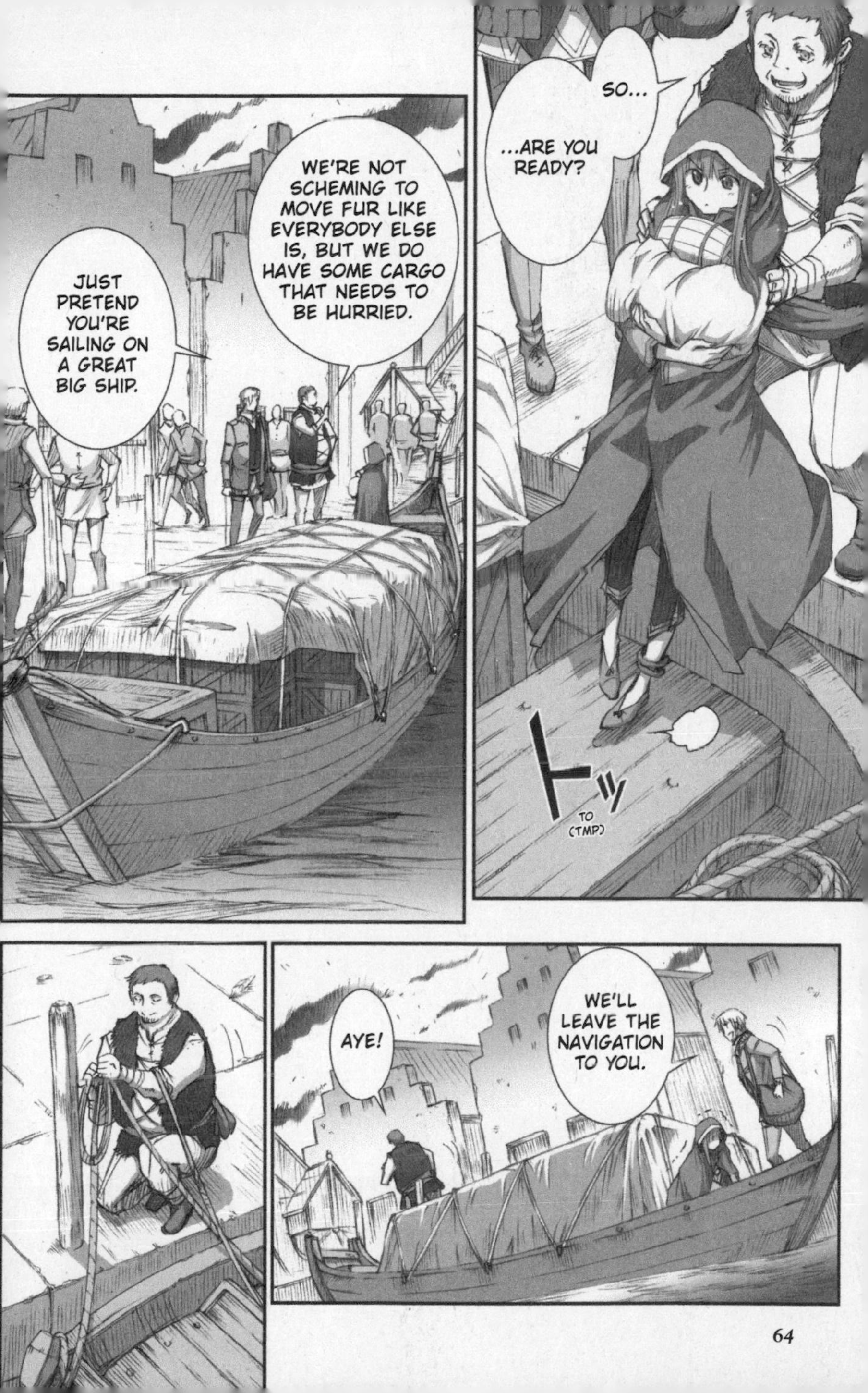
SO...
...ARE YOU READY?
トッ
TO (TMP)
WE'RE NOT SCHEMING TO MOVE FUR LIKE EVERYBODY ELSE IS, BUT WE DO HAVE SOME CARGO THAT NEEDS TO BE HURRIED.
JUST PRETEND YOU'RE SAILING ON A GREAT BIG SHIP.
WE'LL LEAVE THE NAVIGATION TO YOU.
AYE!

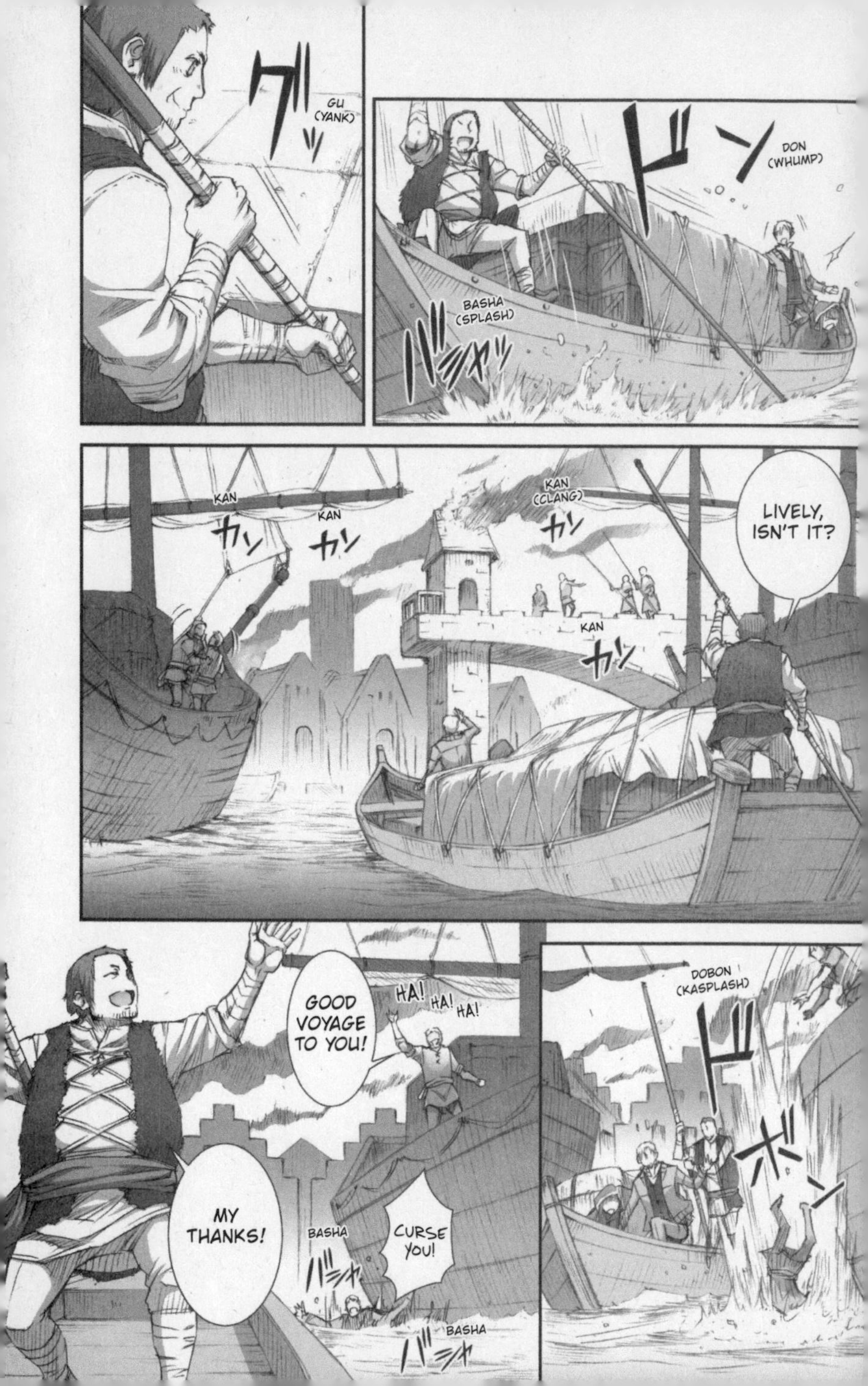
DON (WHUMP)
BASHA (SPLASH)
GU (YANK)
LIVELY, ISN'T IT?
KAN (CLANG)
KAN
KAN
KAN
DOBON (KASPLASH)
GOOD VOYAGE TO YOU!
HA! HA! HA!
CURSE YOU!
BASHA
BASHA
MY THANKS!

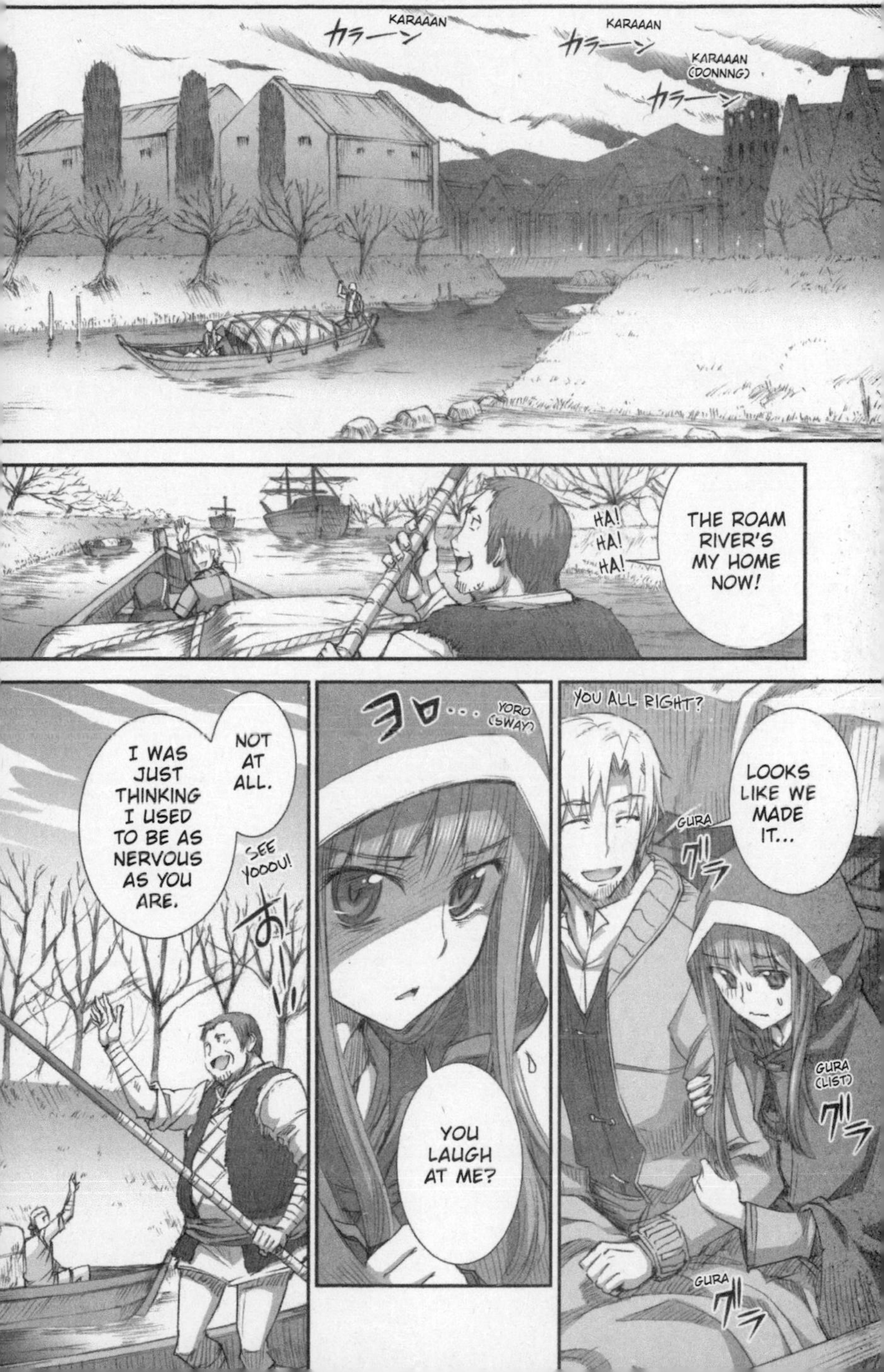
KARAAAN (DONNNG)
カラーン
KARAAAN
カラーン
KARAAAN
カラーン
THE ROAM RIVER'S MY HOME NOW!
HA! HA! HA!
YOU ALL RIGHT?
LOOKS LIKE WE MADE IT...
GURA
グラ
GURA (LIST)
グラ
GURA
グラ
ヨロ...
YORO (SWAY)
YOU LAUGH AT ME?
NOT AT ALL.
I WAS JUST THINKING I USED TO BE AS NERVOUS AS YOU ARE.
SEE YOOOU!
お

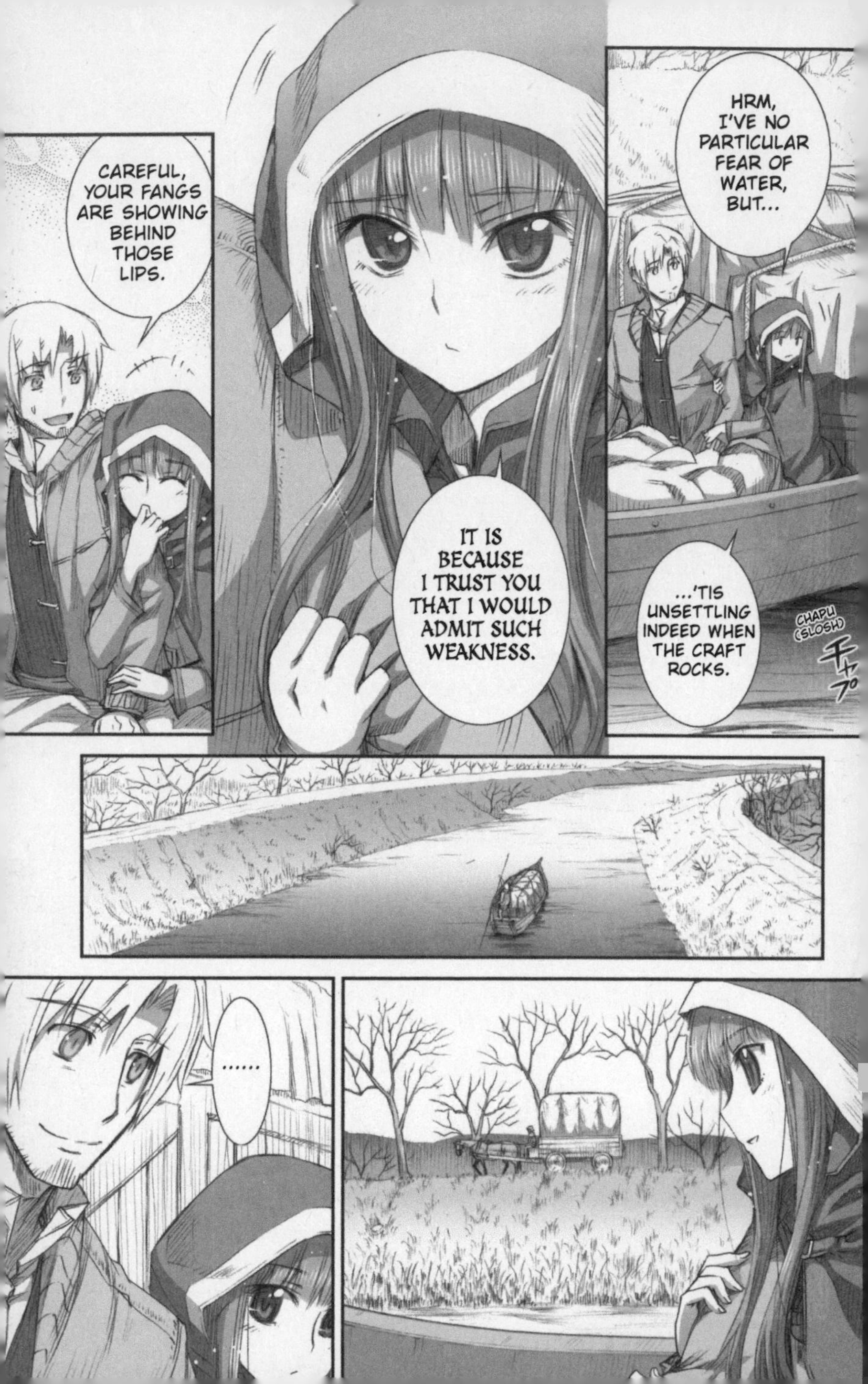
HRM, I'VE NO PARTICULAR FEAR OF WATER, BUT...
...'TIS UNSETTLING INDEED WHEN THE CRAFT ROCKS.
CHAPU (SLOSH)
チャプ
IT IS BECAUSE I TRUST YOU THAT I WOULD ADMIT SUCH WEAKNESS.
CAREFUL, YOUR FANGS ARE SHOWING BEHIND THOSE LIPS.
......

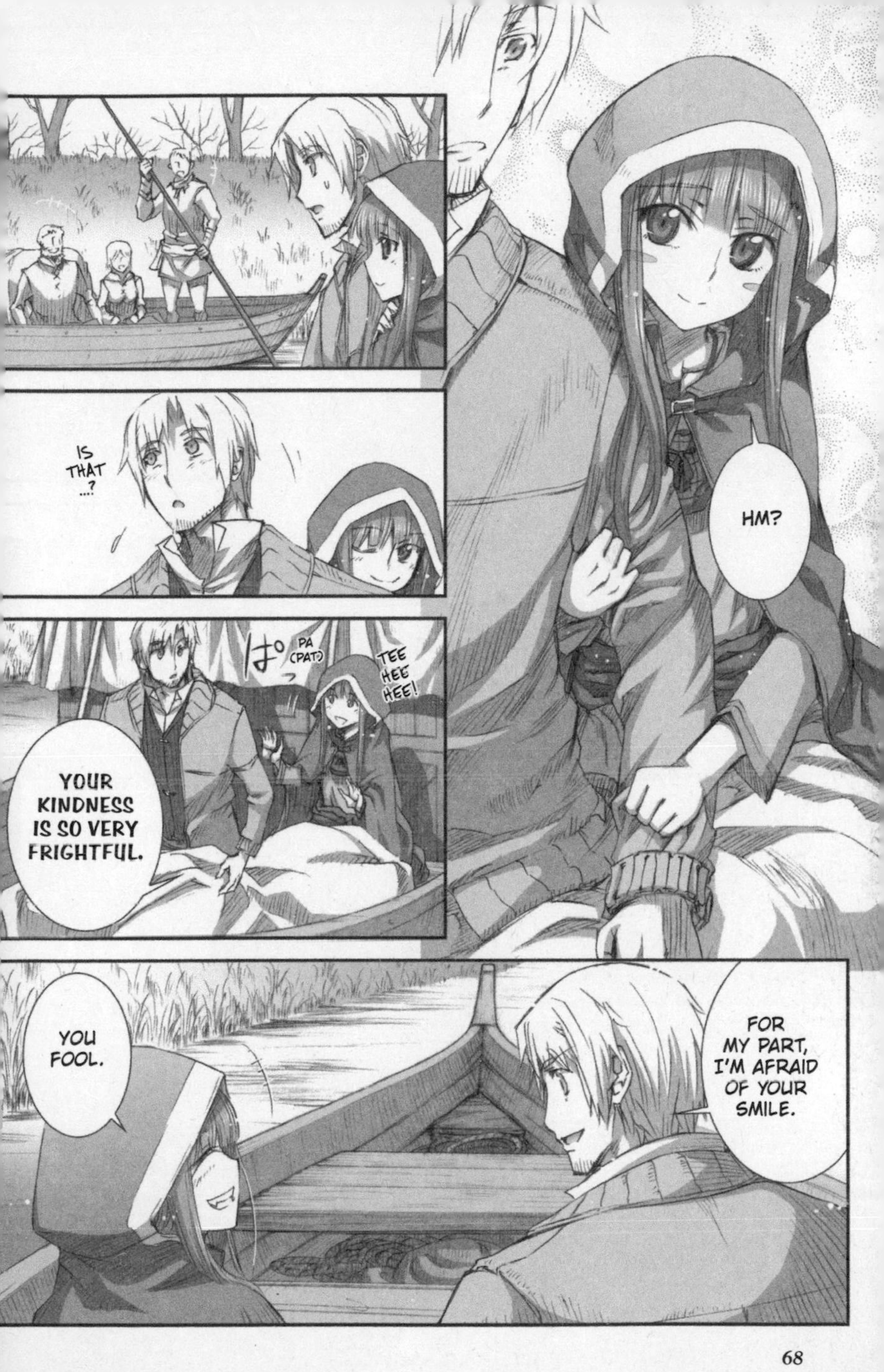
HM?
IS THAT ...?
ぱ
PA (PAT)
TEE HEE HEE!
YOUR KINDNESS IS SO VERY FRIGHTFUL.
FOR MY PART, I'M AFRAID OF YOUR SMILE.
YOU FOOL.

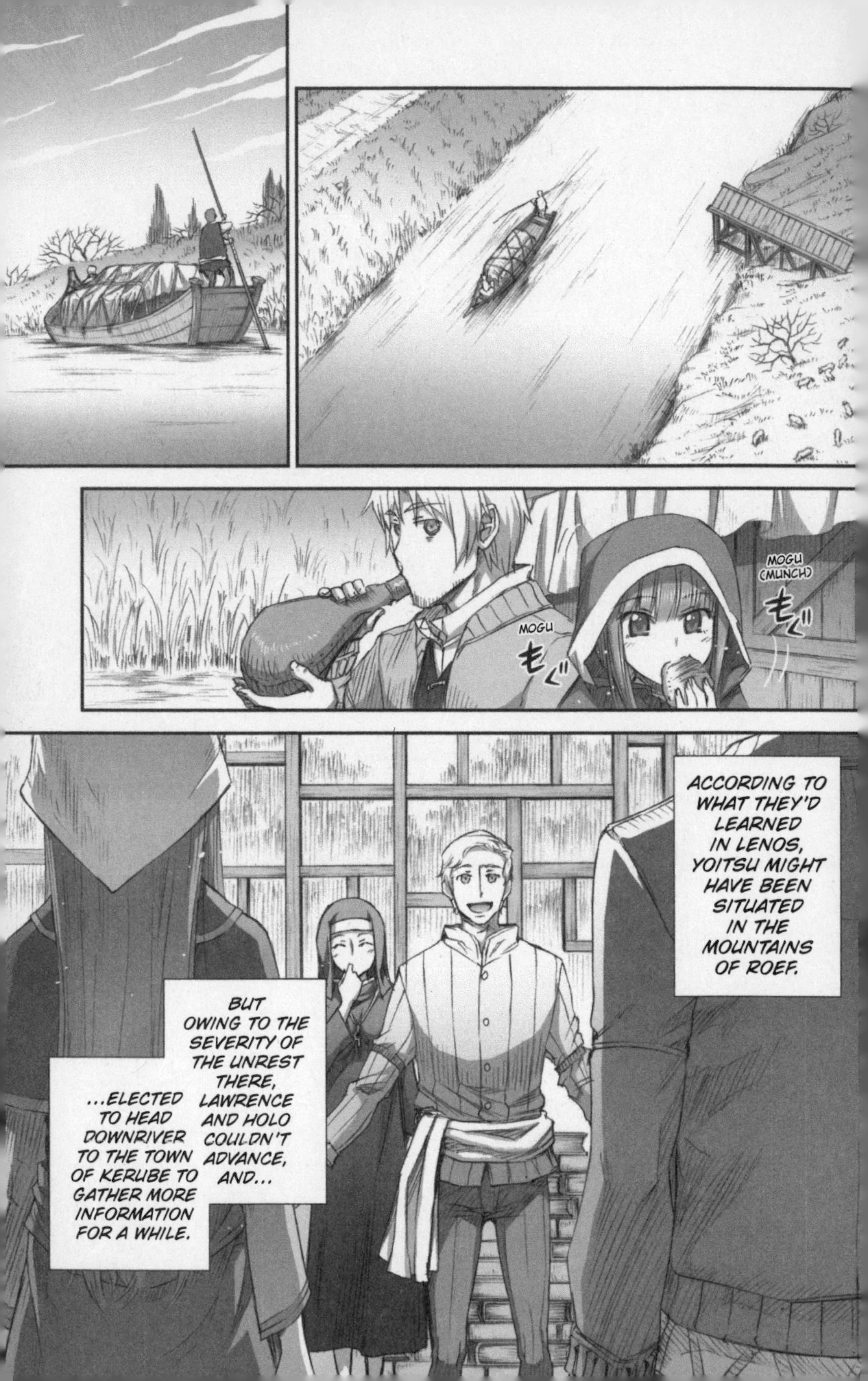

MOGU (MUNCH)
もぐ
MOGU
もぐ
ACCORDING TO WHAT THEY'D LEARNED IN LENOS, YOITSU MIGHT HAVE BEEN SITUATED IN THE MOUNTAINS OF ROEF.
BUT OWING TO THE SEVERITY OF THE UNREST THERE, LAWRENCE AND HOLO COULDN'T ADVANCE, AND...
...ELECTED TO HEAD DOWNRIVER TO THE TOWN OF KERUBE TO GATHER MORE INFORMATION FOR A WHILE.

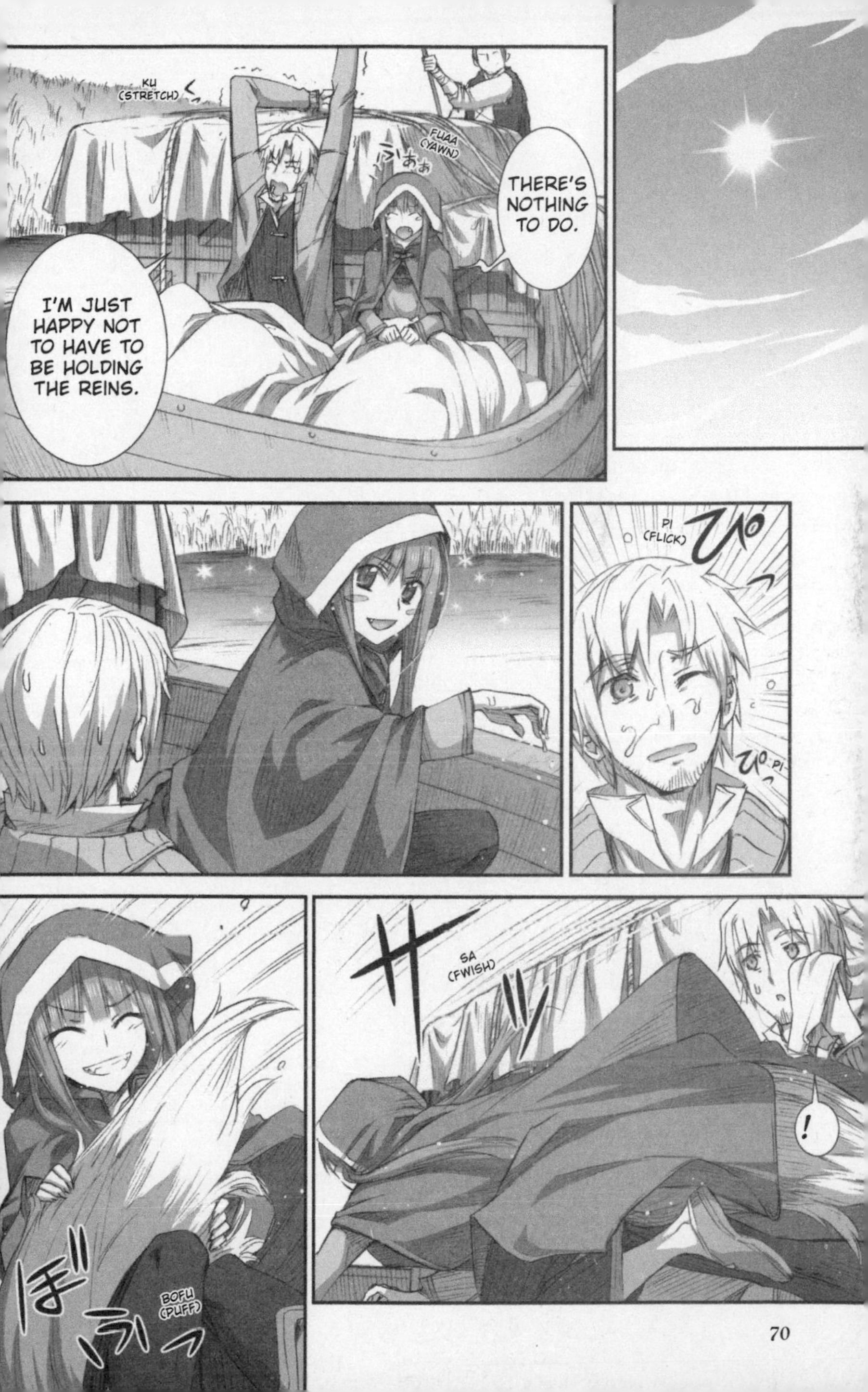
FUAA (YAWN)
THERE'S NOTHING TO DO.
KU (STRETCH)
I'M JUST HAPPY NOT TO HAVE TO BE HOLDING THE REINS.
PI (FLICK)
PI
SA (FWISH)
!
BOFU (PUFF)

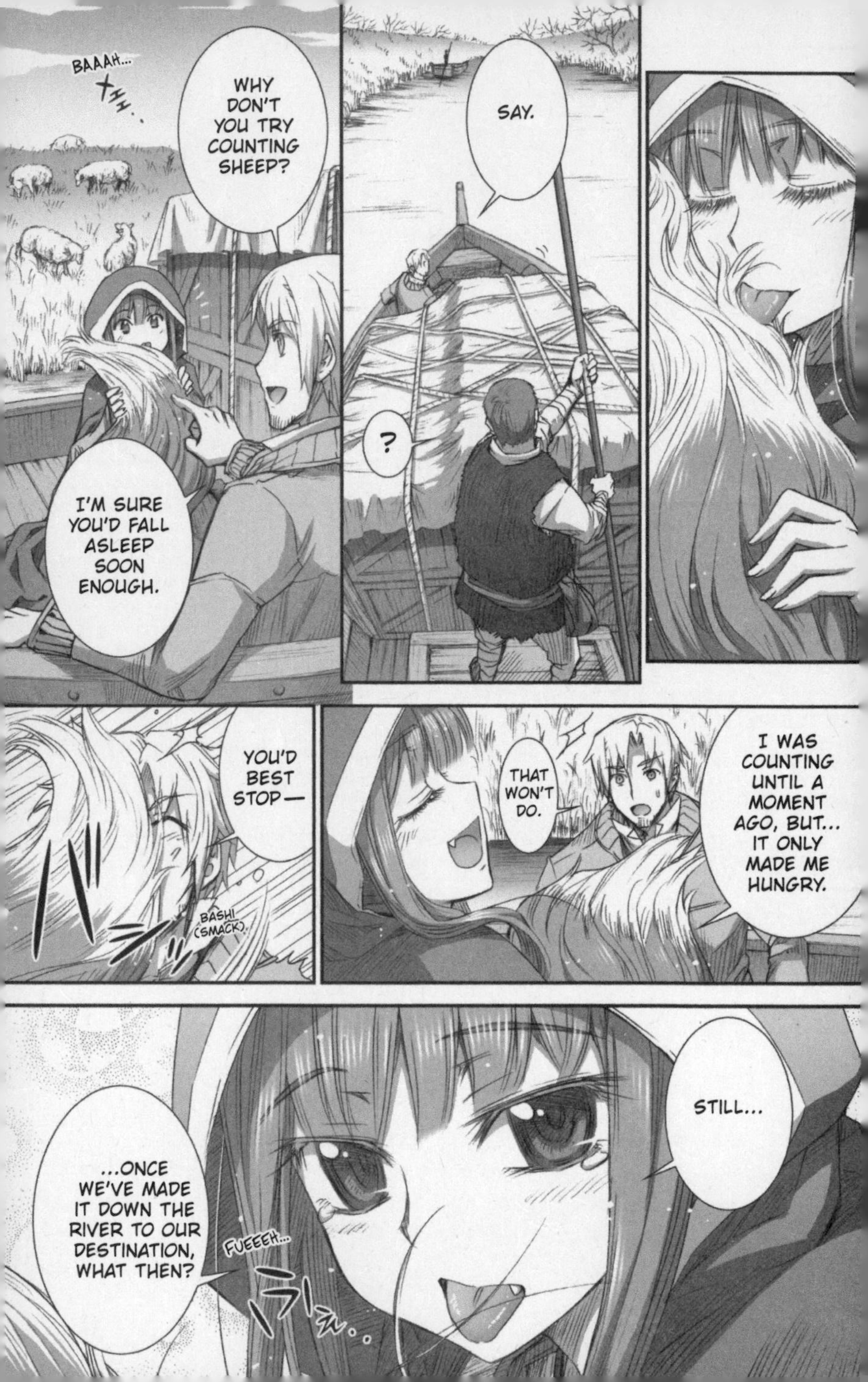
SAY.
?
BAAAH...
WHY DON'T YOU TRY COUNTING SHEEP?
I'M SURE YOU'D FALL ASLEEP SOON ENOUGH.
I WAS COUNTING UNTIL A MOMENT AGO, BUT... IT ONLY MADE ME HUNGRY.
THAT WON'T DO.
YOU'D BEST STOP—
BASHI (SMACK)
STILL...
...ONCE WE'VE MADE IT DOWN THE RIVER TO OUR DESTINATION, WHAT THEN?
FUEEEH...

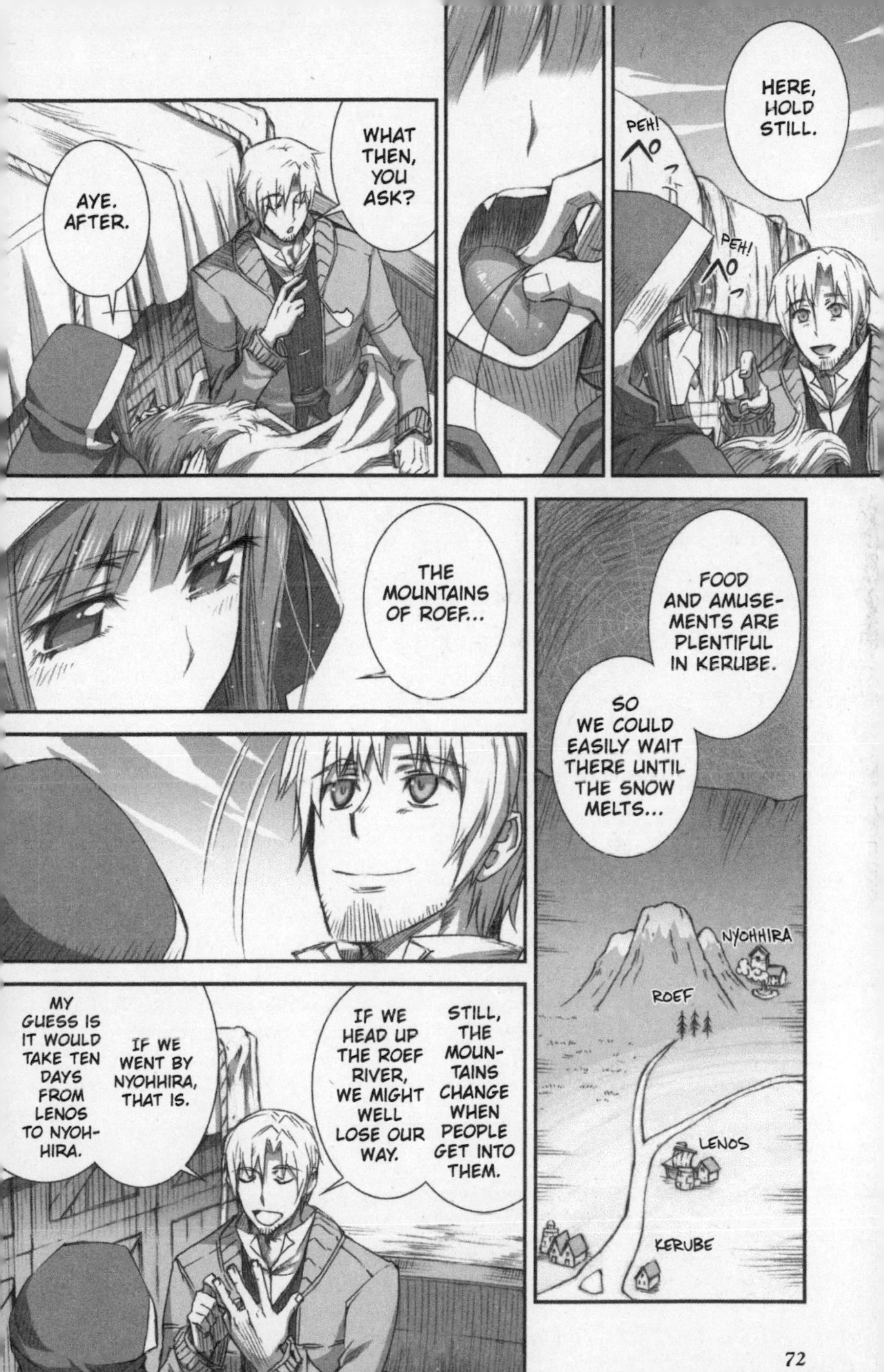
HERE, HOLD STILL.
PEH!
PEH!
WHAT THEN, YOU ASK?
AYE. AFTER.
FOOD AND AMUSEMENTS ARE PLENTIFUL IN KERUBE.
SO WE COULD EASILY WAIT THERE UNTIL THE SNOW MELTS...
NYOHHIRA
ROEF
LENOS
KERUBE
THE MOUNTAINS OF ROEF...
STILL, THE MOUNTAINS CHANGE WHEN PEOPLE GET INTO THEM.
IF WE HEAD UP THE ROEF RIVER, WE MIGHT WELL LOSE OUR WAY.
IF WE WENT BY NYOHHIRA, THAT IS.
MY GUESS IS IT WOULD TAKE TEN DAYS FROM LENOS TO NYOHHIRA.

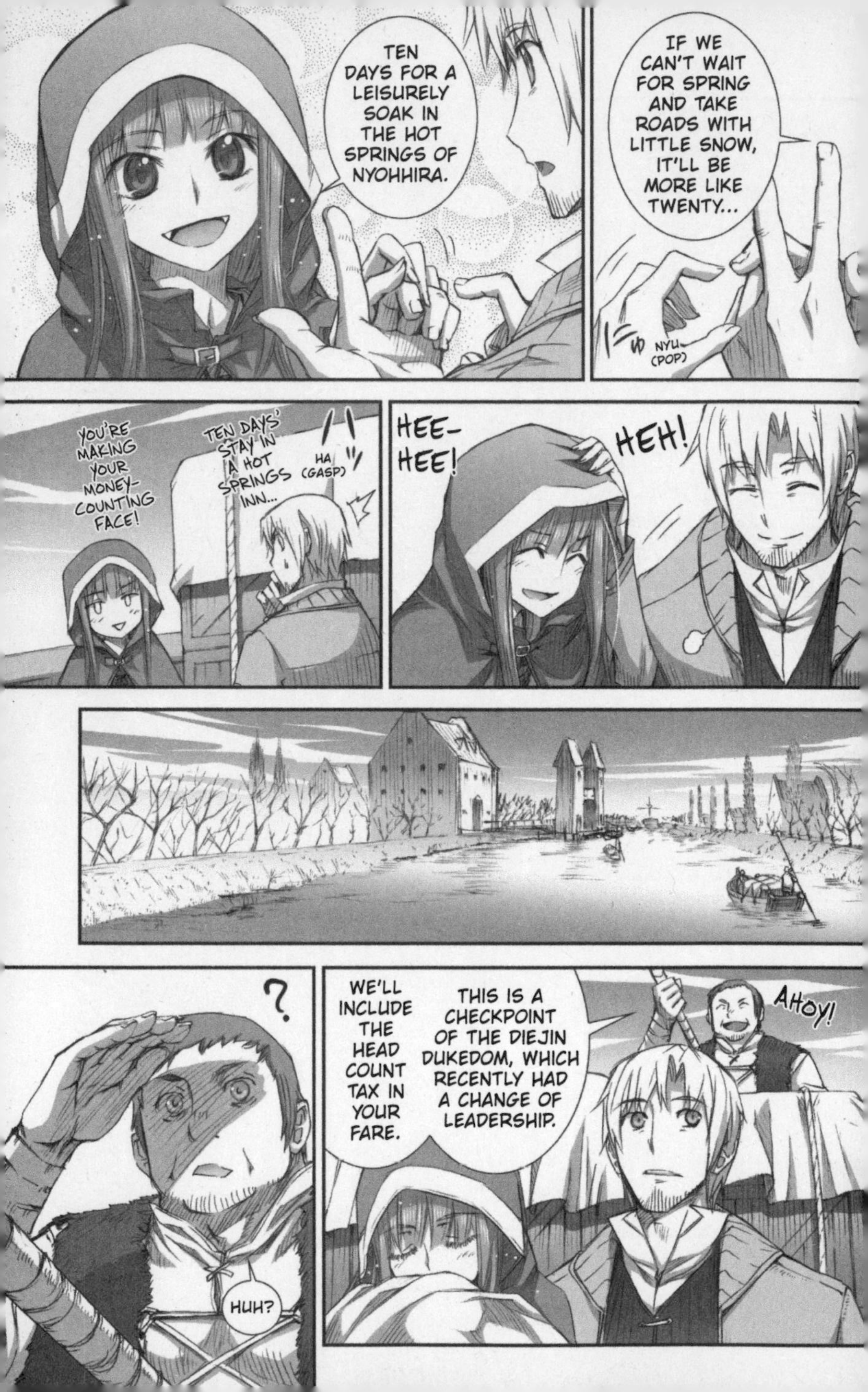
IF WE CAN'T WAIT FOR SPRING AND TAKE ROADS WITH LITTLE SNOW, IT'LL BE MORE LIKE TWENTY...
NYU (POP)
TEN DAYS FOR A LEISURELY SOAK IN THE HOT SPRINGS OF NYOHHIRA.
HEE-HEE!
HEH!
HA (GASP)
TEN DAYS' STAY IN A HOT SPRINGS INN...
YOU'RE MAKING YOUR MONEY-COUNTING FACE!
AHOY!
THIS IS A CHECKPOINT OF THE DIEJIN DUKEDOM, WHICH RECENTLY HAD A CHANGE OF LEADERSHIP.
WE'LL INCLUDE THE HEAD COUNT TAX IN YOUR FARE.
?
HUH?

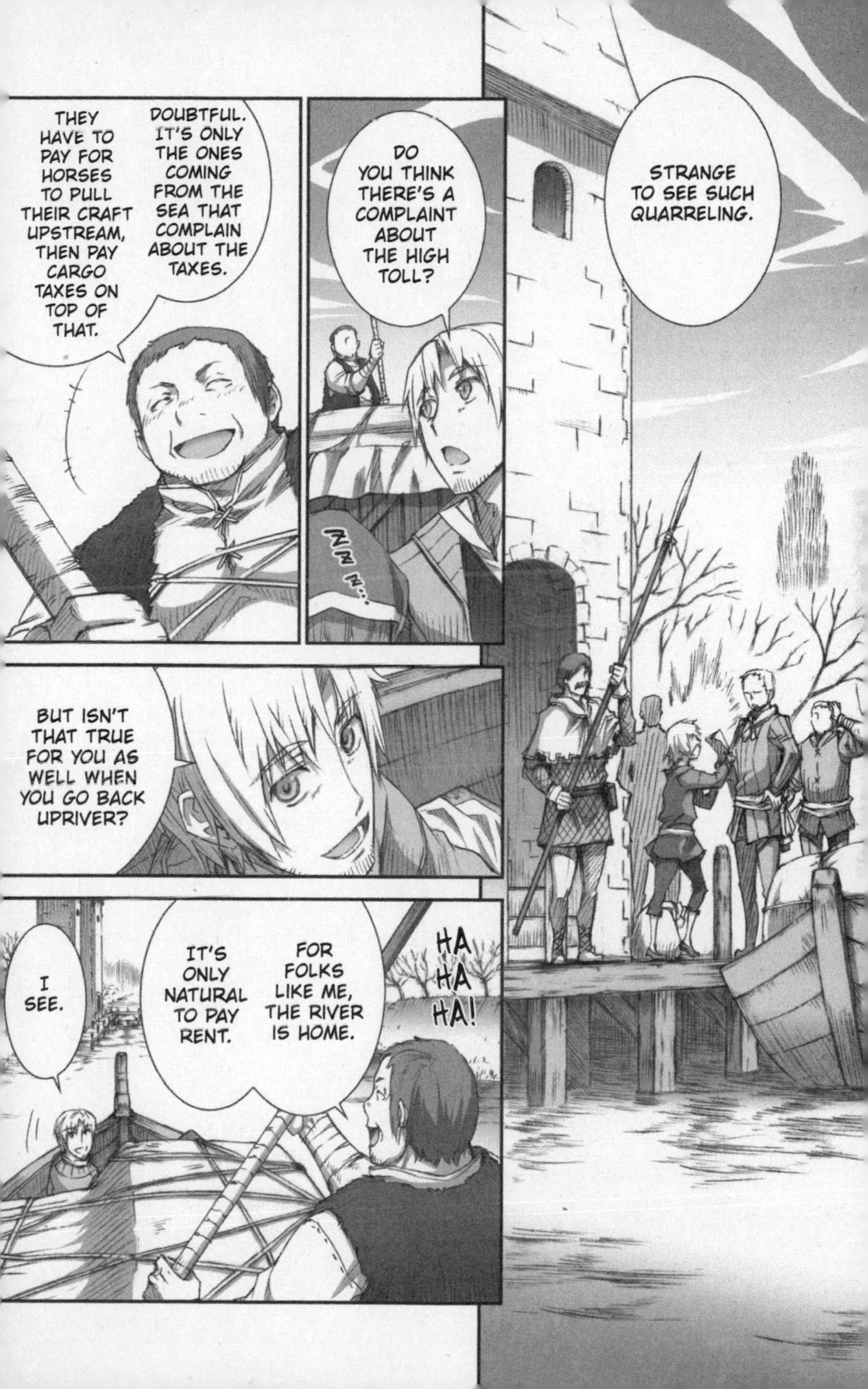

STRANGE TO SEE SUCH QUARRELING.
DO YOU THINK THERE'S A COMPLAINT ABOUT THE HIGH TOLL?
ZZZ Z...
DOUBTFUL. IT'S ONLY THE ONES COMING FROM THE SEA THAT COMPLAIN ABOUT THE TAXES.
THEY HAVE TO PAY FOR HORSES TO PULL THEIR CRAFT UPSTREAM, THEN PAY CARGO TAXES ON TOP OF THAT.
BUT ISN'T THAT TRUE FOR YOU AS WELL WHEN YOU GO BACK UPRIVER?
HA HA HA!
FOR FOLKS LIKE ME, THE RIVER IS HOME.
IT'S ONLY NATURAL TO PAY RENT.
I SEE.

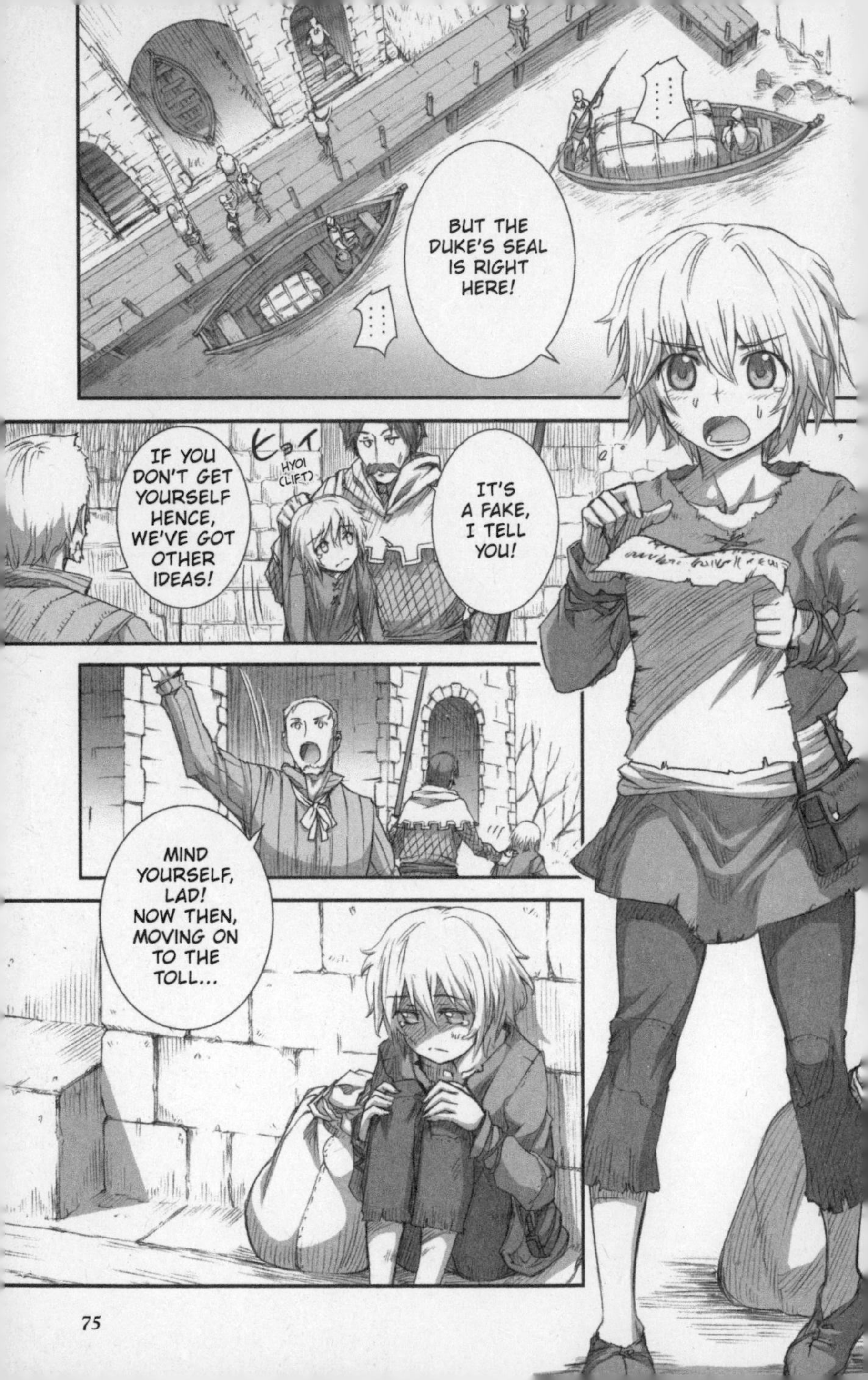
BUT THE DUKE'S SEAL IS RIGHT HERE!
IT'S A FAKE, I TELL YOU!
HYOI (LIFT)
IF YOU DON'T GET YOURSELF HENCE, WE'VE GOT OTHER IDEAS!
MIND YOURSELF, LAD! NOW THEN, MOVING ON TO THE TOLL...

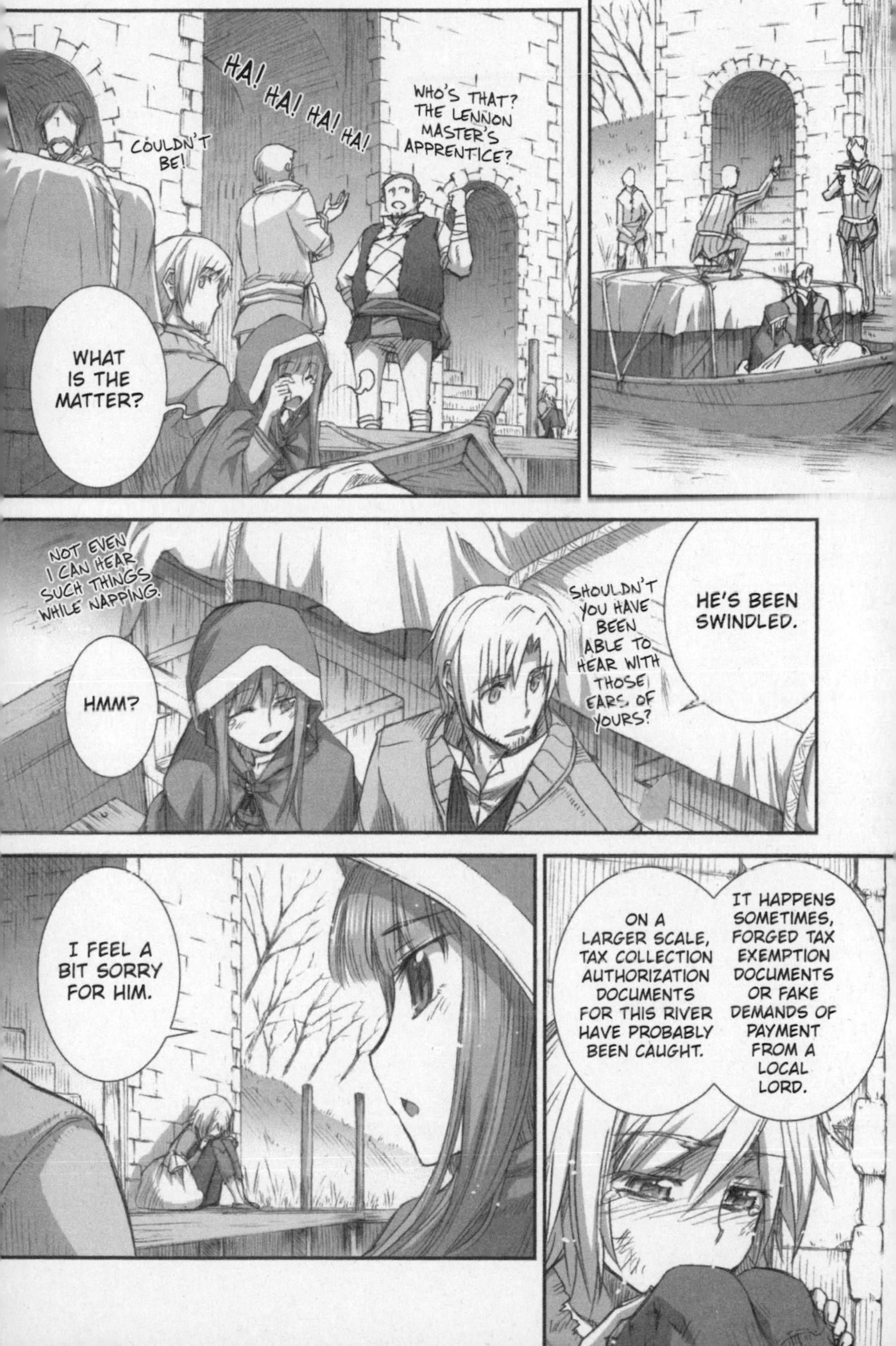
WHO'S THAT? THE LENNON MASTER'S APPRENTICE?
HA! HA! HA! HA!
COULDN'T BE!
WHAT IS THE MATTER?
HE'S BEEN SWINDLED.
SHOULDN'T YOU HAVE BEEN ABLE TO HEAR WITH THOSE EARS OF YOURS?
NOT EVEN I CAN HEAR SUCH THINGS WHILE NAPPING.
HMM?
IT HAPPENS SOMETIMES, FORGED TAX EXEMPTION DOCUMENTS OR FAKE DEMANDS OF PAYMENT FROM A LOCAL LORD.
ON A LARGER SCALE, TAX COLLECTION AUTHORIZATION DOCUMENTS FOR THIS RIVER HAVE PROBABLY BEEN CAUGHT.
I FEEL A BIT SORRY FOR HIM.

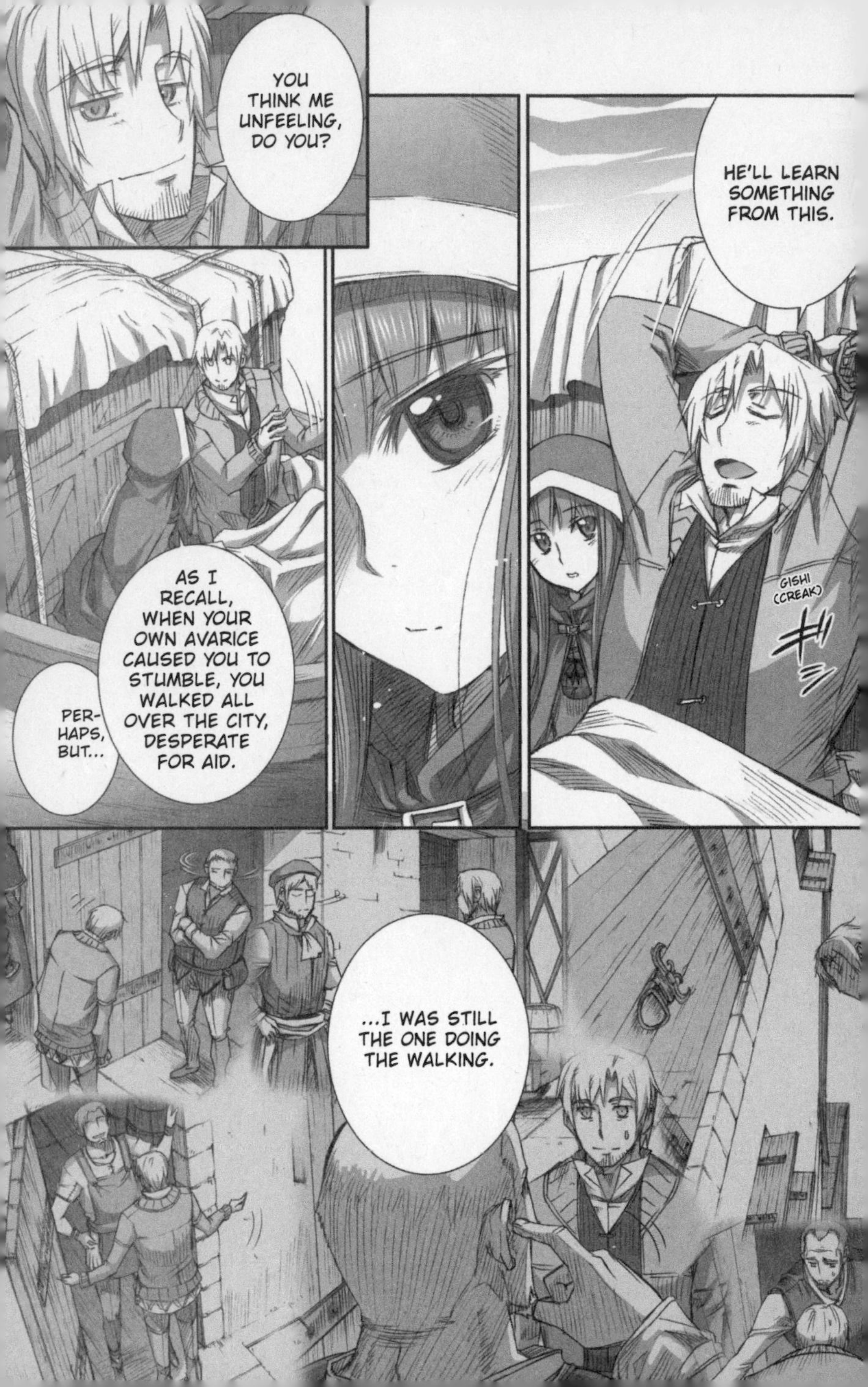
HE'LL LEARN SOMETHING FROM THIS.
GISHI (CREAK)
YOU THINK ME UNFEELING, DO YOU?
PER-HAPS, BUT...
AS I RECALL, WHEN YOUR OWN AVARICE CAUSED YOU TO STUMBLE, YOU WALKED ALL OVER THE CITY, DESPERATE FOR AID.
...I WAS STILL THE ONE DOING THE WALKING.

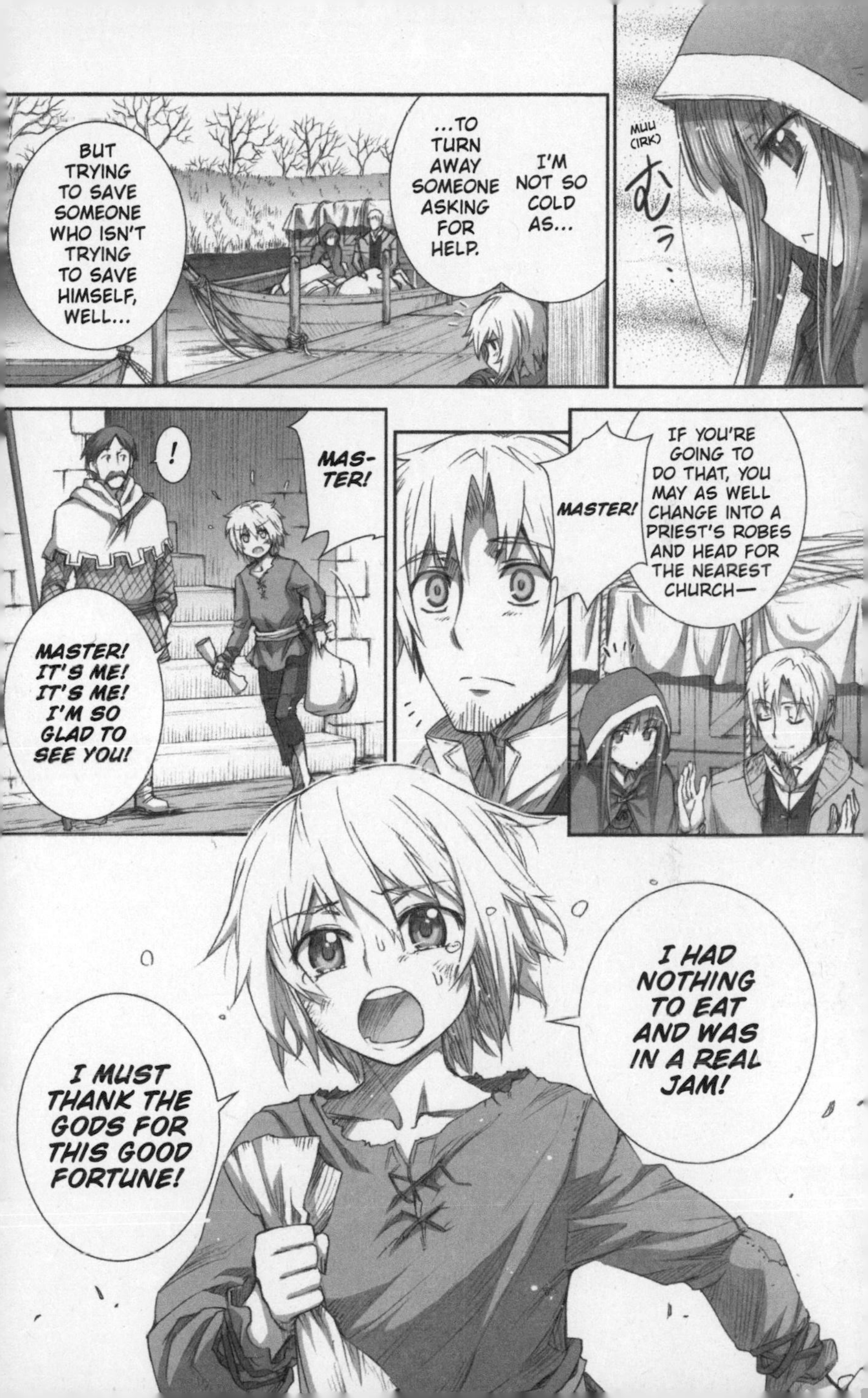
MUU (IRK)
I'M NOT SO COLD AS...
...TO TURN AWAY SOMEONE ASKING FOR HELP.
BUT TRYING TO SAVE SOMEONE WHO ISN'T TRYING TO SAVE HIMSELF, WELL...
IF YOU'RE GOING TO DO THAT, YOU MAY AS WELL CHANGE INTO A PRIEST'S ROBES AND HEAD FOR THE NEAREST CHURCH—
MASTER!
MAS-TER!
!
MASTER! IT'S ME! IT'S ME! I'M SO GLAD TO SEE YOU!
I HAD NOTHING TO EAT AND WAS IN A REAL JAM!
I MUST THANK THE GODS FOR THIS GOOD FORTUNE!

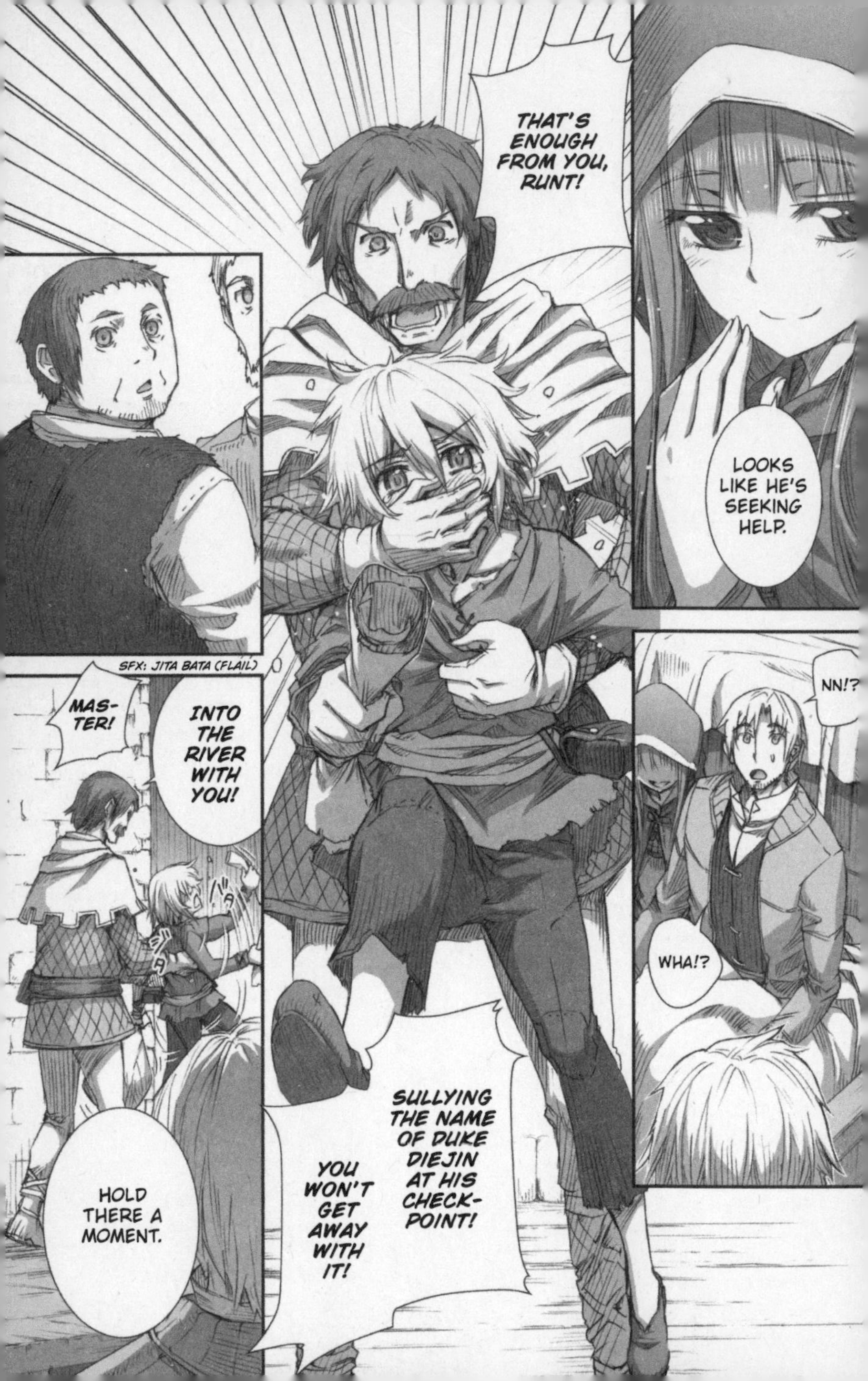
LOOKS LIKE HE'S SEEKING HELP.
NN!?
WHA!?
THAT'S ENOUGH FROM YOU, RUNT!
SULLYING THE NAME OF DUKE DIEJIN AT HIS CHECK-POINT!
YOU WON'T GET AWAY WITH IT!
SFX: JITA BATA (FLAIL)
MAS-TER!
INTO THE RIVER WITH YOU!
HOLD THERE A MOMENT.

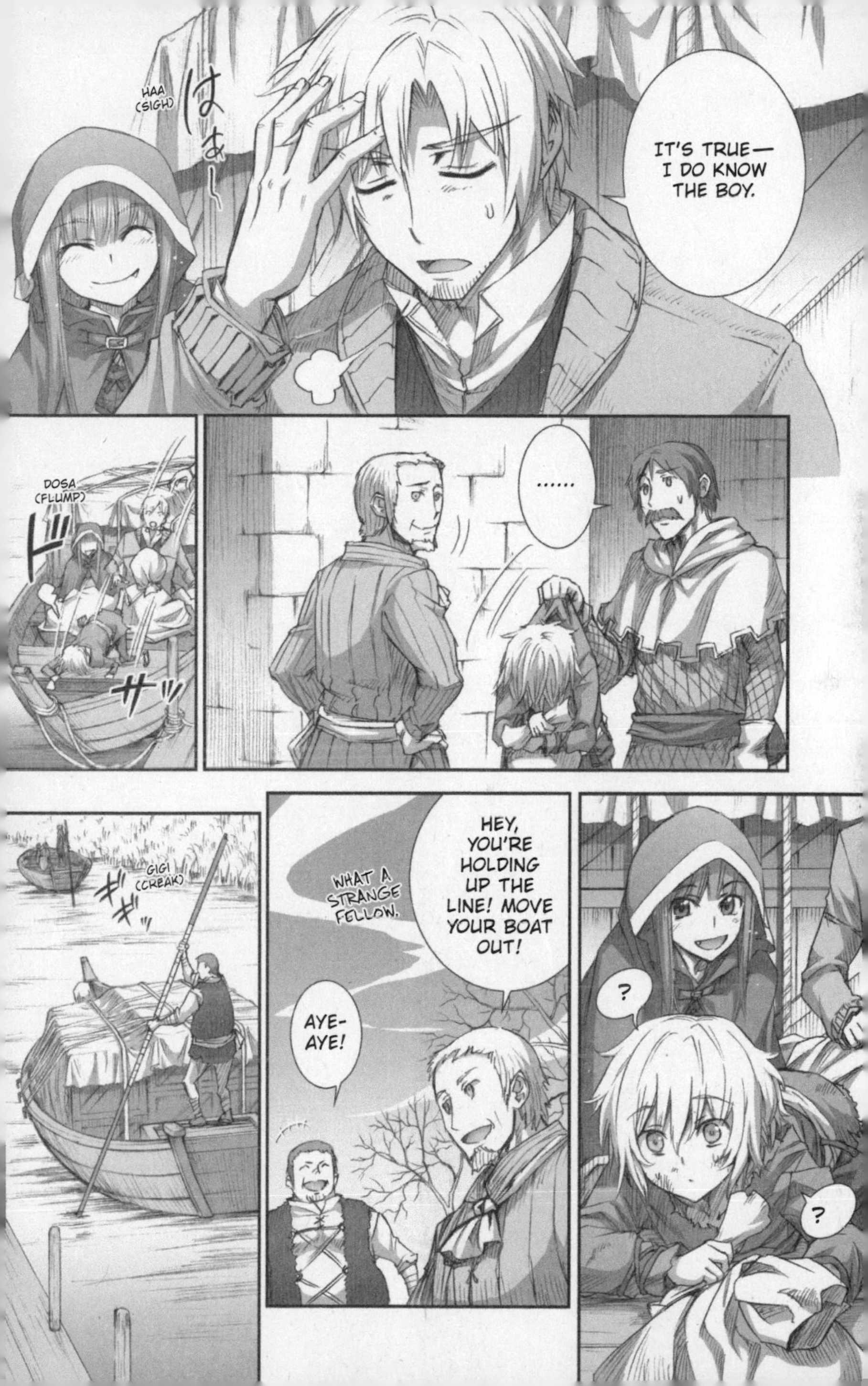
IT'S TRUE—
I DO KNOW
THE BOY.
HAA
(SIGH)
はぁ~
......
DOSA
(FLUMP)
ド
ザッ
HEY, YOU'RE HOLDING UP THE LINE! MOVE YOUR BOAT OUT!
WHAT A STRANGE FELLOW.
AYE-AYE!
?
?
GIGI
(CREAK)
ギギ

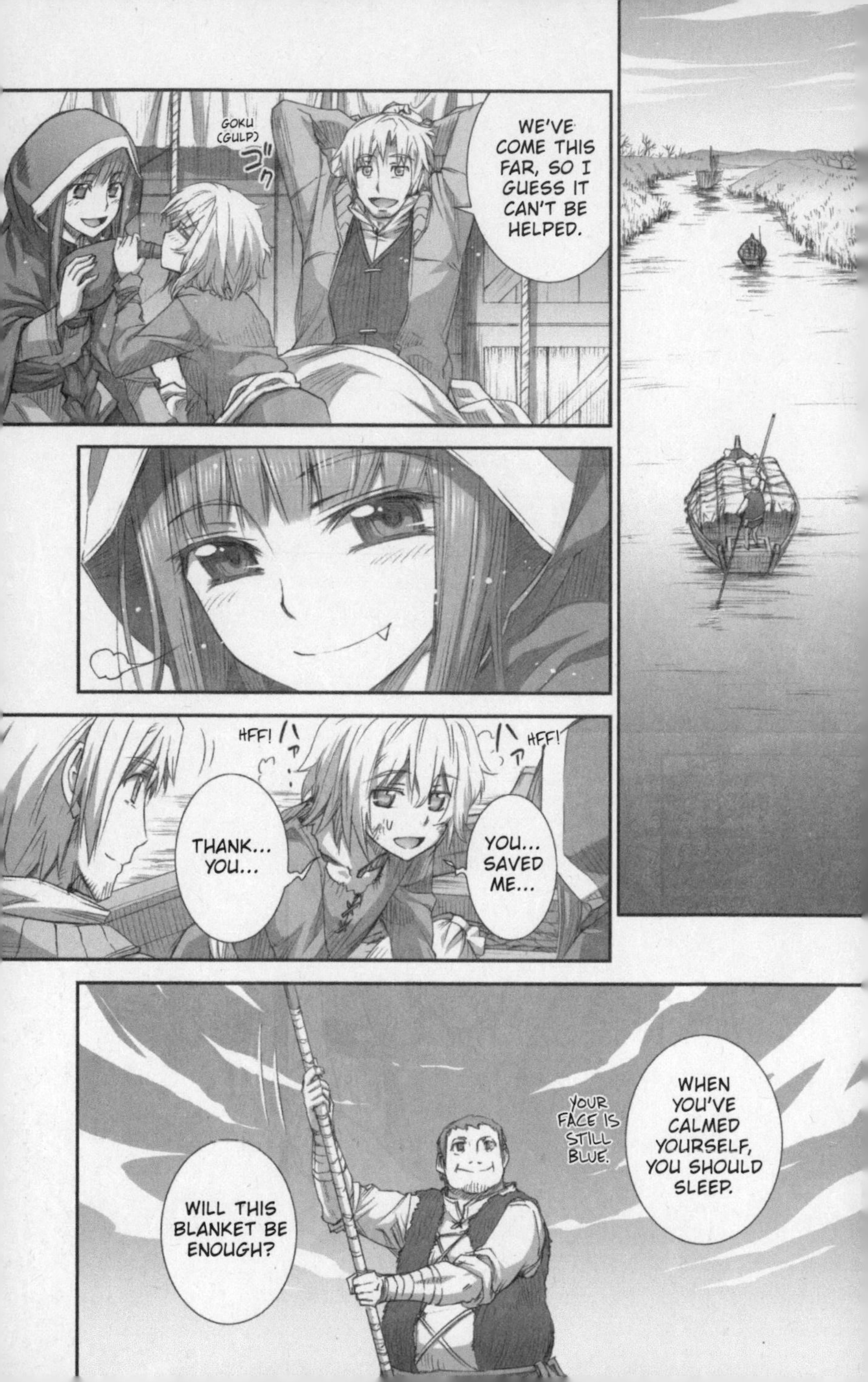
WE'VE COME THIS FAR, SO I GUESS IT CAN'T BE HELPED.
GOKU (GULP)
HFF!
HFF!
YOU... SAVED ME...
THANK... YOU...
WHEN YOU'VE CALMED YOURSELF, YOU SHOULD SLEEP.
YOUR FACE IS STILL BLUE.
WILL THIS BLANKET BE ENOUGH?

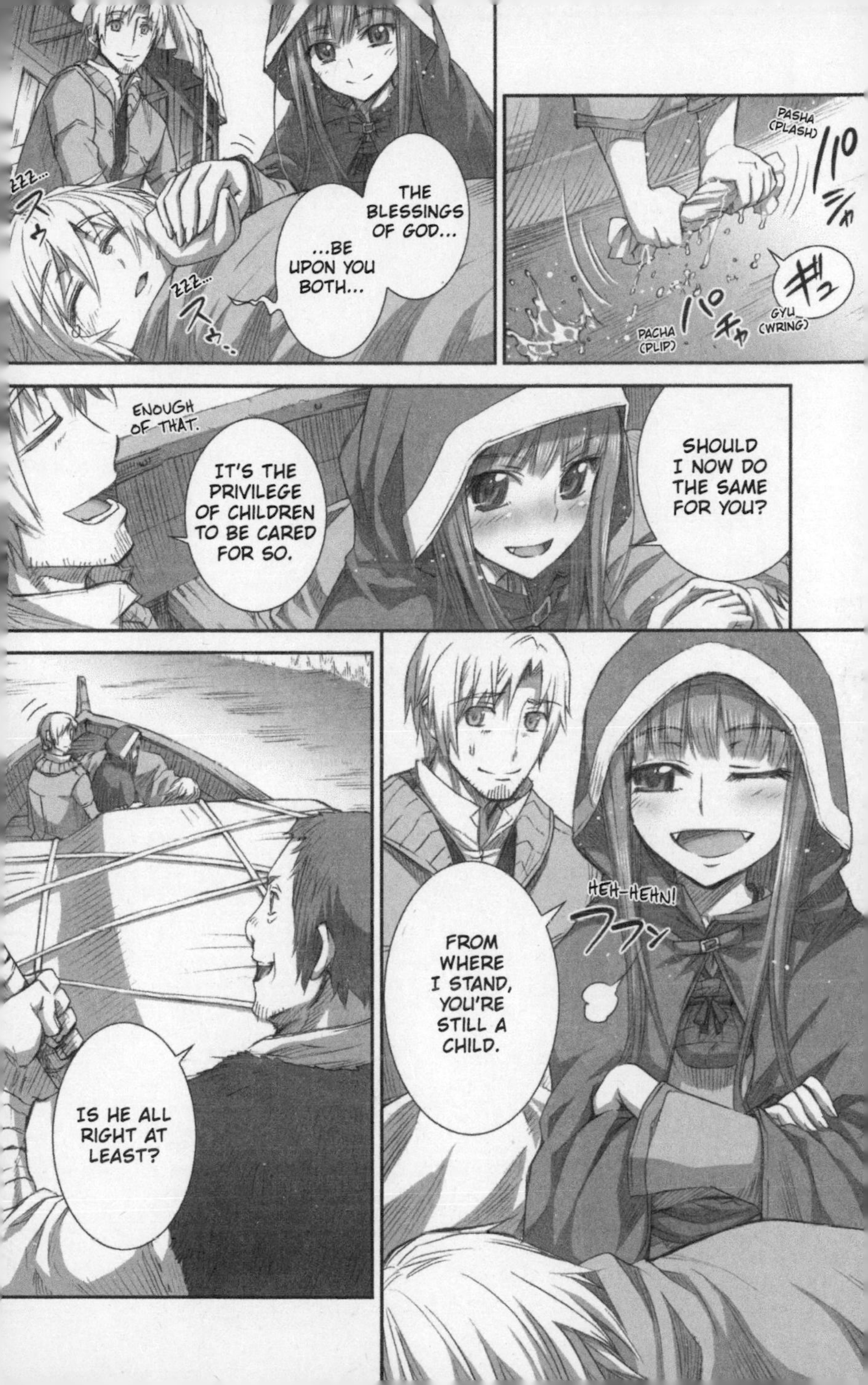
PASHA (PLASH)
GYU (WRING)
PACHA (PLIP)
THE BLESSINGS OF GOD...
...BE UPON YOU BOTH...
ZZZ...
ZZZ...
SHOULD I NOW DO THE SAME FOR YOU?
IT'S THE PRIVILEGE OF CHILDREN TO BE CARED FOR SO.
ENOUGH OF THAT.
HEH-HEHN!
FROM WHERE I STAND, YOU'RE STILL A CHILD.
IS HE ALL RIGHT AT LEAST?

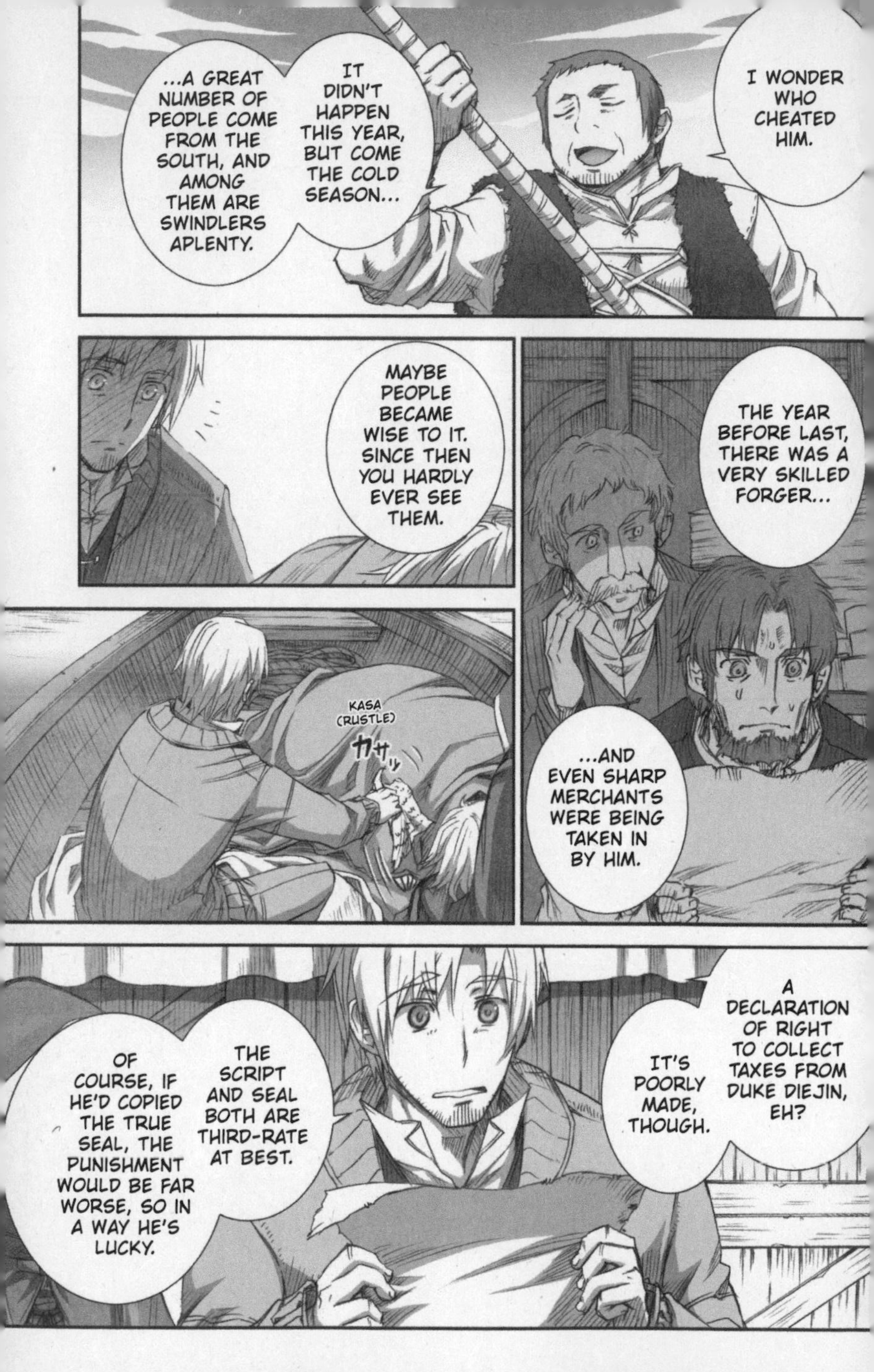
I WONDER WHO CHEATED HIM.
IT DIDN'T HAPPEN THIS YEAR, BUT COME THE COLD SEASON...
...A GREAT NUMBER OF PEOPLE COME FROM THE SOUTH, AND AMONG THEM ARE SWINDLERS APLENTY.
THE YEAR BEFORE LAST, THERE WAS A VERY SKILLED FORGER...
...AND EVEN SHARP MERCHANTS WERE BEING TAKEN IN BY HIM.
MAYBE PEOPLE BECAME WISE TO IT. SINCE THEN YOU HARDLY EVER SEE THEM.
KASA (RUSTLE)
カサッ
A DECLARATION OF RIGHT TO COLLECT TAXES FROM DUKE DIEJIN, EH?
IT'S POORLY MADE, THOUGH.
THE SCRIPT AND SEAL BOTH ARE THIRD-RATE AT BEST.
OF COURSE, IF HE'D COPIED THE TRUE SEAL, THE PUNISHMENT WOULD BE FAR WORSE, SO IN A WAY HE'S LUCKY.

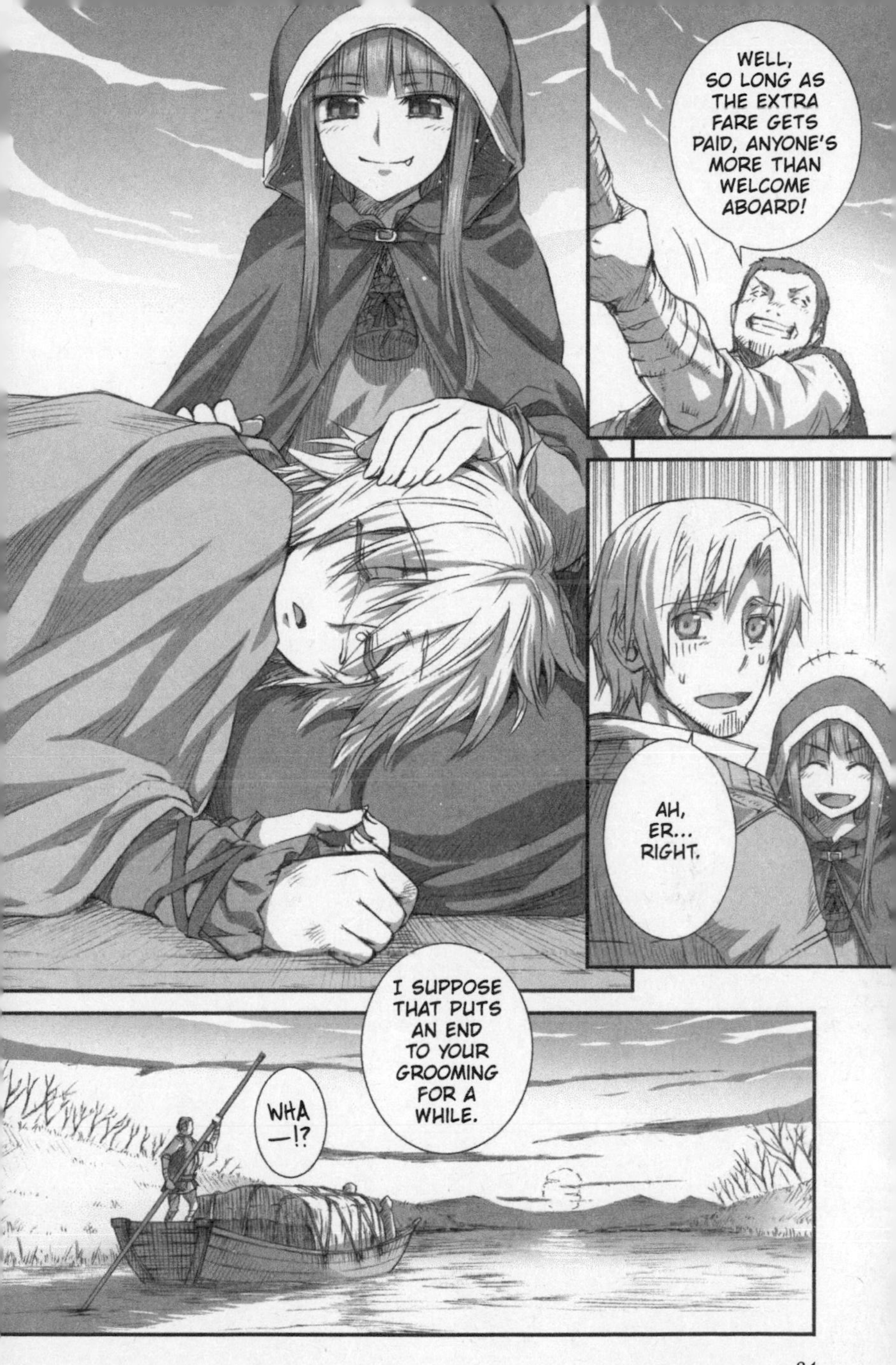
WELL, SO LONG AS THE EXTRA FARE GETS PAID, ANYONE'S MORE THAN WELCOME ABOARD!
AH, ER... RIGHT.
I SUPPOSE THAT PUTS AN END TO YOUR GROOMING FOR A WHILE.
WHA—!?

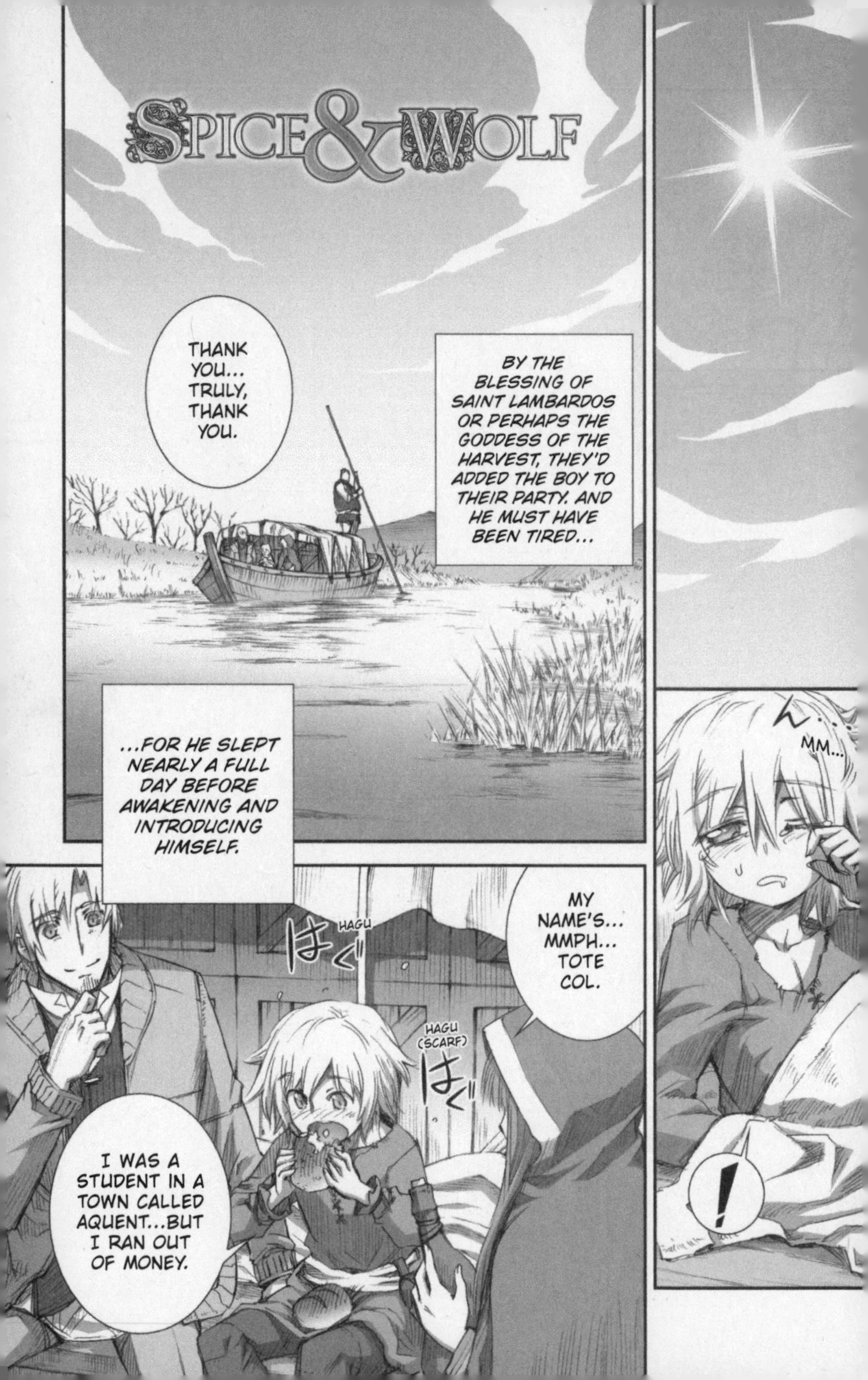
SPICE & WOLF
BY THE BLESSING OF SAINT LAMBARDOS OR PERHAPS THE GODDESS OF THE HARVEST, THEY'D ADDED THE BOY TO THEIR PARTY. AND HE MUST HAVE BEEN TIRED...
THANK YOU... TRULY, THANK YOU.
...FOR HE SLEPT NEARLY A FULL DAY BEFORE AWAKENING AND INTRODUCING HIMSELF.
ん…
MM...
!
MY NAME'S... MMPH... TOTE COL.
はぐ
HAGU
HAGU (SCARF)
はぐ
I WAS A STUDENT IN A TOWN CALLED AQUENT...BUT I RAN OUT OF MONEY.

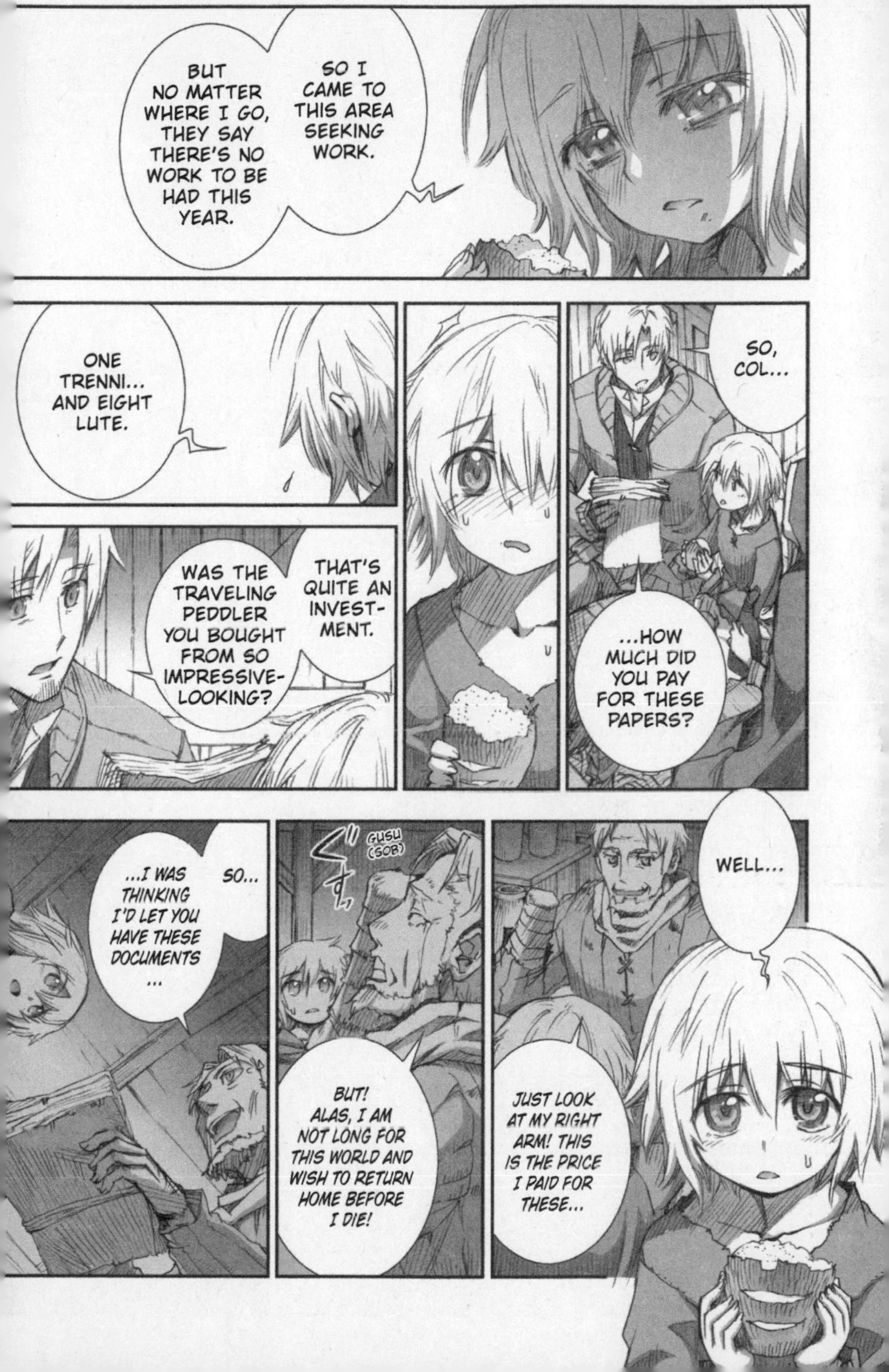
SO I CAME TO THIS AREA SEEKING WORK.
BUT NO MATTER WHERE I GO, THEY SAY THERE'S NO WORK TO BE HAD THIS YEAR.
SO, COL...
...HOW MUCH DID YOU PAY FOR THESE PAPERS?
ONE TRENNI... AND EIGHT LUTE.
THAT'S QUITE AN INVEST-MENT.
WAS THE TRAVELING PEDDLER YOU BOUGHT FROM SO IMPRESSIVE-LOOKING?
WELL...
JUST LOOK AT MY RIGHT ARM! THIS IS THE PRICE I PAID FOR THESE...
GUSU (SOB)
BUT! ALAS, I AM NOT LONG FOR THIS WORLD AND WISH TO RETURN HOME BEFORE I DIE!
SO...
...I WAS THINKING I'D LET YOU HAVE THESE DOCUMENTS ...

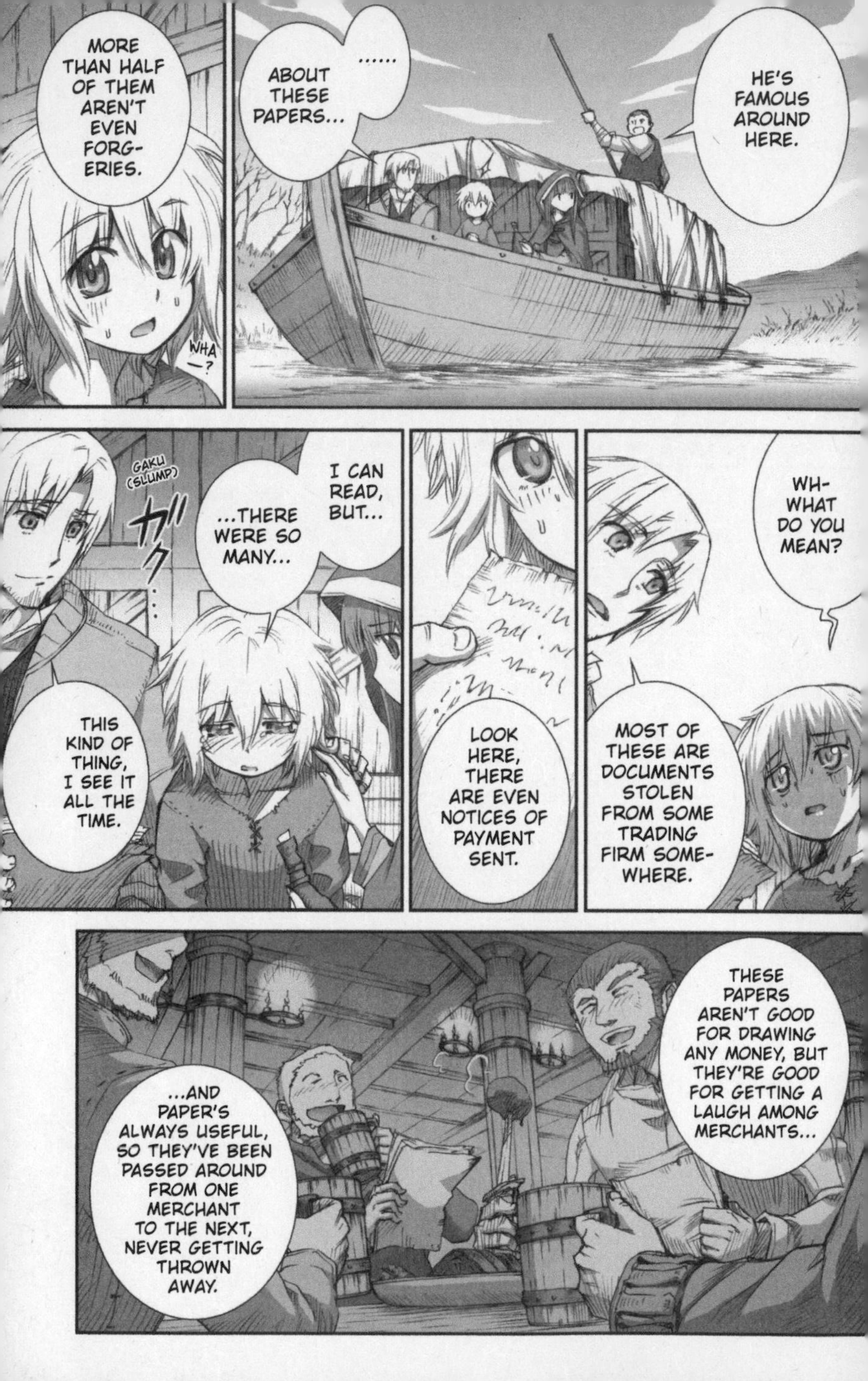
HE'S FAMOUS AROUND HERE.
......
ABOUT THESE PAPERS...
MORE THAN HALF OF THEM AREN'T EVEN FORG-ERIES.
WHA—?
WH-WHAT DO YOU MEAN?
MOST OF THESE ARE DOCUMENTS STOLEN FROM SOME TRADING FIRM SOME-WHERE.
LOOK HERE, THERE ARE EVEN NOTICES OF PAYMENT SENT.
I CAN READ, BUT...
...THERE WERE SO MANY...
GAKU (SLUMP)
THIS KIND OF THING, I SEE IT ALL THE TIME.
THESE PAPERS AREN'T GOOD FOR DRAWING ANY MONEY, BUT THEY'RE GOOD FOR GETTING A LAUGH AMONG MERCHANTS...
...AND PAPER'S ALWAYS USEFUL, SO THEY'VE BEEN PASSED AROUND FROM ONE MERCHANT TO THE NEXT, NEVER GETTING THROWN AWAY.

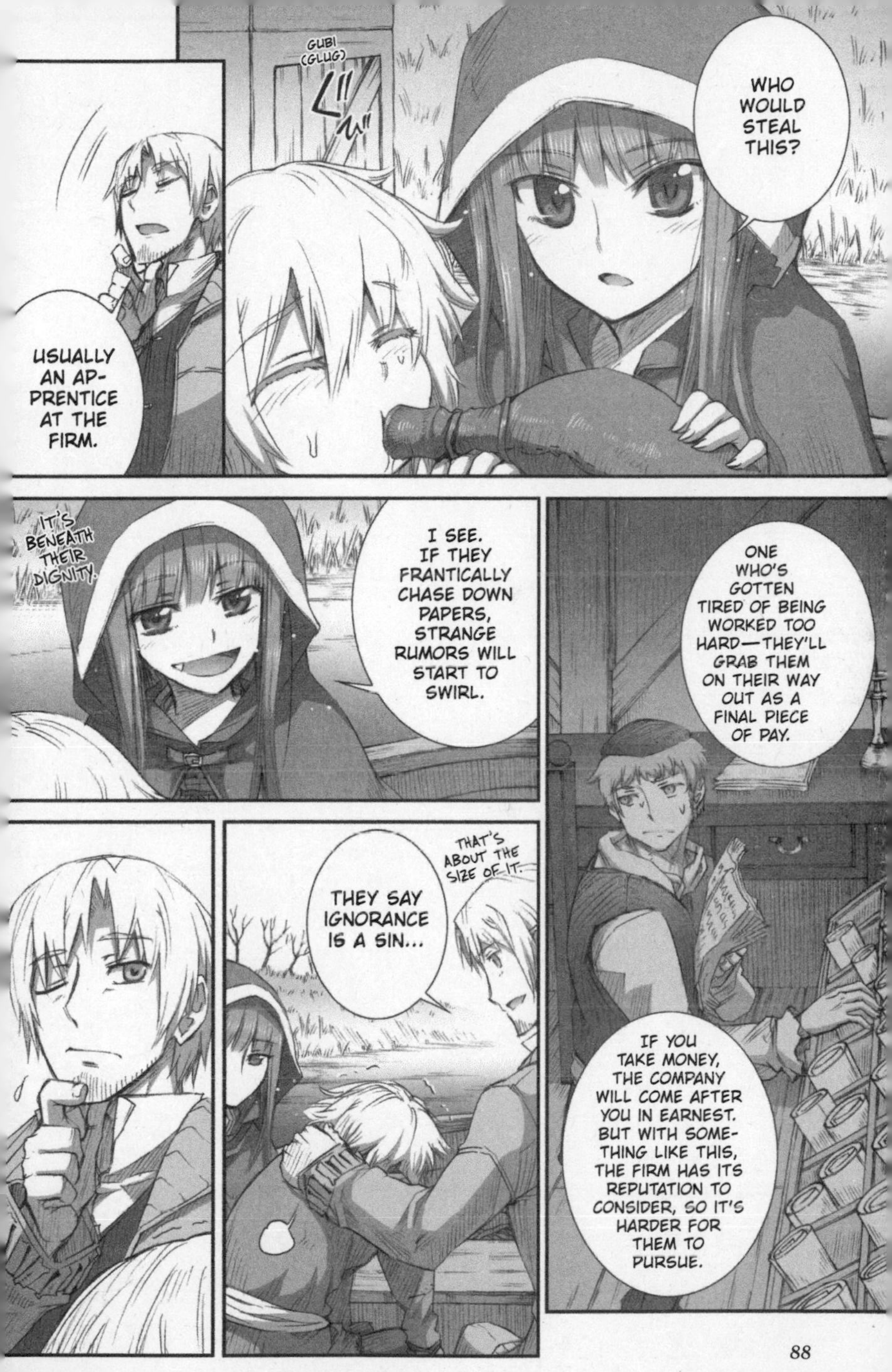
WHO WOULD STEAL THIS?
GUBI (GLUG)
USUALLY AN AP-PRENTICE AT THE FIRM.
ONE WHO'S GOTTEN TIRED OF BEING WORKED TOO HARD—THEY'LL GRAB THEM ON THEIR WAY OUT AS A FINAL PIECE OF PAY.
IF YOU TAKE MONEY, THE COMPANY WILL COME AFTER YOU IN EARNEST. BUT WITH SOME-THING LIKE THIS, THE FIRM HAS ITS REPUTATION TO CONSIDER, SO IT'S HARDER FOR THEM TO PURSUE.
I SEE. IF THEY FRANTICALLY CHASE DOWN PAPERS, STRANGE RUMORS WILL START TO SWIRL.
IT'S BENEATH THEIR DIGNITY.
THAT'S ABOUT THE SIZE OF IT.
THEY SAY IGNORANCE IS A SIN...

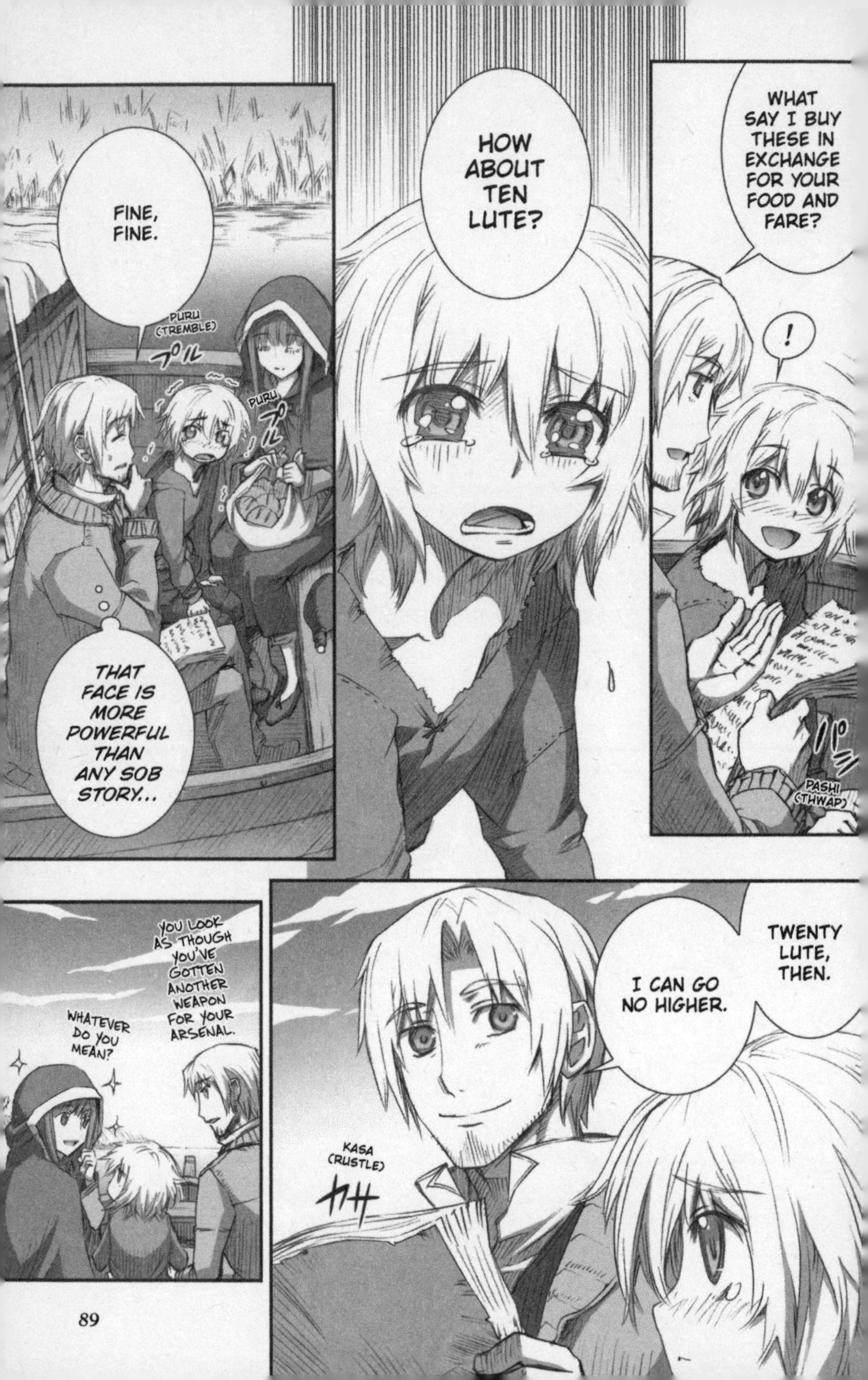
WHAT SAY I BUY THESE IN EXCHANGE FOR YOUR FOOD AND FARE?
!
PASHI (THWAP)
HOW ABOUT TEN LUTE?
FINE, FINE.
PURU (TREMBLE)
PURU
THAT FACE IS MORE POWERFUL THAN ANY SOB STORY...
TWENTY LUTE, THEN.
I CAN GO NO HIGHER.
KASA (RUSTLE)
YOU LOOK AS THOUGH YOU'VE GOTTEN ANOTHER WEAPON FOR YOUR ARSENAL.
WHATEVER DO YOU MEAN?

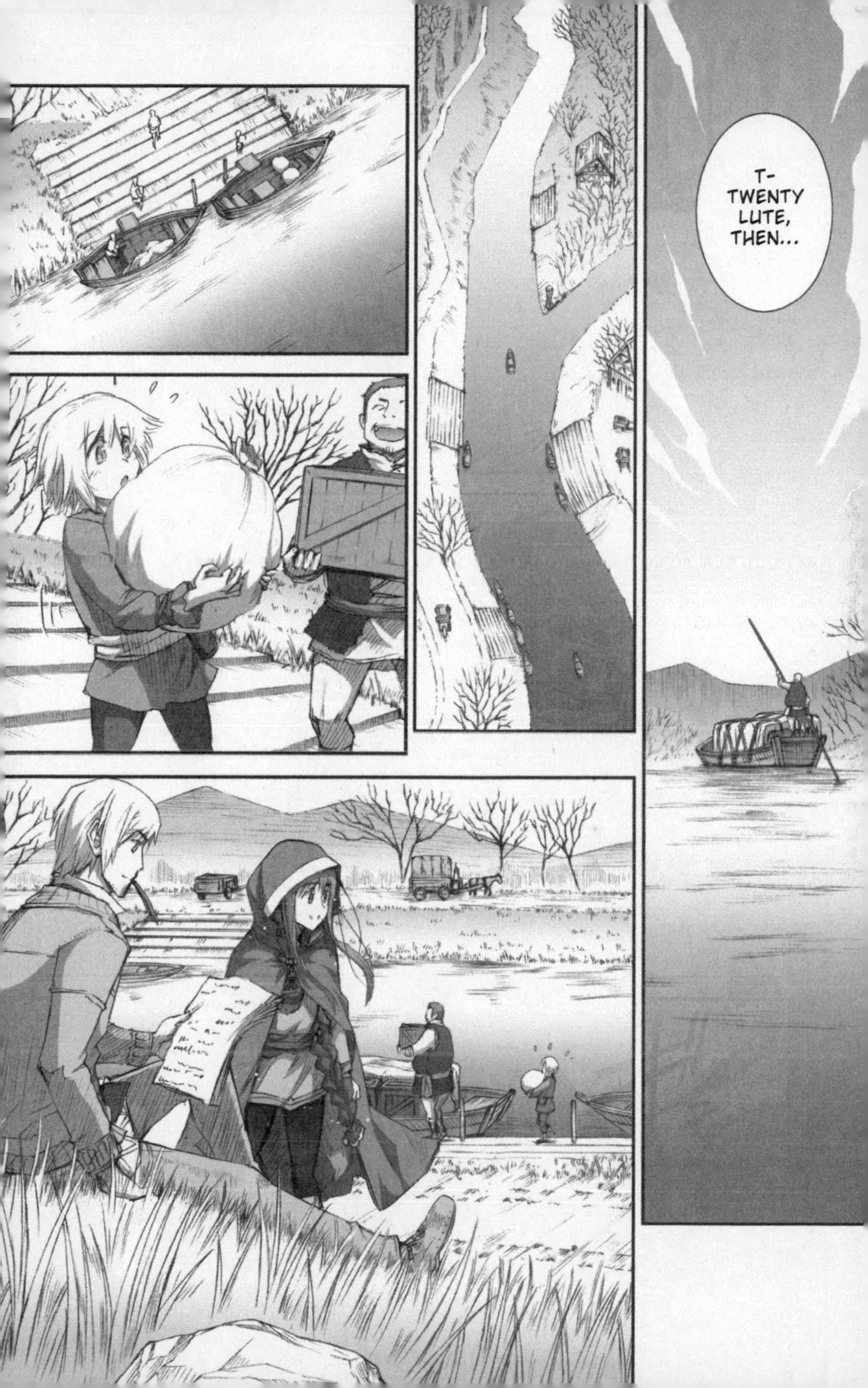
T-
TWENTY
LUTE,
THEN...

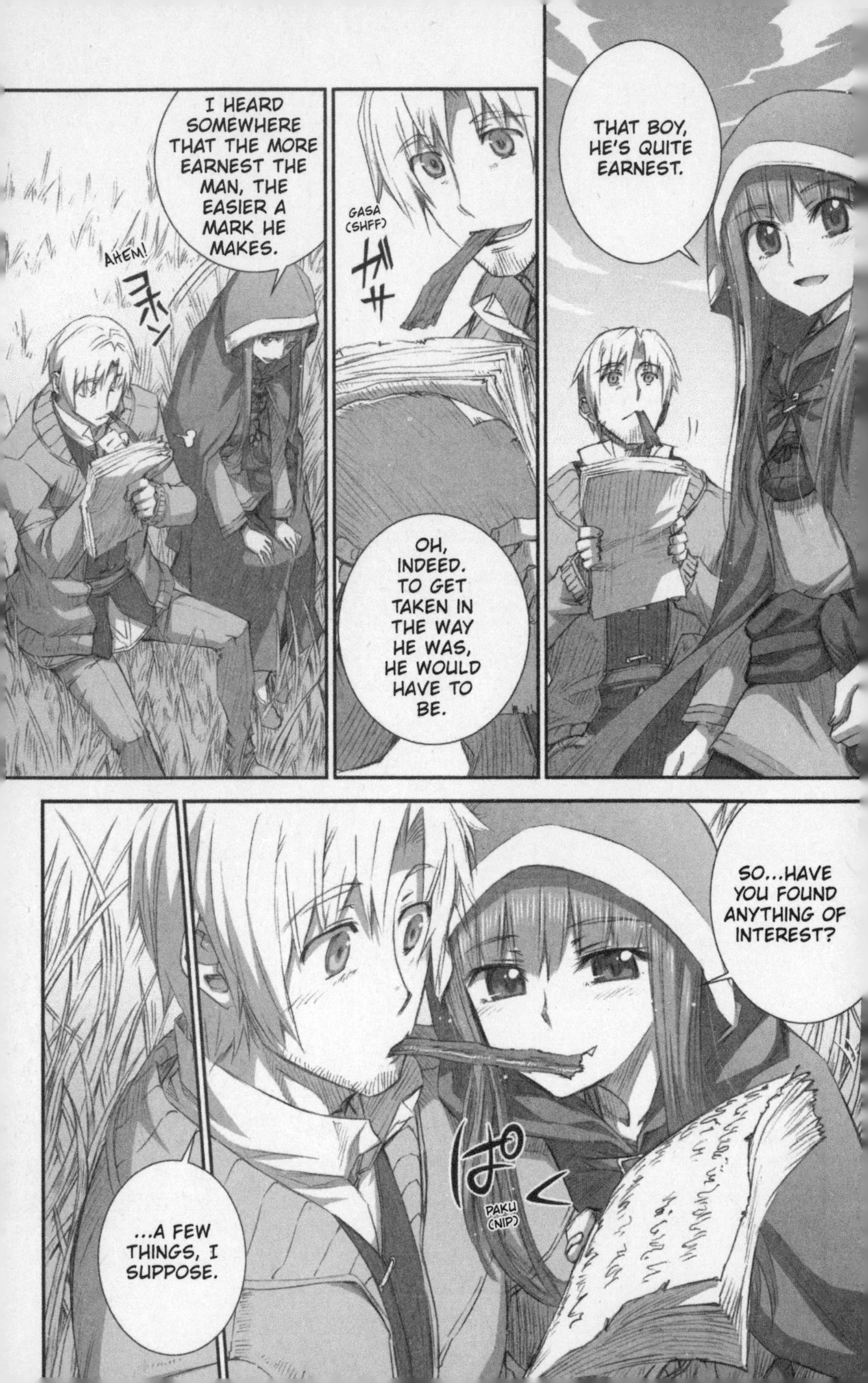

THAT BOY, HE'S QUITE EARNEST.
GASA (SHFF)
OH, INDEED. TO GET TAKEN IN THE WAY HE WAS, HE WOULD HAVE TO BE.
I HEARD SOMEWHERE THAT THE MORE EARNEST THE MAN, THE EASIER A MARK HE MAKES.
AHEM!
SO...HAVE YOU FOUND ANYTHING OF INTEREST?
PAKU (NIP)
...A FEW THINGS, I SUPPOSE.

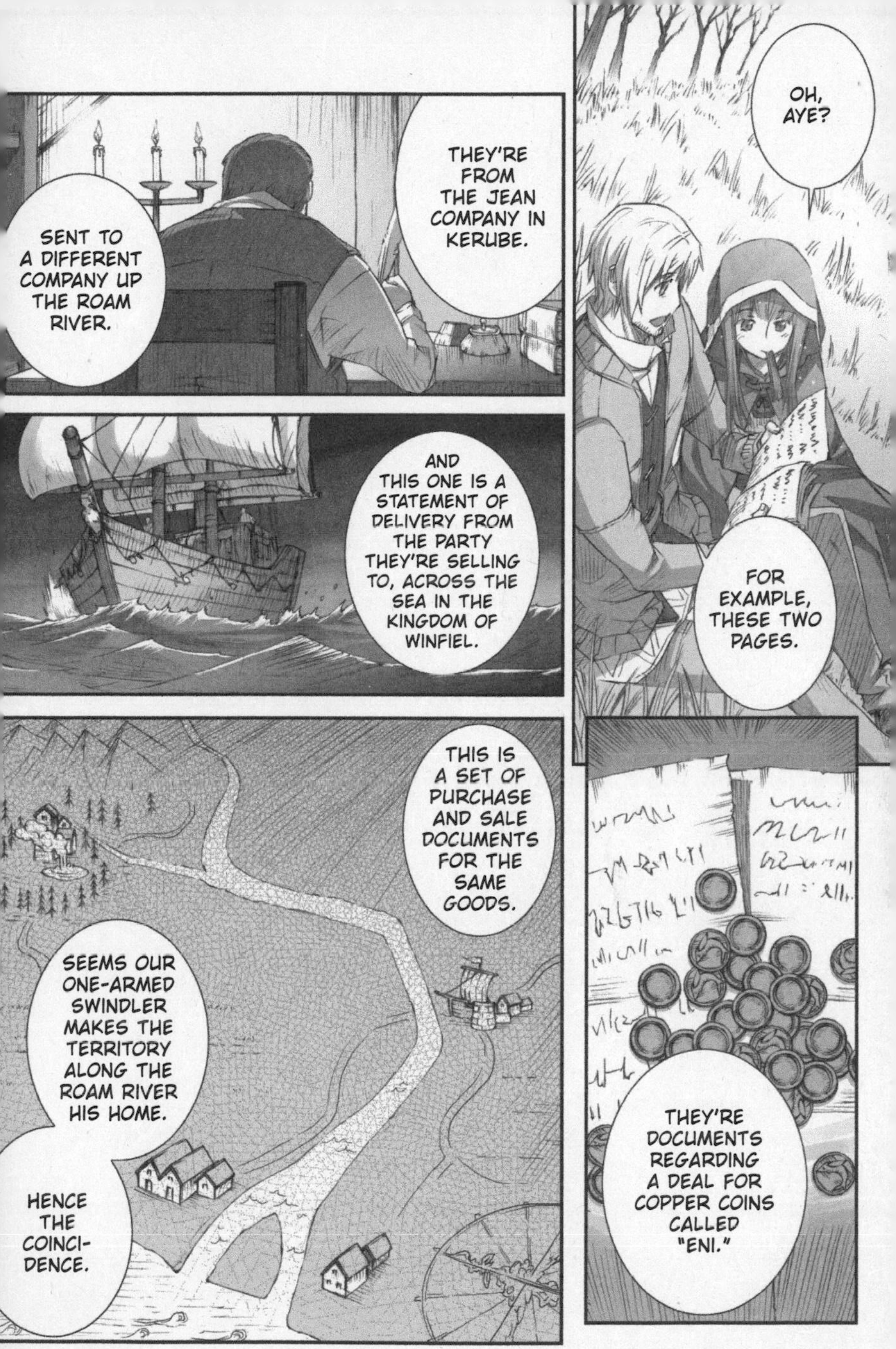
OH, AYE?
FOR EXAMPLE, THESE TWO PAGES.
THEY'RE FROM THE JEAN COMPANY IN KERUBE.
SENT TO A DIFFERENT COMPANY UP THE ROAM RIVER.
AND THIS ONE IS A STATEMENT OF DELIVERY FROM THE PARTY THEY'RE SELLING TO, ACROSS THE SEA IN THE KINGDOM OF WINFIEL.
THEY'RE DOCUMENTS REGARDING A DEAL FOR COPPER COINS CALLED "ENI."
THIS IS A SET OF PURCHASE AND SALE DOCUMENTS FOR THE SAME GOODS.
SEEMS OUR ONE-ARMED SWINDLER MAKES THE TERRITORY ALONG THE ROAM RIVER HIS HOME.
HENCE THE COINCI-DENCE.

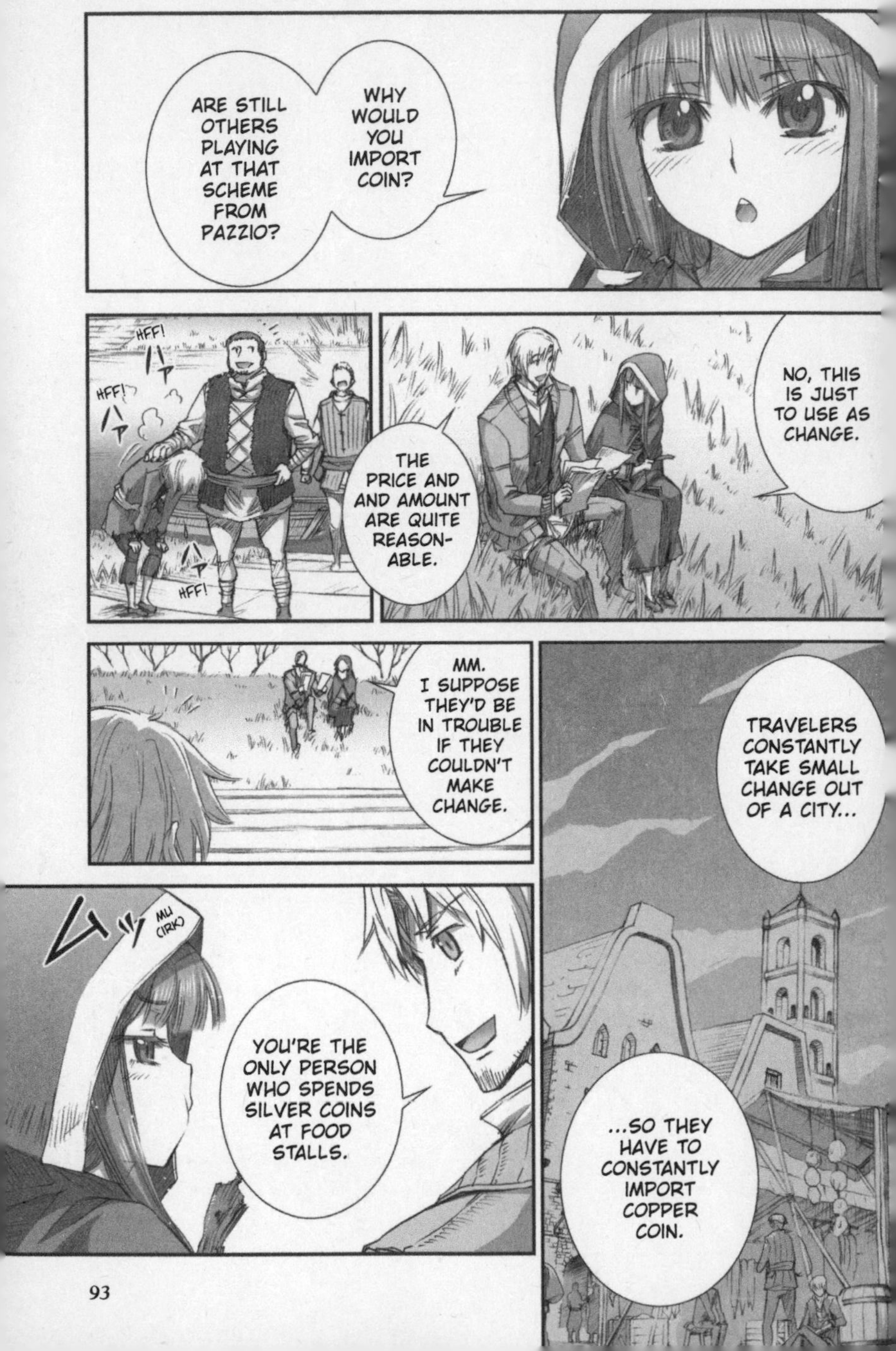
WHY WOULD YOU IMPORT COIN?
ARE STILL OTHERS PLAYING AT THAT SCHEME FROM PAZZIO?
NO, THIS IS JUST TO USE AS CHANGE.
THE PRICE AND AND AMOUNT ARE QUITE REASON-ABLE.
HFF!
HFF!
HFF!
TRAVELERS CONSTANTLY TAKE SMALL CHANGE OUT OF A CITY...
...SO THEY HAVE TO CONSTANTLY IMPORT COPPER COIN.
MM. I SUPPOSE THEY'D BE IN TROUBLE IF THEY COULDN'T MAKE CHANGE.
YOU'RE THE ONLY PERSON WHO SPENDS SILVER COINS AT FOOD STALLS.
MU (IRK)

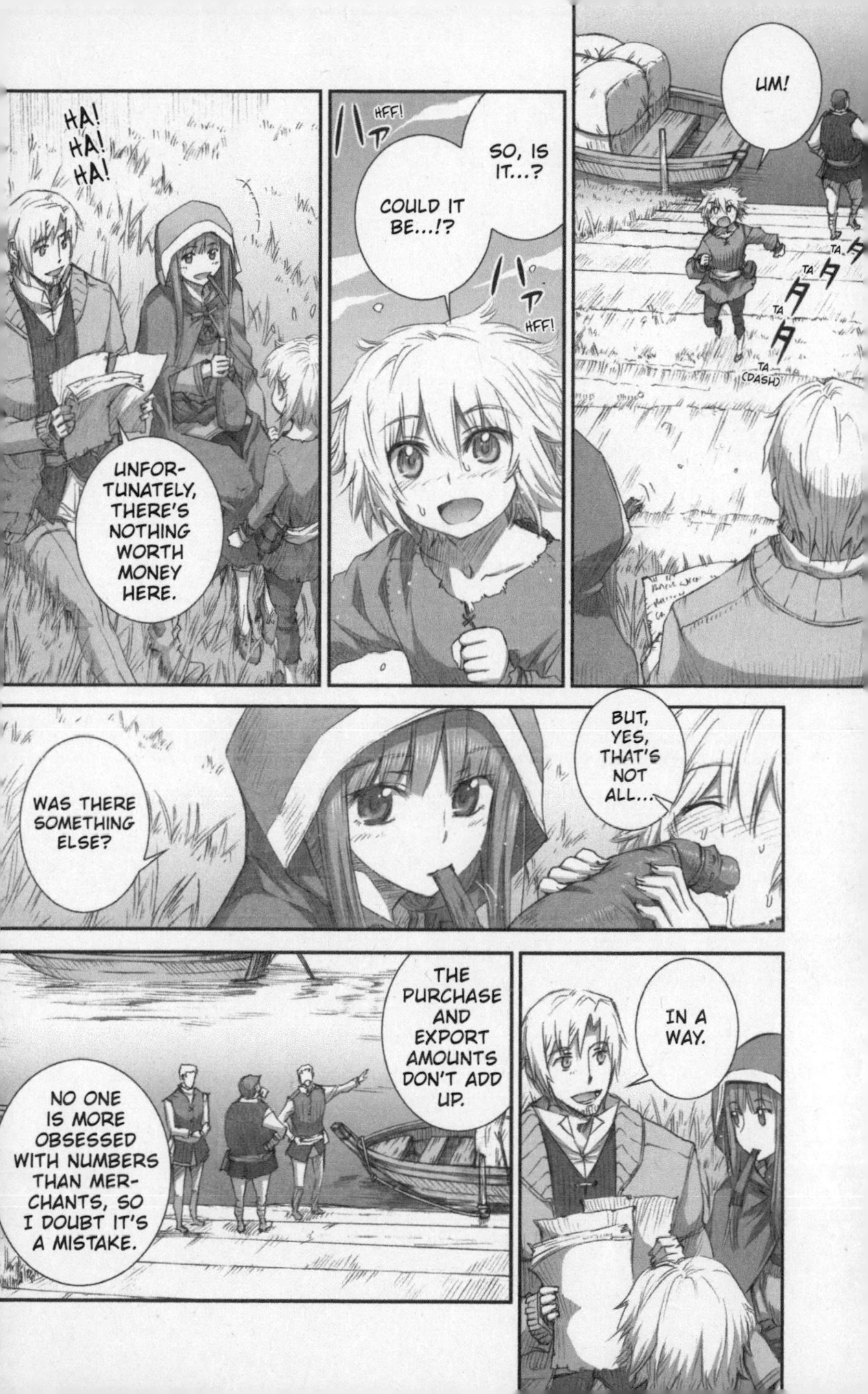
UM!
TA TA TA TA (DASH)
HFF!
SO, IS IT...?
COULD IT BE...!?
HFF!
HA! HA! HA!
UNFOR-TUNATELY, THERE'S NOTHING WORTH MONEY HERE.
BUT, YES, THAT'S NOT ALL...
WAS THERE SOMETHING ELSE?
IN A WAY.
THE PURCHASE AND EXPORT AMOUNTS DON'T ADD UP.
NO ONE IS MORE OBSESSED WITH NUMBERS THAN MER-CHANTS, SO I DOUBT IT'S A MISTAKE.

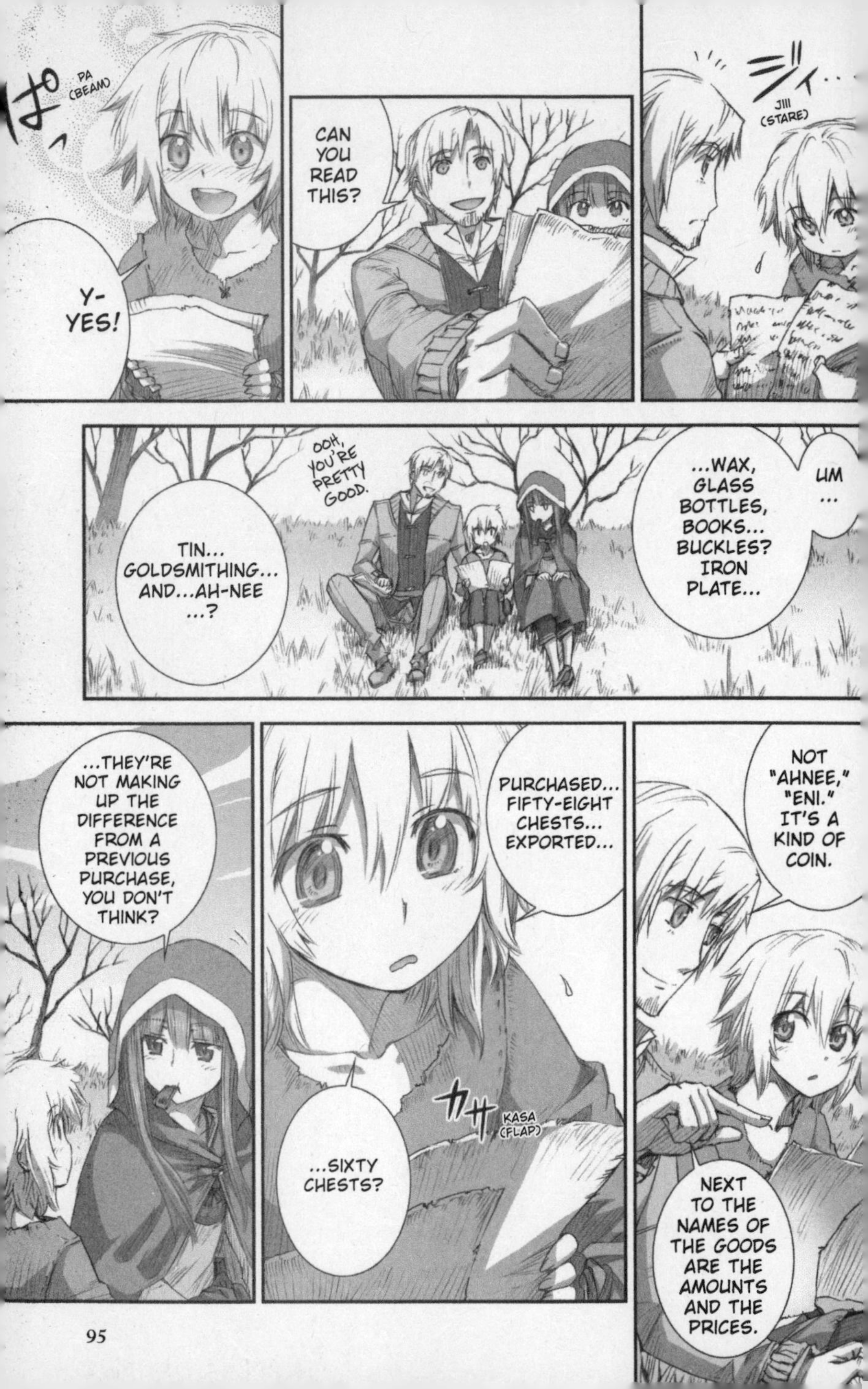
ジィ…
JIII (STARE)
CAN YOU READ THIS?
ぱっ
PA (BEAM)
Y- YES!
UM ...
...WAX, GLASS BOTTLES, BOOKS... BUCKLES? IRON PLATE...
OOH, YOU'RE PRETTY GOOD.
TIN... GOLDSMITHING... AND...AH-NEE ...?
NOT "AHNEE," "ENI." IT'S A KIND OF COIN.
NEXT TO THE NAMES OF THE GOODS ARE THE AMOUNTS AND THE PRICES.
PURCHASED... FIFTY-EIGHT CHESTS... EXPORTED...
カサ
KASA (FLAP)
...SIXTY CHESTS?
...THEY'RE NOT MAKING UP THE DIFFERENCE FROM A PREVIOUS PURCHASE, YOU DON'T THINK?

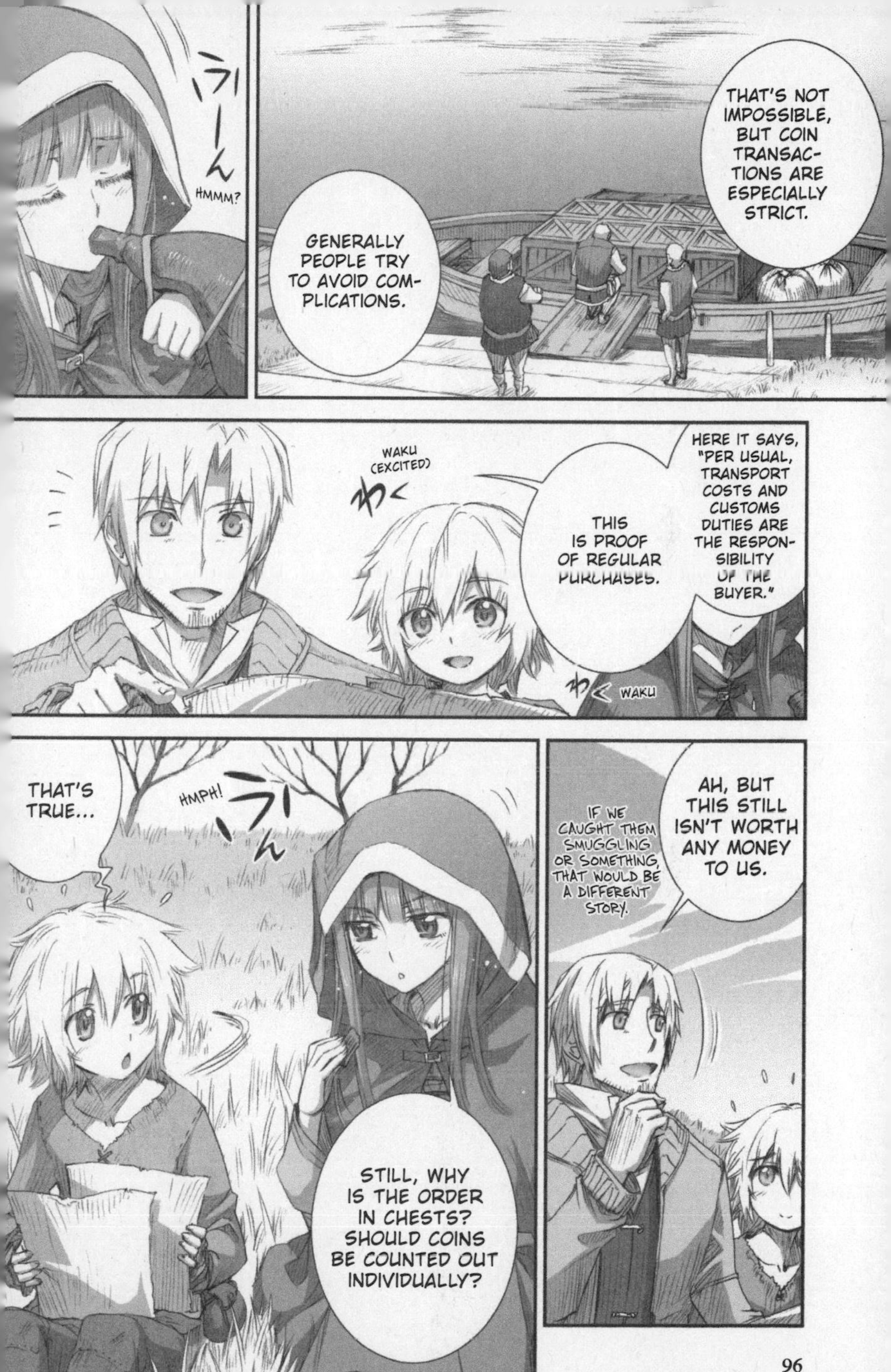
THAT'S NOT IMPOSSIBLE, BUT COIN TRANSACTIONS ARE ESPECIALLY STRICT.
GENERALLY PEOPLE TRY TO AVOID COMPLICATIONS.
HMMM?
HERE IT SAYS, "PER USUAL, TRANSPORT COSTS AND CUSTOMS DUTIES ARE THE RESPONSIBILITY OF THE BUYER."
THIS IS PROOF OF REGULAR PURCHASES.
わく
WAKU (EXCITED)
わく
WAKU
AH, BUT THIS STILL ISN'T WORTH ANY MONEY TO US.
IF WE CAUGHT THEM SMUGGLING OR SOMETHING, THAT WOULD BE A DIFFERENT STORY.
HMPH!
THAT'S TRUE...
STILL, WHY IS THE ORDER IN CHESTS? SHOULD COINS BE COUNTED OUT INDIVIDUALLY?

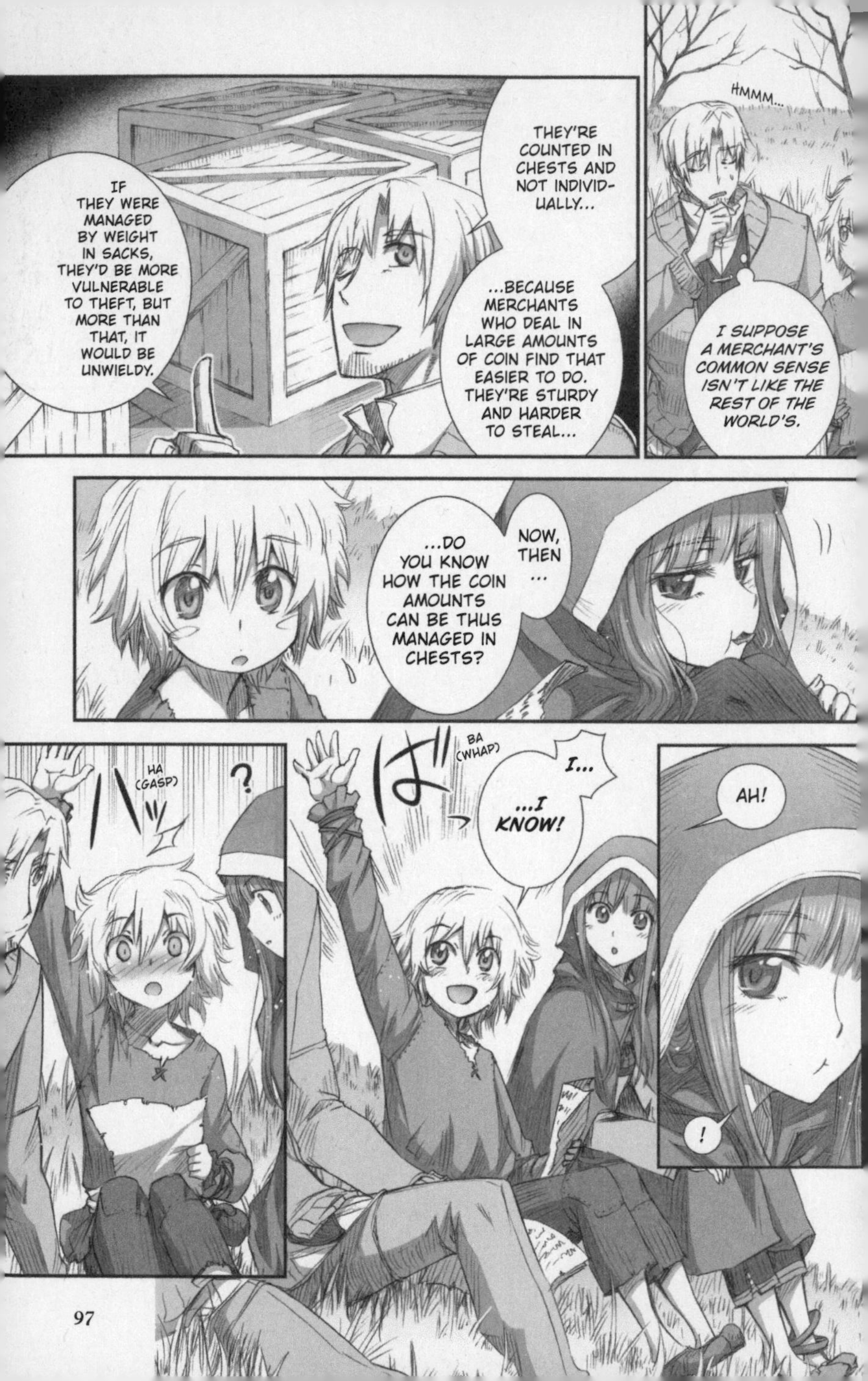
HMMM...
I SUPPOSE A MERCHANT'S COMMON SENSE ISN'T LIKE THE REST OF THE WORLD'S.
THEY'RE COUNTED IN CHESTS AND NOT INDIVID-UALLY...
...BECAUSE MERCHANTS WHO DEAL IN LARGE AMOUNTS OF COIN FIND THAT EASIER TO DO. THEY'RE STURDY AND HARDER TO STEAL...
IF THEY WERE MANAGED BY WEIGHT IN SACKS, THEY'D BE MORE VULNERABLE TO THEFT, BUT MORE THAN THAT, IT WOULD BE UNWIELDY.
NOW, THEN...
...DO YOU KNOW HOW THE COIN AMOUNTS CAN BE THUS MANAGED IN CHESTS?
AH!
!
ば
BA (WHAP)
I...
...I KNOW!
ハ
HA (GASP)
?

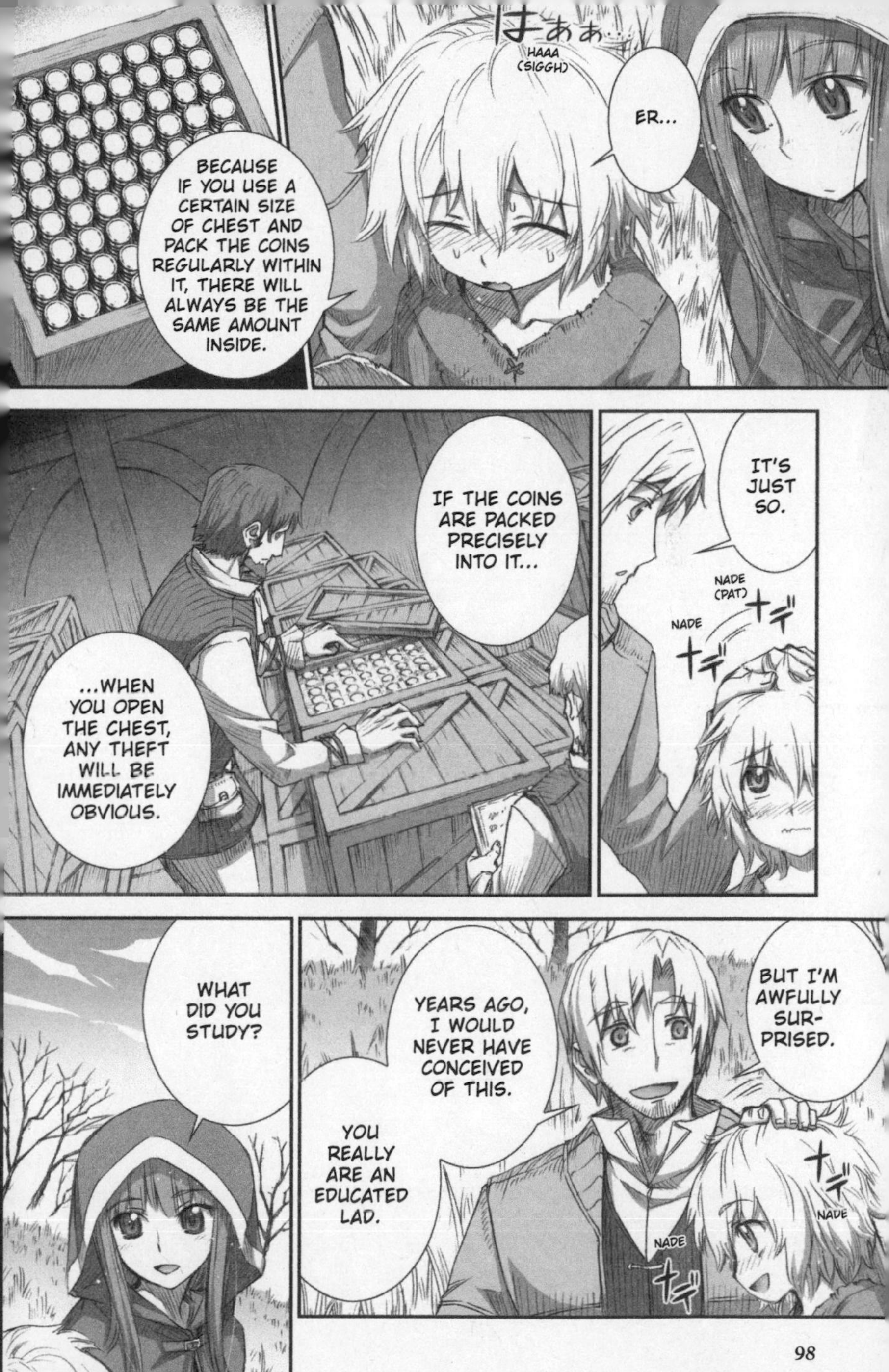
ER...
はぁぁ…
HAAA (SIGGH)
BECAUSE IF YOU USE A CERTAIN SIZE OF CHEST AND PACK THE COINS REGULARLY WITHIN IT, THERE WILL ALWAYS BE THE SAME AMOUNT INSIDE.
IT'S JUST SO.
ナデ
NADE (PAT)
ナデ
NADE
IF THE COINS ARE PACKED PRECISELY INTO IT...
...WHEN YOU OPEN THE CHEST, ANY THEFT WILL BE IMMEDIATELY OBVIOUS.
BUT I'M AWFULLY SUR-PRISED.
YEARS AGO, I WOULD NEVER HAVE CONCEIVED OF THIS.
ナデ
NADE
YOU REALLY ARE AN EDUCATED LAD.
ナデ
NADE
WHAT DID YOU STUDY?

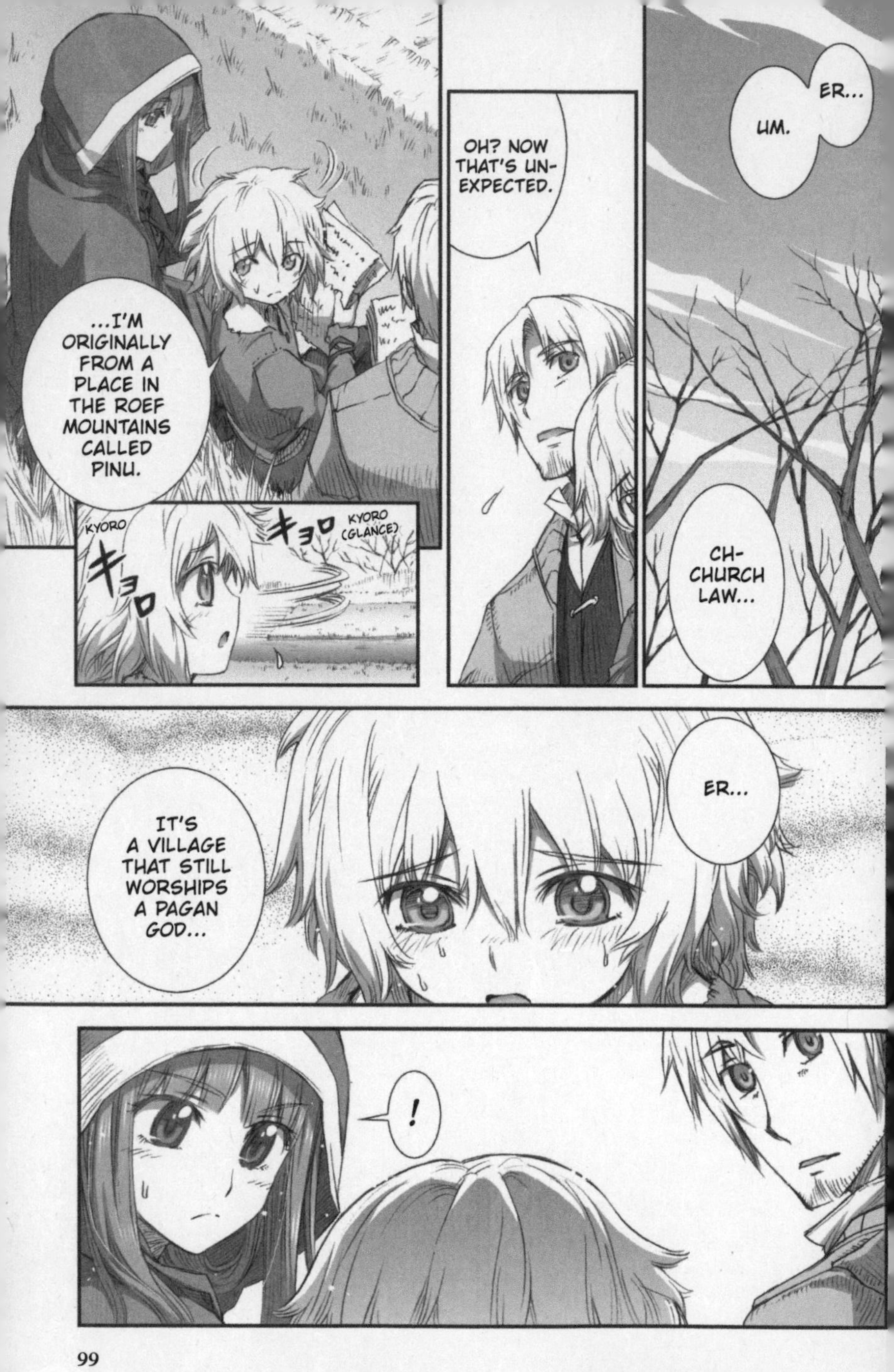
ER...
UM.
CH-CHURCH LAW...
OH? NOW THAT'S UN-EXPECTED.
...I'M ORIGINALLY FROM A PLACE IN THE ROEF MOUNTAINS CALLED PINU.
KYORO (GLANCE)
KYORO
ER...
IT'S A VILLAGE THAT STILL WORSHIPS A PAGAN GOD...
!

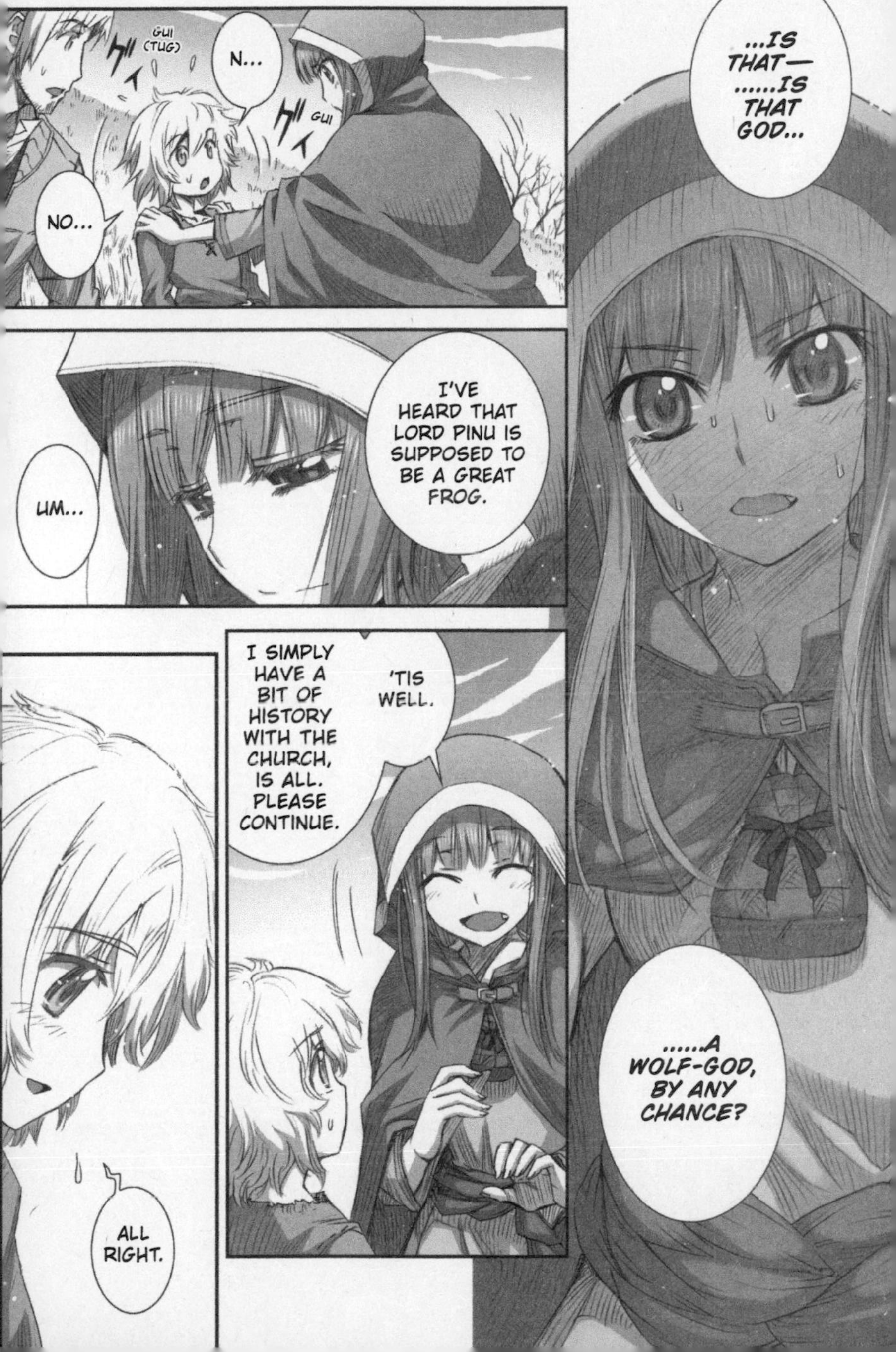
...IS THAT— ......IS THAT GOD...
......A WOLF-GOD, BY ANY CHANCE?
N...
GUI
GUI (TUG)
NO...
I'VE HEARD THAT LORD PINU IS SUPPOSED TO BE A GREAT FROG.
UM...
'TIS WELL.
I SIMPLY HAVE A BIT OF HISTORY WITH THE CHURCH, IS ALL. PLEASE CONTINUE.
ALL RIGHT.

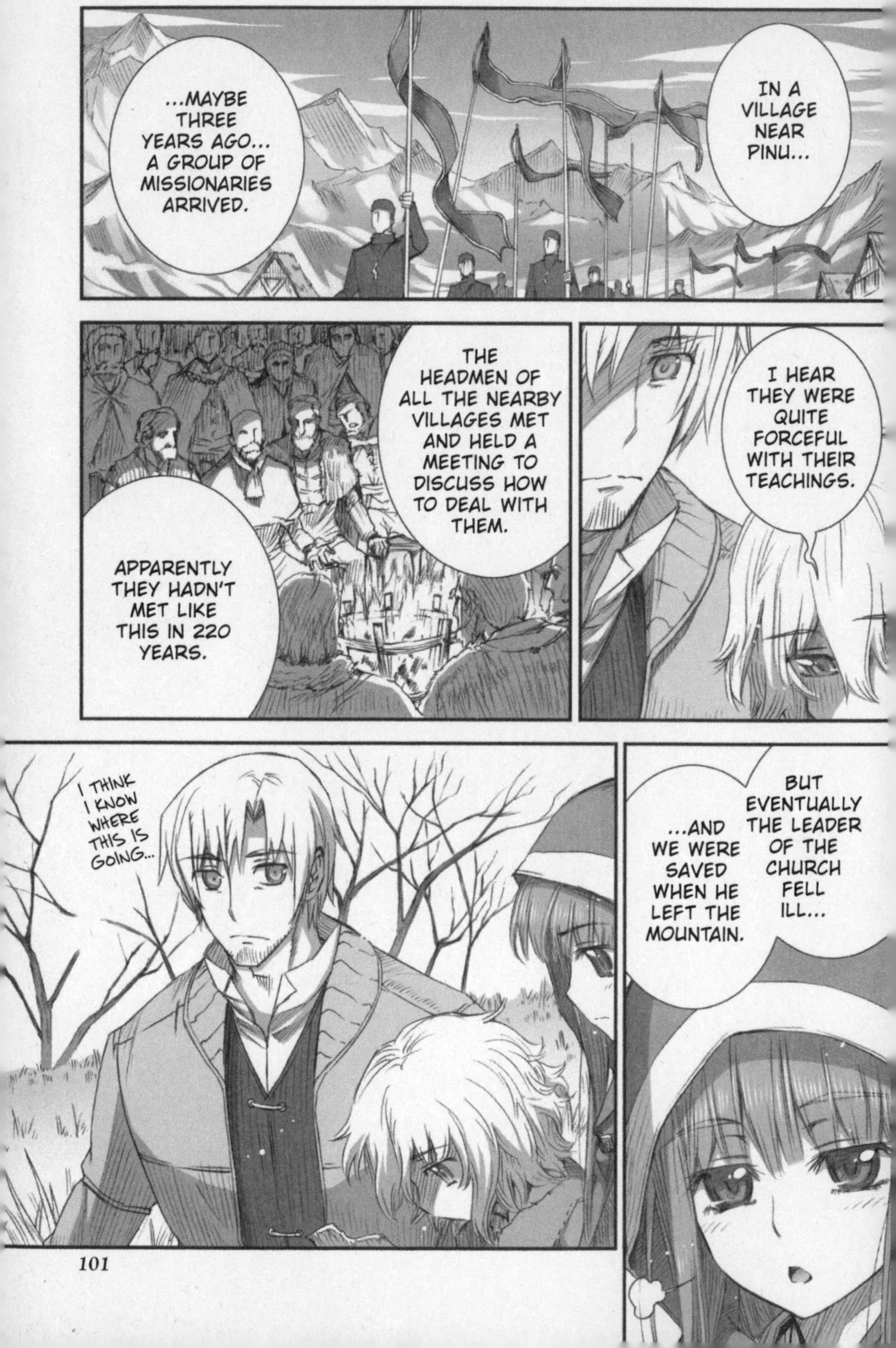
IN A VILLAGE NEAR PINU...
...MAYBE THREE YEARS AGO... A GROUP OF MISSIONARIES ARRIVED.
I HEAR THEY WERE QUITE FORCEFUL WITH THEIR TEACHINGS.
THE HEADMEN OF ALL THE NEARBY VILLAGES MET AND HELD A MEETING TO DISCUSS HOW TO DEAL WITH THEM.
APPARENTLY THEY HADN'T MET LIKE THIS IN 220 YEARS.
BUT EVENTUALLY THE LEADER OF THE CHURCH FELL ILL...
...AND WE WERE SAVED WHEN HE LEFT THE MOUNTAIN.
I THINK I KNOW WHERE THIS IS GOING...

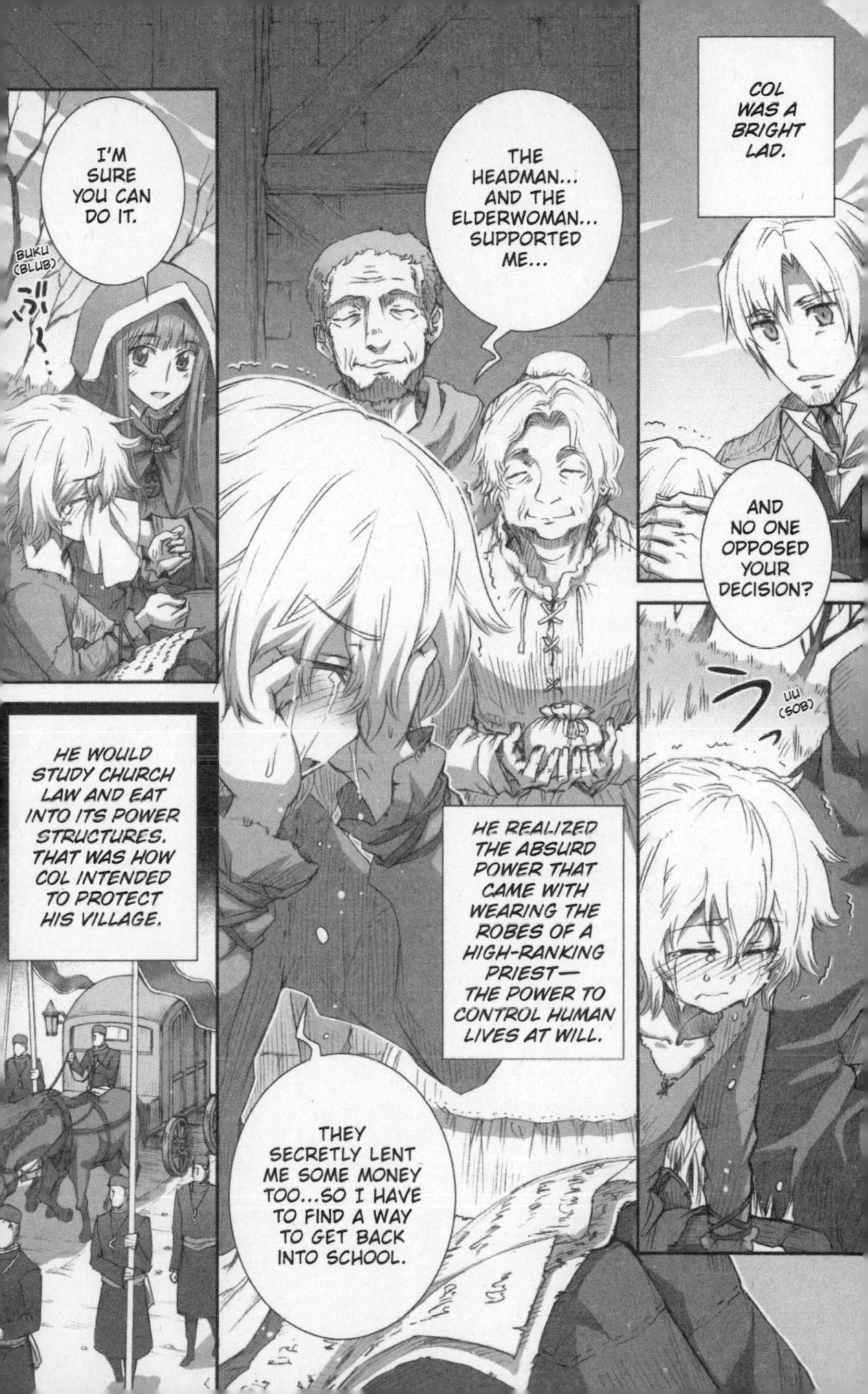
COL WAS A BRIGHT LAD.
AND NO ONE OPPOSED YOUR DECISION?
UU (SOB)
THE HEADMAN... AND THE ELDERWOMAN... SUPPORTED ME...
HE REALIZED THE ABSURD POWER THAT CAME WITH WEARING THE ROBES OF A HIGH-RANKING PRIEST— THE POWER TO CONTROL HUMAN LIVES AT WILL.
THEY SECRETLY LENT ME SOME MONEY TOO...SO I HAVE TO FIND A WAY TO GET BACK INTO SCHOOL.
I'M SURE YOU CAN DO IT.
BUKU (BLUB)
HE WOULD STUDY CHURCH LAW AND EAT INTO ITS POWER STRUCTURES. THAT WAS HOW COL INTENDED TO PROTECT HIS VILLAGE.

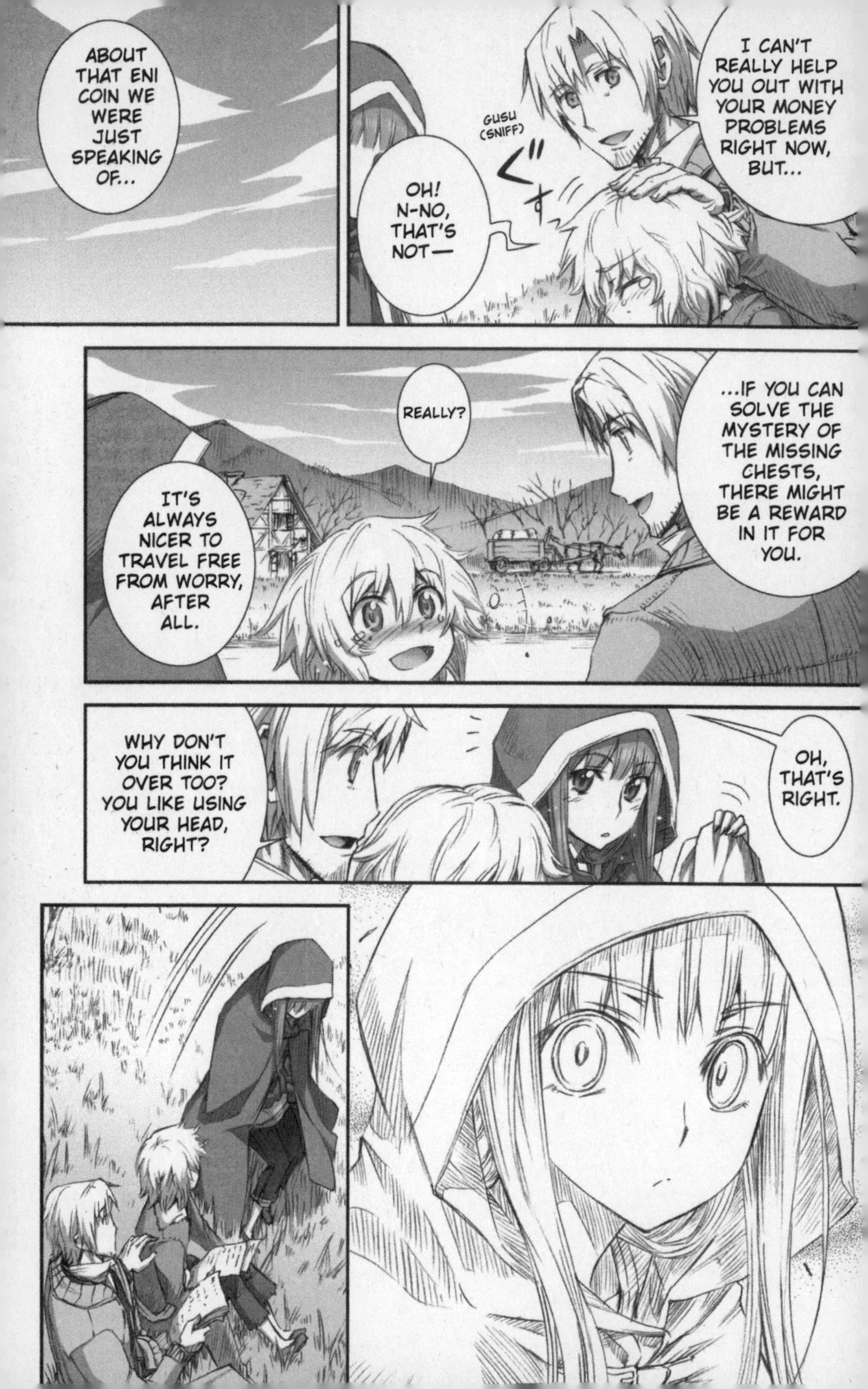
I CAN'T REALLY HELP YOU OUT WITH YOUR MONEY PROBLEMS RIGHT NOW, BUT...
GUSU (SNIFF)
OH! N-NO, THAT'S NOT—
ABOUT THAT ENI COIN WE WERE JUST SPEAKING OF...
...IF YOU CAN SOLVE THE MYSTERY OF THE MISSING CHESTS, THERE MIGHT BE A REWARD IN IT FOR YOU.
REALLY?
IT'S ALWAYS NICER TO TRAVEL FREE FROM WORRY, AFTER ALL.
OH, THAT'S RIGHT.
WHY DON'T YOU THINK IT OVER TOO? YOU LIKE USING YOUR HEAD, RIGHT?

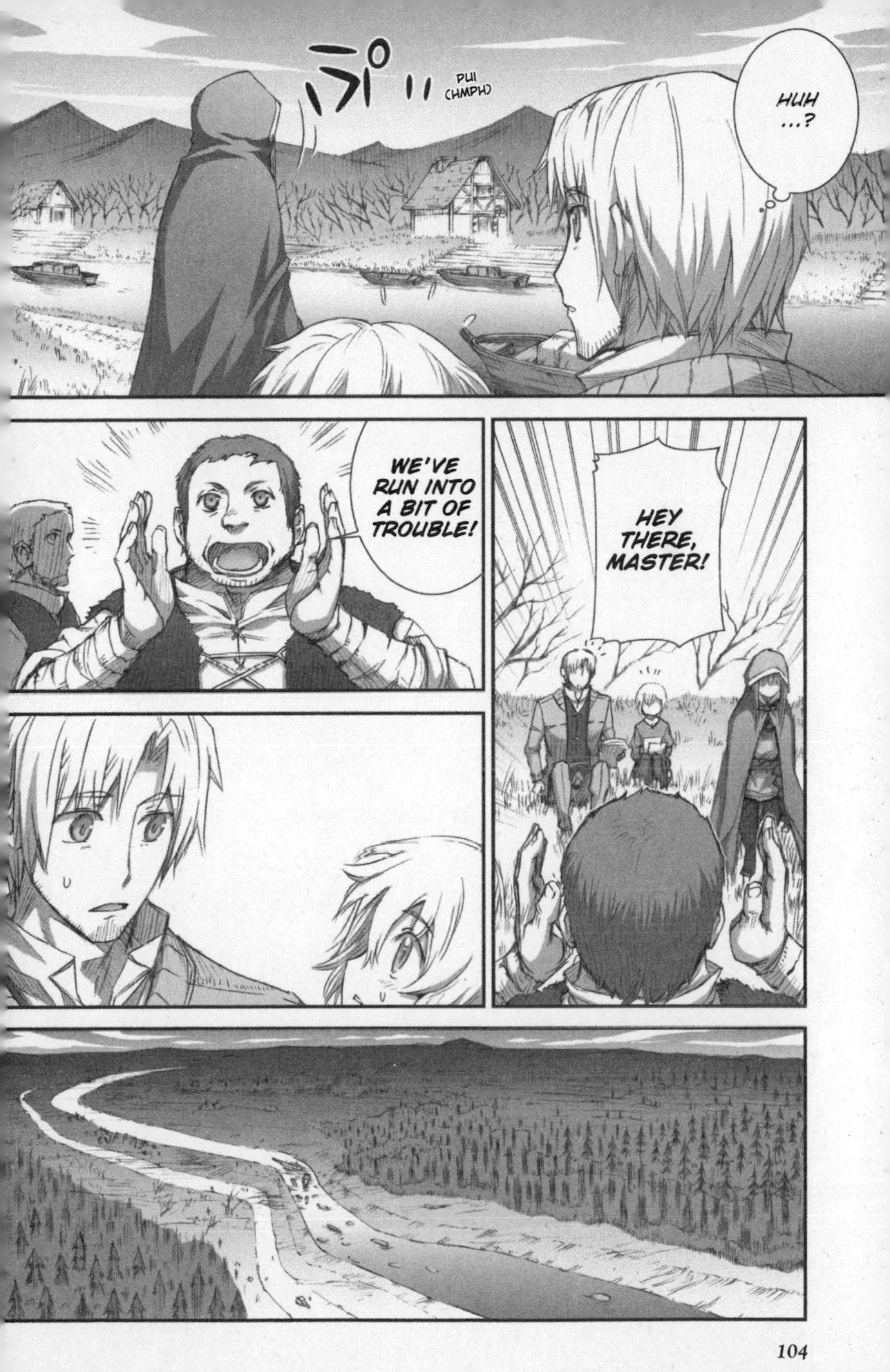
HUH ...?
ぷい
PUI (HMPH)
HEY THERE, MASTER!
WE'VE RUN INTO A BIT OF TROUBLE!

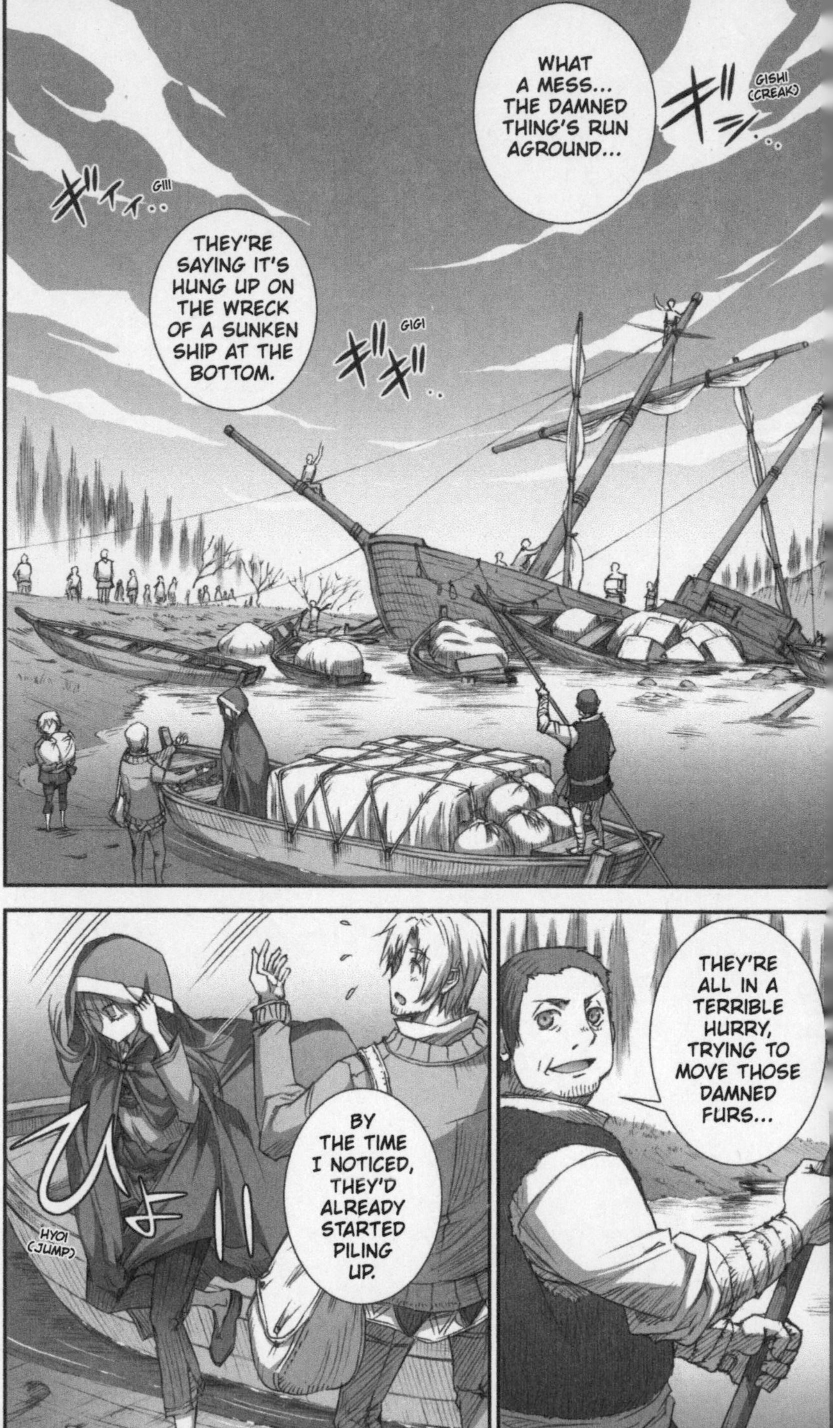
WHAT A MESS... THE DAMNED THING'S RUN AGROUND...
GISHI (CREAK)
GIII
THEY'RE SAYING IT'S HUNG UP ON THE WRECK OF A SUNKEN SHIP AT THE BOTTOM.
GIGI
THEY'RE ALL IN A TERRIBLE HURRY, TRYING TO MOVE THOSE DAMNED FURS...
BY THE TIME I NOTICED, THEY'D ALREADY STARTED PILING UP.
HYOI (JUMP)

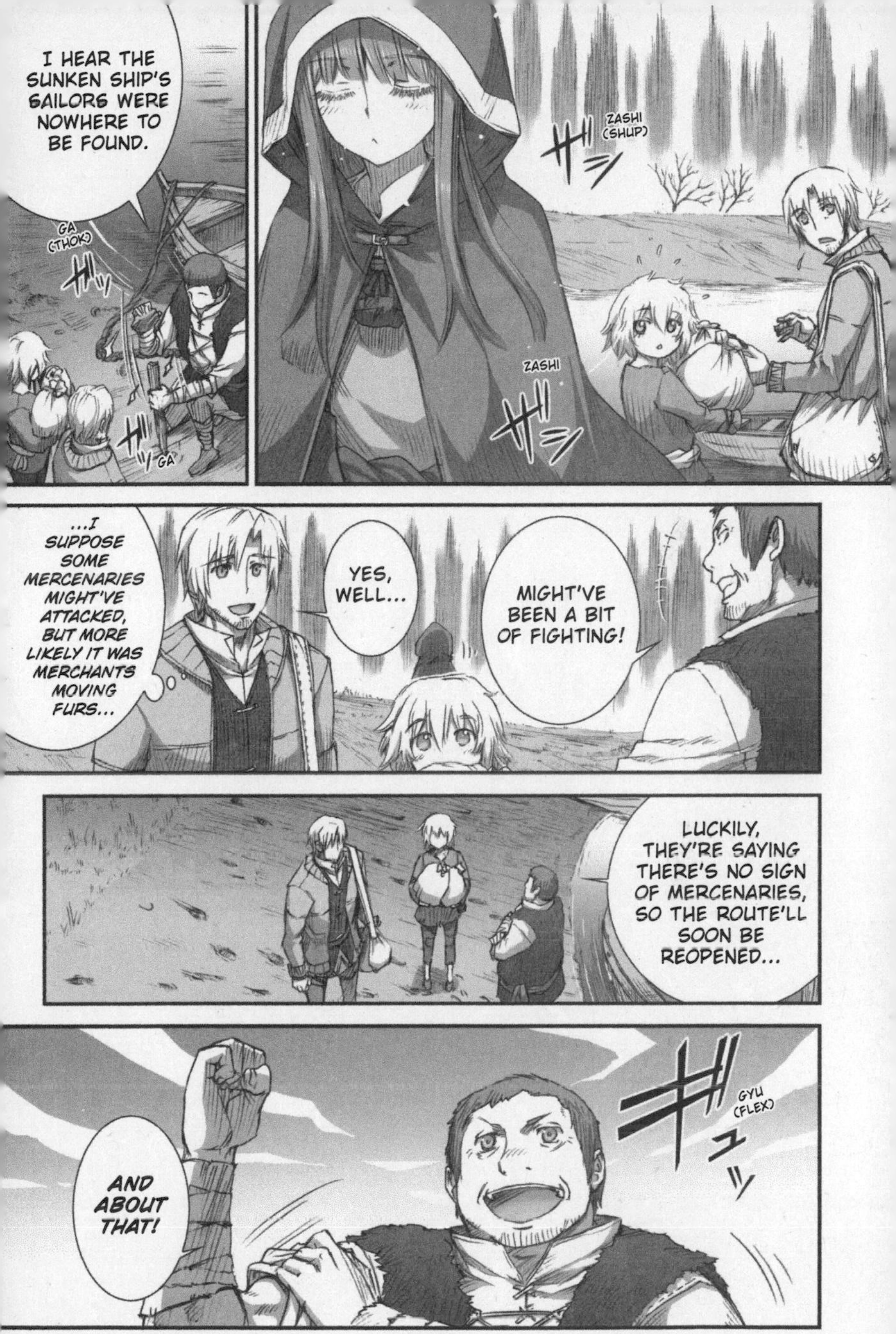
ZASHI (SHUP)
ZASHI
I HEAR THE SUNKEN SHIP'S SAILORS WERE NOWHERE TO BE FOUND.
GA (THOK)
GA
MIGHT'VE BEEN A BIT OF FIGHTING!
YES, WELL...
...I SUPPOSE SOME MERCENARIES MIGHT'VE ATTACKED, BUT MORE LIKELY IT WAS MERCHANTS MOVING FURS...
LUCKILY, THEY'RE SAYING THERE'S NO SIGN OF MERCENARIES, SO THE ROUTE'LL SOON BE REOPENED...
GYU (FLEX)
AND ABOUT THAT!

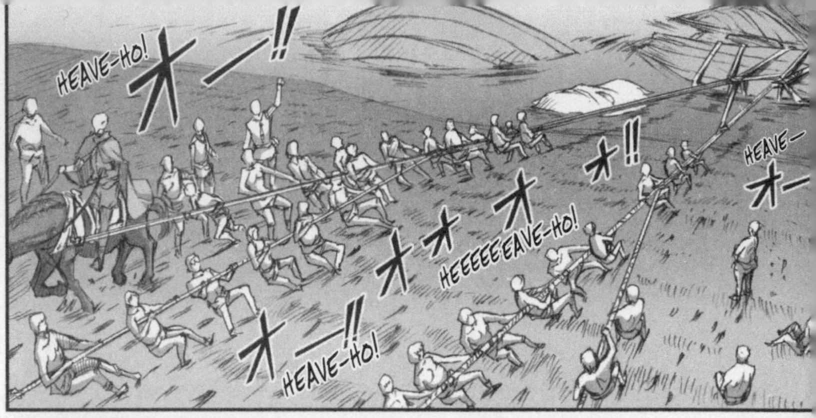
HEAVE—
オー
オ!!
オオオ
HEEEEEEAVE-HO!
オー!!
HEAVE-HO!
オー!!
HEAVE-HO!

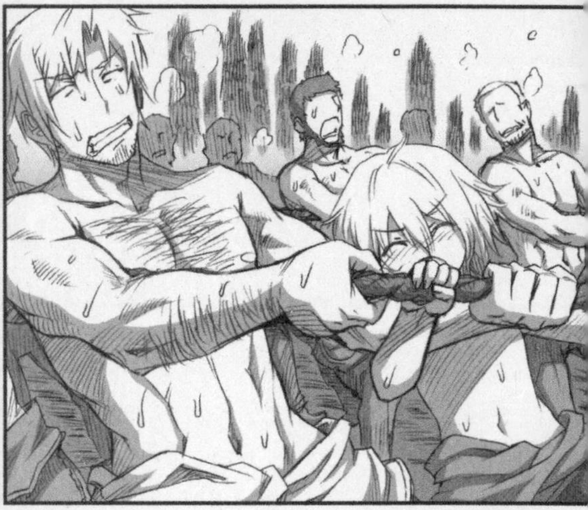

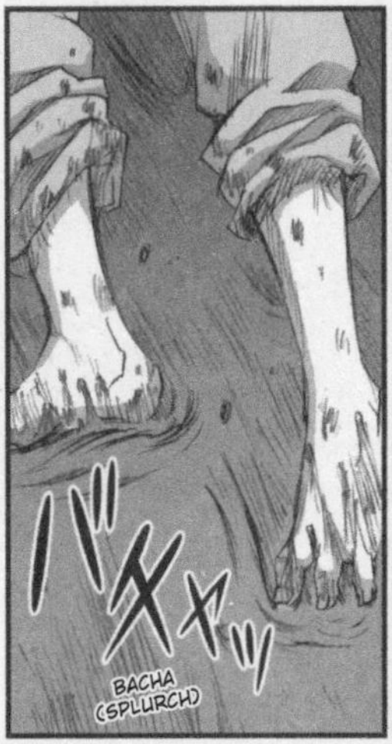
バチャッ
BACHA
(SPLURCH)

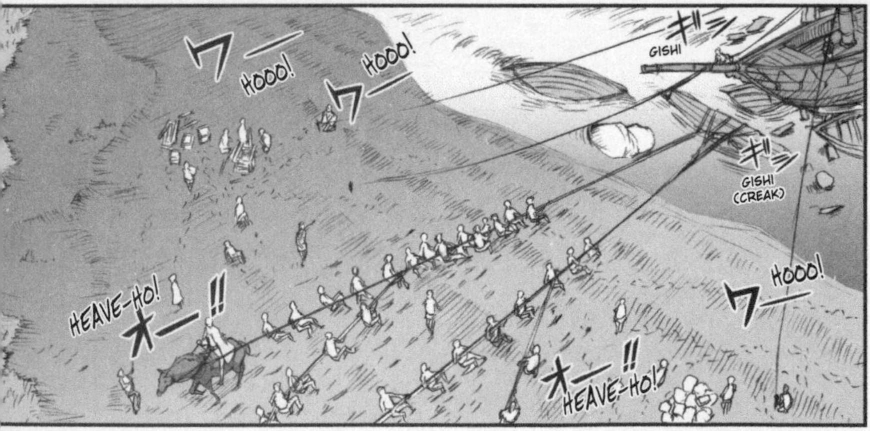
ギシ
GISHI
ギシ
GISHI
(CREAK)
ワー
HOOO!
ワー
HOOO!
ワー
HOOO!
オー!!
HEAVE-HO!
HEAVE-HO!
オー!!

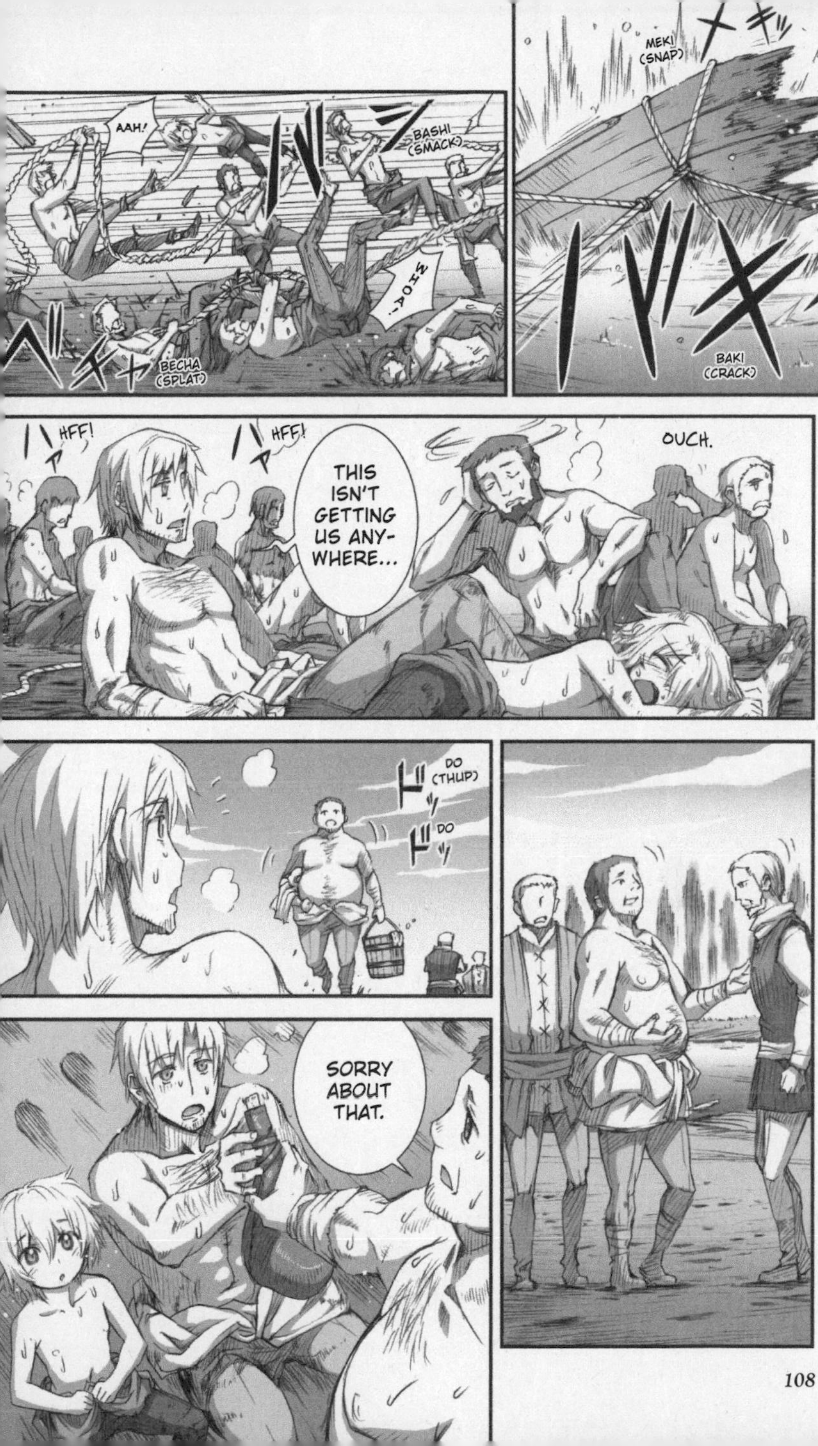

メキッ
MEKI (SNAP)
バキィ
BAKI (CRACK)
AAH!
バシッ
BASHI (SMACK)
WHOA!
ベチャ
BECHA (SPLAT)
OUCH.
HFF!
THIS ISN'T GETTING US ANY-WHERE...
HFF!
DO (THUP)
DO
SORRY ABOUT THAT.

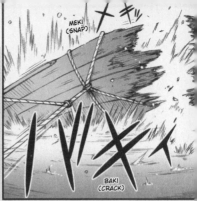

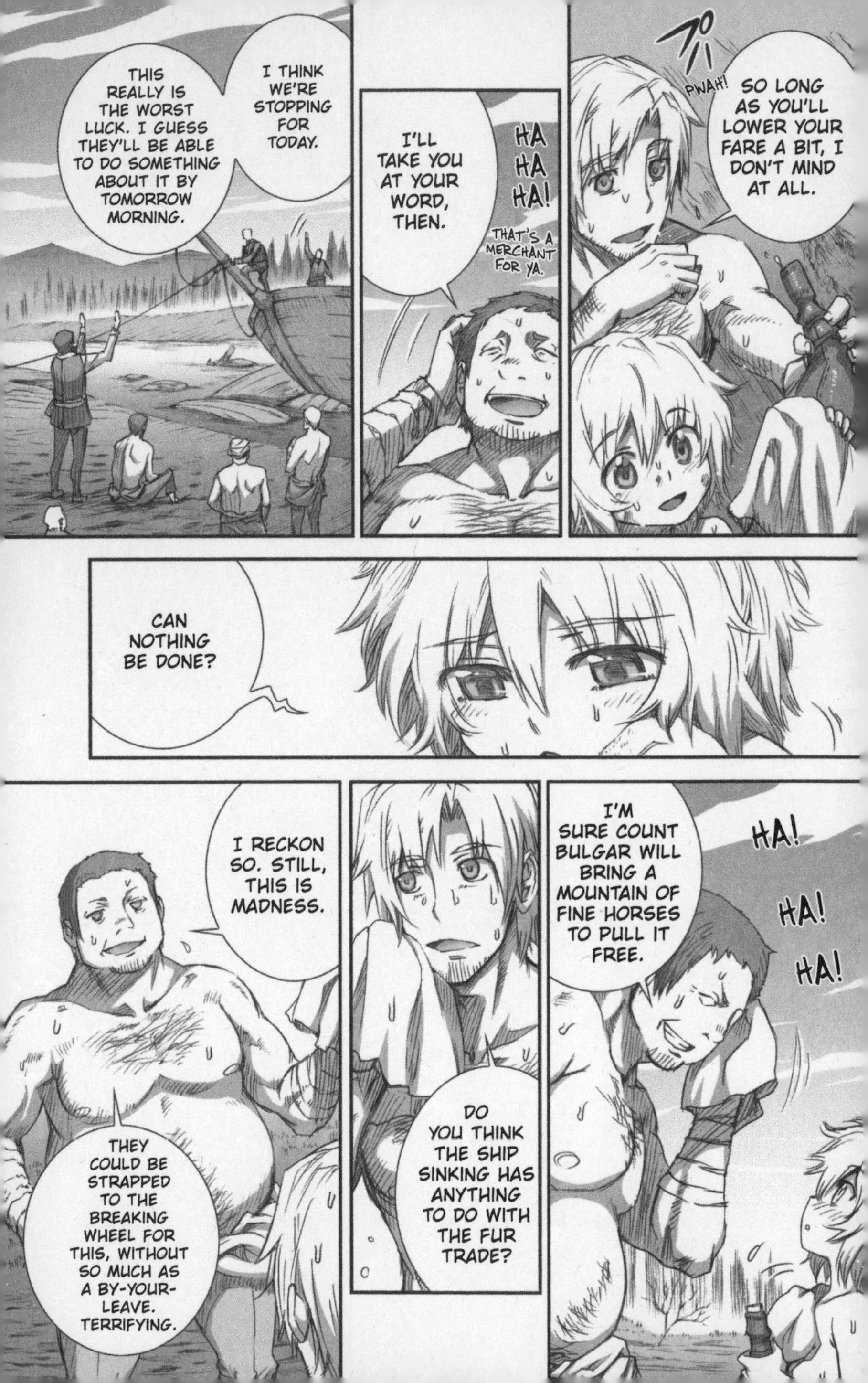
PWAH!
SO LONG AS YOU'LL LOWER YOUR FARE A BIT, I DON'T MIND AT ALL.
I'LL TAKE YOU AT YOUR WORD, THEN.
HA HA HA!
THAT'S A MERCHANT FOR YA.
I THINK WE'RE STOPPING FOR TODAY.
THIS REALLY IS THE WORST LUCK. I GUESS THEY'LL BE ABLE TO DO SOMETHING ABOUT IT BY TOMORROW MORNING.
CAN NOTHING BE DONE?
I'M SURE COUNT BULGAR WILL BRING A MOUNTAIN OF FINE HORSES TO PULL IT FREE.
HA! HA! HA!
DO YOU THINK THE SHIP SINKING HAS ANYTHING TO DO WITH THE FUR TRADE?
I RECKON SO. STILL, THIS IS MADNESS.
THEY COULD BE STRAPPED TO THE BREAKING WHEEL FOR THIS, WITHOUT SO MUCH AS A BY-YOUR-LEAVE. TERRIFYING.

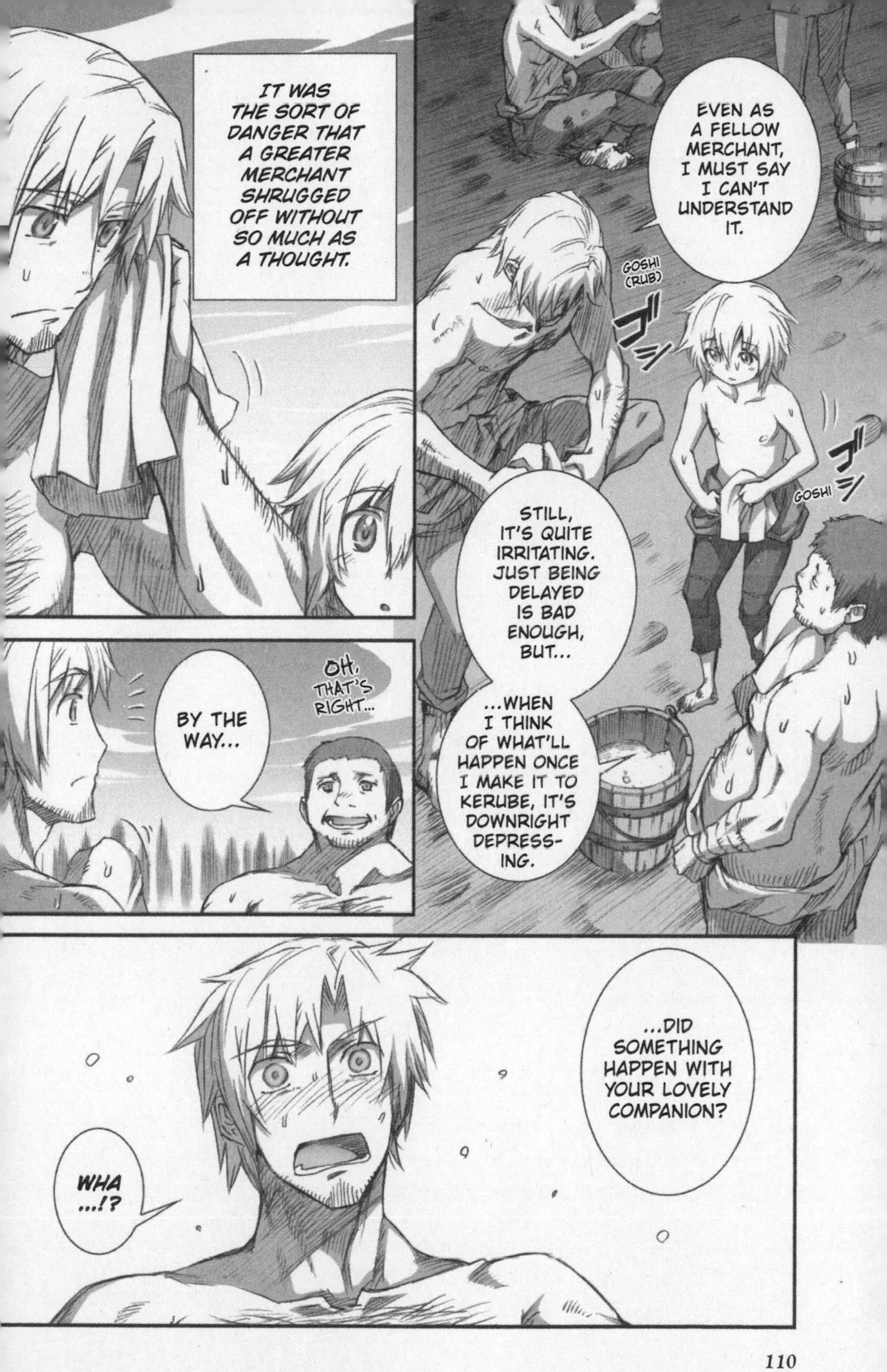
EVEN AS A FELLOW MERCHANT, I MUST SAY I CAN'T UNDERSTAND IT.
GOSHI (RUB)
GOSHI
STILL, IT'S QUITE IRRITATING. JUST BEING DELAYED IS BAD ENOUGH, BUT...
...WHEN I THINK OF WHAT'LL HAPPEN ONCE I MAKE IT TO KERUBE, IT'S DOWNRIGHT DEPRESS-ING.
IT WAS THE SORT OF DANGER THAT A GREATER MERCHANT SHRUGGED OFF WITHOUT SO MUCH AS A THOUGHT.
OH, THAT'S RIGHT...
BY THE WAY...
...DID SOMETHING HAPPEN WITH YOUR LOVELY COMPANION?
WHA ...!?

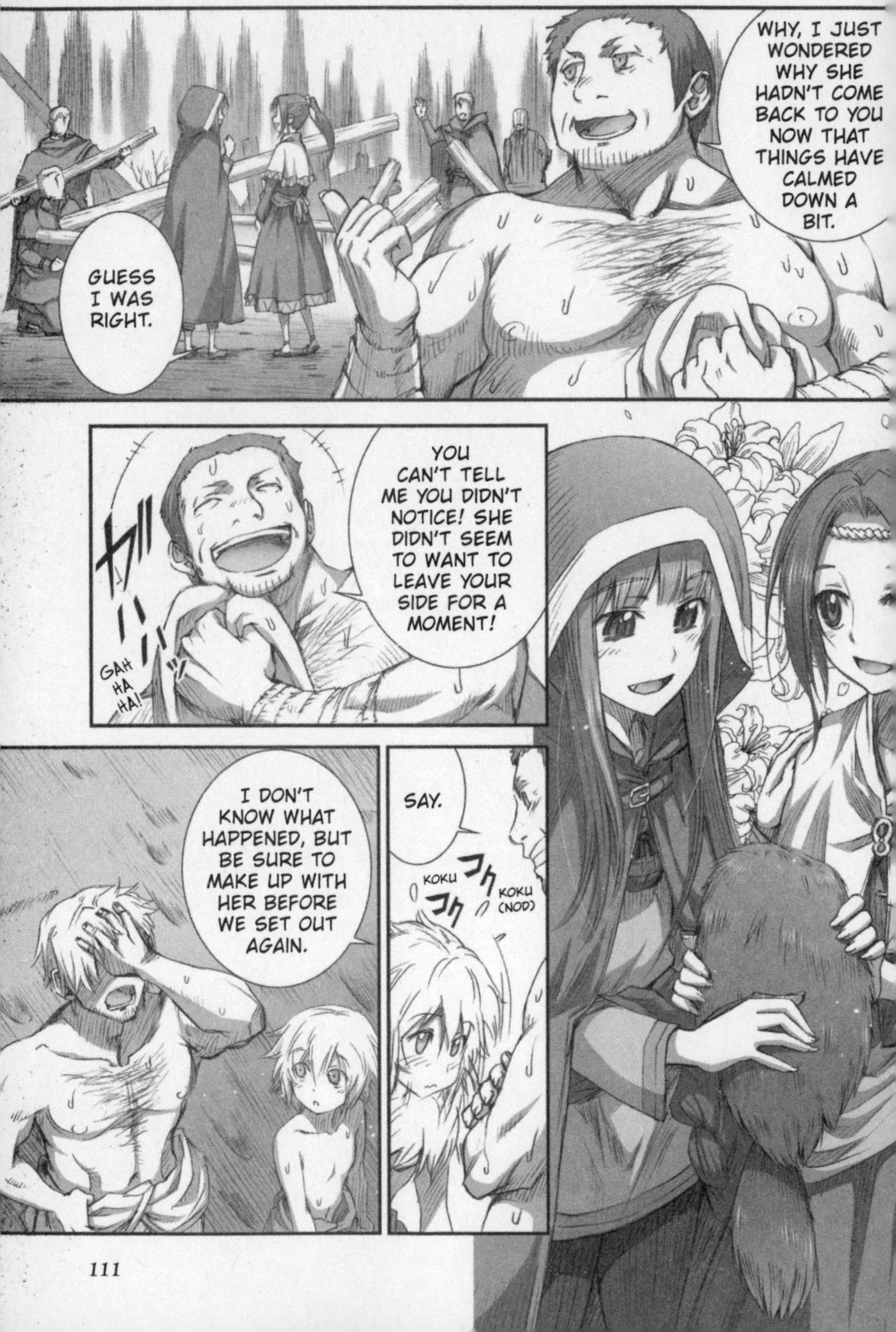
WHY, I JUST WONDERED WHY SHE HADN'T COME BACK TO YOU NOW THAT THINGS HAVE CALMED DOWN A BIT.
GUESS I WAS RIGHT.
YOU CAN'T TELL ME YOU DIDN'T NOTICE! SHE DIDN'T SEEM TO WANT TO LEAVE YOUR SIDE FOR A MOMENT!
GAH HA HA!
SAY.
KOKU
KOKU (NOD)
I DON'T KNOW WHAT HAPPENED, BUT BE SURE TO MAKE UP WITH HER BEFORE WE SET OUT AGAIN.

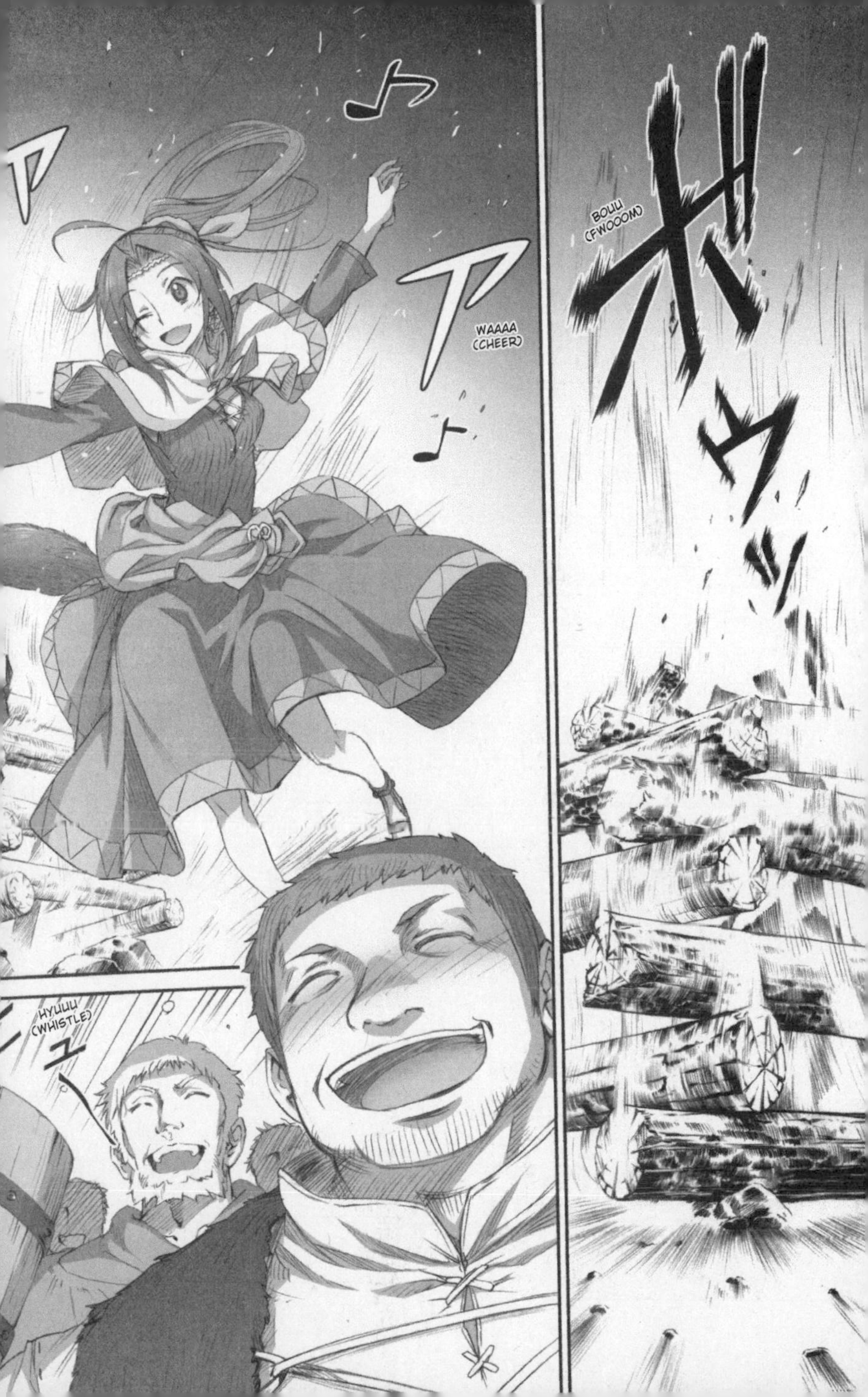
BOUU (FWOOOM)
WAAAA (CHEER)
HYUUU (WHISTLE)

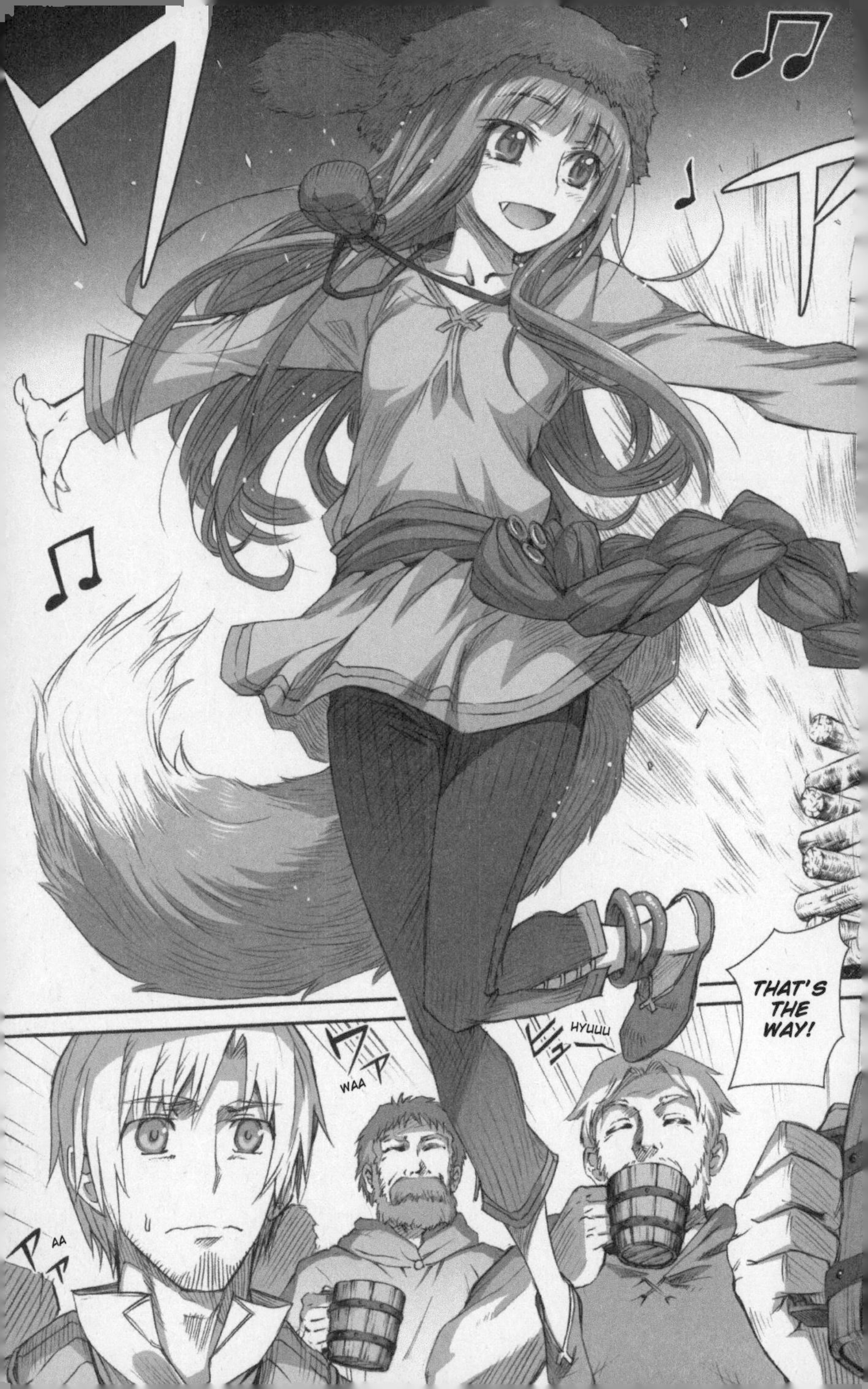
HYUUU
THAT'S THE WAY!
WAA
AA

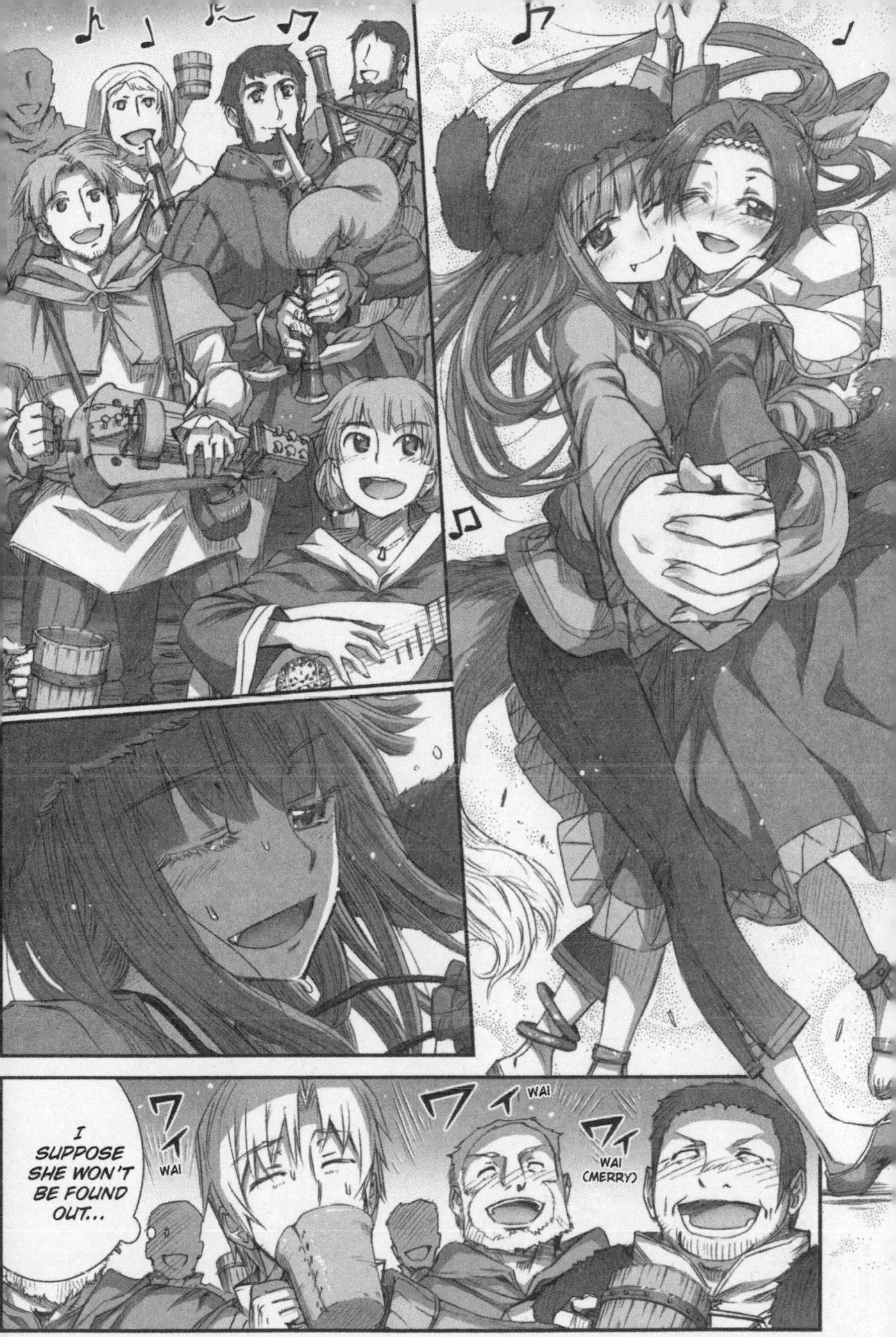
ワイ
WAI
ワイ
WAI (MERRY)
ワイ
WAI
I SUPPOSE SHE WON'T BE FOUND OUT...

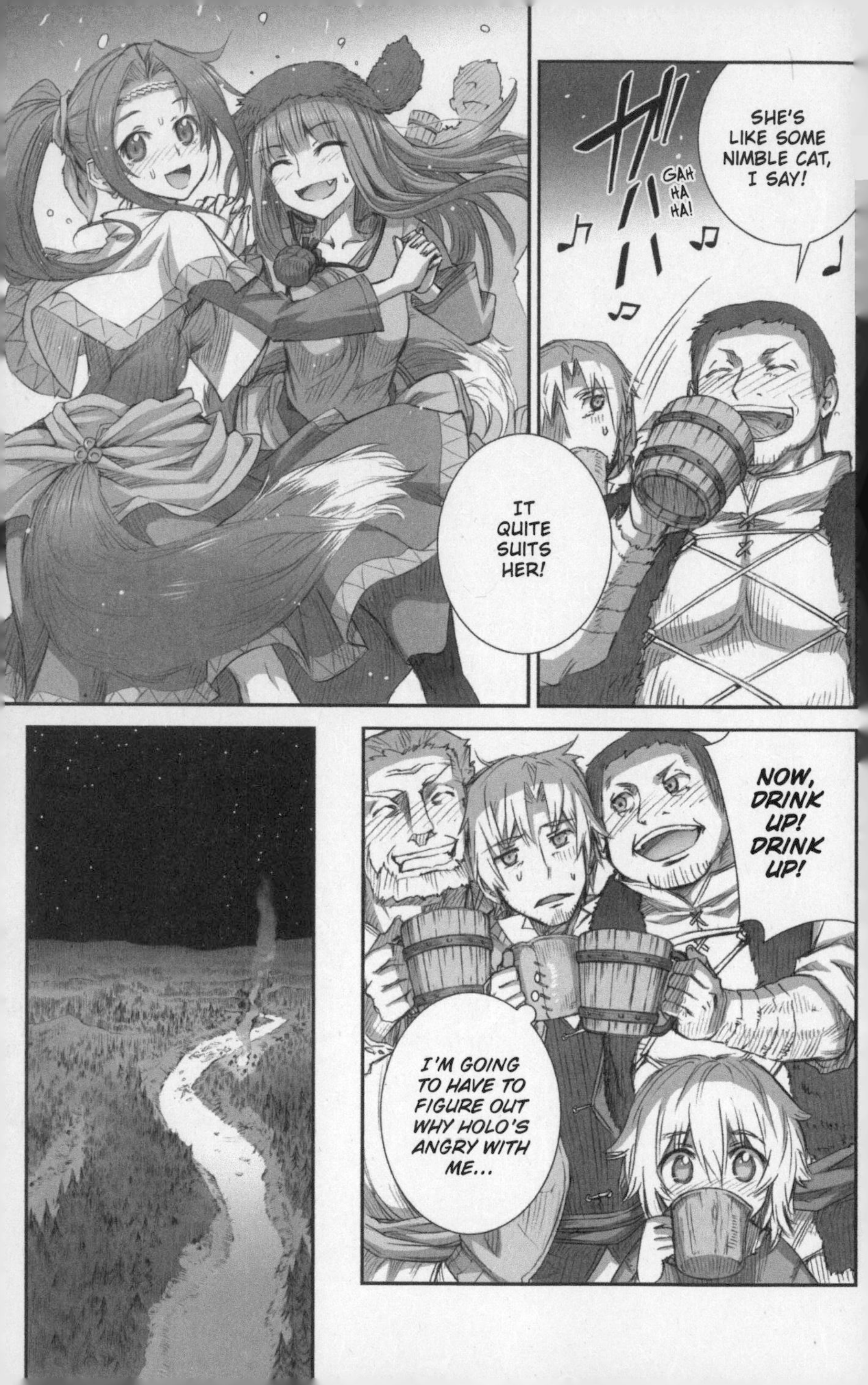
SHE'S LIKE SOME NIMBLE CAT, I SAY!
ガハハ
GAH HA HA!
IT QUITE SUITS HER!
NOW, DRINK UP! DRINK UP!
I'M GOING TO HAVE TO FIGURE OUT WHY HOLO'S ANGRY WITH ME...

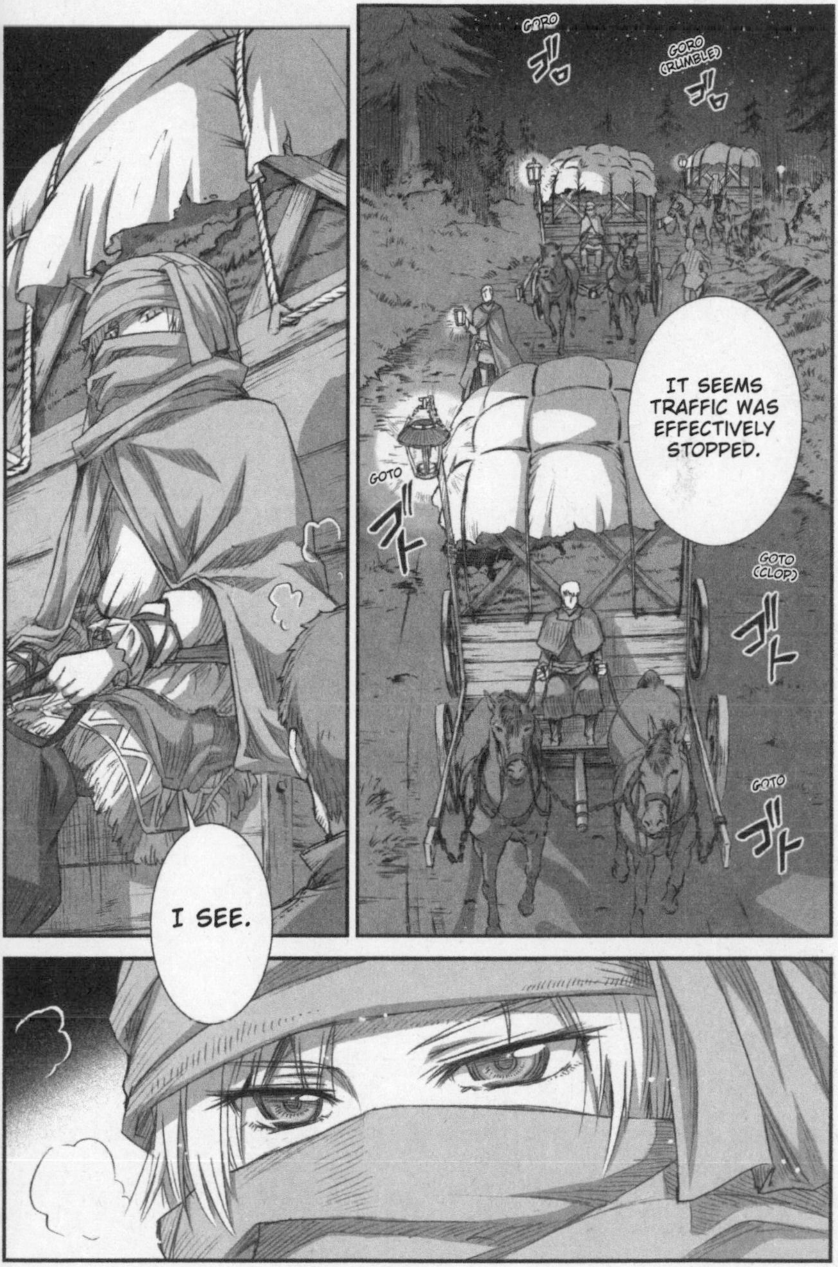
GORO
GORO (RUMBLE)
IT SEEMS TRAFFIC WAS EFFECTIVELY STOPPED.
GOTO
GOTO (CLOP)
GOTO
I SEE.

SPICE & WOLF

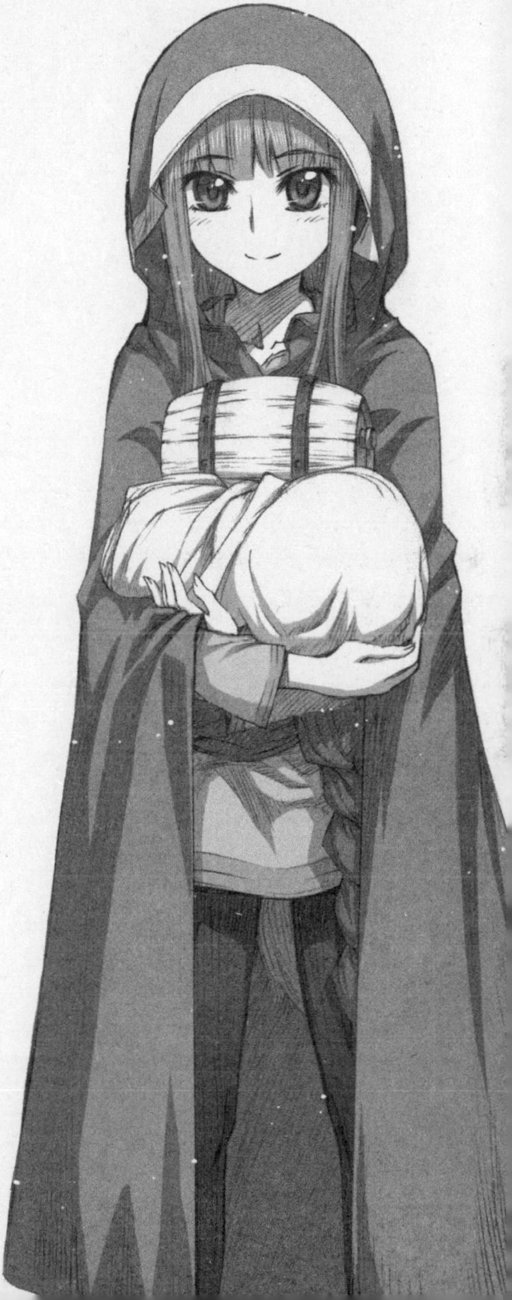

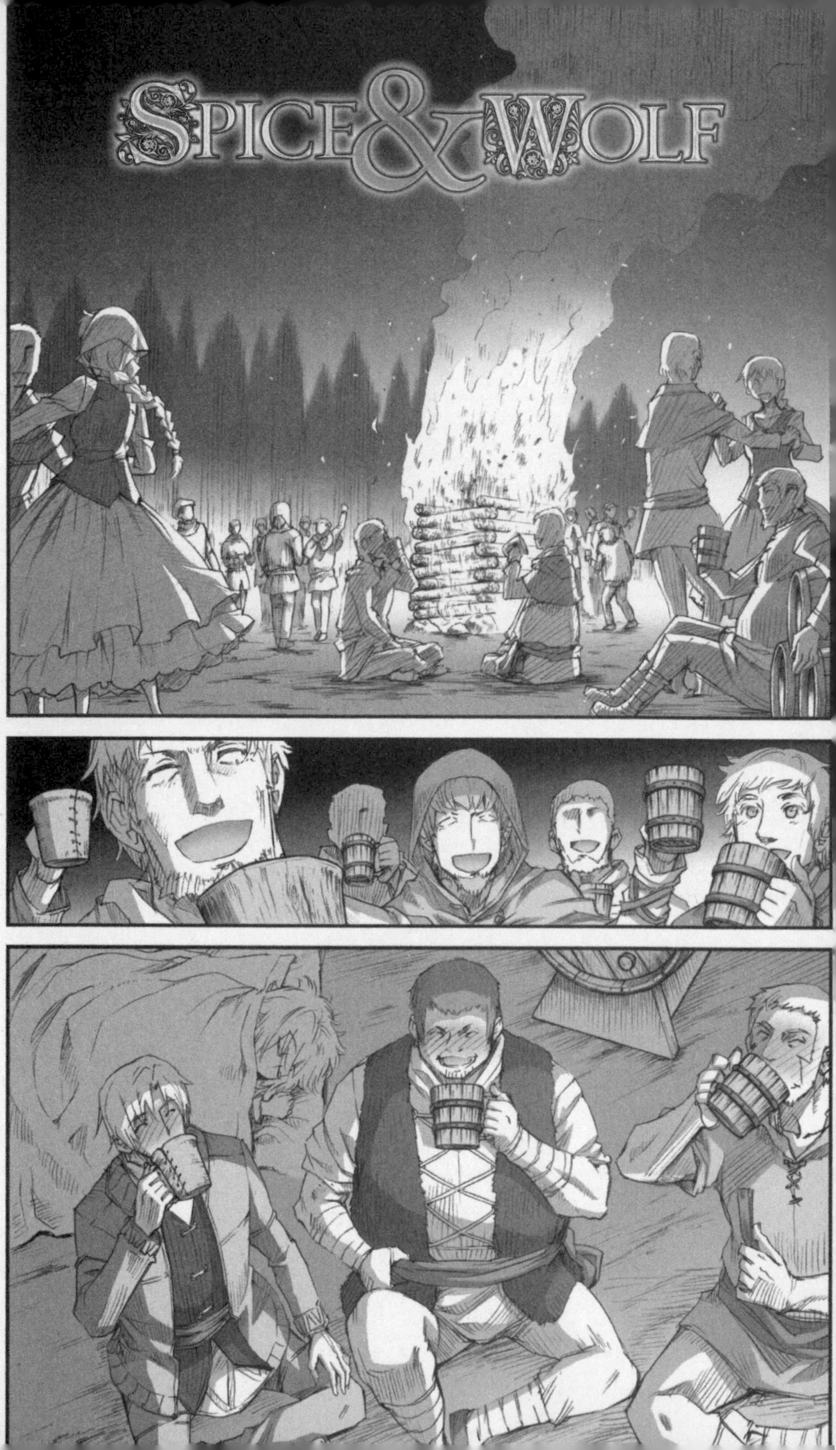
SPICE & WOLF

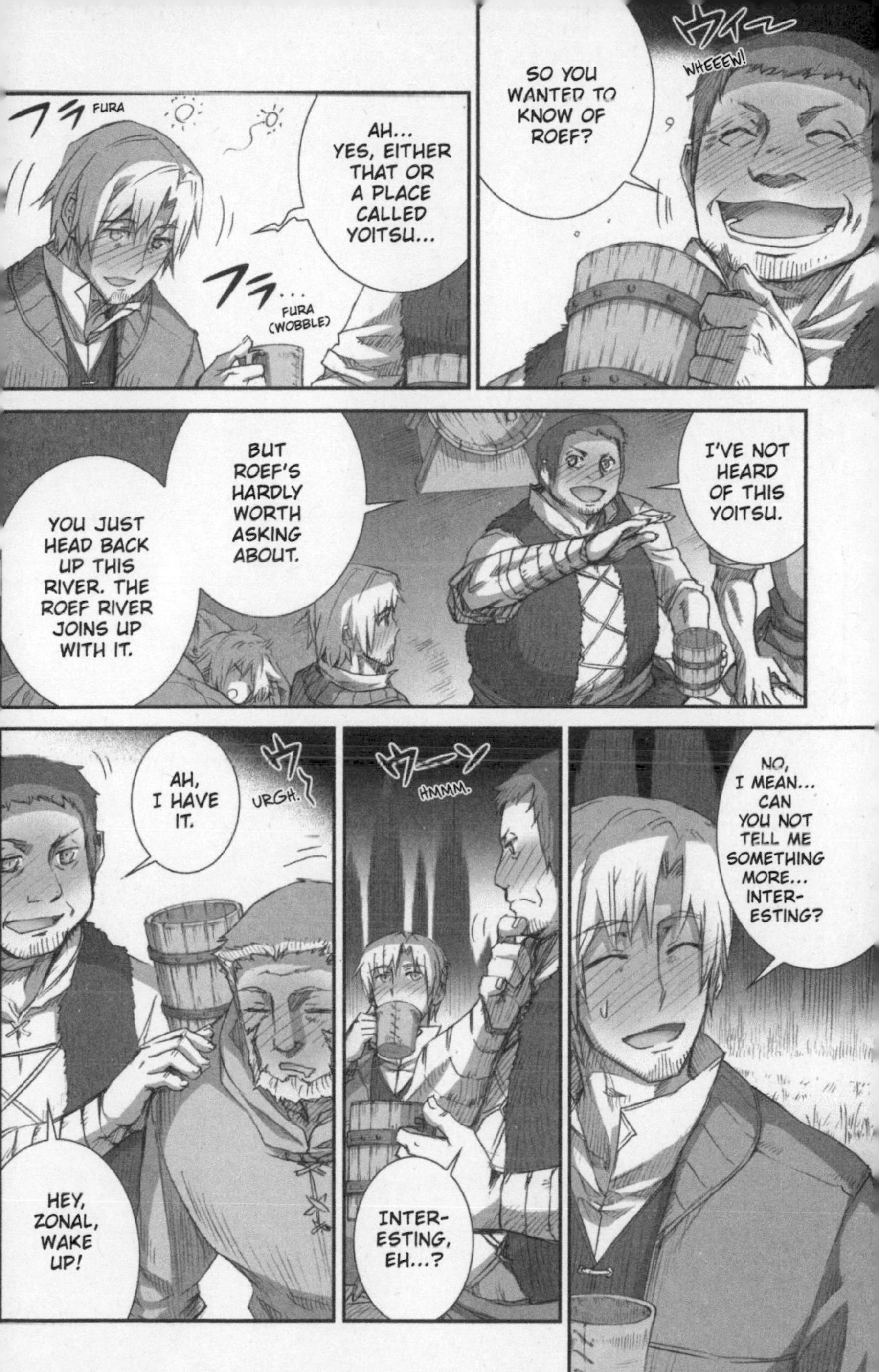
WHEEEW!
SO YOU WANTED TO KNOW OF ROEF?
FURA
AH... YES, EITHER THAT OR A PLACE CALLED YOITSU...
FURA (WOBBLE)
I'VE NOT HEARD OF THIS YOITSU.
BUT ROEF'S HARDLY WORTH ASKING ABOUT.
YOU JUST HEAD BACK UP THIS RIVER. THE ROEF RIVER JOINS UP WITH IT.
NO, I MEAN... CAN YOU NOT TELL ME SOMETHING MORE... INTER-ESTING?
HMMM.
INTER-ESTING, EH...?
URGH.
AH, I HAVE IT.
HEY, ZONAL, WAKE UP!

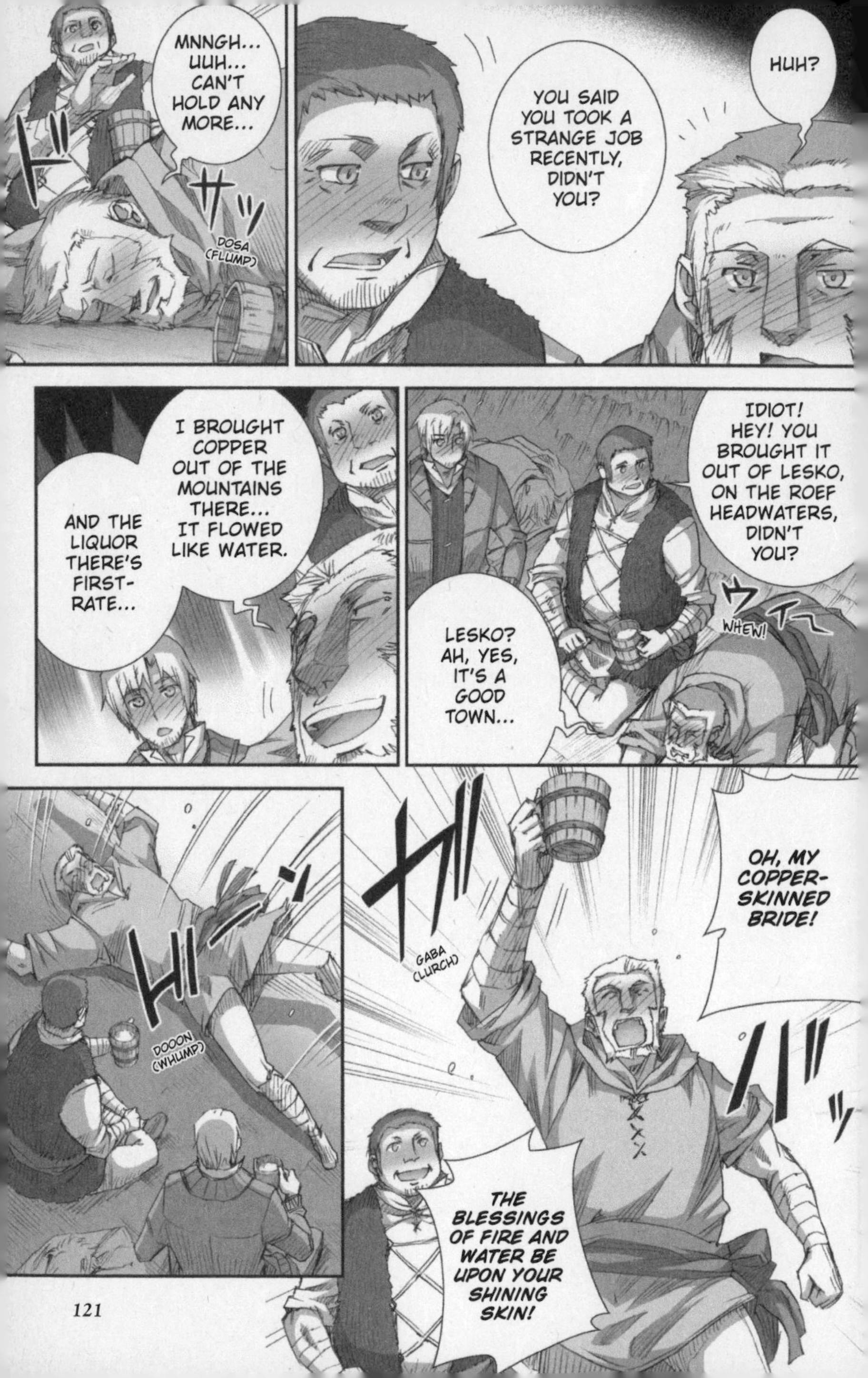
HUH?
YOU SAID YOU TOOK A STRANGE JOB RECENTLY, DIDN'T YOU?
MNNGH... UUH... CAN'T HOLD ANY MORE...
DOSA (FLUMP)
IDIOT! HEY! YOU BROUGHT IT OUT OF LESKO, ON THE ROEF HEADWATERS, DIDN'T YOU?
WHEW!
LESKO? AH, YES, IT'S A GOOD TOWN...
I BROUGHT COPPER OUT OF THE MOUNTAINS THERE... IT FLOWED LIKE WATER.
AND THE LIQUOR THERE'S FIRST-RATE...
OH, MY COPPER-SKINNED BRIDE!
GABA (LURCH)
THE BLESSINGS OF FIRE AND WATER BE UPON YOUR SHINING SKIN!
DOOON (WHUMP)

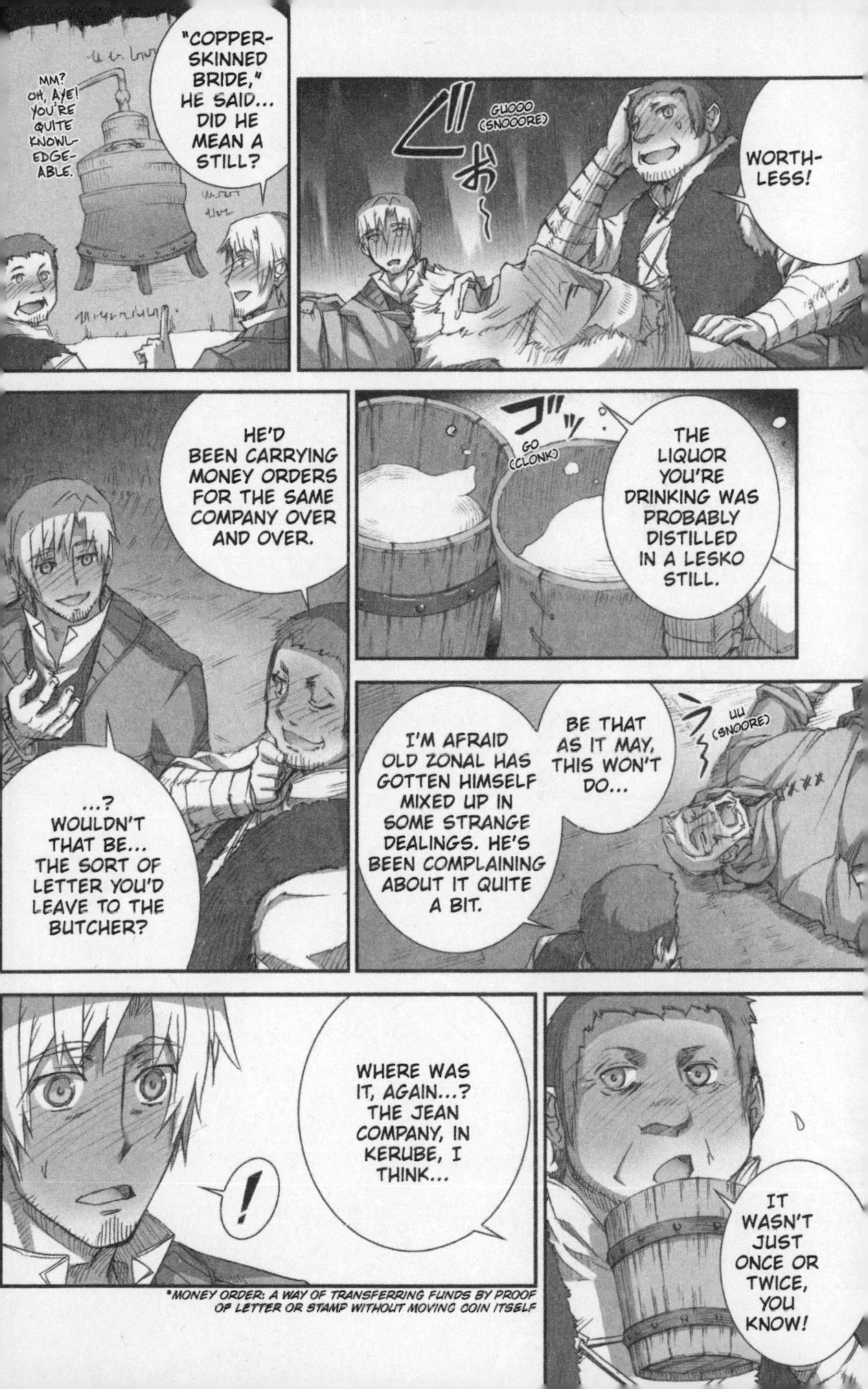
GUOOO (SNOOORE)
WORTHLESS!
"COPPER-SKINNED BRIDE," HE SAID... DID HE MEAN A STILL?
MM? OH, AYE! YOU'RE QUITE KNOWLEDGEABLE.
GO (CLONK)
THE LIQUOR YOU'RE DRINKING WAS PROBABLY DISTILLED IN A LESKO STILL.
UU (SNOORE)
BE THAT AS IT MAY, THIS WON'T DO...
I'M AFRAID OLD ZONAL HAS GOTTEN HIMSELF MIXED UP IN SOME STRANGE DEALINGS. HE'S BEEN COMPLAINING ABOUT IT QUITE A BIT.
HE'D BEEN CARRYING MONEY ORDERS FOR THE SAME COMPANY OVER AND OVER.
...? WOULDN'T THAT BE... THE SORT OF LETTER YOU'D LEAVE TO THE BUTCHER?
IT WASN'T JUST ONCE OR TWICE, YOU KNOW!
WHERE WAS IT, AGAIN...? THE JEAN COMPANY, IN KERUBE, I THINK...
!

*MONEY ORDER: A WAY OF TRANSFERRING FUNDS BY PROOF OF LETTER OR STAMP WITHOUT MOVING COIN ITSELF

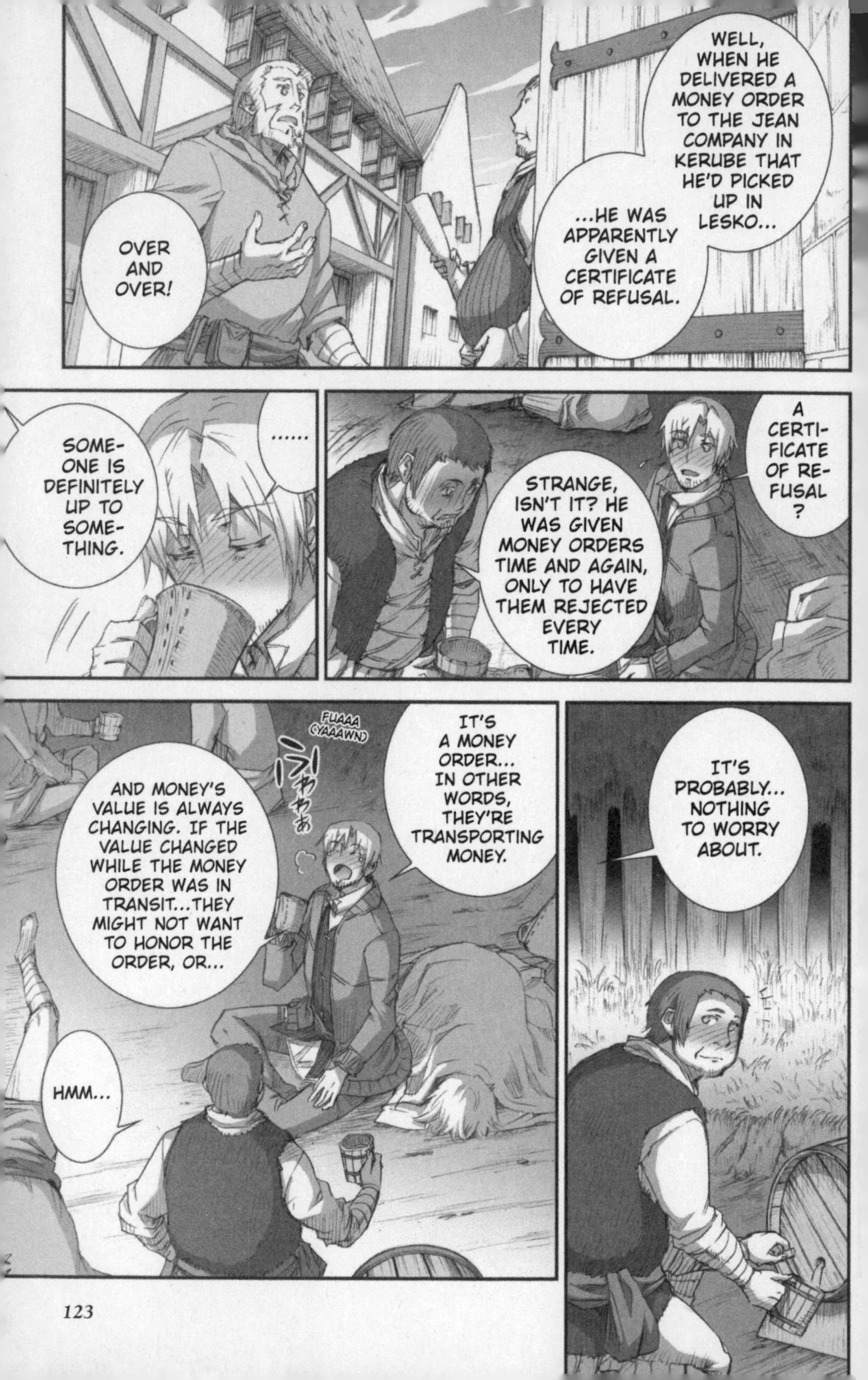
WELL, WHEN HE DELIVERED A MONEY ORDER TO THE JEAN COMPANY IN KERUBE THAT HE'D PICKED UP IN LESKO...
...HE WAS APPARENTLY GIVEN A CERTIFICATE OF REFUSAL.
OVER AND OVER!
A CERTIFICATE OF REFUSAL?
STRANGE, ISN'T IT? HE WAS GIVEN MONEY ORDERS TIME AND AGAIN, ONLY TO HAVE THEM REJECTED EVERY TIME.
......
SOMEONE IS DEFINITELY UP TO SOMETHING.
IT'S PROBABLY... NOTHING TO WORRY ABOUT.
IT'S A MONEY ORDER... IN OTHER WORDS, THEY'RE TRANSPORTING MONEY.
FUAAA (YAAAWN)
AND MONEY'S VALUE IS ALWAYS CHANGING. IF THE VALUE CHANGED WHILE THE MONEY ORDER WAS IN TRANSIT...THEY MIGHT NOT WANT TO HONOR THE ORDER, OR...
HMM...

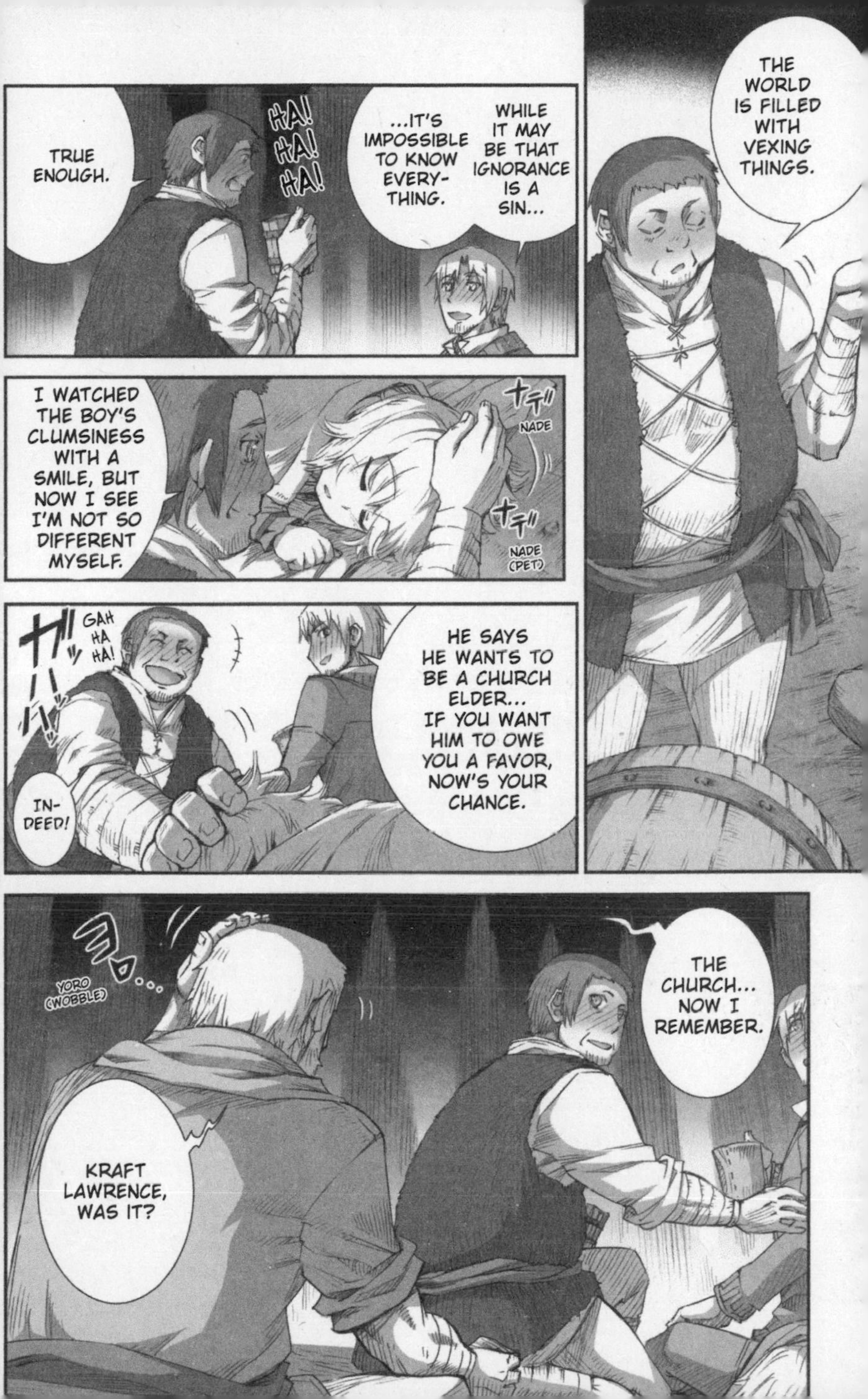
THE WORLD IS FILLED WITH VEXING THINGS.
WHILE IT MAY BE THAT IGNORANCE IS A SIN...
...IT'S IMPOSSIBLE TO KNOW EVERY-THING.
HA! HA! HA!
TRUE ENOUGH.
NADE
NADE (PET)
I WATCHED THE BOY'S CLUMSINESS WITH A SMILE, BUT NOW I SEE I'M NOT SO DIFFERENT MYSELF.
HE SAYS HE WANTS TO BE A CHURCH ELDER... IF YOU WANT HIM TO OWE YOU A FAVOR, NOW'S YOUR CHANCE.
GAH HA HA!
IN-DEED!
THE CHURCH... NOW I REMEMBER.
YORO (WOBBLE)
KRAFT LAWRENCE, WAS IT?

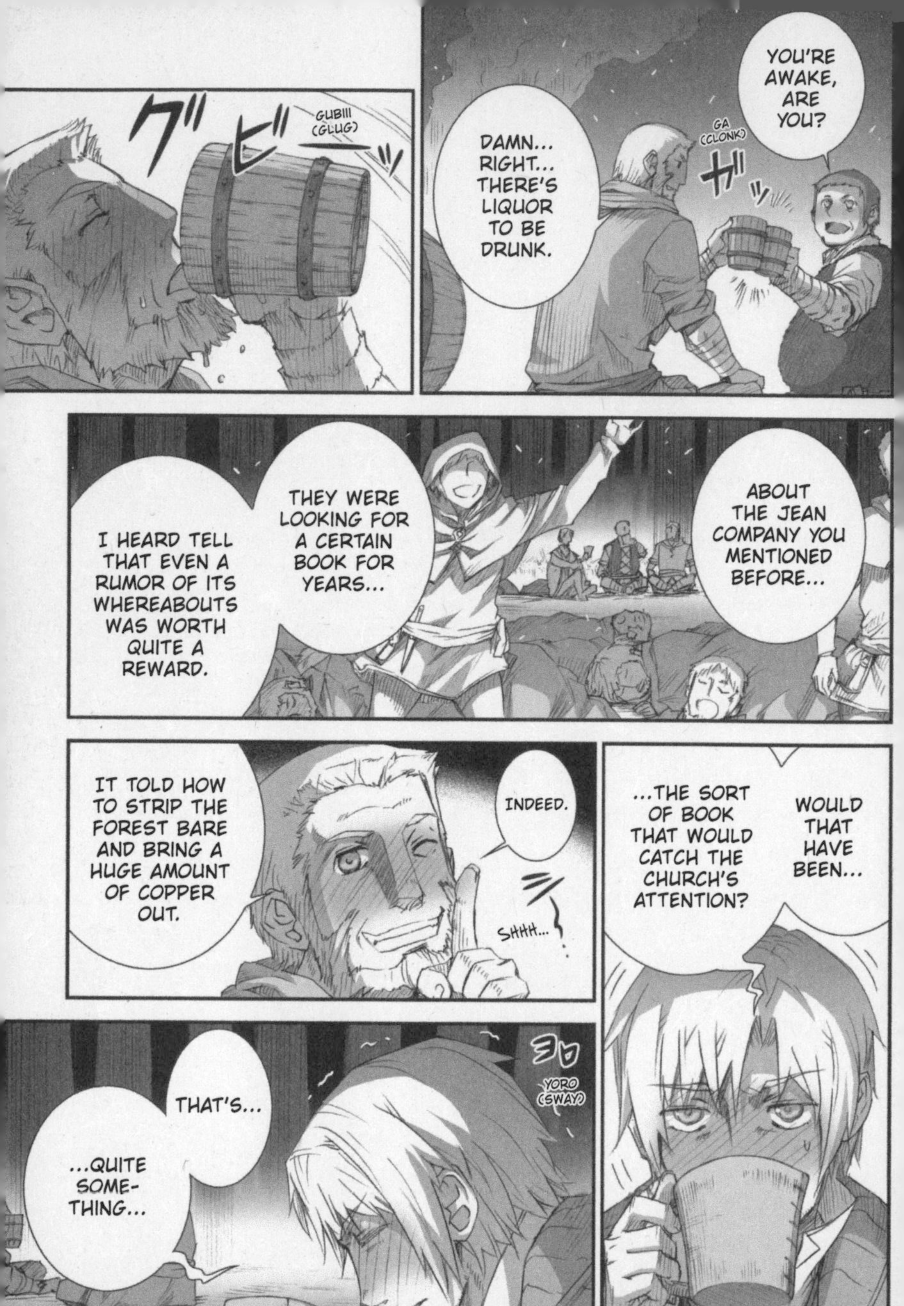

YOU'RE AWAKE, ARE YOU?
GA (CLONK)
DAMN... RIGHT... THERE'S LIQUOR TO BE DRUNK.
GUBIII (GLUG)
ABOUT THE JEAN COMPANY YOU MENTIONED BEFORE...
THEY WERE LOOKING FOR A CERTAIN BOOK FOR YEARS...
I HEARD TELL THAT EVEN A RUMOR OF ITS WHEREABOUTS WAS WORTH QUITE A REWARD.
WOULD THAT HAVE BEEN...
...THE SORT OF BOOK THAT WOULD CATCH THE CHURCH'S ATTENTION?
INDEED.
IT TOLD HOW TO STRIP THE FOREST BARE AND BRING A HUGE AMOUNT OF COPPER OUT.
SHHH...
YORO (SWAY)
THAT'S...
...QUITE SOME-THING...

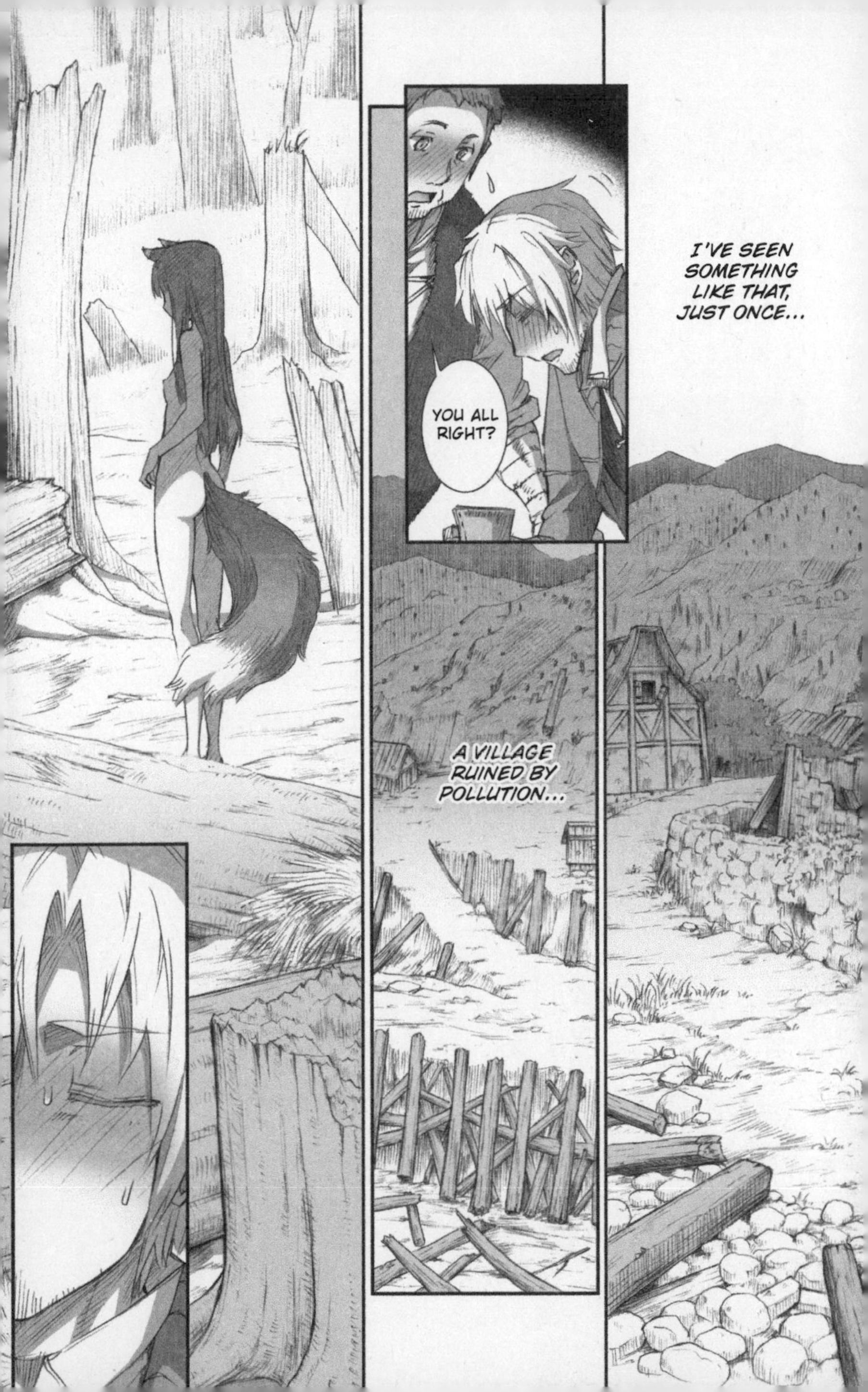
I'VE SEEN SOMETHING LIKE THAT, JUST ONCE...
YOU ALL RIGHT?
A VILLAGE RUINED BY POLLUTION...

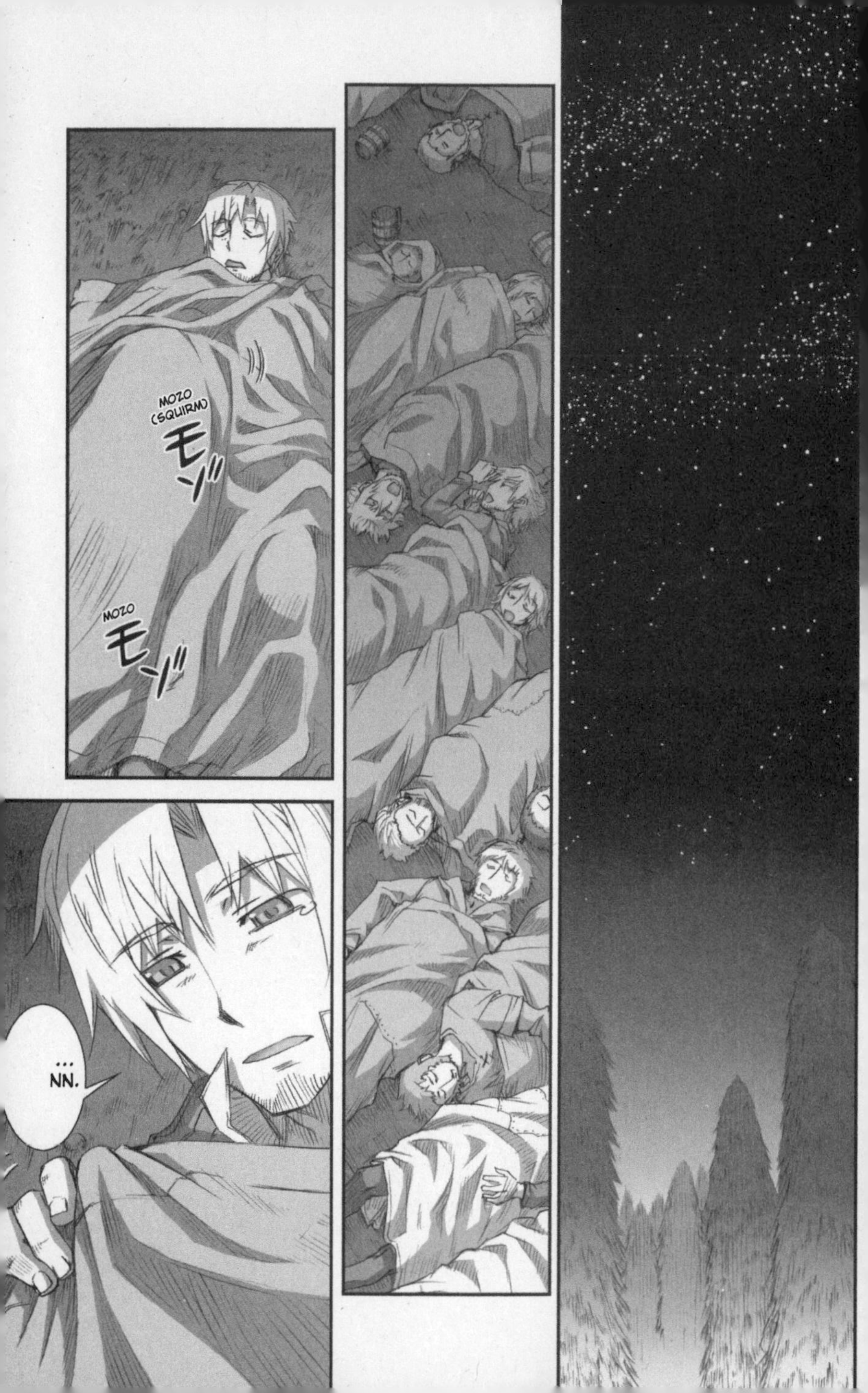
MOZO (SQUIRM)
モゾ
MOZO
モゾ
... NN.

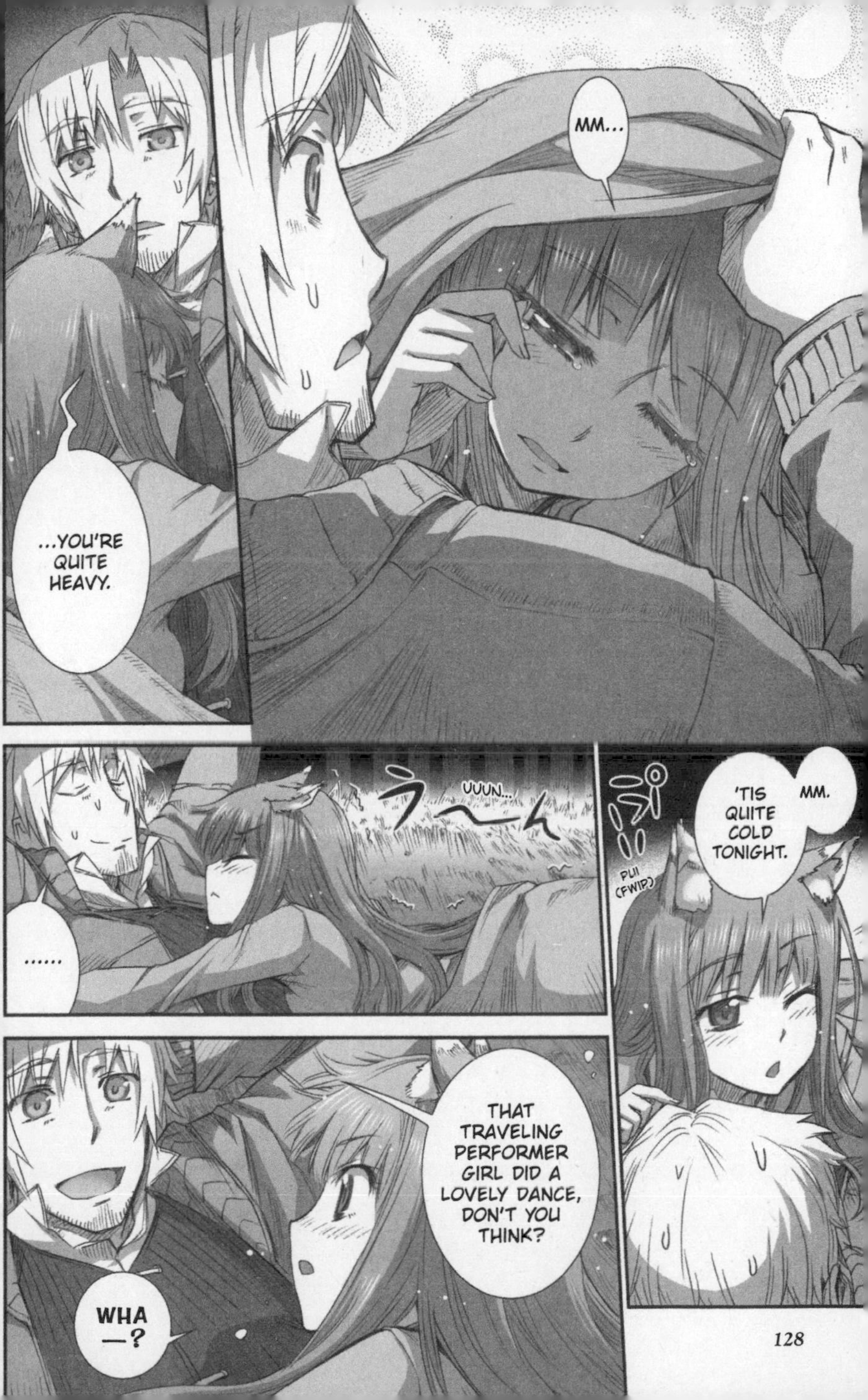
MM...
...YOU'RE QUITE HEAVY.
PUI (FWIP)
MM.
'TIS QUITE COLD TONIGHT.
UUUN...
......
THAT TRAVELING PERFORMER GIRL DID A LOVELY DANCE, DON'T YOU THINK?
WHA—?

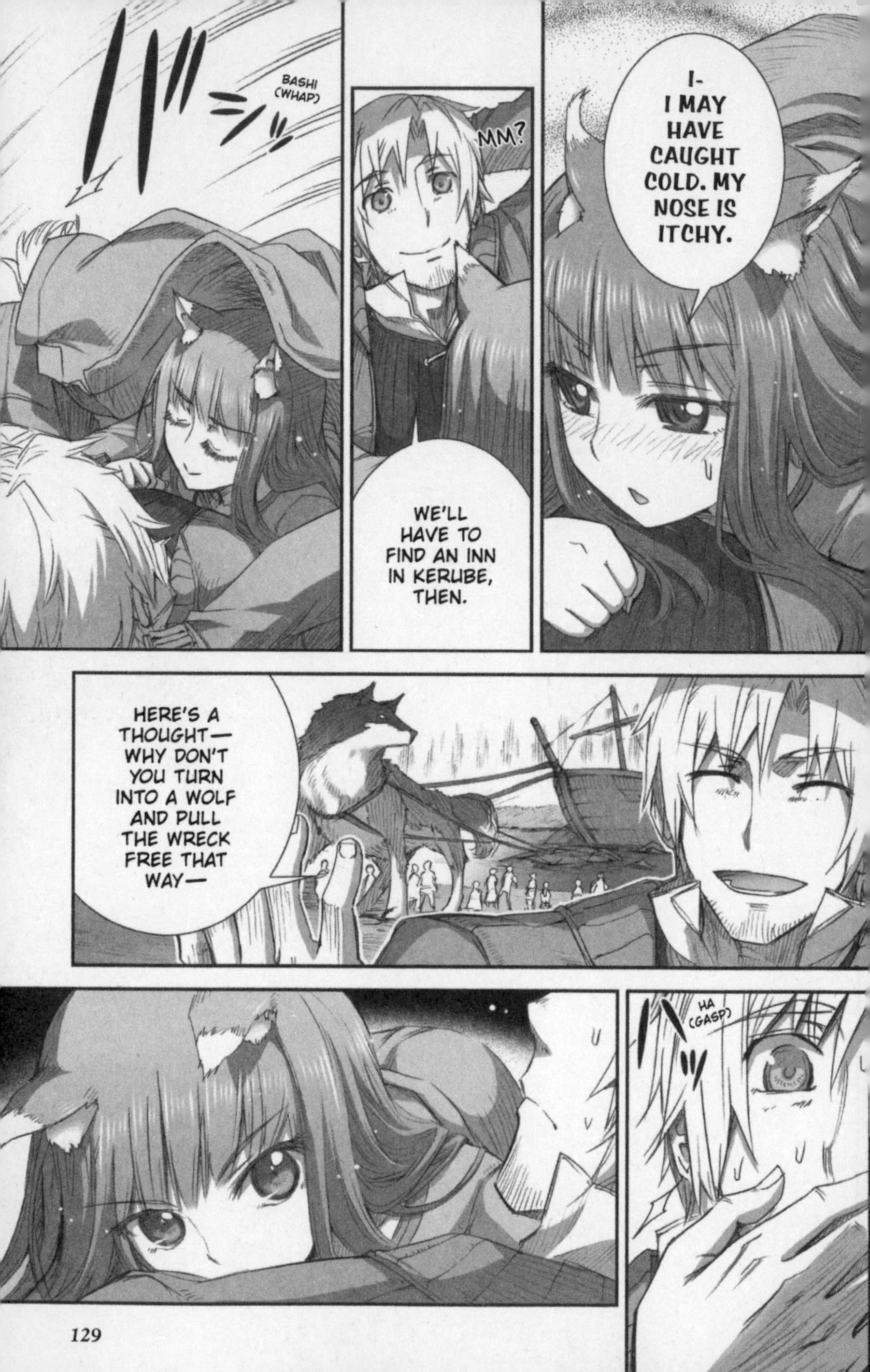
I- I MAY HAVE CAUGHT COLD. MY NOSE IS ITCHY.
MM?
WE'LL HAVE TO FIND AN INN IN KERUBE, THEN.
BASHI (WHAP)
HERE'S A THOUGHT—WHY DON'T YOU TURN INTO A WOLF AND PULL THE WRECK FREE THAT WAY—
HA (GASP)

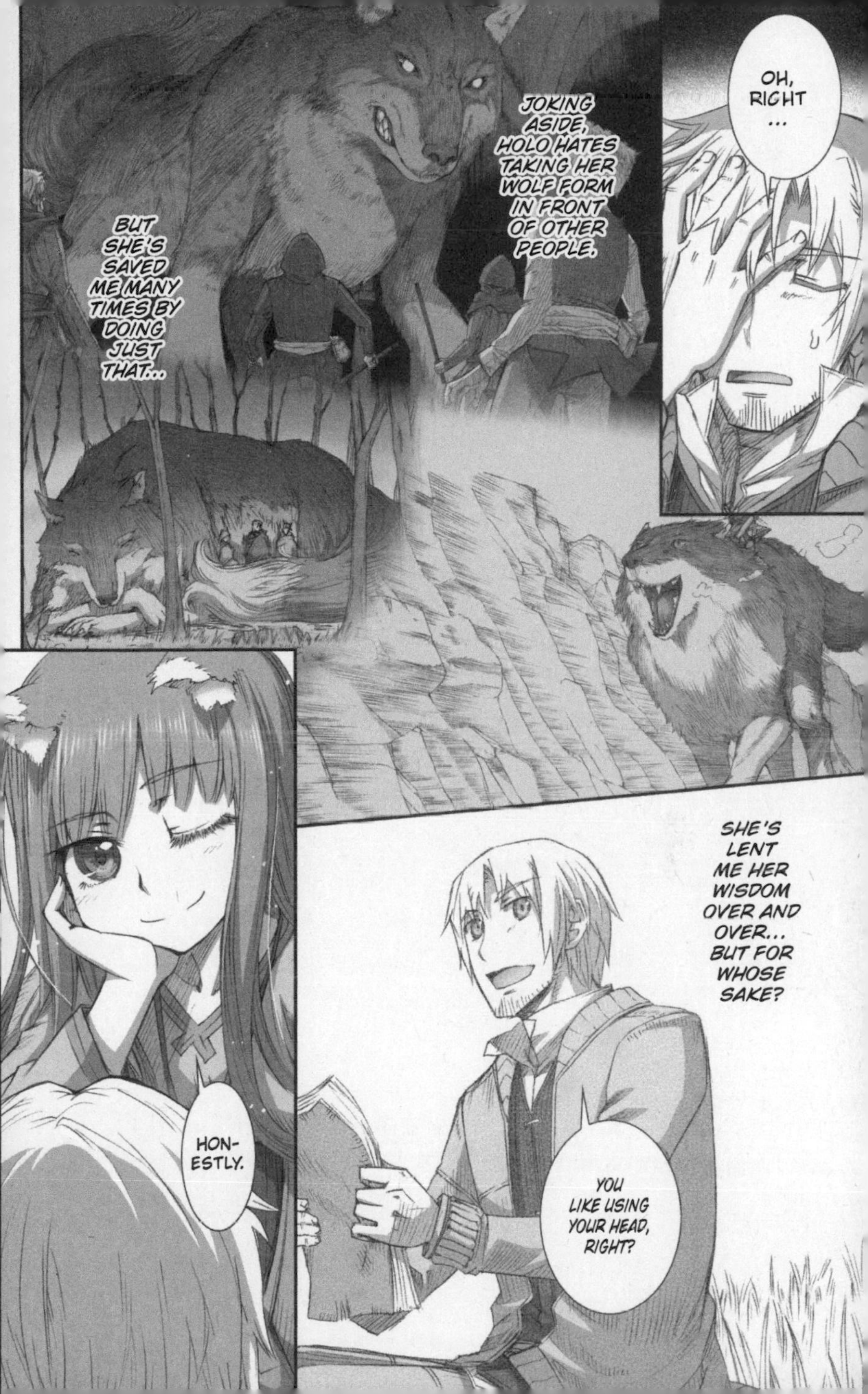
OH, RIGHT ...
JOKING ASIDE, HOLO HATES TAKING HER WOLF FORM IN FRONT OF OTHER PEOPLE.
BUT SHE'S SAVED ME MANY TIMES BY DOING JUST THAT...
SHE'S LENT ME HER WISDOM OVER AND OVER... BUT FOR WHOSE SAKE?
YOU LIKE USING YOUR HEAD, RIGHT?
HON-ESTLY.

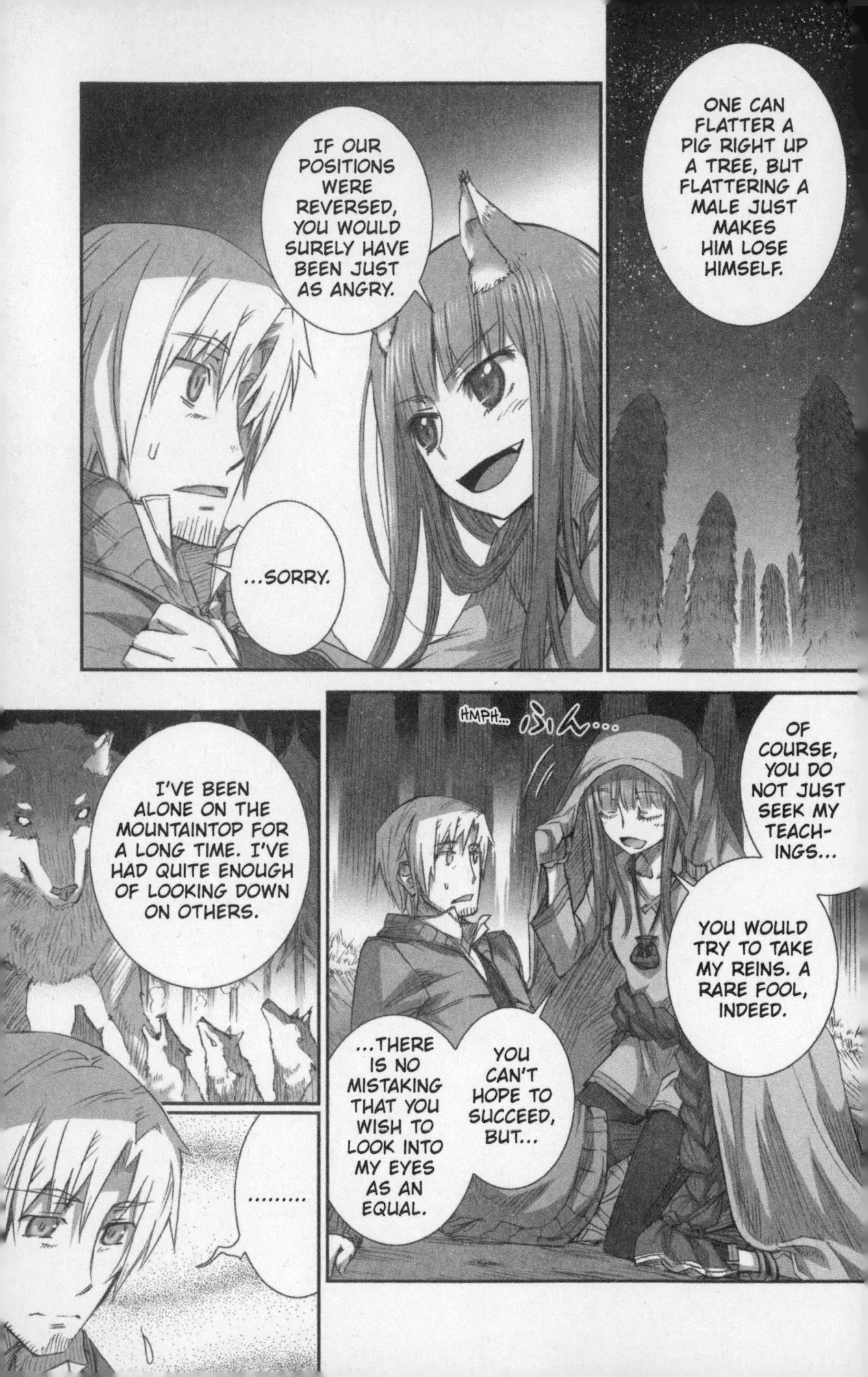
ONE CAN FLATTER A PIG RIGHT UP A TREE, BUT FLATTERING A MALE JUST MAKES HIM LOSE HIMSELF.
IF OUR POSITIONS WERE REVERSED, YOU WOULD SURELY HAVE BEEN JUST AS ANGRY.
...SORRY.
HMPH... ふん...
OF COURSE, YOU DO NOT JUST SEEK MY TEACHINGS...
YOU WOULD TRY TO TAKE MY REINS. A RARE FOOL, INDEED.
YOU CAN'T HOPE TO SUCCEED, BUT...
...THERE IS NO MISTAKING THAT YOU WISH TO LOOK INTO MY EYES AS AN EQUAL.
I'VE BEEN ALONE ON THE MOUNTAINTOP FOR A LONG TIME. I'VE HAD QUITE ENOUGH OF LOOKING DOWN ON OTHERS.
....

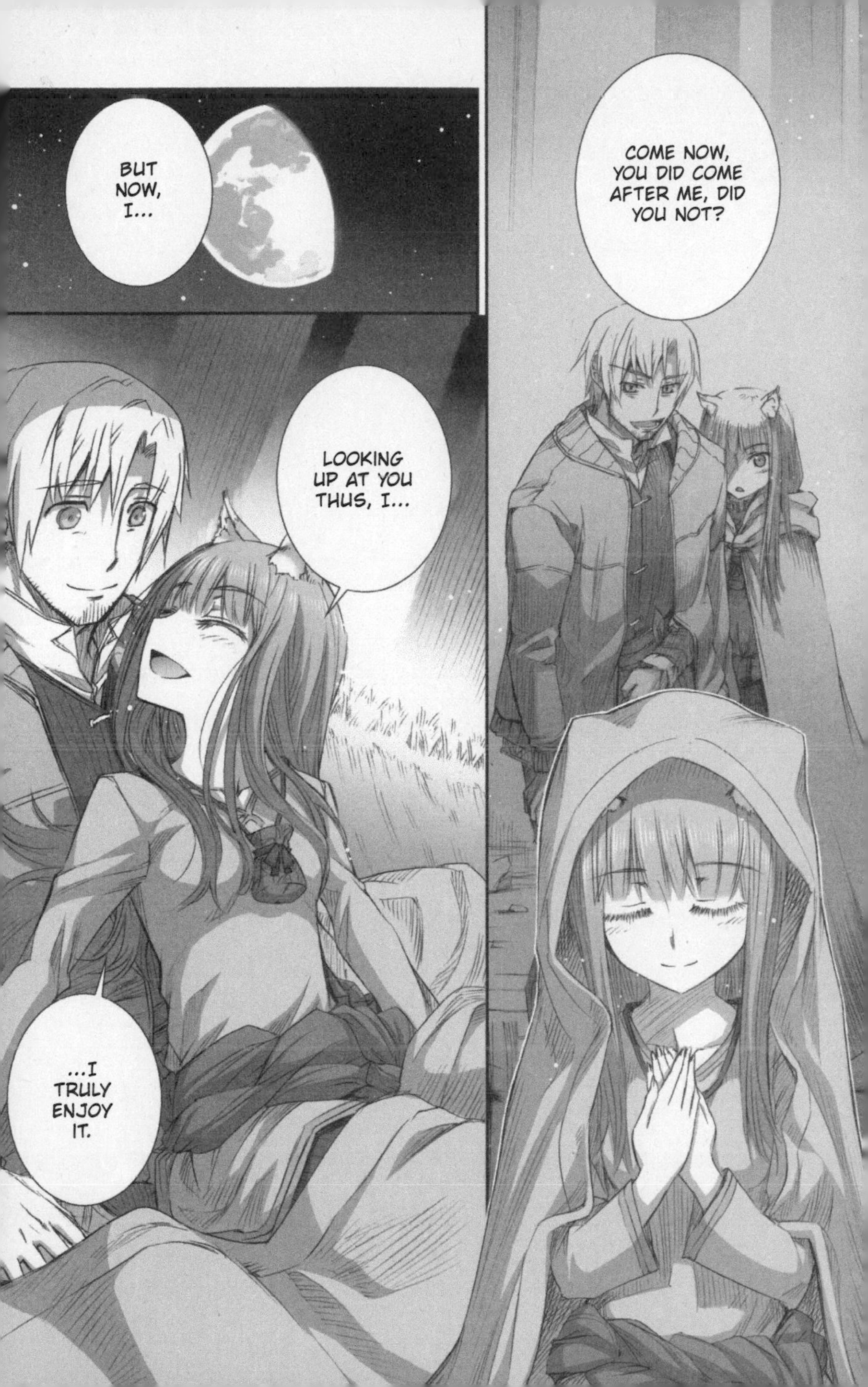
COME NOW, YOU DID COME AFTER ME, DID YOU NOT?
BUT NOW, I...
LOOKING UP AT YOU THUS, I...
...I TRULY ENJOY IT.

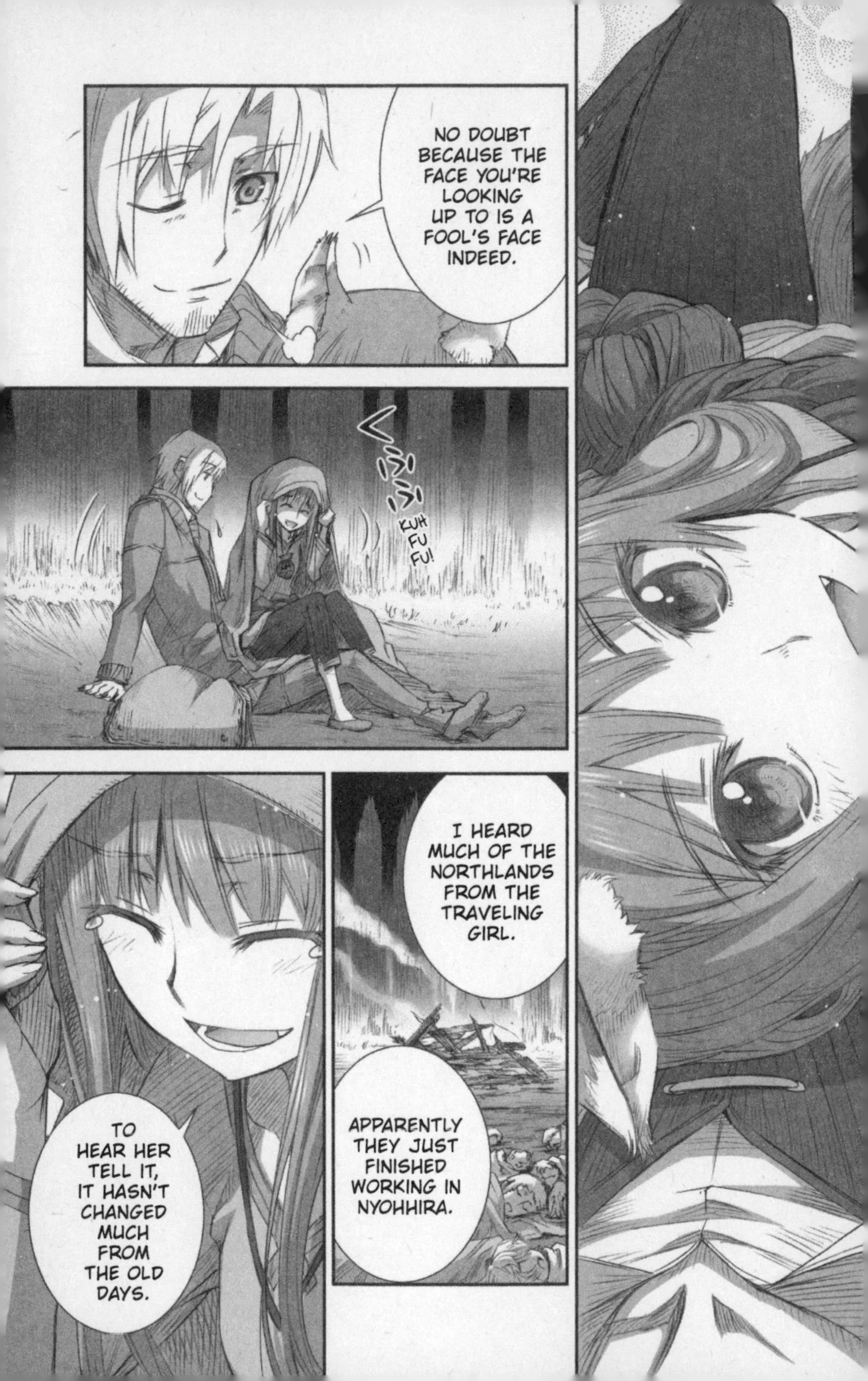
NO DOUBT BECAUSE THE FACE YOU'RE LOOKING UP TO IS A FOOL'S FACE INDEED.
KUH FU FU!
I HEARD MUCH OF THE NORTHLANDS FROM THE TRAVELING GIRL.
APPARENTLY THEY JUST FINISHED WORKING IN NYOHHIRA.
TO HEAR HER TELL IT, IT HASN'T CHANGED MUCH FROM THE OLD DAYS.

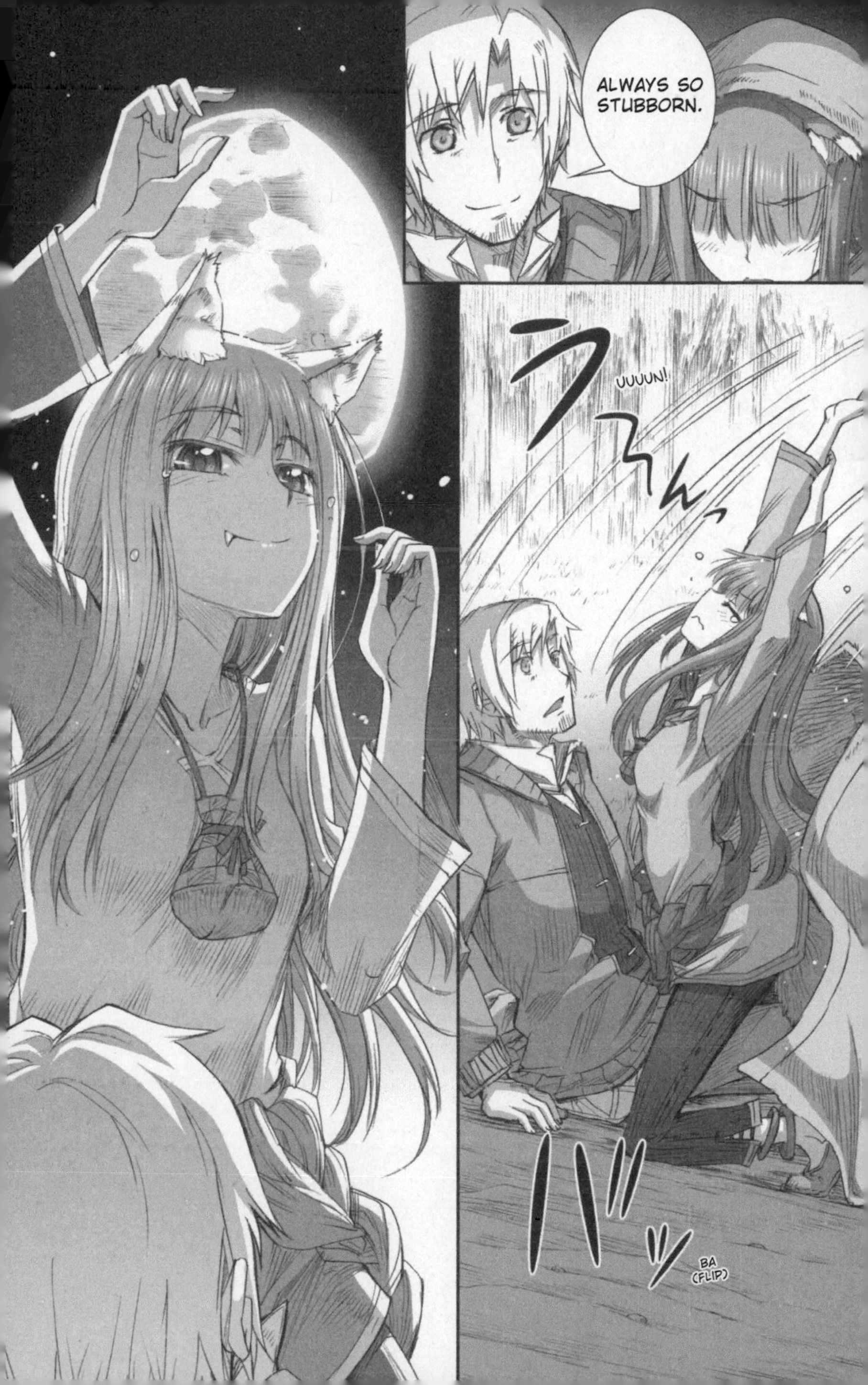
ALWAYS SO STUBBORN.
う
UUUUN!
ーん
バッ
BA (FLIP)

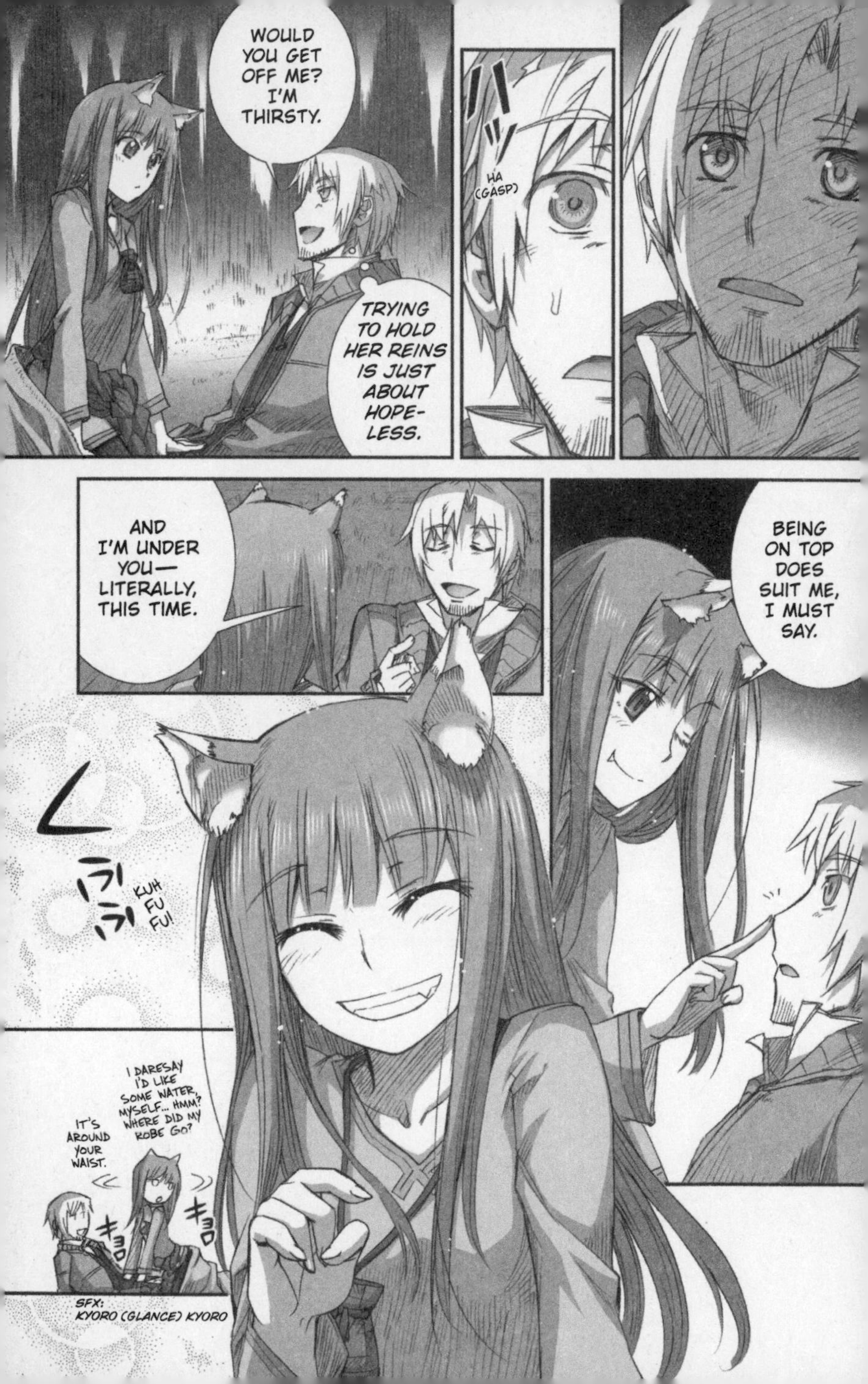
HA (GASP)
WOULD YOU GET OFF ME? I'M THIRSTY.
TRYING TO HOLD HER REINS IS JUST ABOUT HOPE-LESS.
BEING ON TOP DOES SUIT ME, I MUST SAY.
AND I'M UNDER YOU— LITERALLY, THIS TIME.
KUH FU FU!
I DARESAY I'D LIKE SOME WATER, MYSELF... HMM? WHERE DID MY ROBE GO?
IT'S AROUND YOUR WAIST.
SFX: KYORO (GLANCE) KYORO

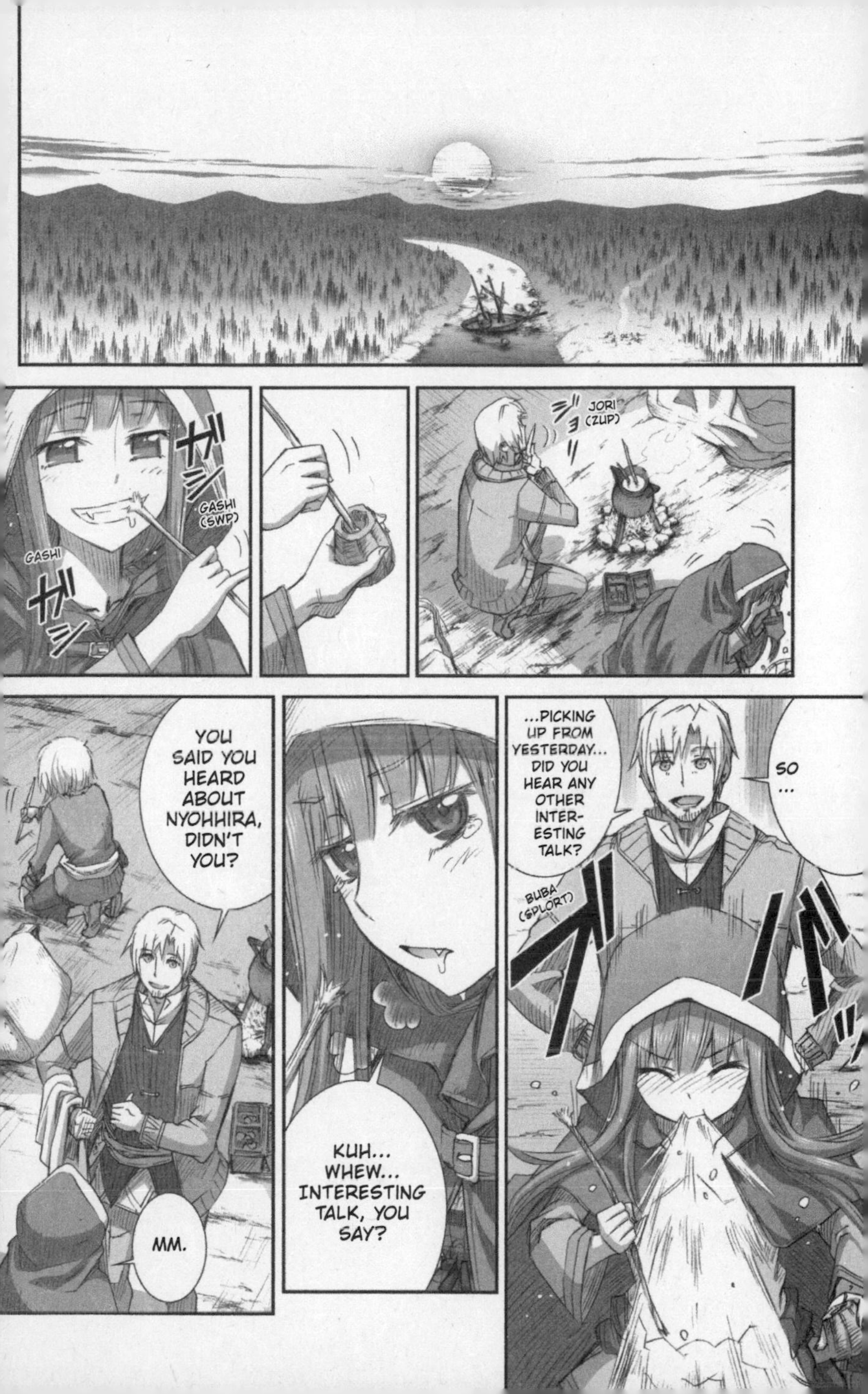
JORI (ZUP)
GASHI (SWP)
GASHI
SO ...
...PICKING UP FROM YESTERDAY... DID YOU HEAR ANY OTHER INTERESTING TALK?
BUBA (SPLORT)
KUH... WHEW... INTERESTING TALK, YOU SAY?
YOU SAID YOU HEARD ABOUT NYOHHIRA, DIDN'T YOU?
MM.

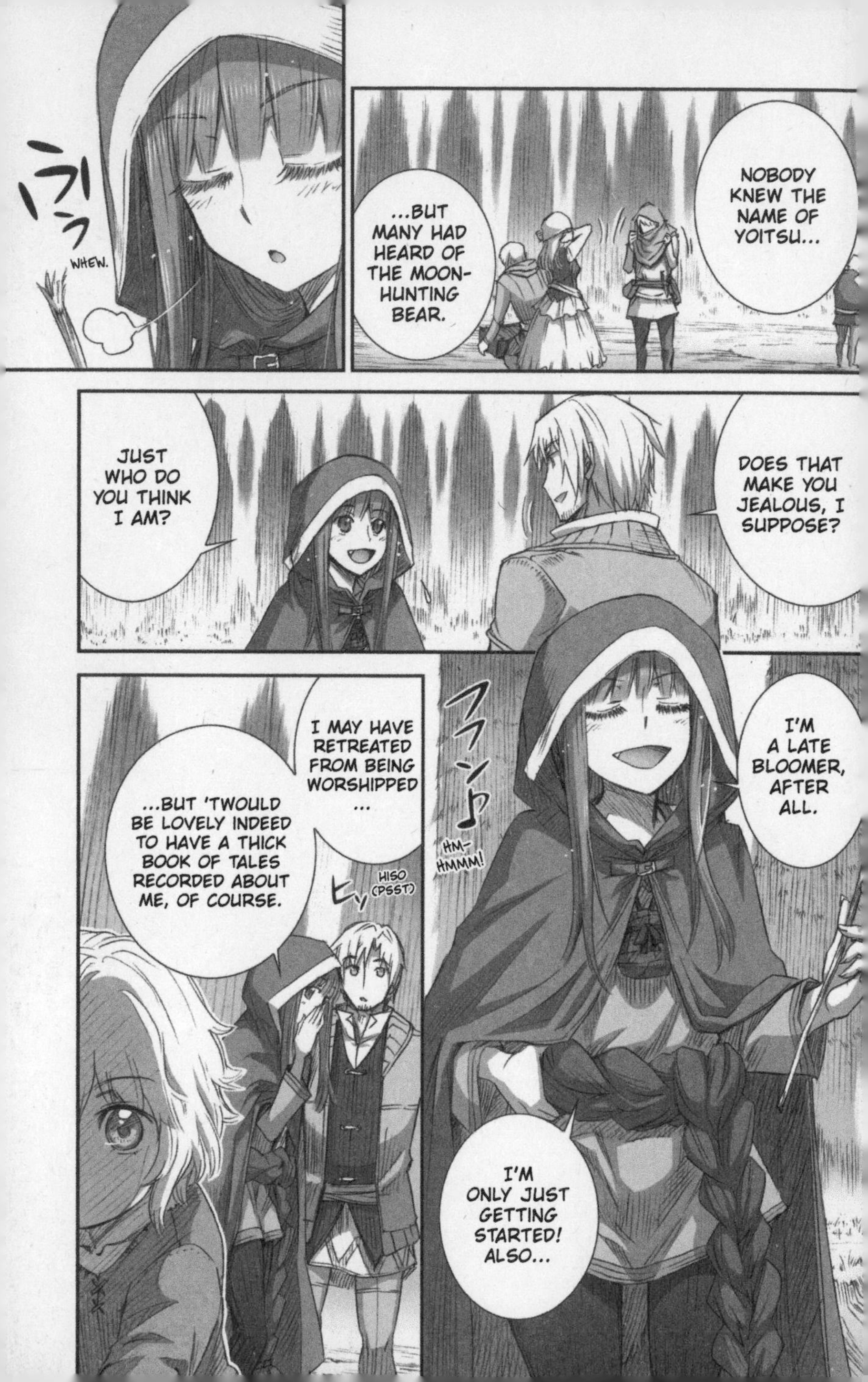
NOBODY KNEW THE NAME OF YOITSU...
...BUT MANY HAD HEARD OF THE MOON-HUNTING BEAR.
WHEW.
DOES THAT MAKE YOU JEALOUS, I SUPPOSE?
JUST WHO DO YOU THINK I AM?
I'M A LATE BLOOMER, AFTER ALL.
HM-HMMM!
I'M ONLY JUST GETTING STARTED! ALSO...
I MAY HAVE RETREATED FROM BEING WORSHIPPED...
...BUT 'TWOULD BE LOVELY INDEED TO HAVE A THICK BOOK OF TALES RECORDED ABOUT ME, OF COURSE.
HISO (PSST)

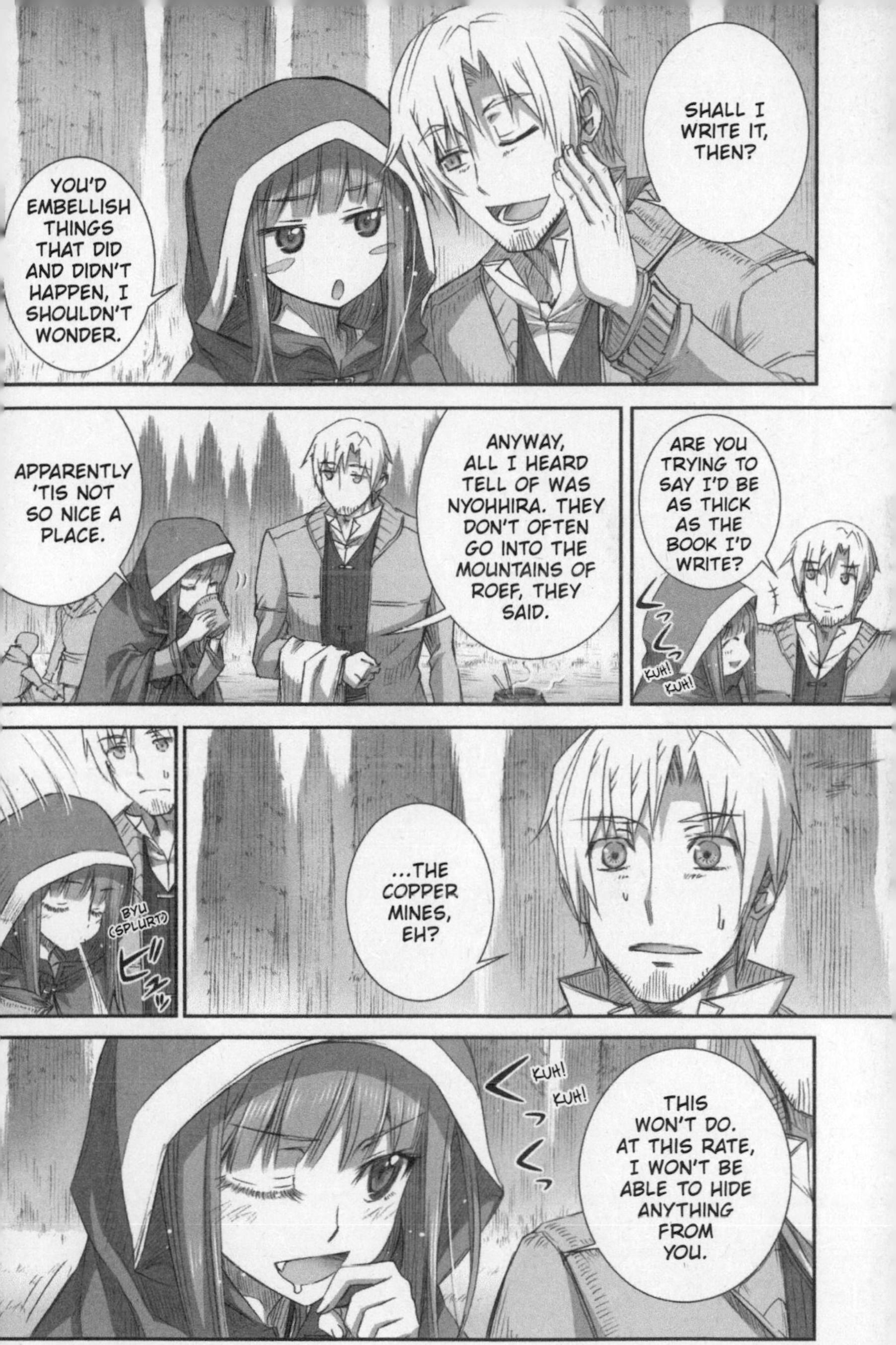
SHALL I WRITE IT, THEN?
YOU'D EMBELLISH THINGS THAT DID AND DIDN'T HAPPEN, I SHOULDN'T WONDER.
ARE YOU TRYING TO SAY I'D BE AS THICK AS THE BOOK I'D WRITE?
KUH! KUH!
ANYWAY, ALL I HEARD TELL OF WAS NYOHHIRA. THEY DON'T OFTEN GO INTO THE MOUNTAINS OF ROEF, THEY SAID.
APPARENTLY 'TIS NOT SO NICE A PLACE.
...THE COPPER MINES, EH?
BYU (SPLURT)
THIS WON'T DO. AT THIS RATE, I WON'T BE ABLE TO HIDE ANYTHING FROM YOU.
KUH! KUH!

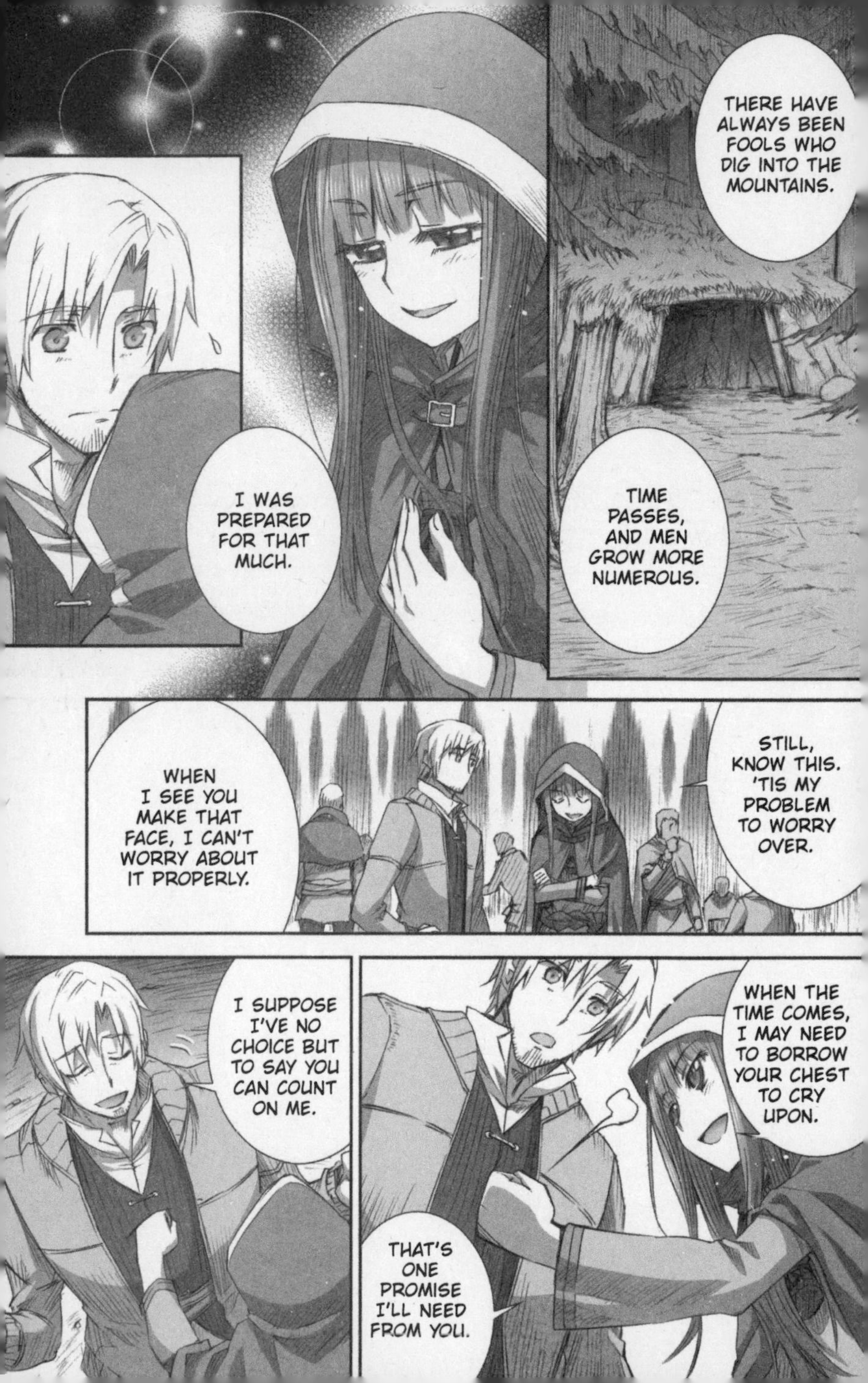
THERE HAVE ALWAYS BEEN FOOLS WHO DIG INTO THE MOUNTAINS.
TIME PASSES, AND MEN GROW MORE NUMEROUS.
I WAS PREPARED FOR THAT MUCH.
STILL, KNOW THIS. 'TIS MY PROBLEM TO WORRY OVER.
WHEN I SEE YOU MAKE THAT FACE, I CAN'T WORRY ABOUT IT PROPERLY.
WHEN THE TIME COMES, I MAY NEED TO BORROW YOUR CHEST TO CRY UPON.
THAT'S ONE PROMISE I'LL NEED FROM YOU.
I SUPPOSE I'VE NO CHOICE BUT TO SAY YOU CAN COUNT ON ME.

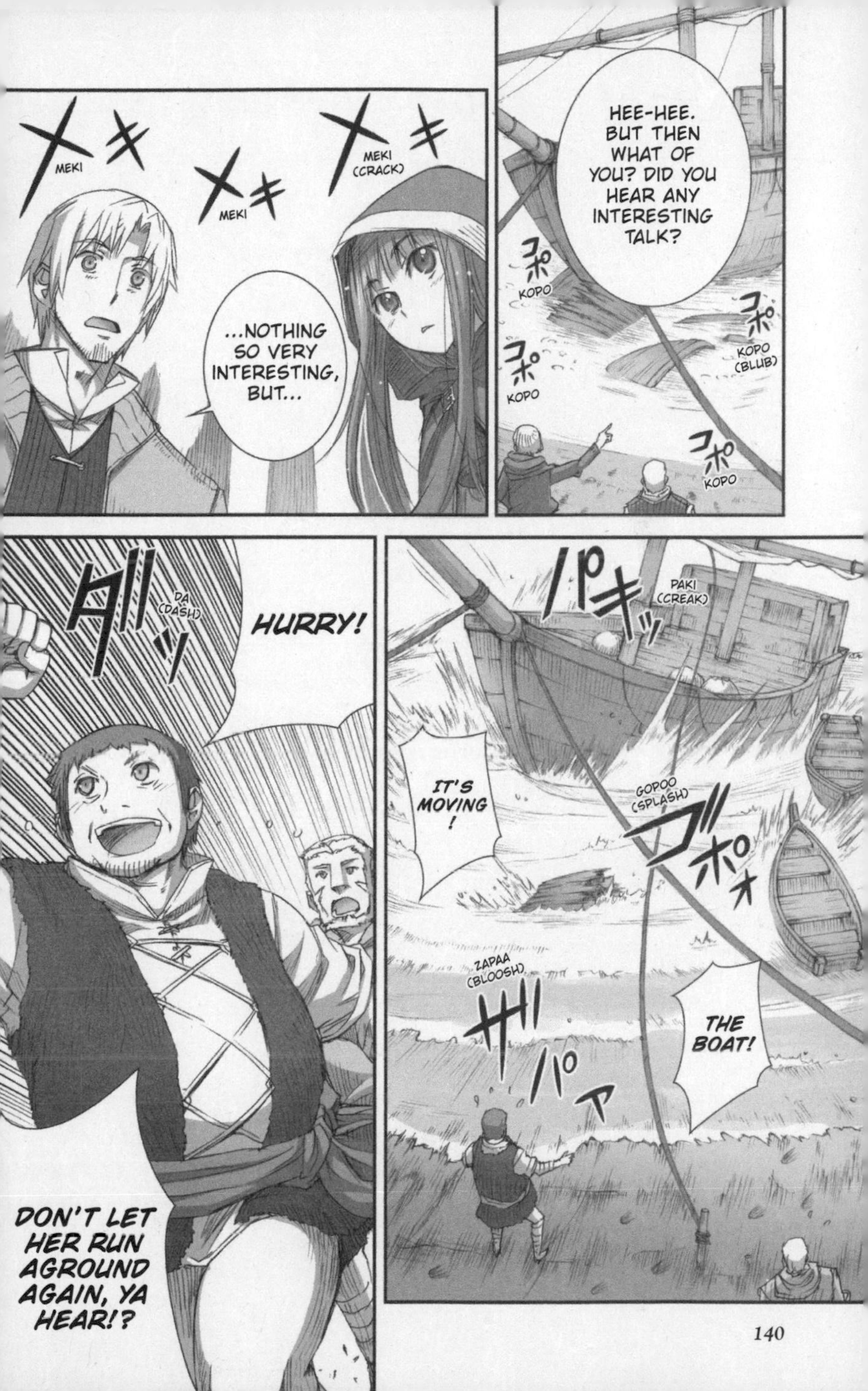
HEE-HEE. BUT THEN WHAT OF YOU? DID YOU HEAR ANY INTERESTING TALK?
KOPO (BLUB)
KOPO
KOPO
KOPO
MEKI (CRACK)
MEKI
MEKI
...NOTHING SO VERY INTERESTING, BUT...
PAKI (CREAK)
IT'S MOVING!
GOPOO (SPLASH)
THE BOAT!
ZAPAA (BLOOSH)
DA (DASH)
HURRY!
DON'T LET HER RUN AGROUND AGAIN, YA HEAR!?

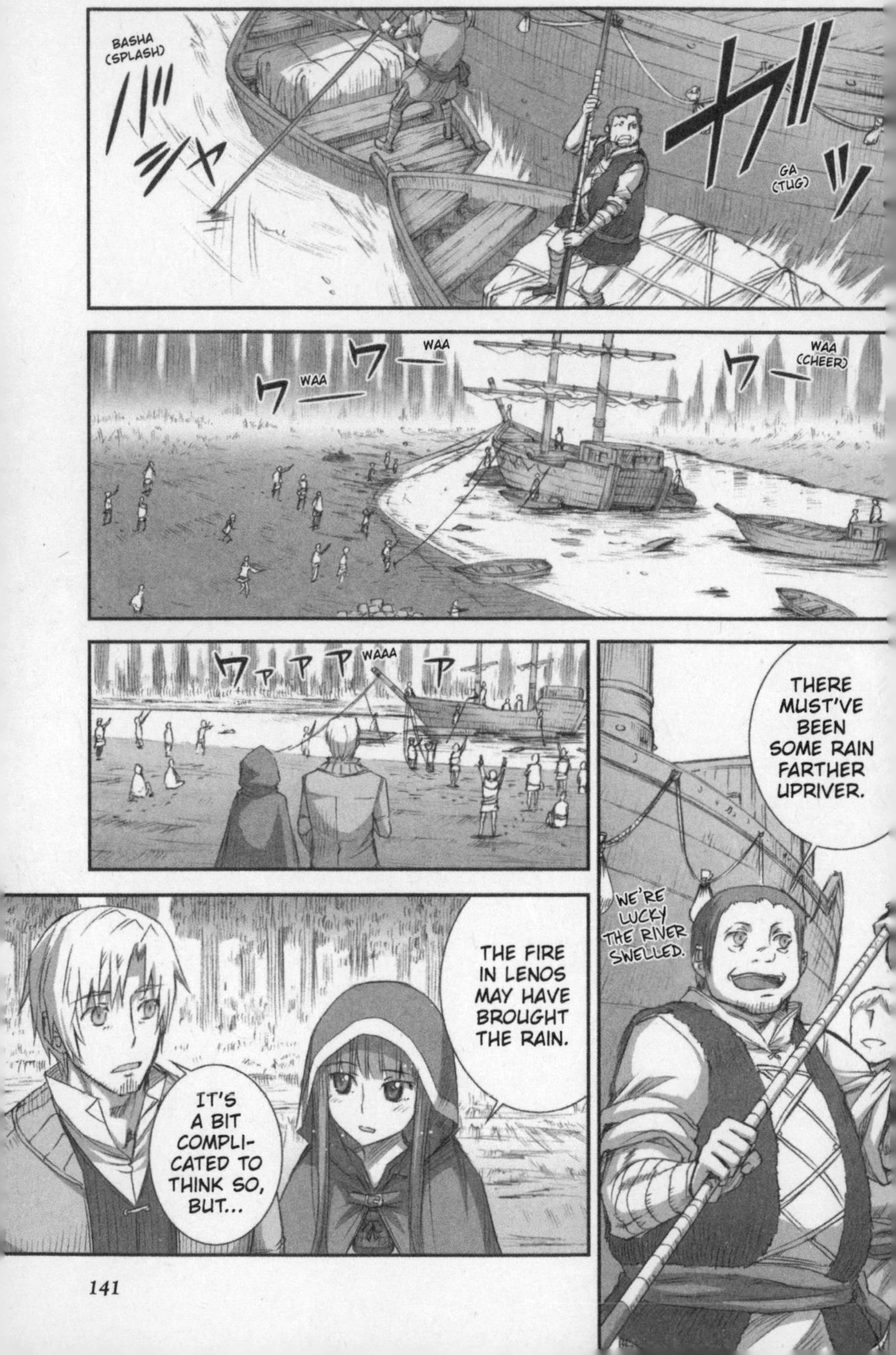
GA (TUG)
BASHA (SPLASH)
WAA (CHEER)
WAA
WAA
THERE MUST'VE BEEN SOME RAIN FARTHER UPRIVER.
WE'RE LUCKY THE RIVER SWELLED.
WAAA
THE FIRE IN LENOS MAY HAVE BROUGHT THE RAIN.
IT'S A BIT COMPLICATED TO THINK SO, BUT...

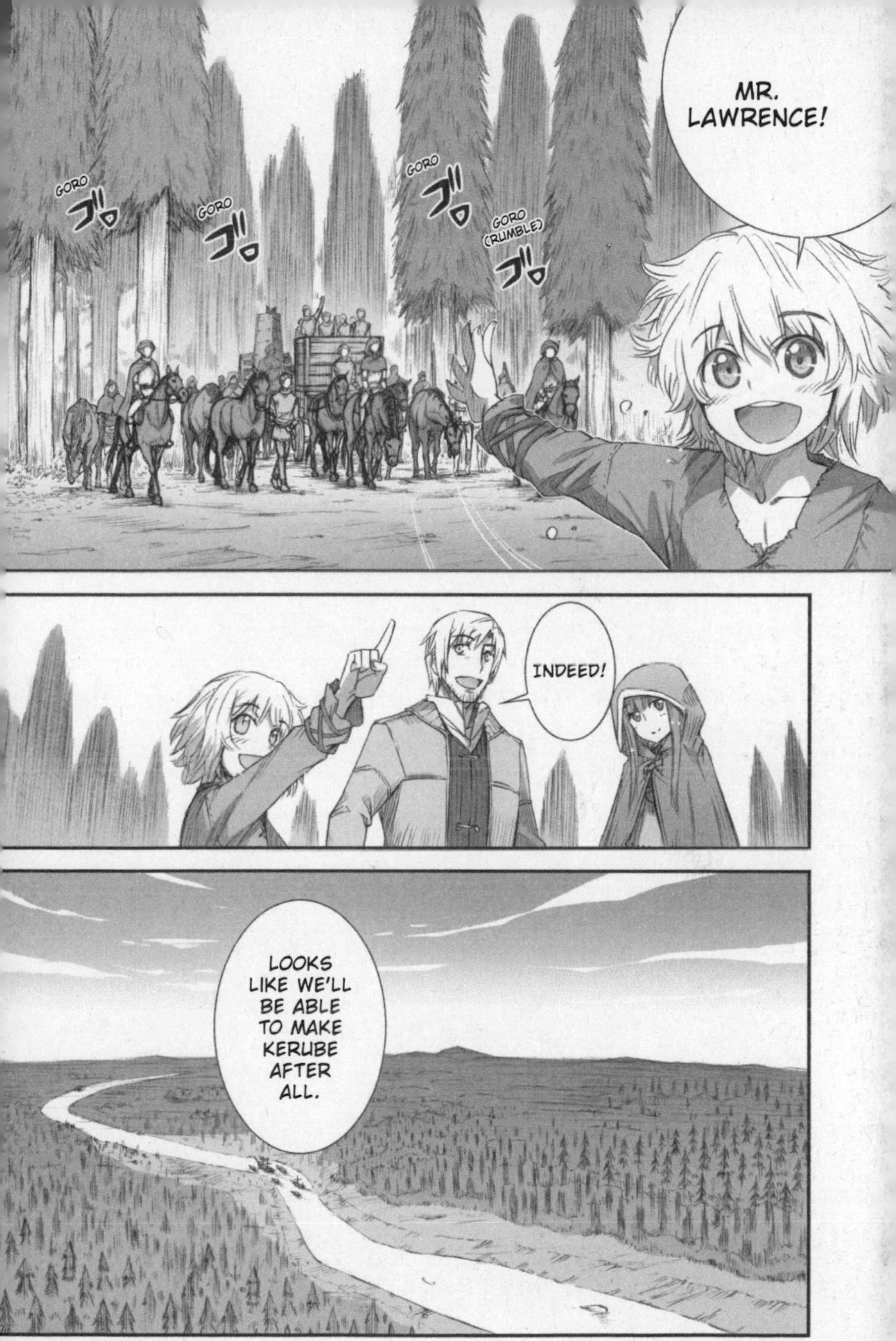
MR. LAWRENCE!
GORO (RUMBLE)
ゴロ
GORO
ゴロ
GORO
ゴロ
GORO
ゴロ
INDEED!
LOOKS LIKE WE'LL BE ABLE TO MAKE KERUBE AFTER ALL.

SPICE&WOLF

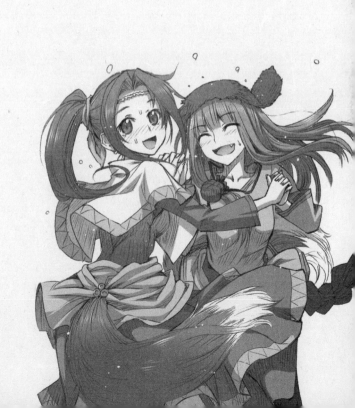

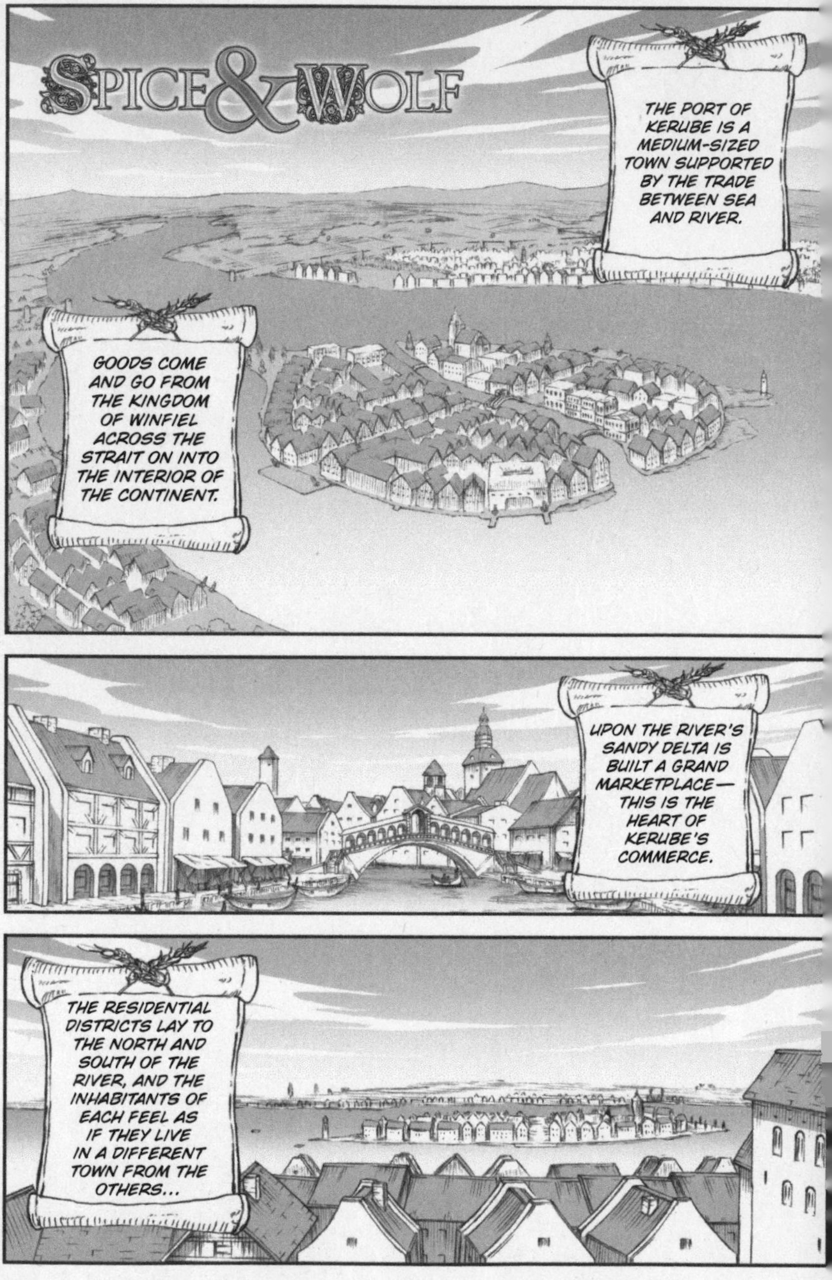
SPICE & WOLF
THE PORT OF KERUBE IS A MEDIUM-SIZED TOWN SUPPORTED BY THE TRADE BETWEEN SEA AND RIVER.
GOODS COME AND GO FROM THE KINGDOM OF WINFIEL ACROSS THE STRAIT ON INTO THE INTERIOR OF THE CONTINENT.
UPON THE RIVER'S SANDY DELTA IS BUILT A GRAND MARKETPLACE—THIS IS THE HEART OF KERUBE'S COMMERCE.
THE RESIDENTIAL DISTRICTS LAY TO THE NORTH AND SOUTH OF THE RIVER, AND THE INHABITANTS OF EACH FEEL AS IF THEY LIVE IN A DIFFERENT TOWN FROM THE OTHERS...

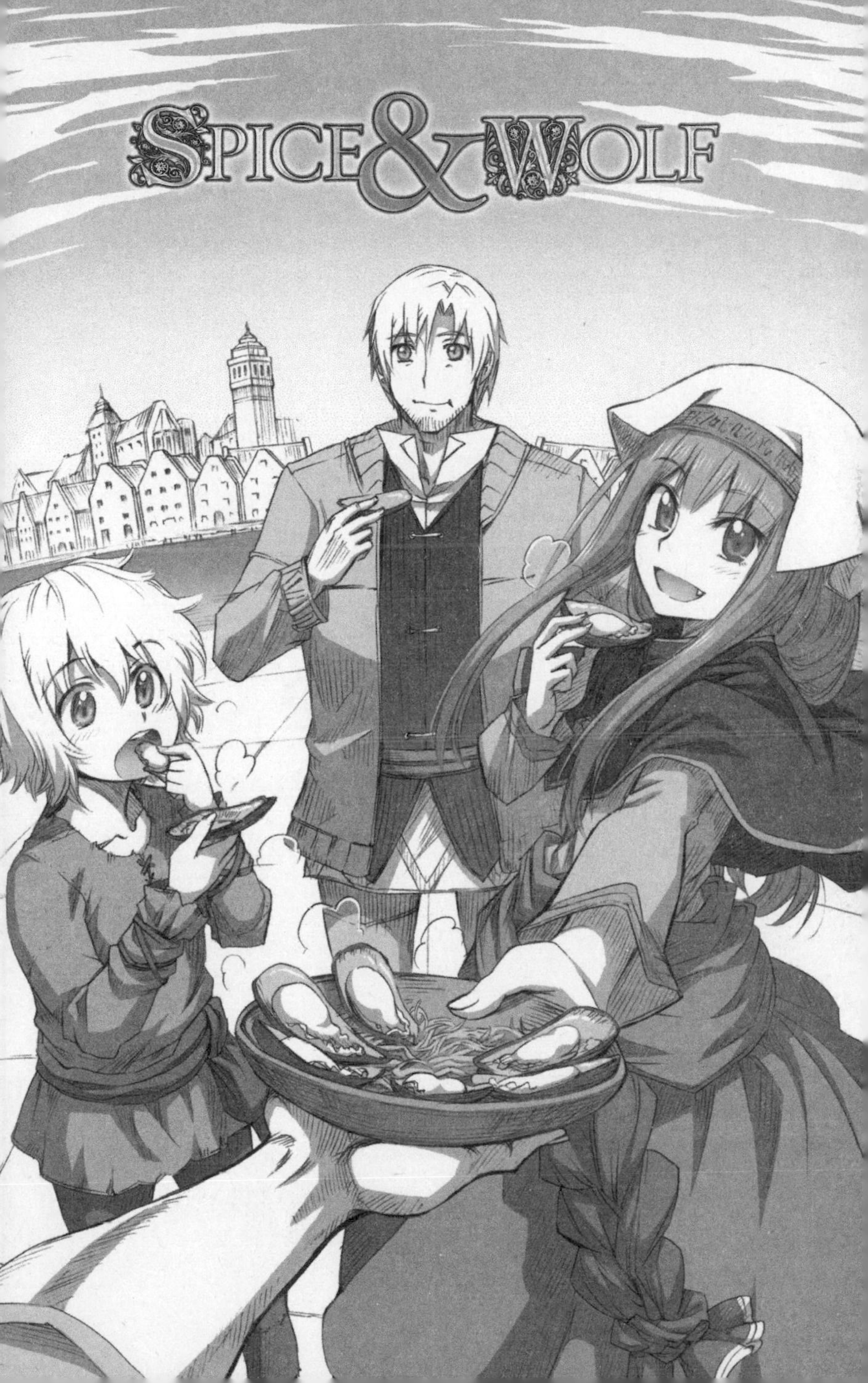
SPICE&WOLF

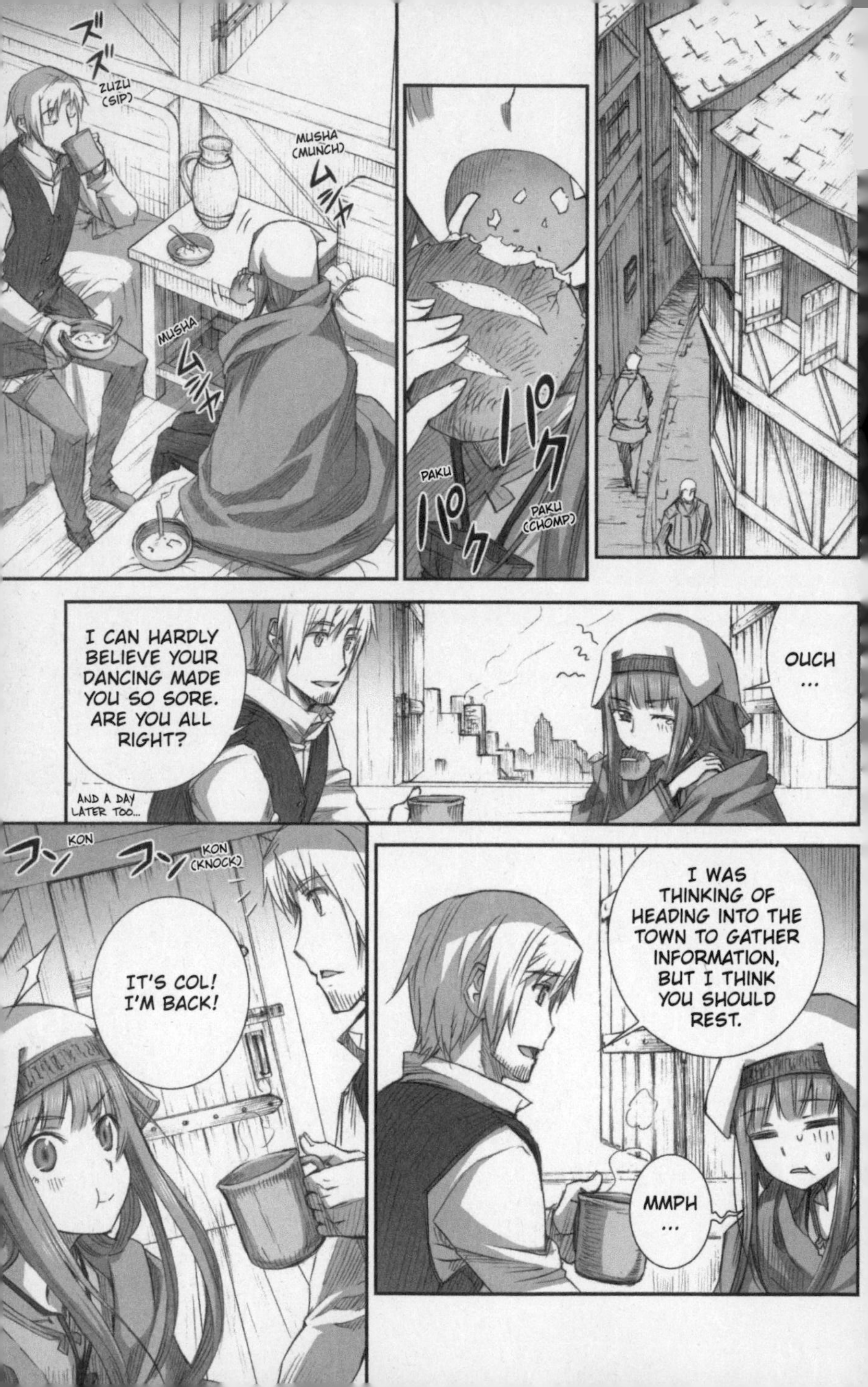
PAKU (CHOMP)
PAKU
MUSHA (MUNCH)
ZUZU (SIP)
MUSHA
OUCH ...
I CAN HARDLY BELIEVE YOUR DANCING MADE YOU SO SORE. ARE YOU ALL RIGHT?
AND A DAY LATER TOO...
I WAS THINKING OF HEADING INTO THE TOWN TO GATHER INFORMATION, BUT I THINK YOU SHOULD REST.
MMPH ...
KON
KON (KNOCK)
IT'S COL! I'M BACK!

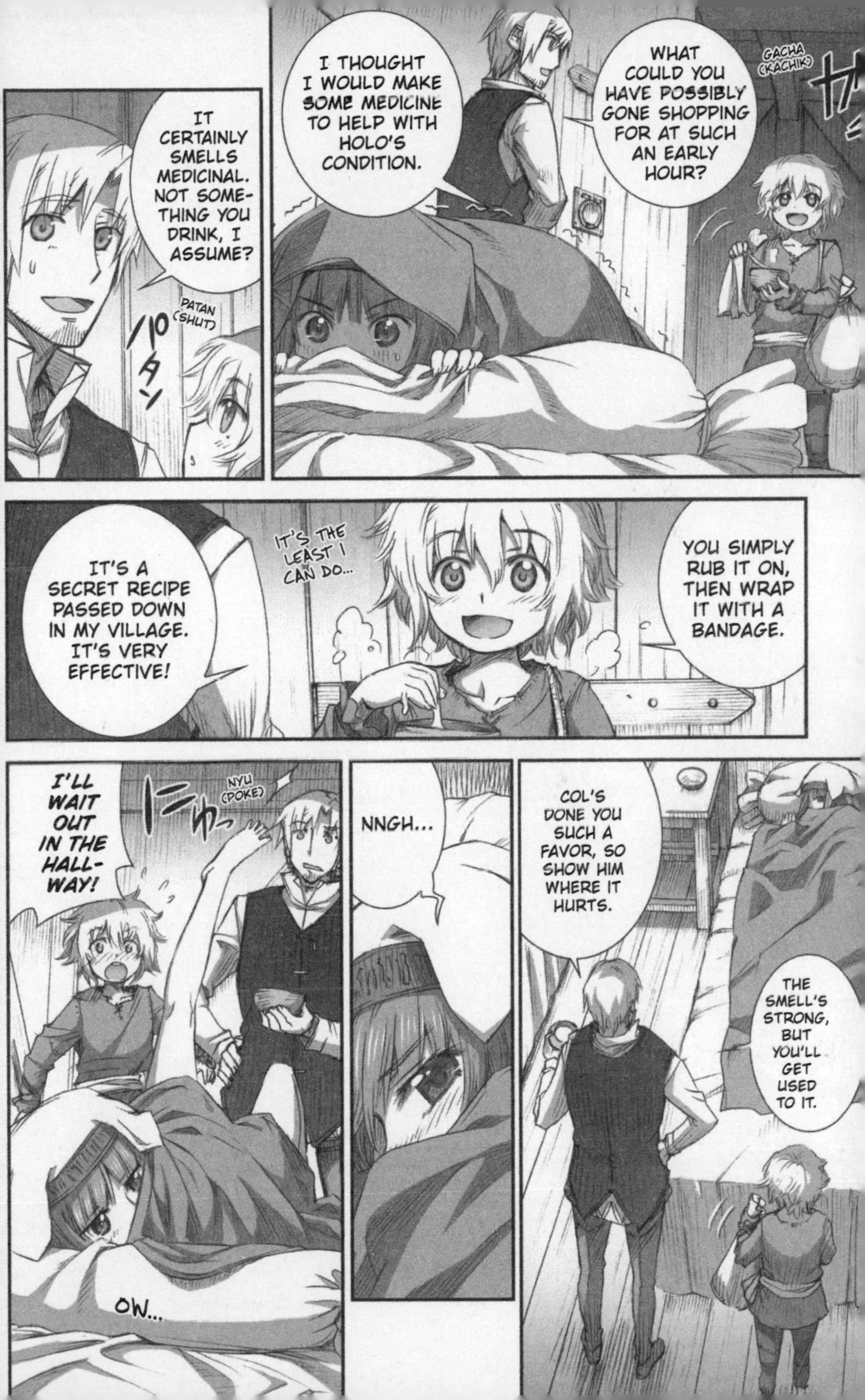
GACHA (KACHIK)
WHAT COULD YOU HAVE POSSIBLY GONE SHOPPING FOR AT SUCH AN EARLY HOUR?
I THOUGHT I WOULD MAKE SOME MEDICINE TO HELP WITH HOLO'S CONDITION.
IT CERTAINLY SMELLS MEDICINAL. NOT SOMETHING YOU DRINK, I ASSUME?
PATAN (SHUT)
YOU SIMPLY RUB IT ON, THEN WRAP IT WITH A BANDAGE.
IT'S THE LEAST I CAN DO...
IT'S A SECRET RECIPE PASSED DOWN IN MY VILLAGE. IT'S VERY EFFECTIVE!
COL'S DONE YOU SUCH A FAVOR, SO SHOW HIM WHERE IT HURTS.
THE SMELL'S STRONG, BUT YOU'LL GET USED TO IT.
NNGH...
NYU (POKE)
I'LL WAIT OUT IN THE HALLWAY!
OW...

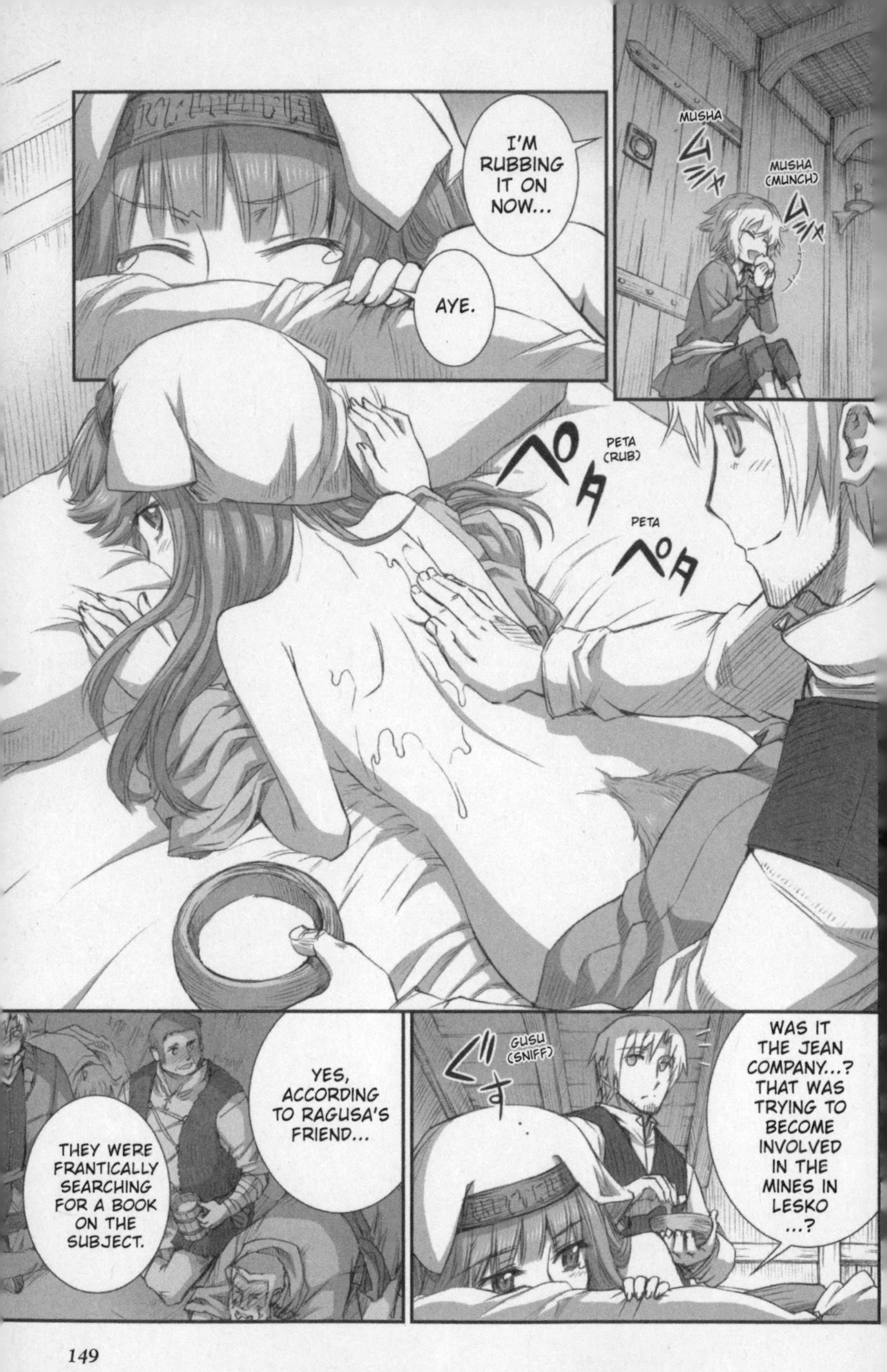
MUSHA
ムシャ
MUSHA (MUNCH)
ムシャ
I'M RUBBING IT ON NOW...
AYE.
ペタ
PETA (RUB)
ペタ
PETA
ぐす
GUSU (SNIFF)
WAS IT THE JEAN COMPANY...? THAT WAS TRYING TO BECOME INVOLVED IN THE MINES IN LESKO ...?
YES, ACCORDING TO RAGUSA'S FRIEND...
THEY WERE FRANTICALLY SEARCHING FOR A BOOK ON THE SUBJECT.

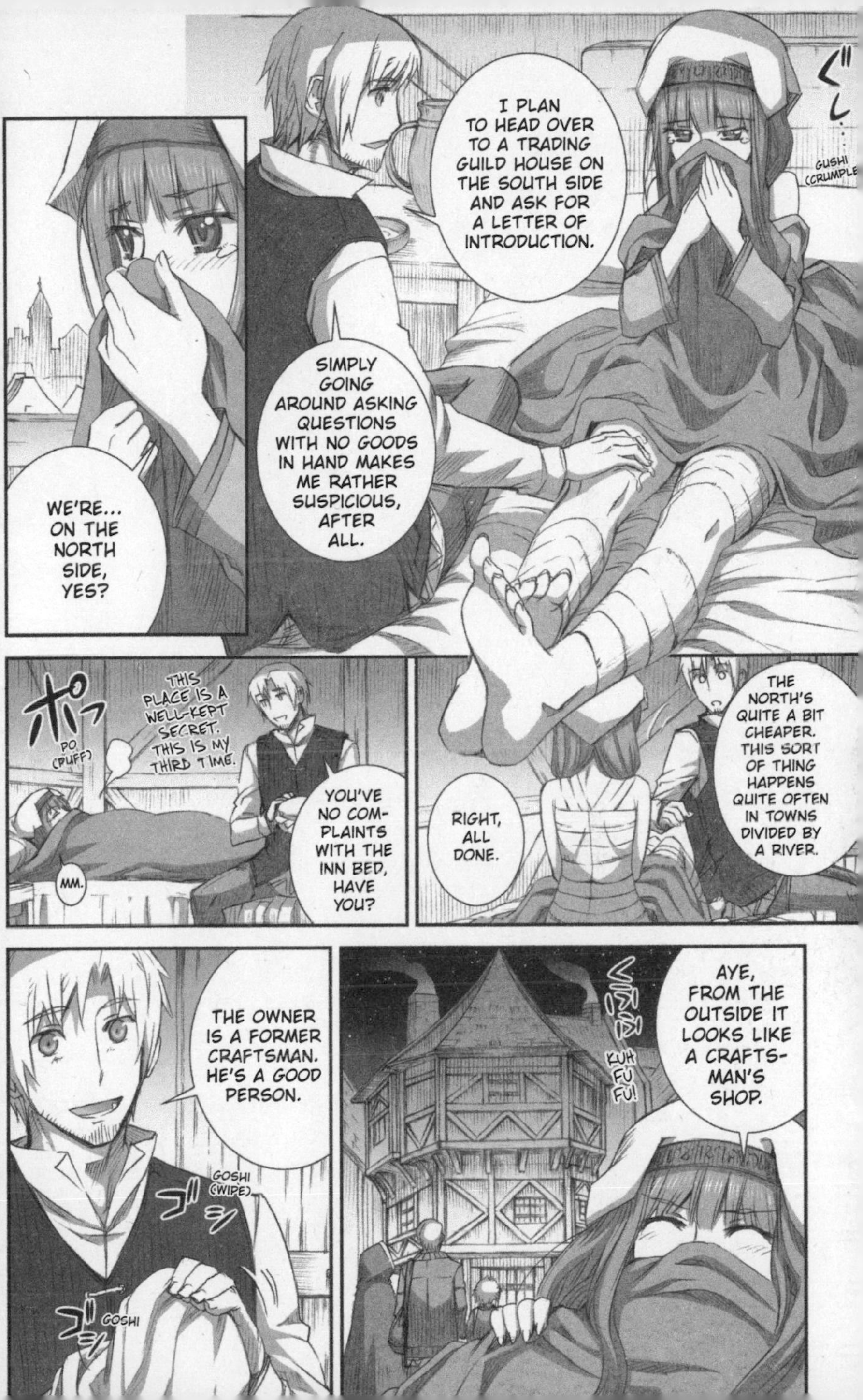
ぐし…
GUSHI (CRUMPLE)
I PLAN TO HEAD OVER TO A TRADING GUILD HOUSE ON THE SOUTH SIDE AND ASK FOR A LETTER OF INTRODUCTION.
SIMPLY GOING AROUND ASKING QUESTIONS WITH NO GOODS IN HAND MAKES ME RATHER SUSPICIOUS, AFTER ALL.
WE'RE... ON THE NORTH SIDE, YES?
THE NORTH'S QUITE A BIT CHEAPER. THIS SORT OF THING HAPPENS QUITE OFTEN IN TOWNS DIVIDED BY A RIVER.
RIGHT, ALL DONE.
ポッ
PO (PUFF)
THIS PLACE IS A WELL-KEPT SECRET. THIS IS MY THIRD TIME.
YOU'VE NO COMPLAINTS WITH THE INN BED, HAVE YOU?
MM.
くふふ
KUH FU FU!
AYE, FROM THE OUTSIDE IT LOOKS LIKE A CRAFTSMAN'S SHOP.
THE OWNER IS A FORMER CRAFTSMAN. HE'S A GOOD PERSON.
ゴシ
GOSHI (WIPE)
ゴシ
GOSHI

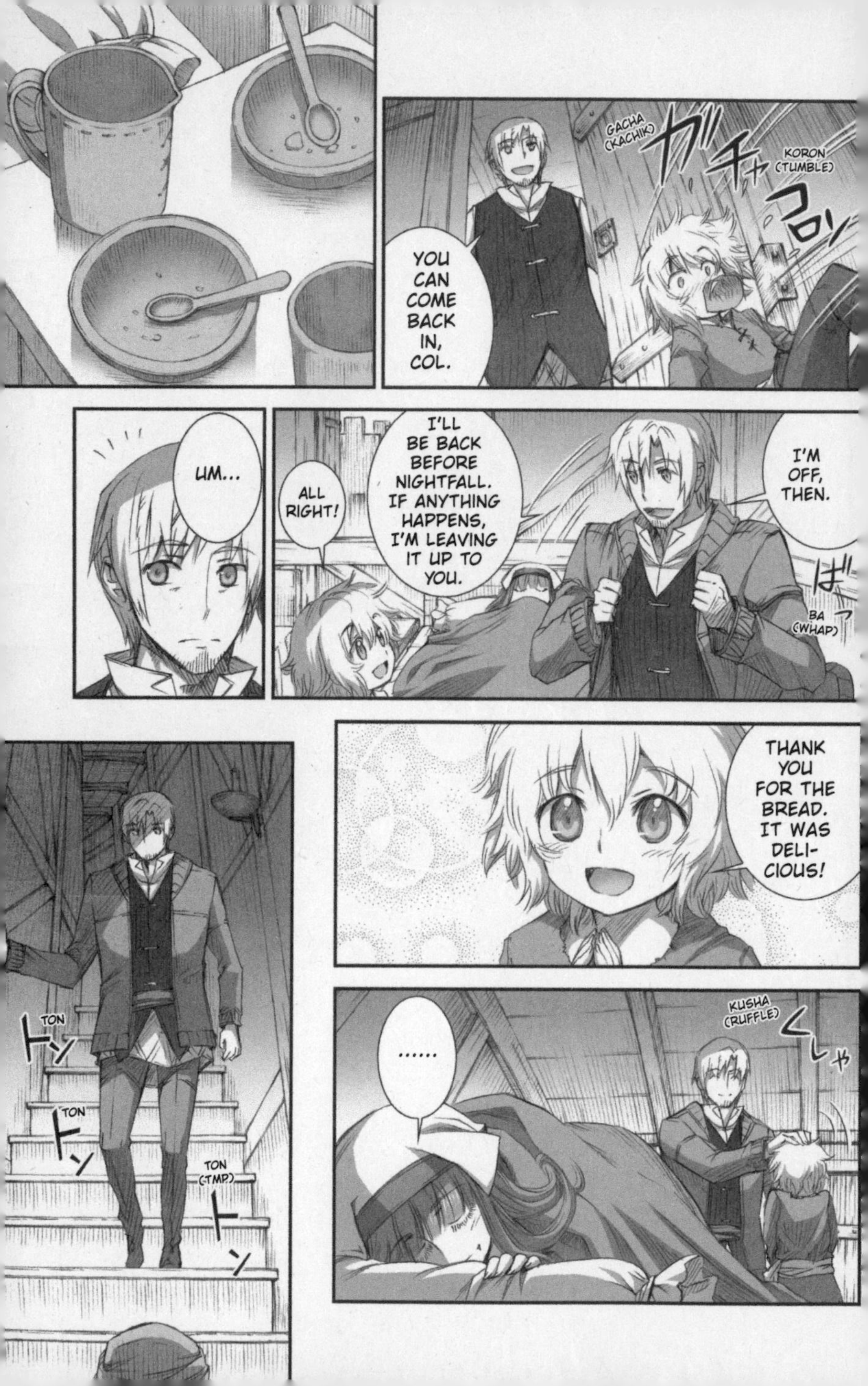

ガチャ
GACHA (KACHIK)
コロン
KORON (TUMBLE)
YOU CAN COME BACK IN, COL.
I'M OFF, THEN.
ばっ
BA (WHAP)
I'LL BE BACK BEFORE NIGHTFALL. IF ANYTHING HAPPENS, I'M LEAVING IT UP TO YOU.
ALL RIGHT!
UM...
THANK YOU FOR THE BREAD. IT WAS DELICIOUS!
くしゃ
KUSHA (RUFFLE)
....
トン
TON
トン
TON
トン
TON (TMP)

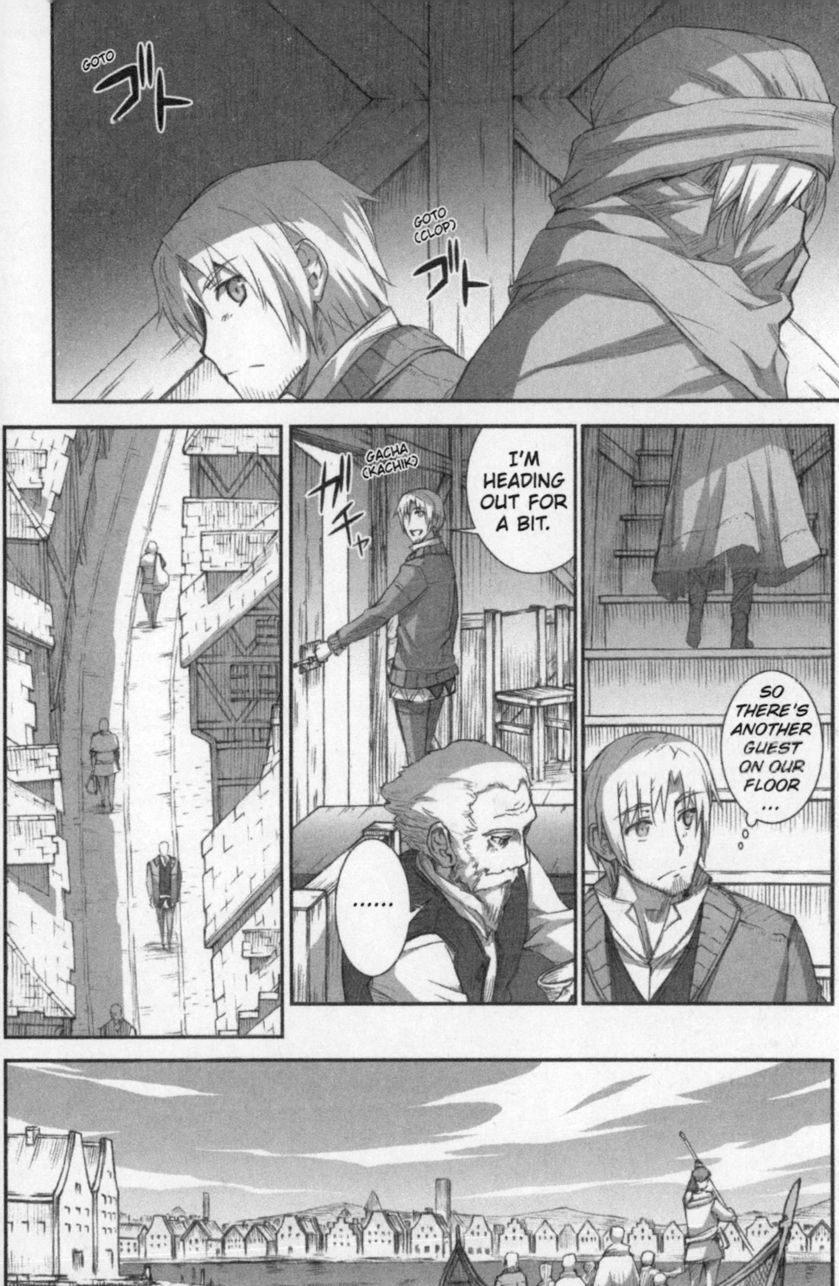
GOTO
GOTO (CLOP)
SO THERE'S ANOTHER GUEST ON OUR FLOOR ...
GACHA (KACHIK)
I'M HEADING OUT FOR A BIT.
......

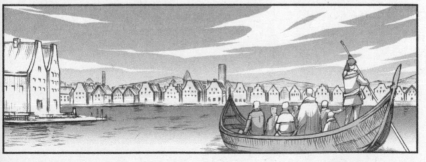

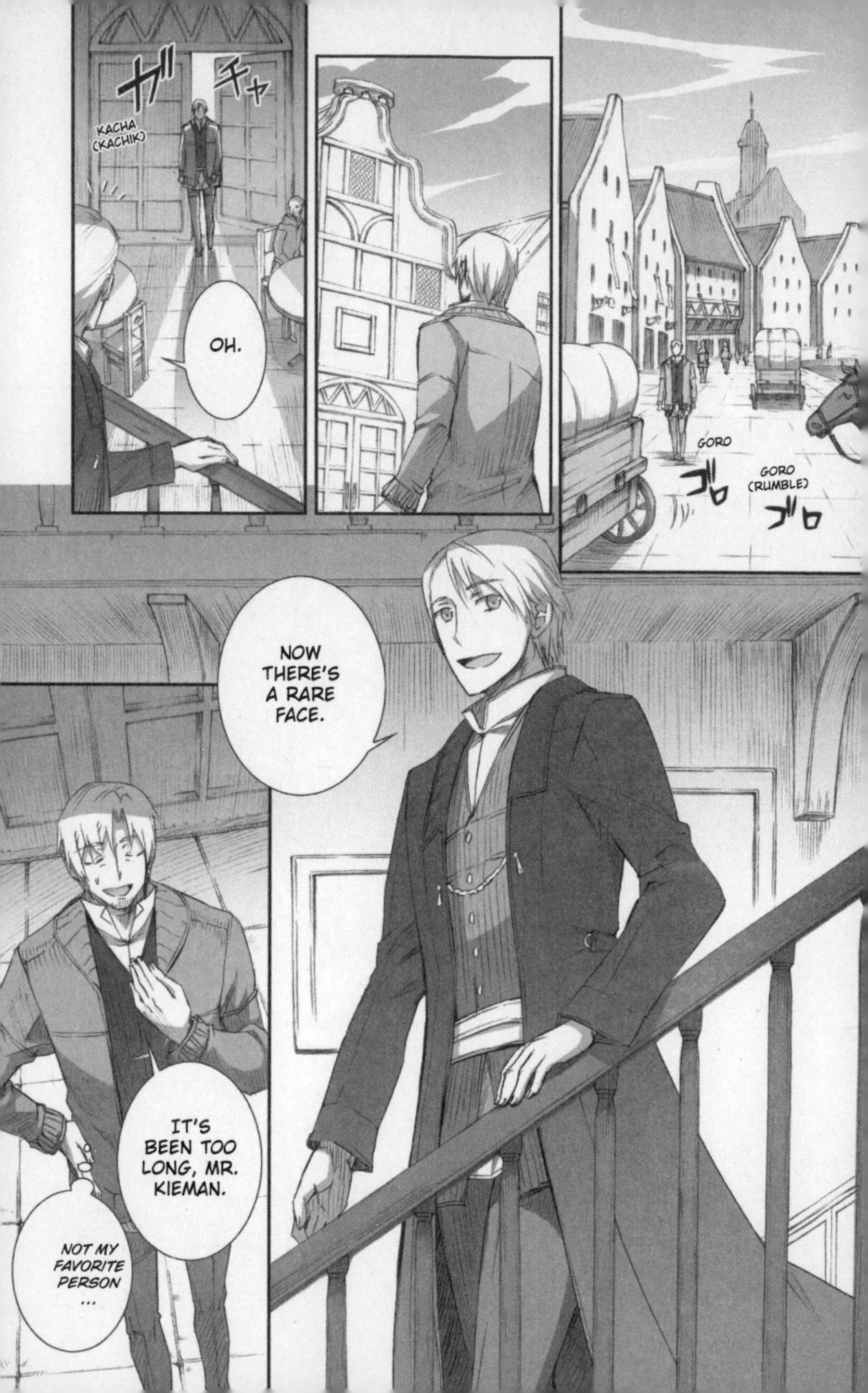

ゴロ
GORO
ゴロ
GORO (RUMBLE)
ガチャ
KACHA (KACHIK)
OH.
NOW THERE'S A RARE FACE.
IT'S BEEN TOO LONG, MR. KIEMAN.
NOT MY FAVORITE PERSON ...

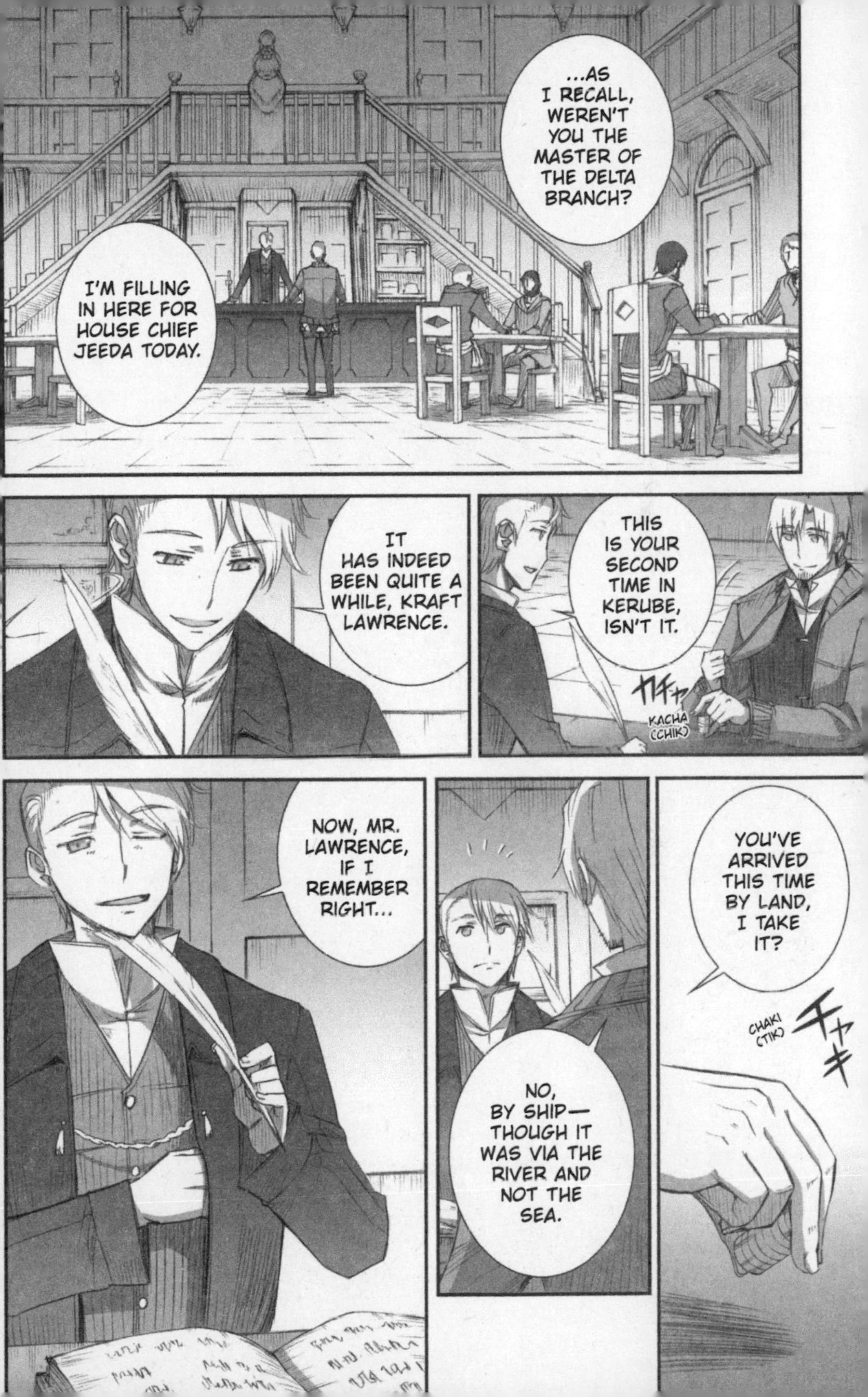
...AS I RECALL, WEREN'T YOU THE MASTER OF THE DELTA BRANCH?
I'M FILLING IN HERE FOR HOUSE CHIEF JEEDA TODAY.
THIS IS YOUR SECOND TIME IN KERUBE, ISN'T IT.
KACHA (CHIK)
IT HAS INDEED BEEN QUITE A WHILE, KRAFT LAWRENCE.
YOU'VE ARRIVED THIS TIME BY LAND, I TAKE IT?
CHAKI (TIK)
NO, BY SHIP— THOUGH IT WAS VIA THE RIVER AND NOT THE SEA.
NOW, MR. LAWRENCE, IF I REMEMBER RIGHT...

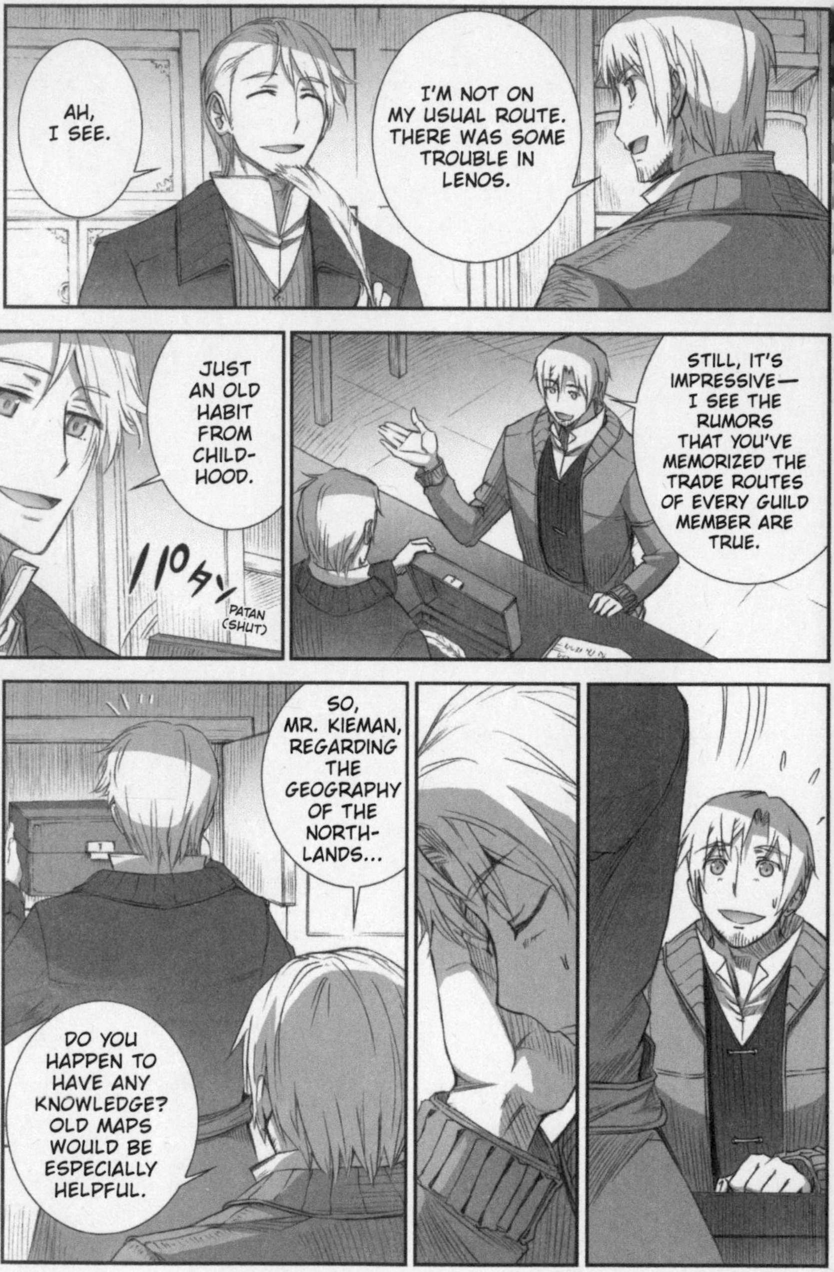
I'M NOT ON MY USUAL ROUTE. THERE WAS SOME TROUBLE IN LENOS.
AH, I SEE.
STILL, IT'S IMPRESSIVE— I SEE THE RUMORS THAT YOU'VE MEMORIZED THE TRADE ROUTES OF EVERY GUILD MEMBER ARE TRUE.
JUST AN OLD HABIT FROM CHILD-HOOD.
PATAN (SHUT)
SO, MR. KIEMAN, REGARDING THE GEOGRAPHY OF THE NORTH-LANDS...
DO YOU HAPPEN TO HAVE ANY KNOWLEDGE? OLD MAPS WOULD BE ESPECIALLY HELPFUL.

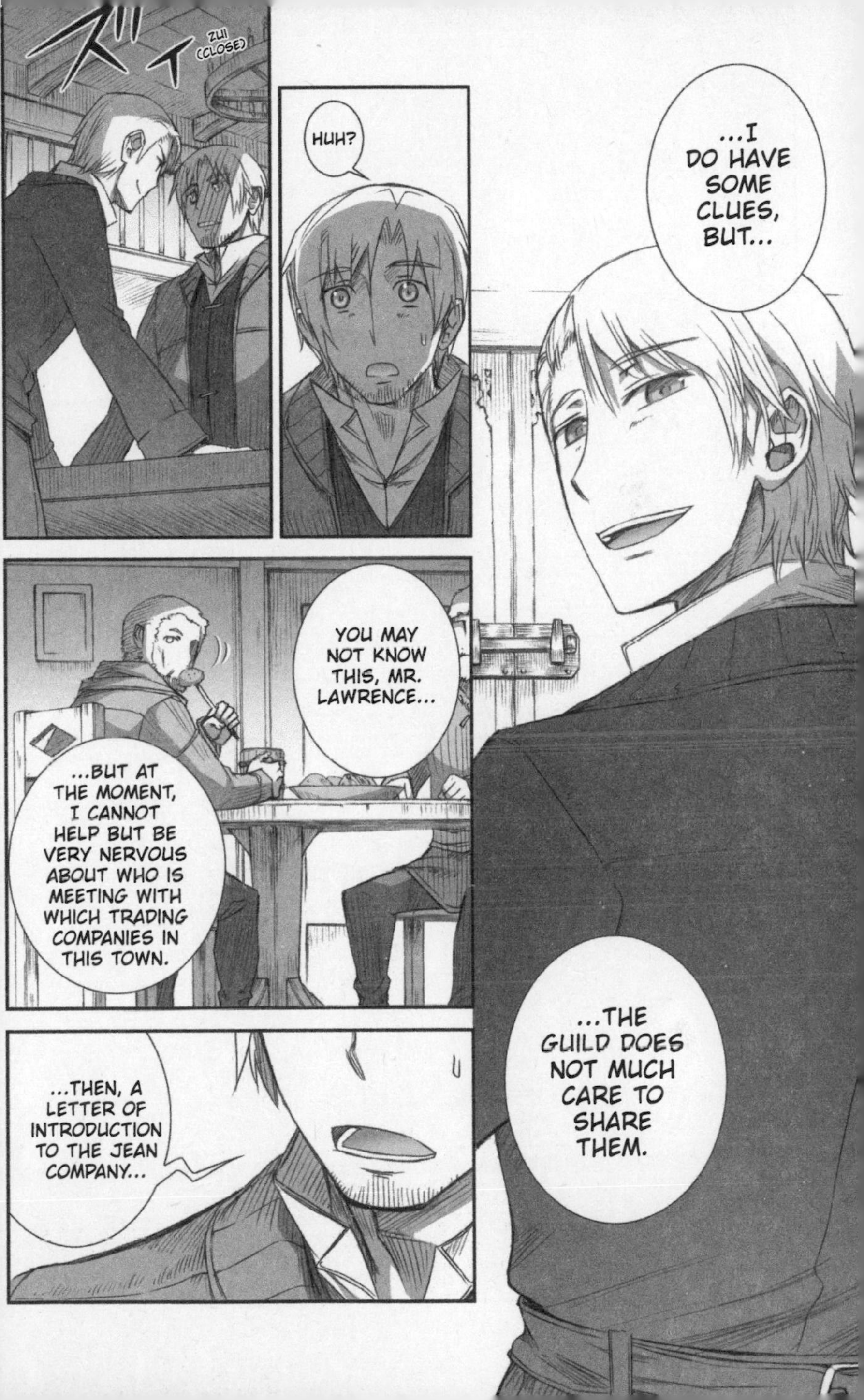
...I DO HAVE SOME CLUES, BUT...
...THE GUILD DOES NOT MUCH CARE TO SHARE THEM.
HUH?
ズイ
ZUI (CLOSE)
YOU MAY NOT KNOW THIS, MR. LAWRENCE...
...BUT AT THE MOMENT, I CANNOT HELP BUT BE VERY NERVOUS ABOUT WHO IS MEETING WITH WHICH TRADING COMPANIES IN THIS TOWN.
...THEN, A LETTER OF INTRODUCTION TO THE JEAN COMPANY...

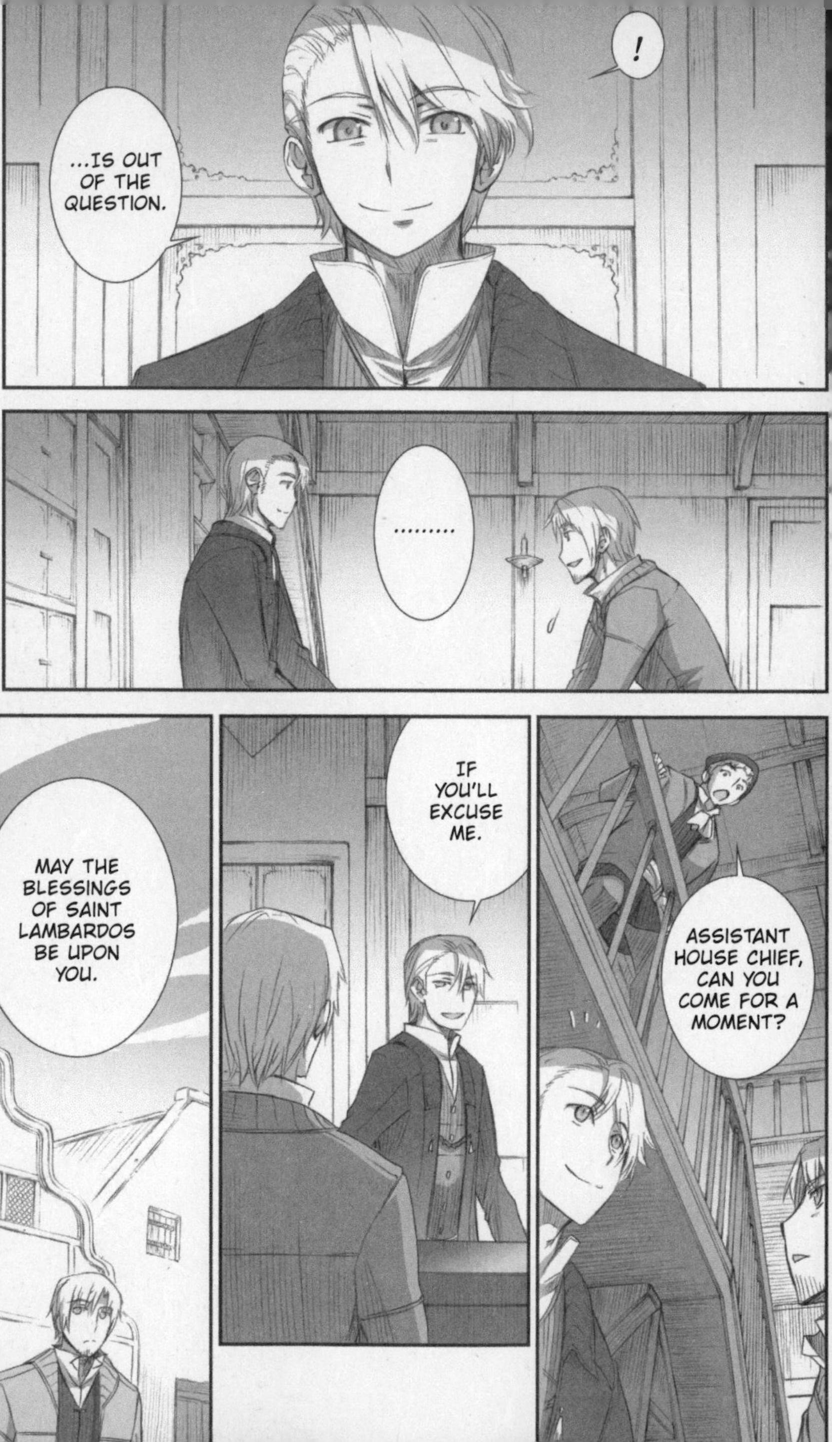
!
...IS OUT OF THE QUESTION.
....
ASSISTANT HOUSE CHIEF, CAN YOU COME FOR A MOMENT?
IF YOU'LL EXCUSE ME.
MAY THE BLESSINGS OF SAINT LAMBARDOS BE UPON YOU.

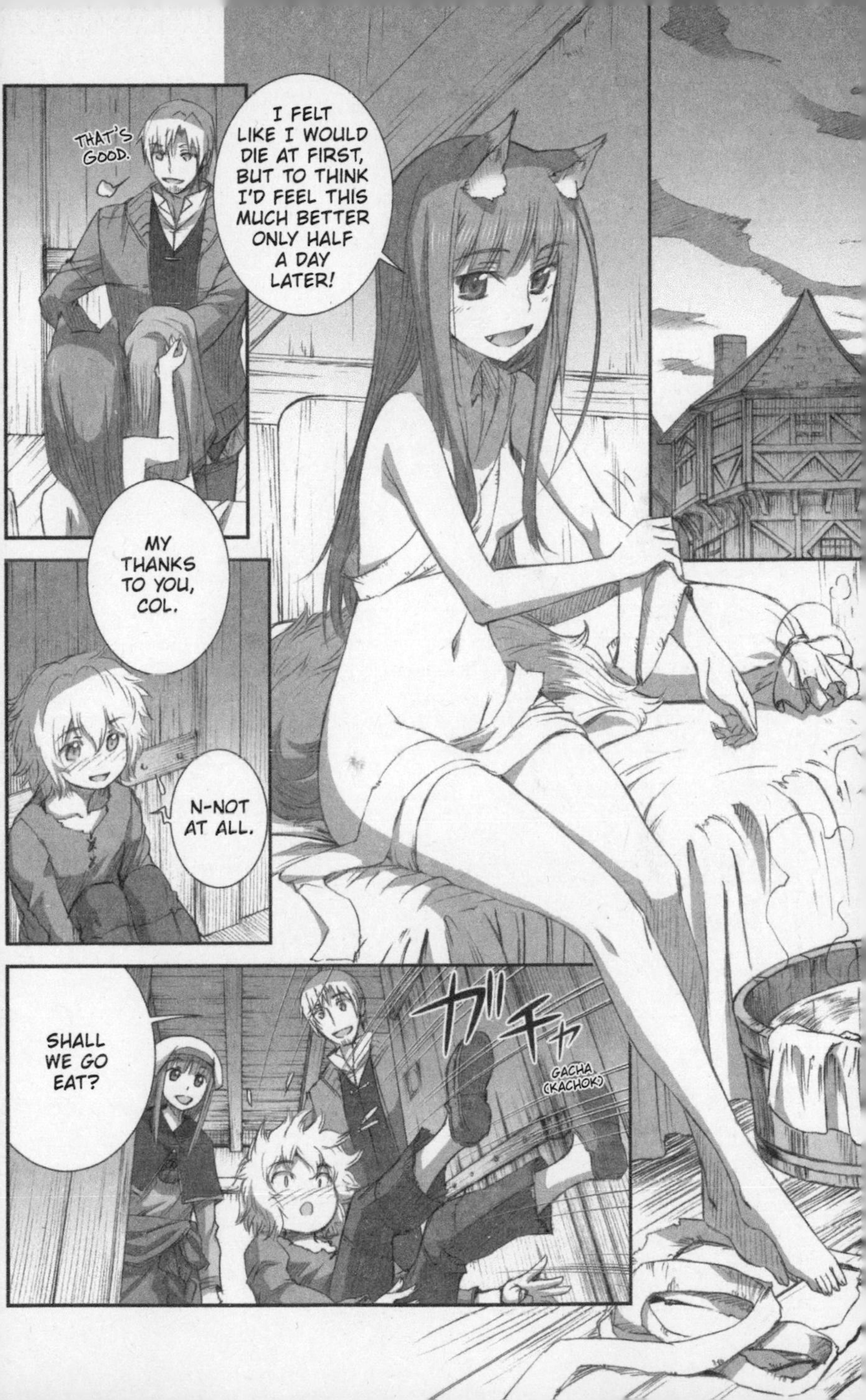
I FELT LIKE I WOULD DIE AT FIRST, BUT TO THINK I'D FEEL THIS MUCH BETTER ONLY HALF A DAY LATER!
THAT'S GOOD.
MY THANKS TO YOU, COL.
N-NOT AT ALL.
ガチャ
GACHA (KACHOK)
SHALL WE GO EAT?

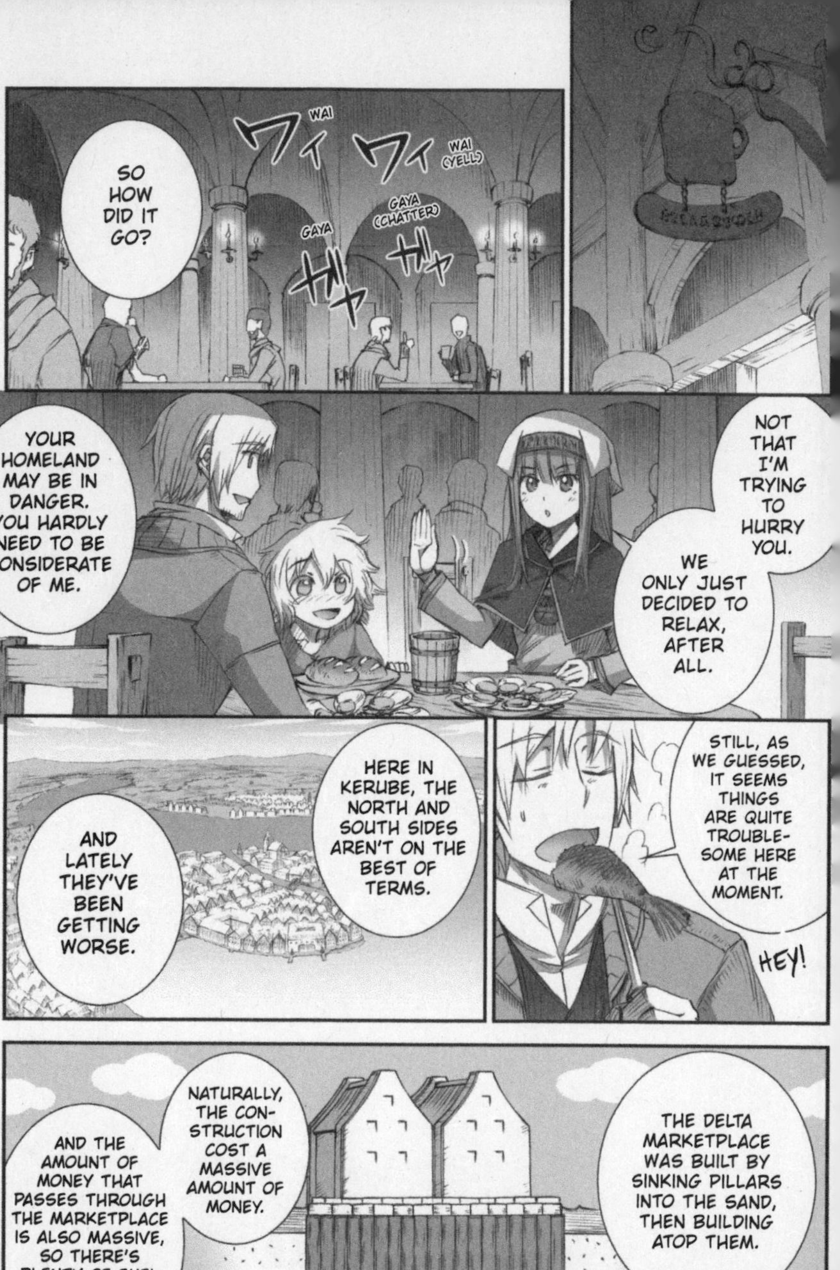
WAI (YELL)
WAI
GAYA (CHATTER)
GAYA
SO HOW DID IT GO?
NOT THAT I'M TRYING TO HURRY YOU.
WE ONLY JUST DECIDED TO RELAX, AFTER ALL.
YOUR HOMELAND MAY BE IN DANGER. YOU HARDLY NEED TO BE CONSIDERATE OF ME.
STILL, AS WE GUESSED, IT SEEMS THINGS ARE QUITE TROUBLE-SOME HERE AT THE MOMENT.
HEY!
HERE IN KERUBE, THE NORTH AND SOUTH SIDES AREN'T ON THE BEST OF TERMS.
AND LATELY THEY'VE BEEN GETTING WORSE.
THE DELTA MARKETPLACE WAS BUILT BY SINKING PILLARS INTO THE SAND, THEN BUILDING ATOP THEM.
NATURALLY, THE CON-STRUCTION COST A MASSIVE AMOUNT OF MONEY.
AND THE AMOUNT OF MONEY THAT PASSES THROUGH THE MARKETPLACE IS ALSO MASSIVE, SO THERE'S PLENTY OF FUEL FOR DISAGREE-MENT.

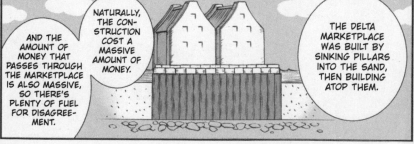

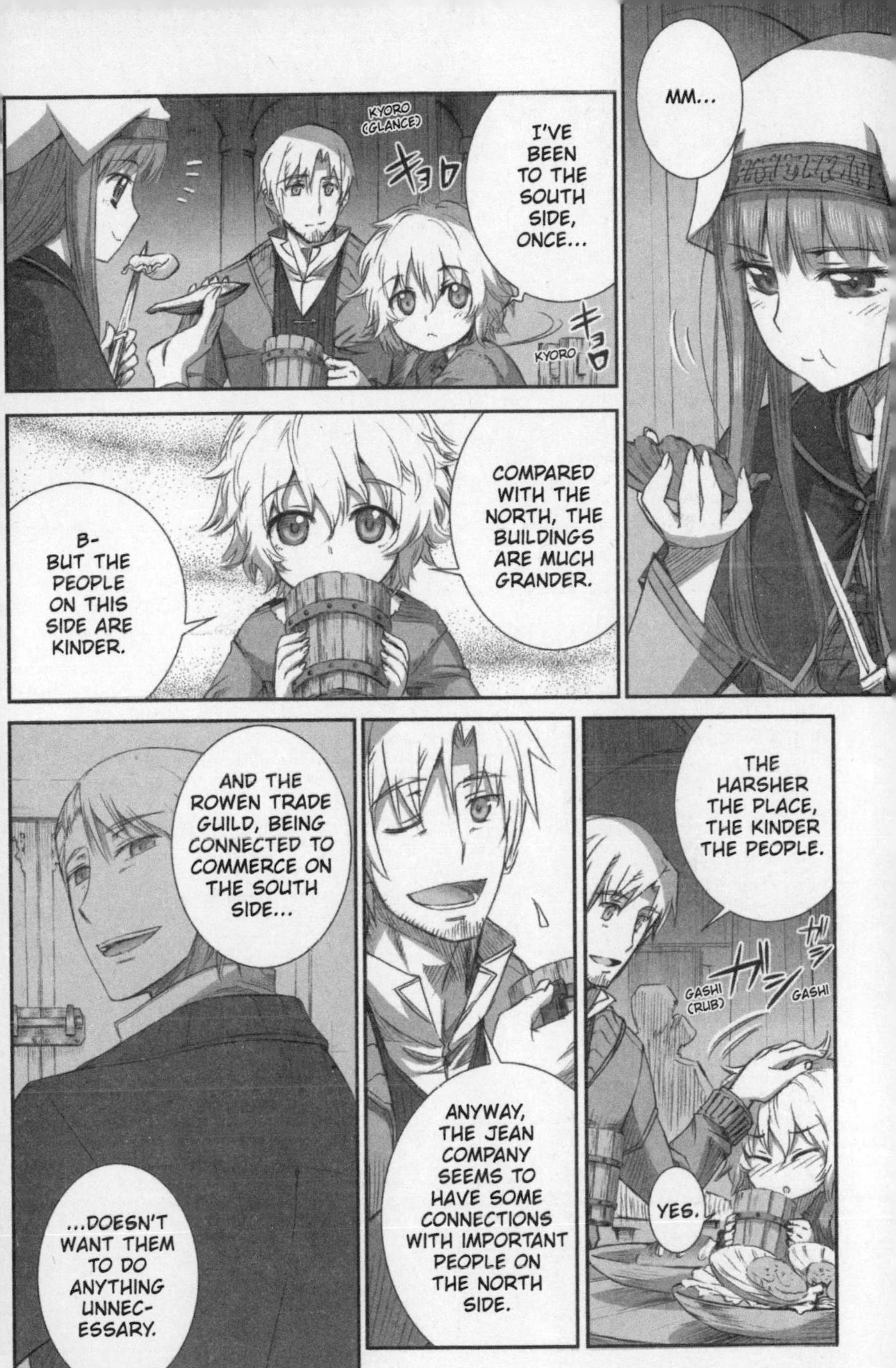
MM...
I'VE BEEN TO THE SOUTH SIDE, ONCE...
KYORO (GLANCE)
KYORO
COMPARED WITH THE NORTH, THE BUILDINGS ARE MUCH GRANDER.
B-BUT THE PEOPLE ON THIS SIDE ARE KINDER.
THE HARSHER THE PLACE, THE KINDER THE PEOPLE.
GASHI
GASHI (RUB)
YES.
ANYWAY, THE JEAN COMPANY SEEMS TO HAVE SOME CONNECTIONS WITH IMPORTANT PEOPLE ON THE NORTH SIDE.
AND THE ROWEN TRADE GUILD, BEING CONNECTED TO COMMERCE ON THE SOUTH SIDE...
...DOESN'T WANT THEM TO DO ANYTHING UNNEC-ESSARY.

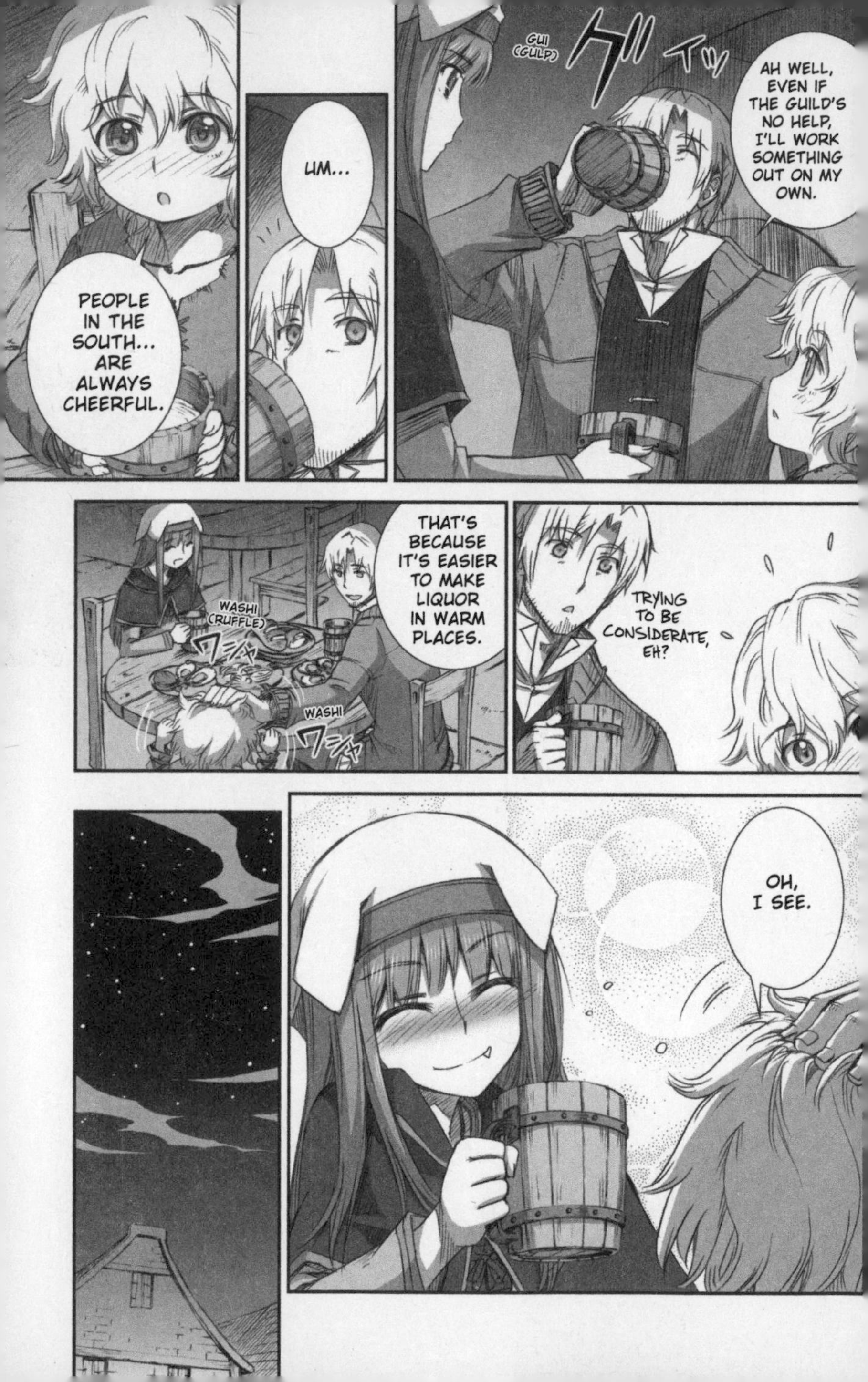
GUI (GULP)
AH WELL, EVEN IF THE GUILD'S NO HELP, I'LL WORK SOMETHING OUT ON MY OWN.
UM...
PEOPLE IN THE SOUTH... ARE ALWAYS CHEERFUL.
TRYING TO BE CONSIDERATE, EH?
THAT'S BECAUSE IT'S EASIER TO MAKE LIQUOR IN WARM PLACES.
WASHI (RUFFLE)
WASHI
OH, I SEE.

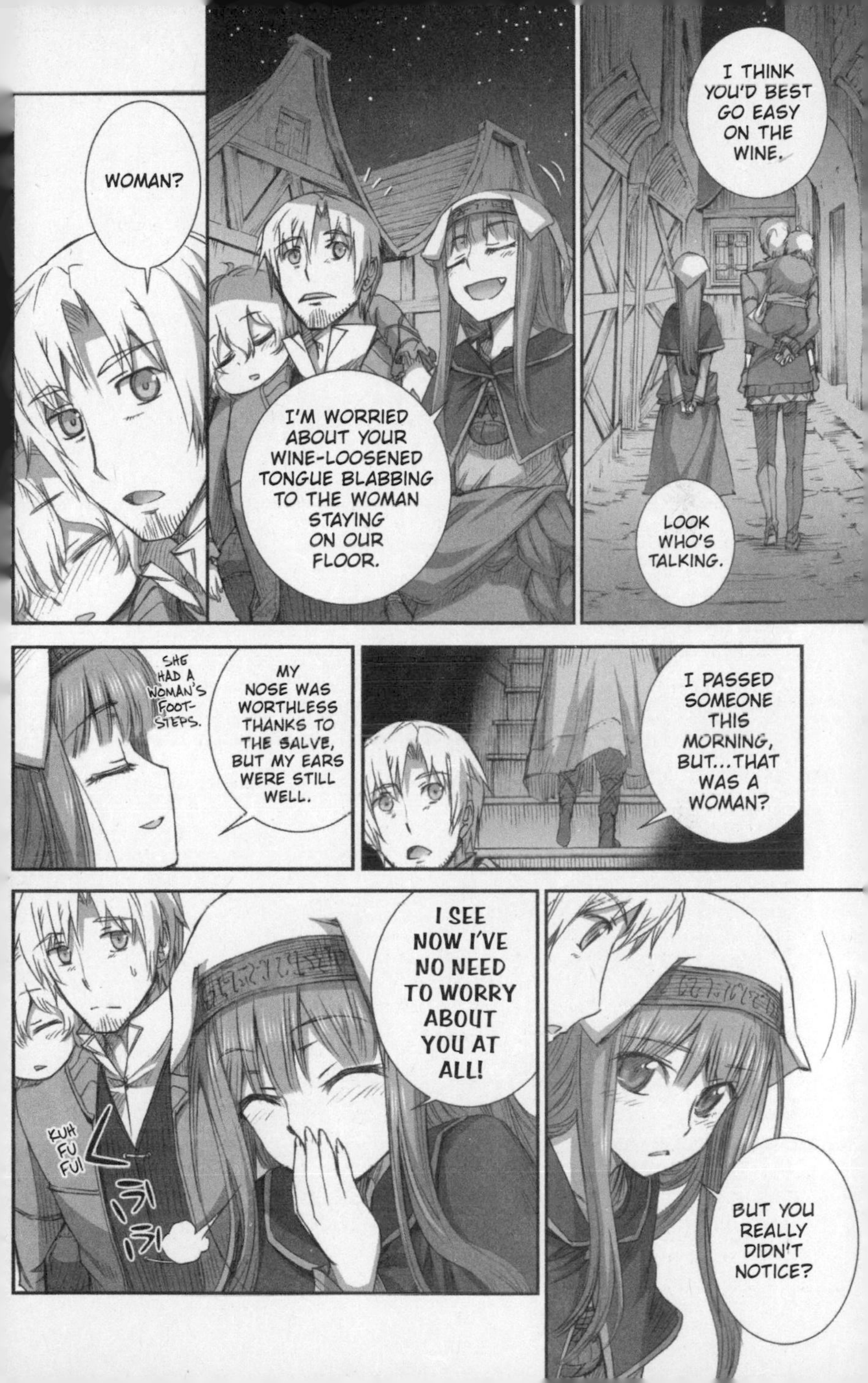
I THINK YOU'D BEST GO EASY ON THE WINE.
LOOK WHO'S TALKING.
I'M WORRIED ABOUT YOUR WINE-LOOSENED TONGUE BLABBING TO THE WOMAN STAYING ON OUR FLOOR.
WOMAN?
I PASSED SOMEONE THIS MORNING, BUT...THAT WAS A WOMAN?
MY NOSE WAS WORTHLESS THANKS TO THE SALVE, BUT MY EARS WERE STILL WELL.
SHE HAD A WOMAN'S FOOT-STEPS.
BUT YOU REALLY DIDN'T NOTICE?
I SEE NOW I'VE NO NEED TO WORRY ABOUT YOU AT ALL!
KUH FU FU!

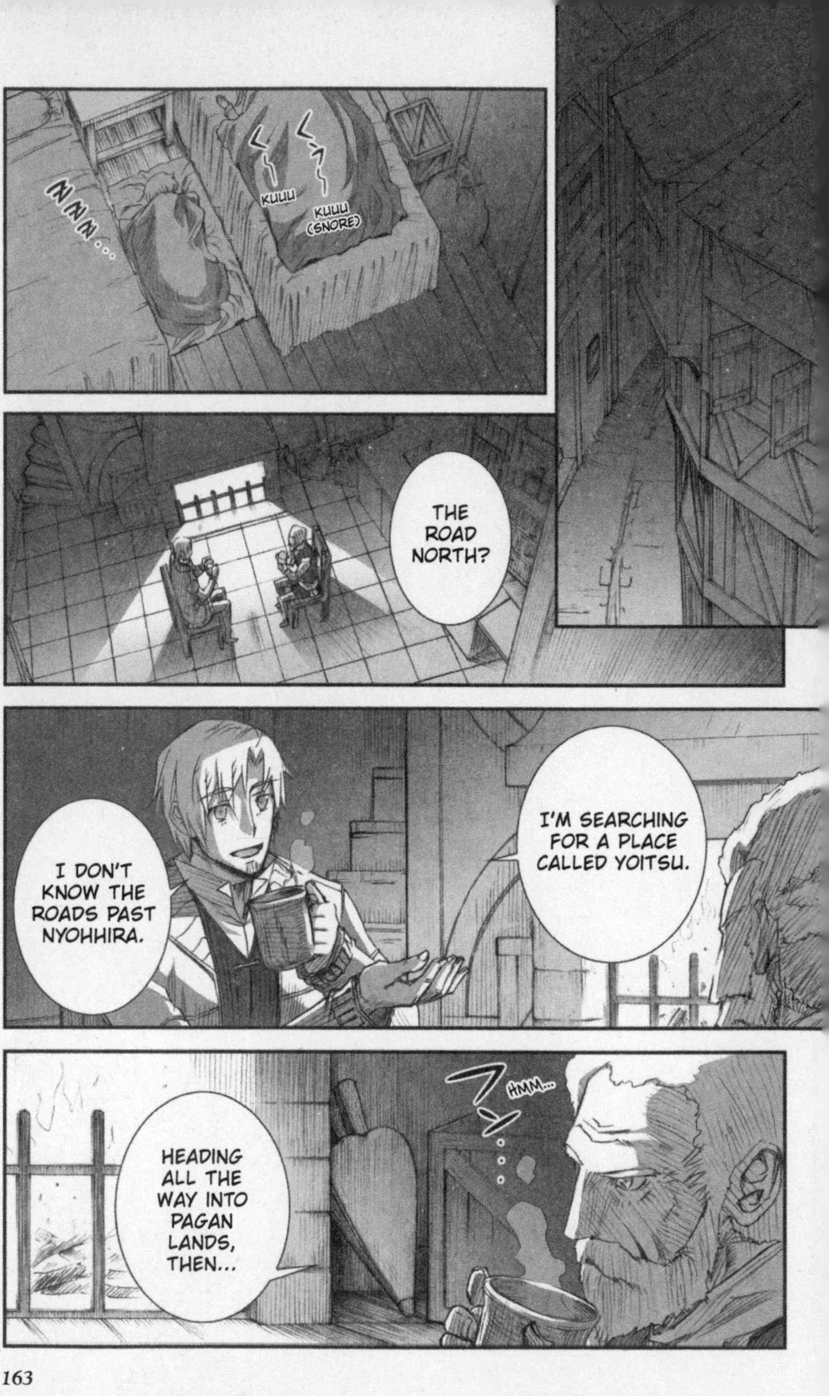
KUUU
KUUU (SNORE)
ZZZ...
THE ROAD NORTH?
I'M SEARCHING FOR A PLACE CALLED YOITSU.
I DON'T KNOW THE ROADS PAST NYOHHIRA.
HMM...
HEADING ALL THE WAY INTO PAGAN LANDS, THEN...

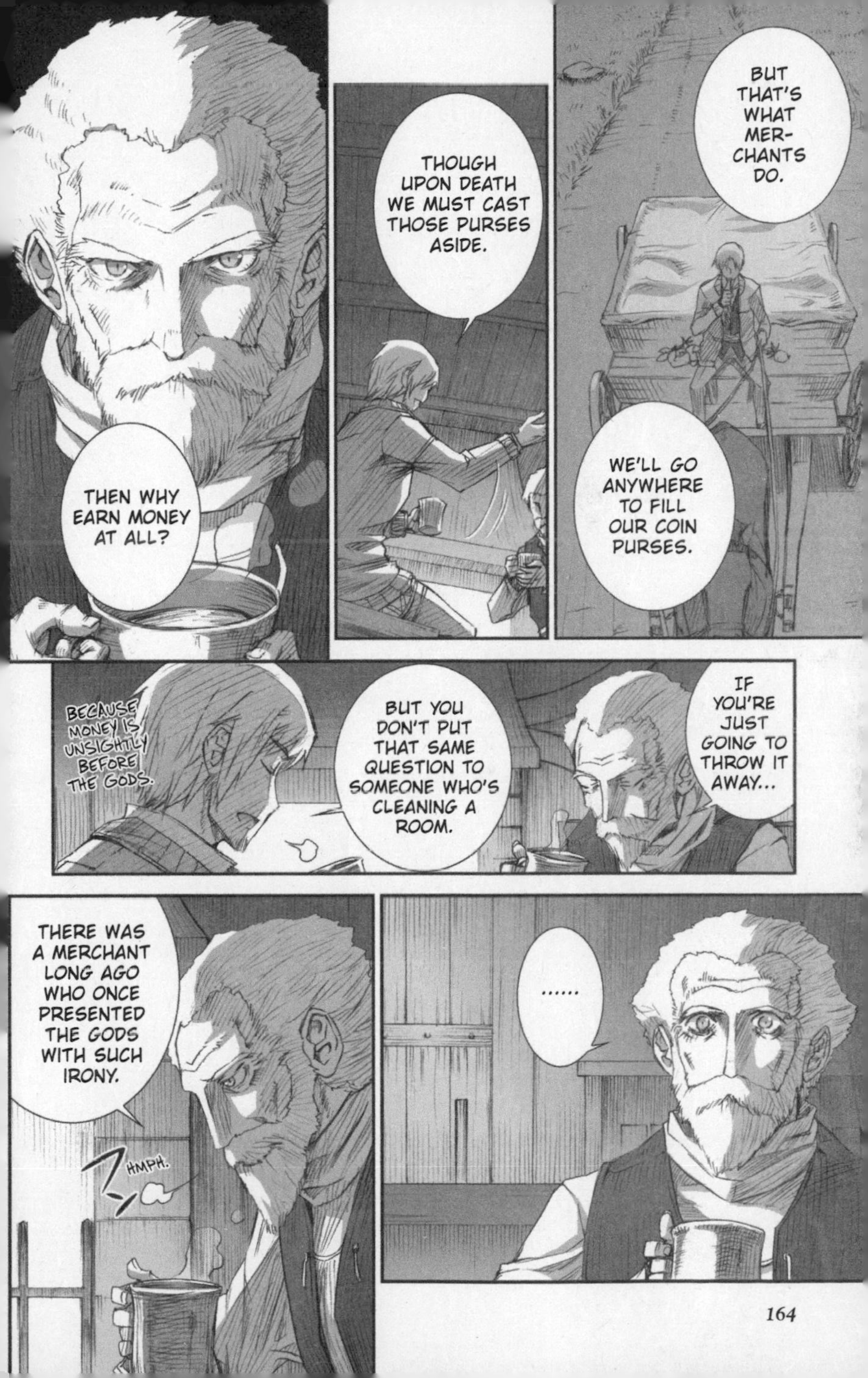
BUT THAT'S WHAT MER-CHANTS DO.
WE'LL GO ANYWHERE TO FILL OUR COIN PURSES.
THOUGH UPON DEATH WE MUST CAST THOSE PURSES ASIDE.
THEN WHY EARN MONEY AT ALL?
IF YOU'RE JUST GOING TO THROW IT AWAY...
BUT YOU DON'T PUT THAT SAME QUESTION TO SOMEONE WHO'S CLEANING A ROOM.
BECAUSE MONEY IS UNSIGHTLY BEFORE THE GODS.
......
THERE WAS A MERCHANT LONG AGO WHO ONCE PRESENTED THE GODS WITH SUCH IRONY.
HMPH.

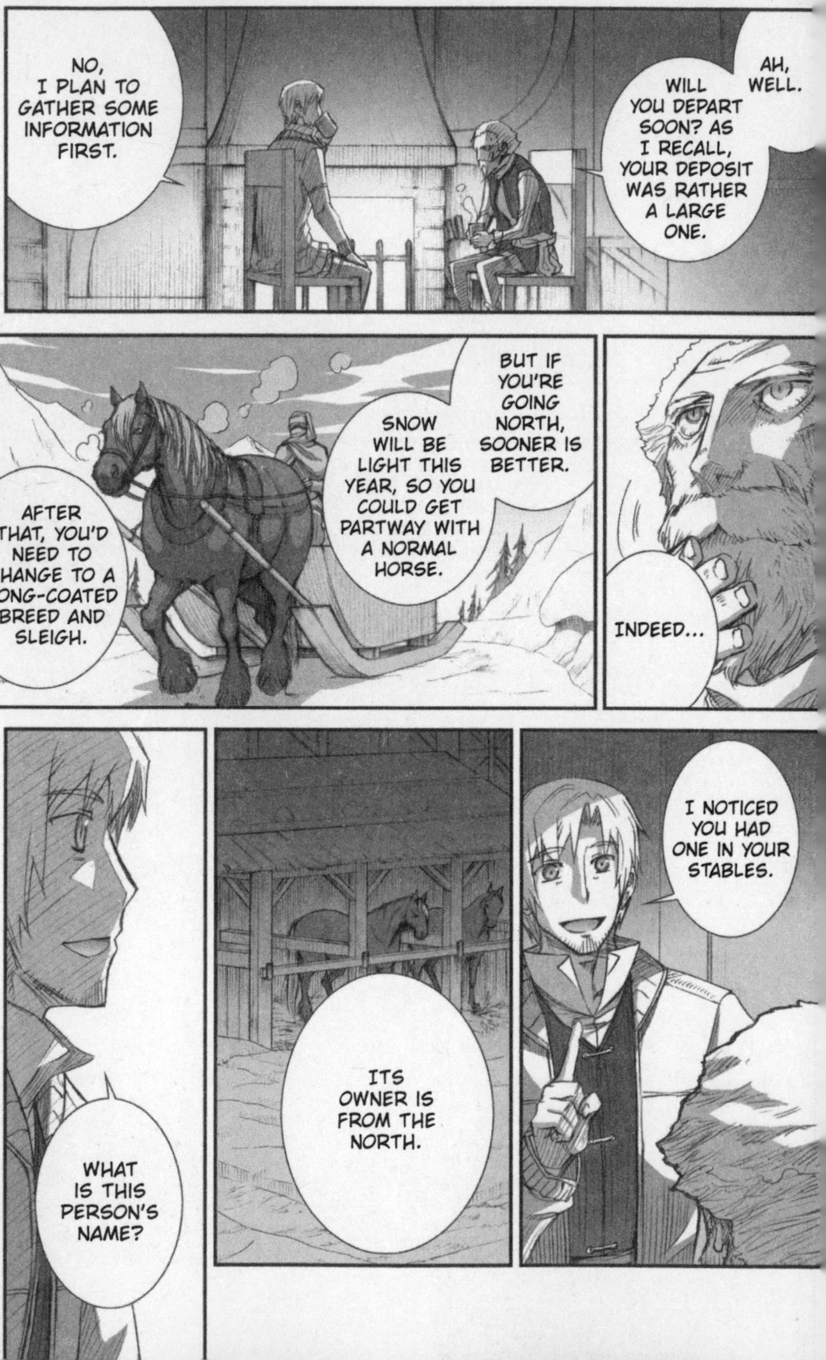
AH, WELL. WILL YOU DEPART SOON? AS I RECALL, YOUR DEPOSIT WAS RATHER A LARGE ONE.
NO, I PLAN TO GATHER SOME INFORMATION FIRST.
INDEED...
BUT IF YOU'RE GOING NORTH, SOONER IS BETTER.
SNOW WILL BE LIGHT THIS YEAR, SO YOU COULD GET PARTWAY WITH A NORMAL HORSE.
AFTER THAT, YOU'D NEED TO CHANGE TO A LONG-COATED BREED AND SLEIGH.
I NOTICED YOU HAD ONE IN YOUR STABLES.
ITS OWNER IS FROM THE NORTH.
WHAT IS THIS PERSON'S NAME?

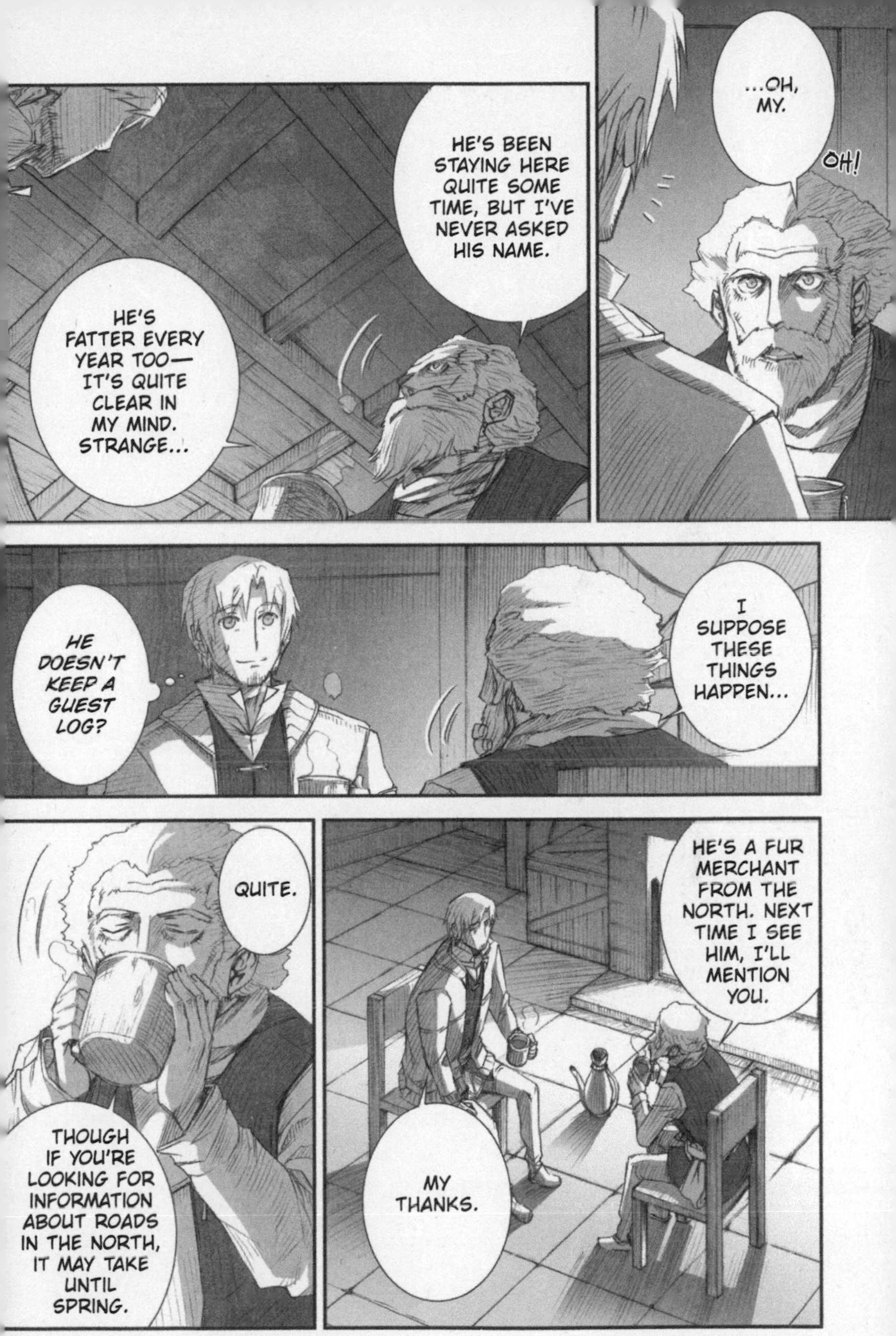
...OH, MY.
OH!
HE'S BEEN STAYING HERE QUITE SOME TIME, BUT I'VE NEVER ASKED HIS NAME.
HE'S FATTER EVERY YEAR TOO— IT'S QUITE CLEAR IN MY MIND. STRANGE...
I SUPPOSE THESE THINGS HAPPEN...
HE DOESN'T KEEP A GUEST LOG?
HE'S A FUR MERCHANT FROM THE NORTH. NEXT TIME I SEE HIM, I'LL MENTION YOU.
MY THANKS.
QUITE.
THOUGH IF YOU'RE LOOKING FOR INFORMATION ABOUT ROADS IN THE NORTH, IT MAY TAKE UNTIL SPRING.

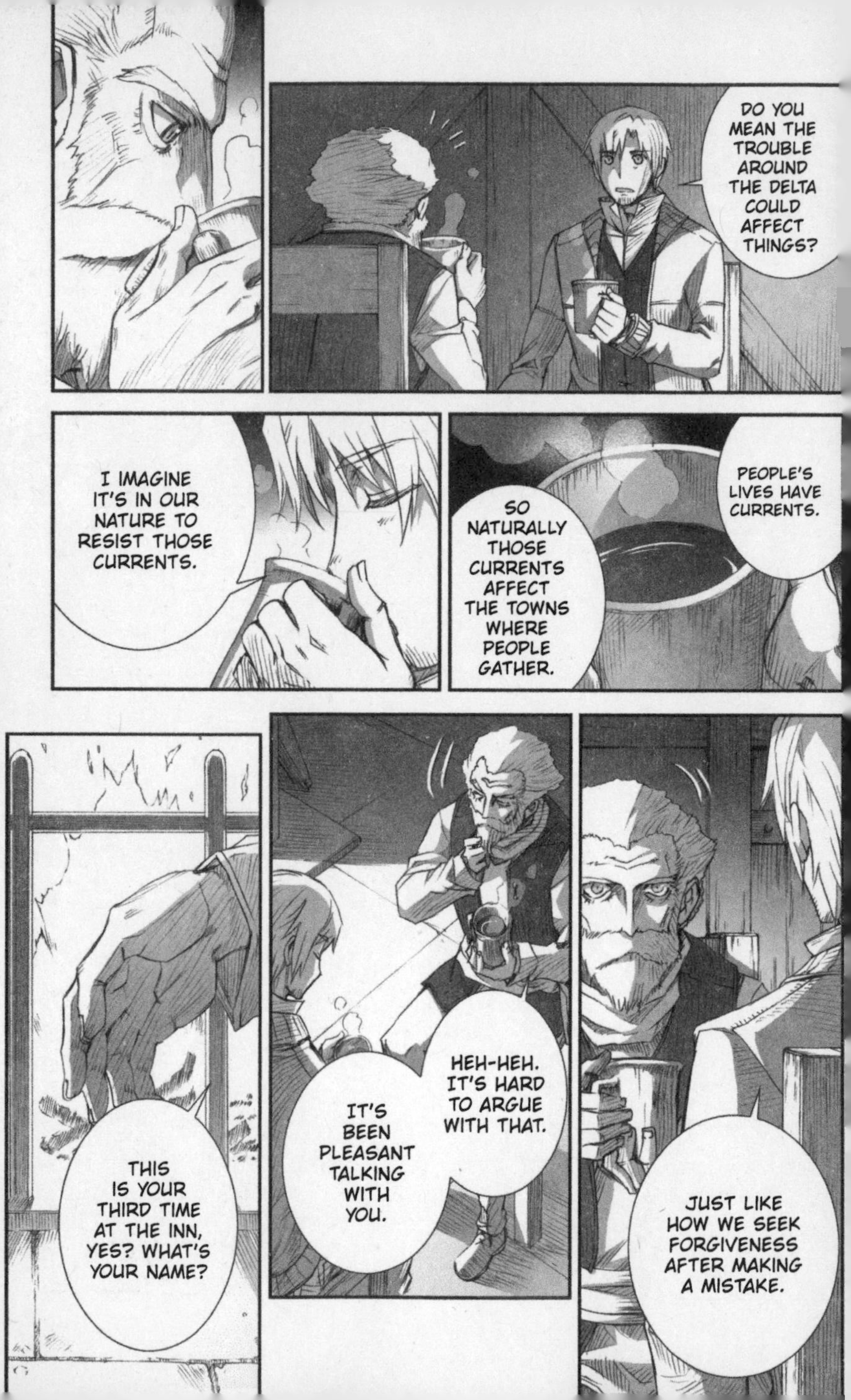
DO YOU MEAN THE TROUBLE AROUND THE DELTA COULD AFFECT THINGS?
PEOPLE'S LIVES HAVE CURRENTS.
SO NATURALLY THOSE CURRENTS AFFECT THE TOWNS WHERE PEOPLE GATHER.
I IMAGINE IT'S IN OUR NATURE TO RESIST THOSE CURRENTS.
JUST LIKE HOW WE SEEK FORGIVENESS AFTER MAKING A MISTAKE.
HEH-HEH. IT'S HARD TO ARGUE WITH THAT.
IT'S BEEN PLEASANT TALKING WITH YOU.
THIS IS YOUR THIRD TIME AT THE INN, YES? WHAT'S YOUR NAME?

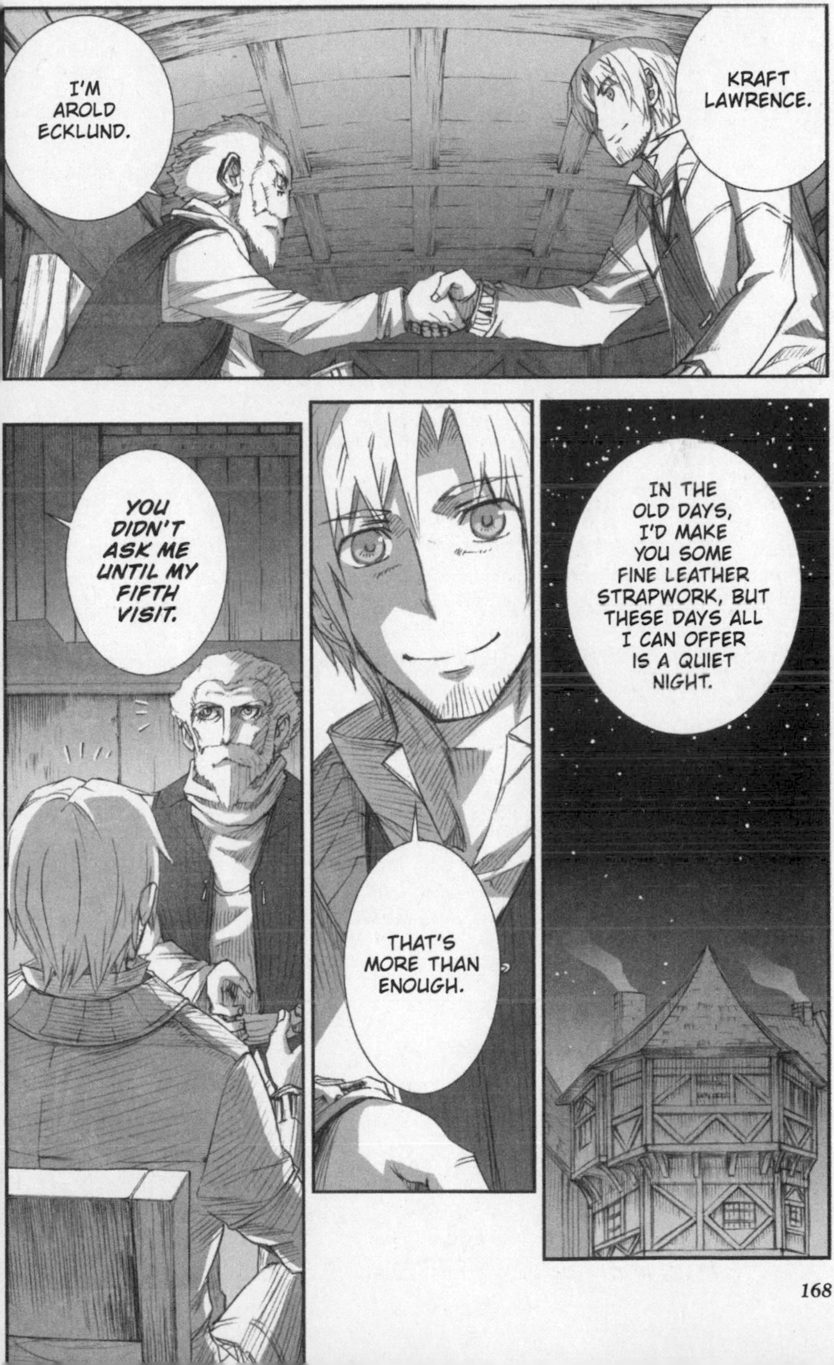
KRAFT LAWRENCE.
I'M AROLD ECKLUND.
IN THE OLD DAYS, I'D MAKE YOU SOME FINE LEATHER STRAPWORK, BUT THESE DAYS ALL I CAN OFFER IS A QUIET NIGHT.
THAT'S MORE THAN ENOUGH.
YOU DIDN'T ASK ME UNTIL MY FIFTH VISIT.

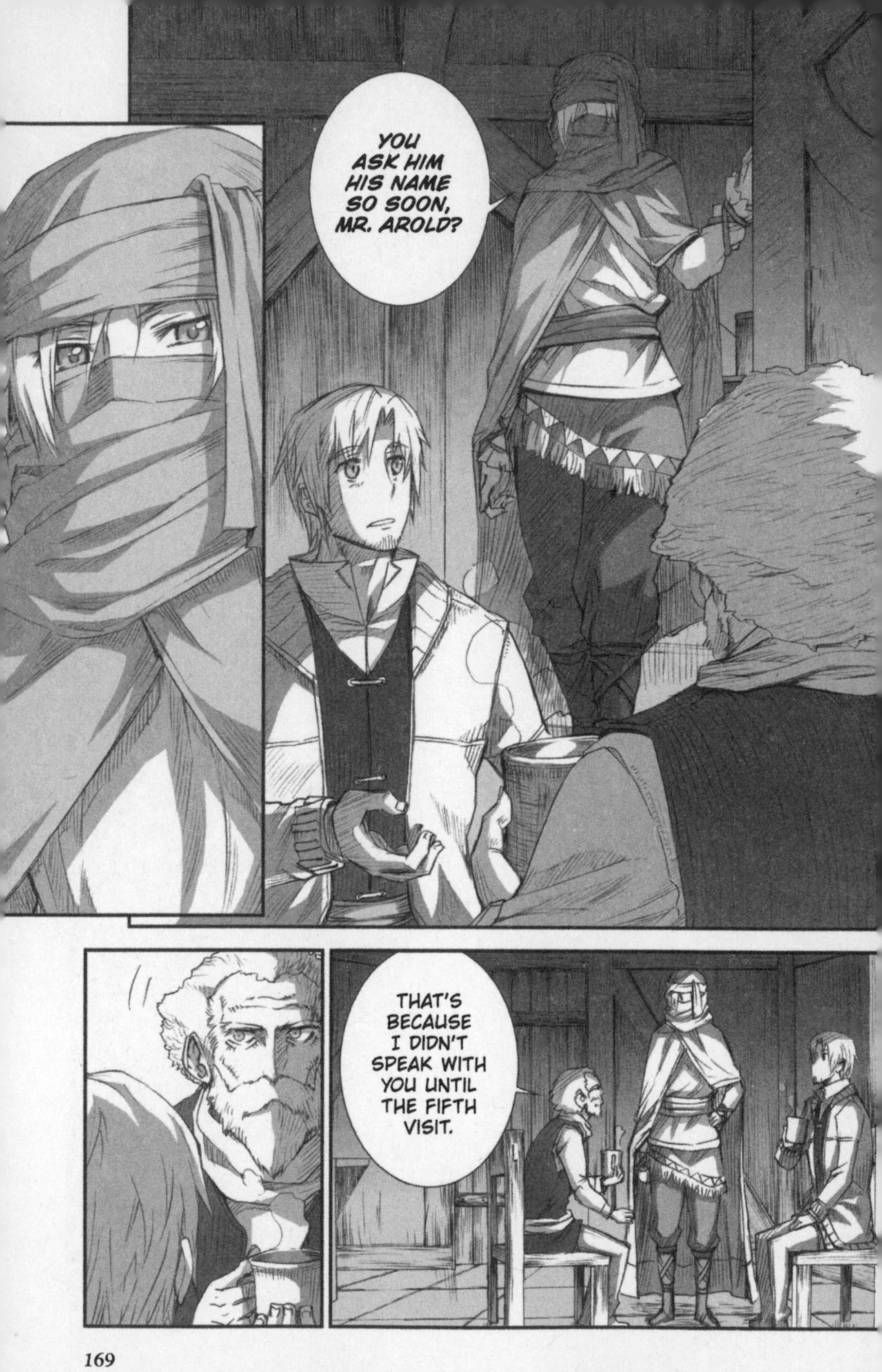
YOU ASK HIM HIS NAME SO SOON, MR. AROLD?
THAT'S BECAUSE I DIDN'T SPEAK WITH YOU UNTIL THE FIFTH VISIT.

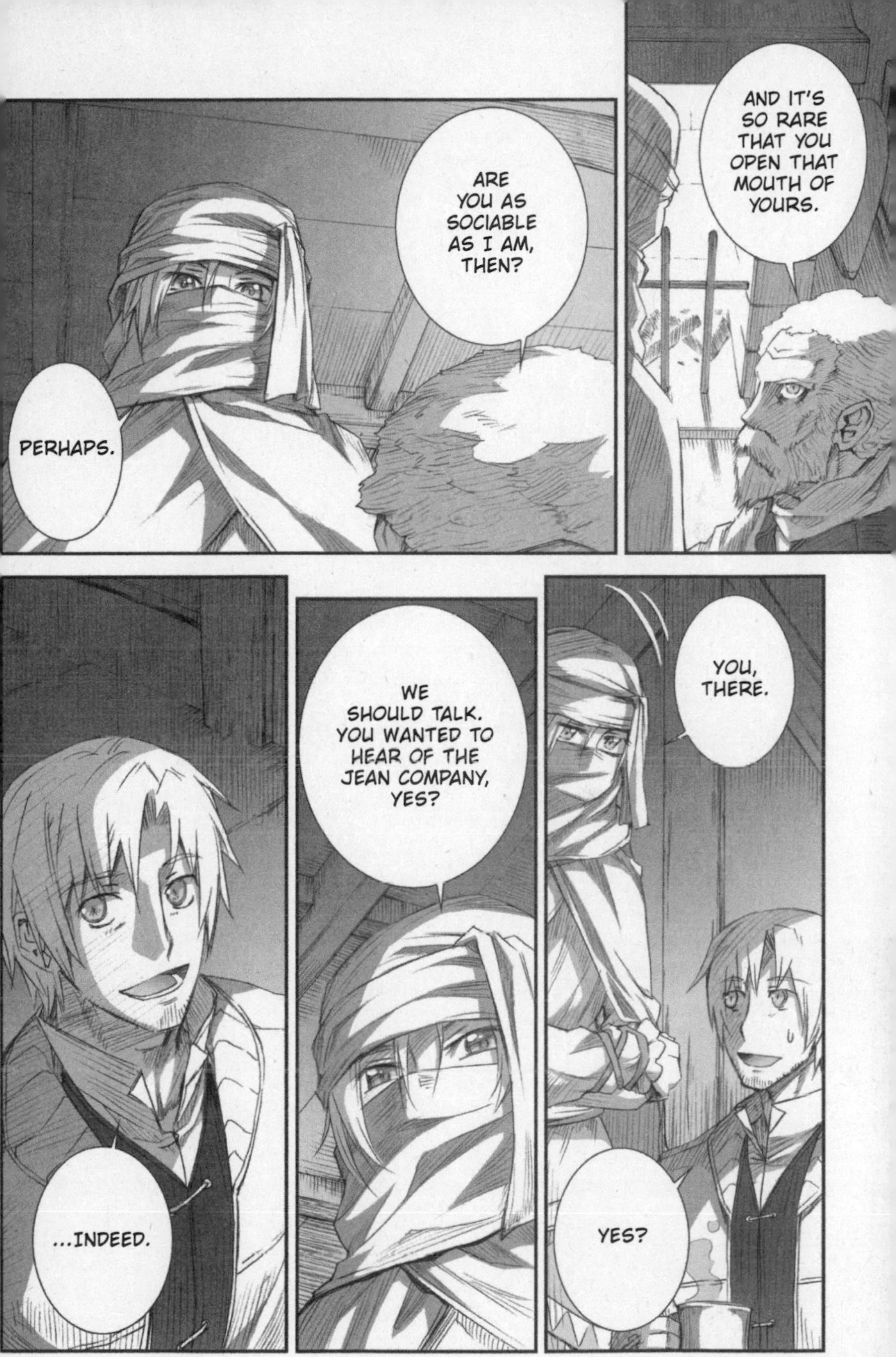
AND IT'S SO RARE THAT YOU OPEN THAT MOUTH OF YOURS.
ARE YOU AS SOCIABLE AS I AM, THEN?
PERHAPS.
YOU, THERE.
YES?
WE SHOULD TALK. YOU WANTED TO HEAR OF THE JEAN COMPANY, YES?
...INDEED.

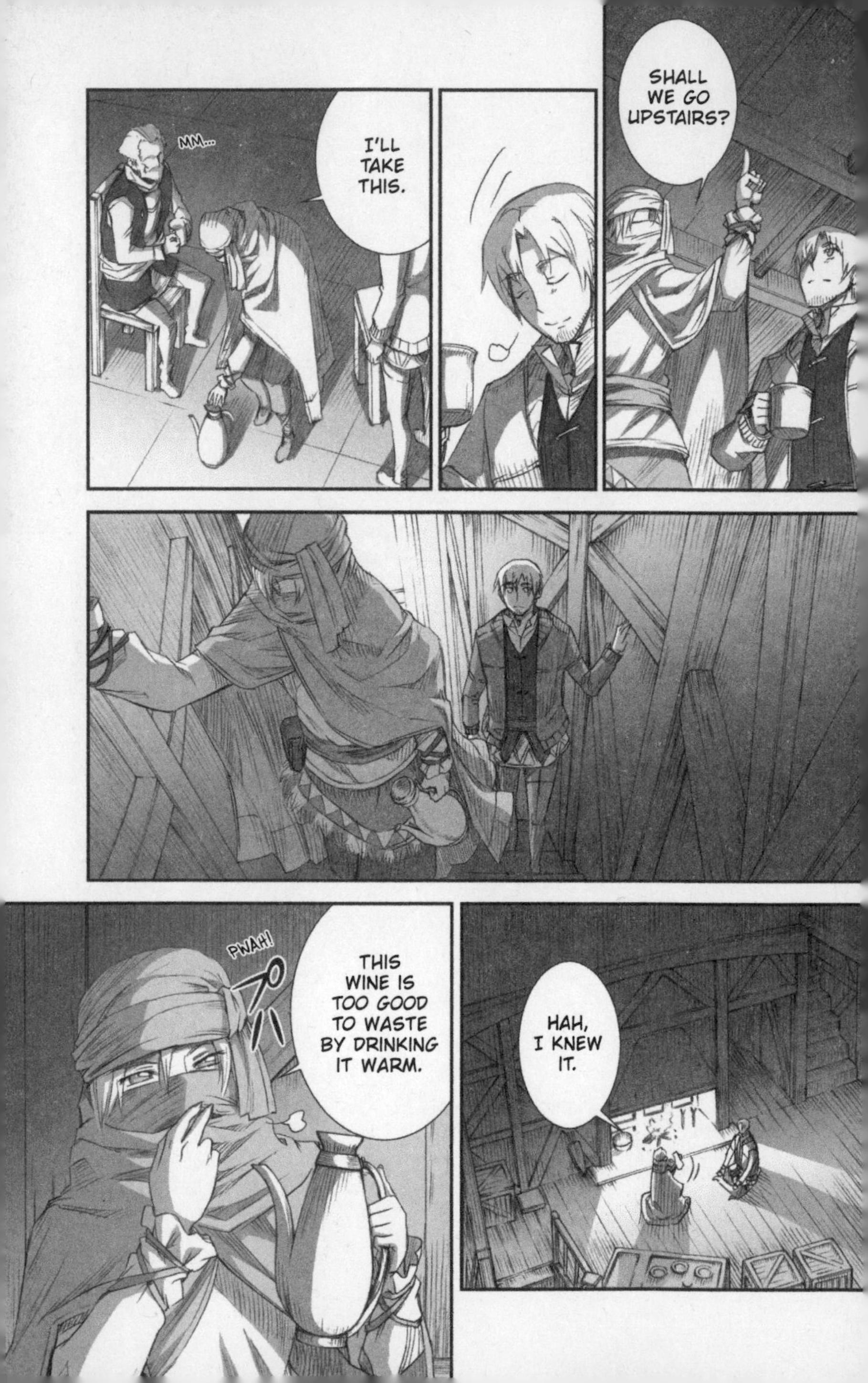
SHALL WE GO UPSTAIRS?
I'LL TAKE THIS.
MM...
THIS WINE IS TOO GOOD TO WASTE BY DRINKING IT WARM.
PWAH!
HAH, I KNEW IT.

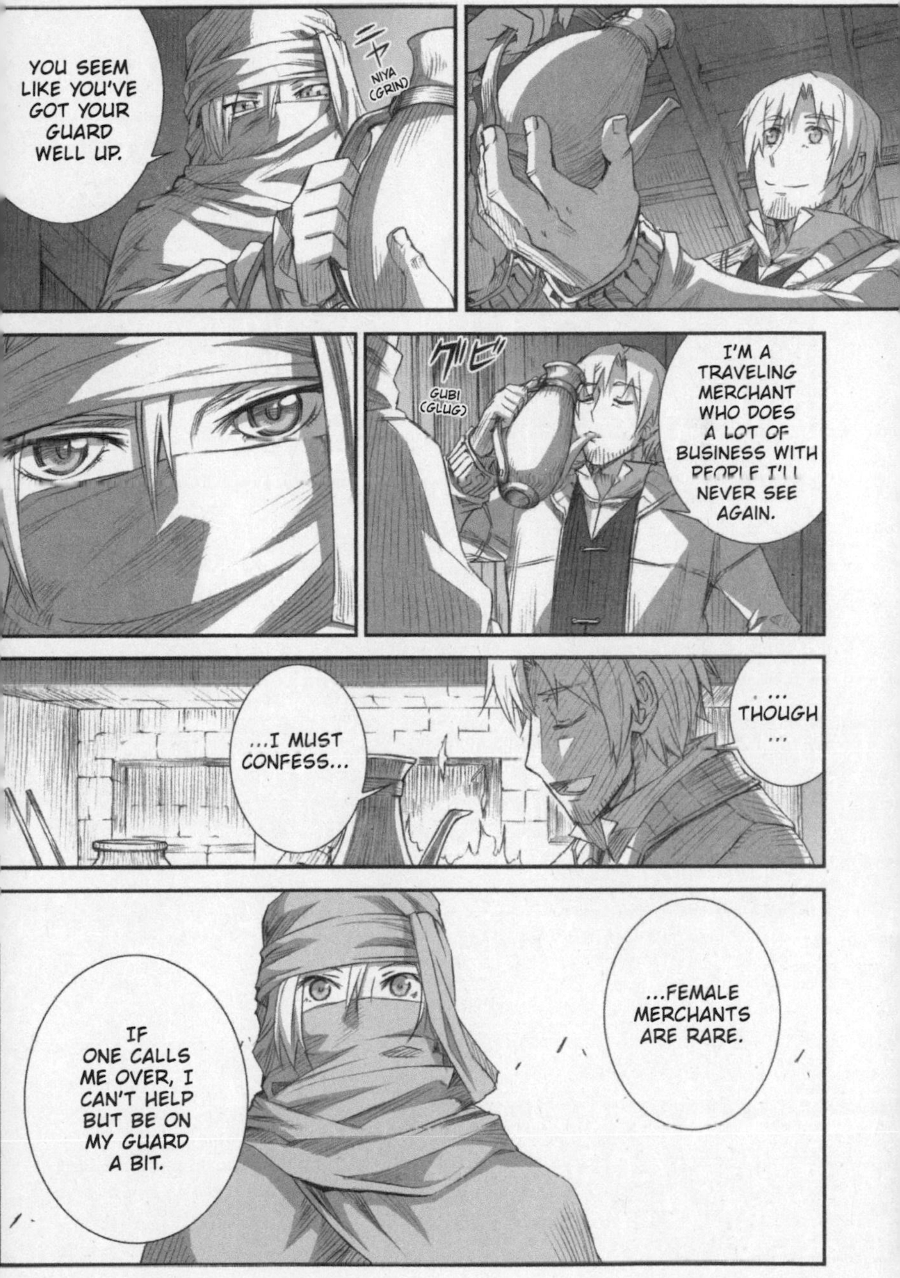
ニヤ NIYA (GRIN)
YOU SEEM LIKE YOU'VE GOT YOUR GUARD WELL UP.
I'M A TRAVELING MERCHANT WHO DOES A LOT OF BUSINESS WITH PEOPLE I'LL NEVER SEE AGAIN.
グビ GUBI (GLUG)
... ... THOUGH ...
...I MUST CONFESS...
...FEMALE MERCHANTS ARE RARE.
IF ONE CALLS ME OVER, I CAN'T HELP BUT BE ON MY GUARD A BIT.

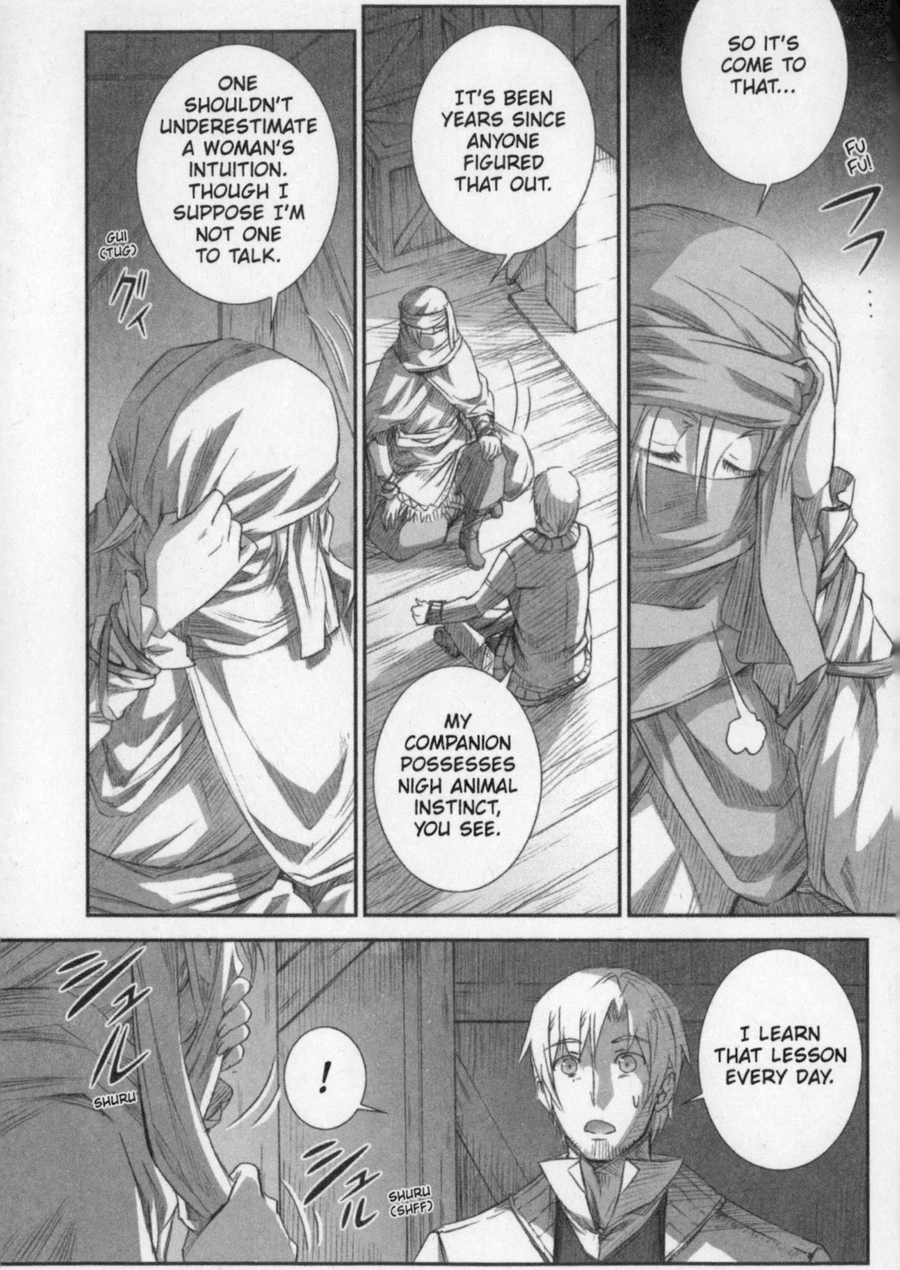
SO IT'S COME TO THAT...
FU FU!
IT'S BEEN YEARS SINCE ANYONE FIGURED THAT OUT.
MY COMPANION POSSESSES NIGH ANIMAL INSTINCT, YOU SEE.
ONE SHOULDN'T UNDERESTIMATE A WOMAN'S INTUITION. THOUGH I SUPPOSE I'M NOT ONE TO TALK.
GUI (TUG)
I LEARN THAT LESSON EVERY DAY.
!
SHURU (SHFF)
SHURU

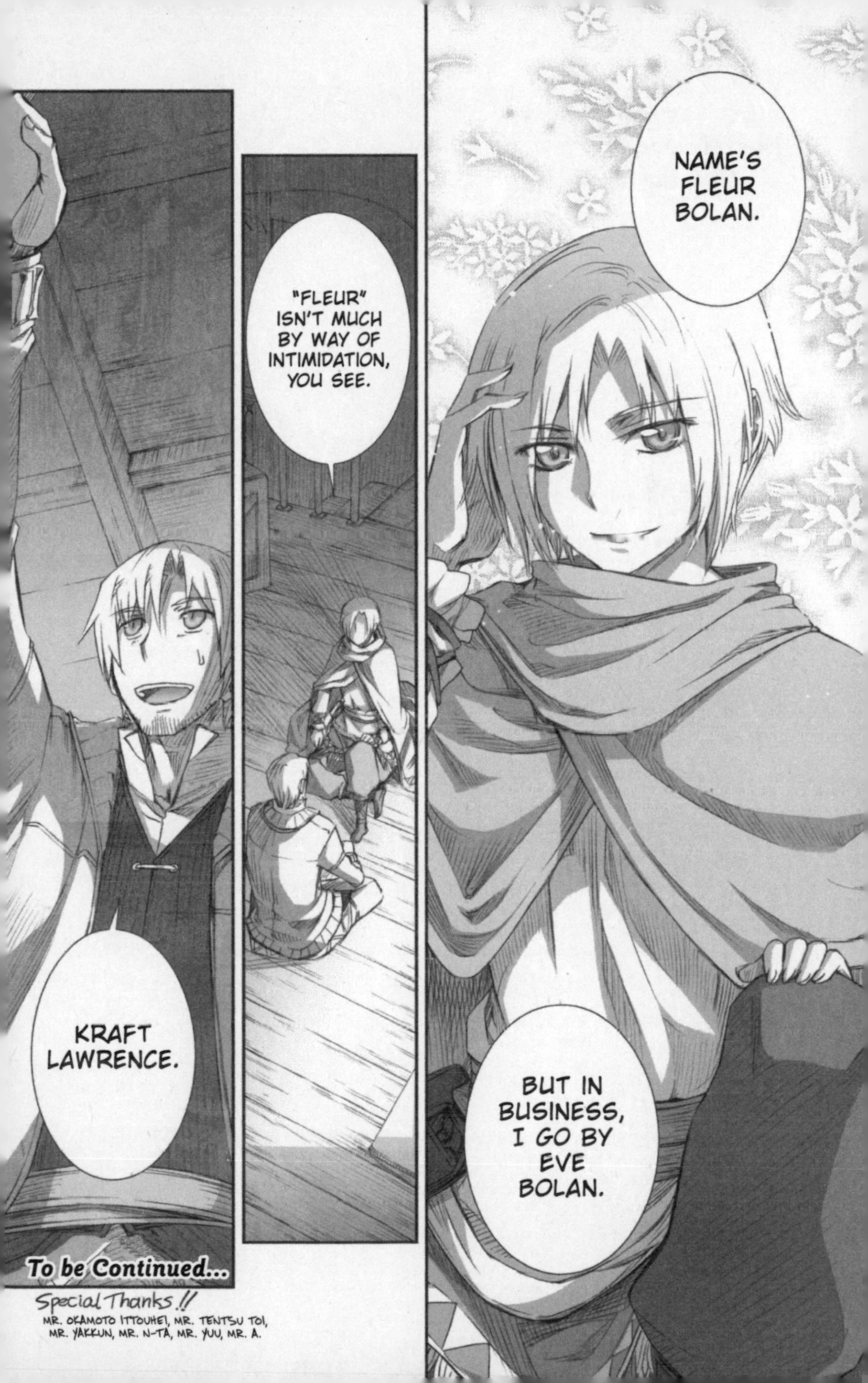
NAME'S FLEUR BOLAN.
BUT IN BUSINESS, I GO BY EVE BOLAN.
"FLEUR" ISN'T MUCH BY WAY OF INTIMIDATION, YOU SEE.
KRAFT LAWRENCE.

To be Continued...

Special Thanks!!
MR. OKAMOTO ITTOUHEI, MR. TENTSU TOI, MR. YAKKUN, MR. N-TA, MR. YUU, MR. A.

Congratulations on Volume 8! The world of Koume-sensei's art is so vivid, I felt like I could smell the dust! Can't wait to see what happens next!

支倉凍砂

Isuna Hasekura

SPICE & WOLF

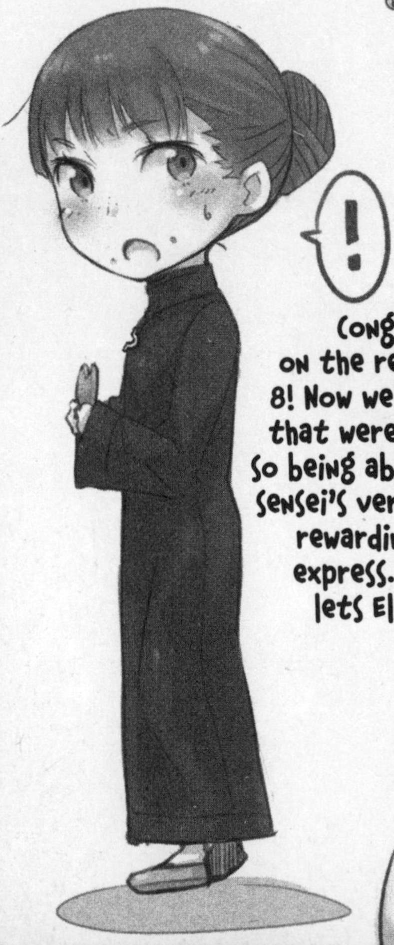
!

Congratulations on the release of Volume 8! Now we're into episodes that weren't in the anime, so being able to read Koume-sensei's version is simply too rewarding to properly express. I just hope he lets Elsa be happy...

Jyuu Ayakura

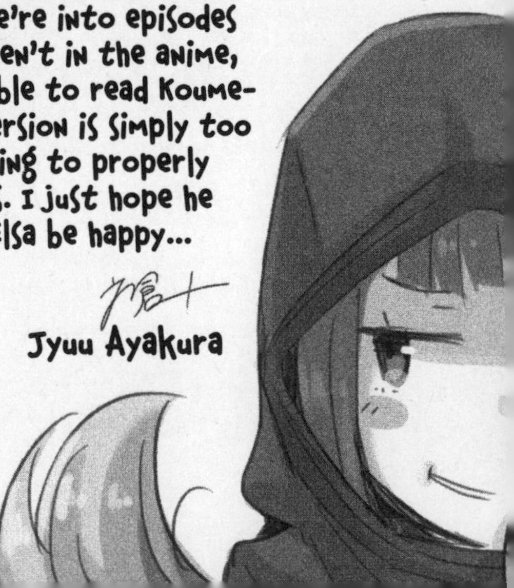

SPICE & WO

ISUNA HASEKURA
KEITO KOUME
CHARACTER DESIGN:
JYUU AYAKURA

TRANSLATION: PAUL STARR

LETTERING: TERRI DELGADO

OOKAMI TO KOUSHINRYOU VOL. 8
©ISUNA HASEKURA/KEITO KOUME 2012
EDITED BY ASCII MEDIA WORKS
FIRST PUBLISHED IN JAPAN IN 2012 BY
KADOKAWA CORPORATION, TOKYO.
ENGLISH TRANSLATION RIGHTS ARRANGED WITH
KADOKAWA CORPORATION, TOKYO,
THROUGH TUTTLE-MORI AGENCY, INC., TOKYO.

TRANSLATION © 2013 BY HACHETTE BOOK GROUP

YEN PRESS
HACHETTE BOOK GROUP
1290 AVENUE OF THE AMERICAS, NEW YORK, NY 10104

WWW.HACHETTEBOOKGROUP.COM
WWW.YENPRESS.COM

YEN PRESS IS AN IMPRINT OF HACHETTE BOOK GROUP, INC. THE YEN PRESS NAME AND LOGO ARE TRADEMARKS OF HACHETTE BOOK GROUP, INC.

FIRST YEN PRESS EDITION: JUNE 2013

ISBN: 978-0-316-25085-6

10 9 8 7 6 5

BVG

PRINTED IN THE UNITED STATES OF AMERICA